Without Borders
The Haqqani Network and the Road to Kabul

By
Jere Van Dyk

Without Borders
The Haqqani Network and the Road to Kabul

By
Jere Van Dyk

"The most important qualification
for a leader is to not want to be the leader."
Plato

"In our family Jalaluddin Sab is the eldest and because of his
age and because he has had a stroke and cannot talk well
and is very weak, Sirajuddin is his representative. Yes,
we call him the Khalifa."
Ibrahim Haqqani, April 2015, Islamabad

Academica Press
Washington~London

Library of Congress Cataloging-in-Publication Data

Names: Van Dyk, Jere (author)

Title: Without borders : the haqqani network and the road to kabul | Van Dyk, Jere.

Description: Washington : Academica Press, 2022. | Includes references.

Identifiers: LCCN 2022944785 | ISBN 9781680538656 (hardcover) | 9781680538663 (paperback) | 9781680538649 (e-book)

Copyright 2022 Jere Van Dyk

Dedication

To Craig Whitney, who, in 1981, as Deputy Foreign Editor, and Bob Semple, as Foreign Editor, at the *New York Times*, gave me a letter of introduction, and a check for $500 to help pay my way to Afghanistan. They trusted me. I am forever grateful.

To Mike Kaufman: (1938-2010), South Asia correspondent (1979-1982), the *New York Times*.

To Aunt Elva (Woods), who after an argument with my grandmother, left the University of Washington and took a slow boat to Shanghai, and got a job at the U.S. Consulate. It was her stories, and those of Uncle (Hugh) Woody, General Manager of the China National Aviation Corporation, the first man to fly over the Himalayas, and the first man shot down by the Japanese, and of my father, in the Marine Corps, who after island hoping in the Pacific fought Mao Tse Tung, told me about the fiercest men he ever saw, riding Bactrian camels off the Gobi Desert through a gate in the Great Wall, that resonated when I was a boy.

To (Uncle) Roy Major, navigator on President Franklin Roosevelt's flight to Yalta, after which he met with King Abdul Aziz of Saudi Arabia on the USS Quincy in the Suez Canal. After the war he charted flight routes for TWA around the world including to Afghanistan.

To Henry Van Dyk, U.S. Seventh Army, betrayed by Berber nomads, captured by Erwin Rommel's Afrika Korps, and held as a POW for two years in Germany.

To Vartan Gregorian (1934-2021), president of the Carnegie Corporation, author, and Afghan hand, who provided supplemental funding from his own budget for this book.[1]

I have changed the names of some people, and their features, to protect them.

---

[1] Vartan Gregorian. *The Emergence of Modern Afghanistan; Politics of Reform and Modernization, 1880-1946,*(Redwood City, Stanford University Press, 1969)

I want to thank my agent, Michael Carlisle for his indispensable help, and friendship, his rising assistant, Michael Mungiello, for all his hard work, and Soumyadev Bose for his design and indexing skills, and Paul du Quenoy for his unwavering support.

Contents

Preface

This is the story of my search to understand the reach in the Arab Middle East of the Haqqani family, born in the foothills of the Suleiman (Solomon) Mountains of eastern Afghanistan, and from which rose in the early 1970s, to fight Communism, this secular religion, a threat to their faith, the Haqqani Mujahideen (Holy Warriors), what the U.S. today calls the Haqqani Network, but which they still call The Haqqani Mujahideen, one of the oldest, and maybe the most powerful jihadist group, and family, in the world, which rose, through its alliance with Pakistan, Saudi Arabia, other Arab nations, the United States, and its anti-Soviet allies, to become a symbol of an ideology, born in the early days of Islam, which became a force after the Mongol conquest in the 13th Century in Baghdad, reemerged in Arabia in the 18th Century, in the anti-European, particularly British colonial rebellions of the 19th and the 20th centuries, which led to the Irregulars in 1947 in Pakistan, to the Afghan Mujahideen in the 1970s and 1980s, which led to al-Qaida, to the Taliban, to the Islamic State and to jihadist groups from Asia to Arabia to Africa to the Levant and to Europe, and beyond.

The Sheikh
May 2019

We entered what looked like a large empty restaurant, with bare round wood tables. A big burly man, standing behind an empty bar, with no bottles, the only person I saw, in a white shirt, black bow tie and a black vest, saw the Sheikh, placed his hand on his heart, and bowed his head. Sheikh Hameed al-Ahmar, of the Hashed tribal federation, a businessman, more ambitious and political than his older brother Saddiq, the Sheikh of the Sheikhs of the Hashed, the most powerful tribe in Yemen, walked to the front and sat by a window. Did I want coffee or tea? The bartender came over and the Sheikh ordered, and then and in a deep, confident voice welcomed me.

An Ethiopian taxi driver in Washington said a few months ago coffee originated in Ethiopia, not in Yemen. The Sheikh smiled. They had the same culture as Ethiopia. The Yemenis were descended from Sheba, who maybe lived in Ethiopia. When she returned from her journey to Palestine to see King Solomon she wanted to take the throne from Marib. The Yemenis were Jewish then but became Christians when the Ethiopians became, under the Eastern Orthodox Church, the first nation.

It appears that Christian missionaries first preached in Ethiopia, and in southern Arabia, about 45 A.D. The Christians were south of Sana'a all the way to Aden. The Yemenis believe that they descended from Shem (Sam) the son of Noah and that his ship was somewhere around where Turkey and Iran have their borders today. Sana'a means the city of Sam—Medina Sam. We believe that Sam built Sana'a and lived there until he died.

The Sheikh drank his coffee. Christians also believe that Noah's ark is there.[2] We watched the sun move closer to the west. It took two years to arrange this meeting. A former Yemeni ambassador was my go-between. If anyone could help me it would be the Sheikh. I was told that Jalaluddin Haqqani was married to a Yemeni. The Pashtuns, the largest ethnic group in Afghanistan and western Pakistan—the Taliban were mostly Pashtuns— rarely married outsiders. I wanted to know the name of her tribe, and what

---

[2] *Bible and Spade*, vol. 21, no. 3 2008

he knew about her family. I didn't learn about Jalaluddin's marriage to a Yemeni until after I left Yemen in 2014.

The Sheikh continued. The first prophet after Sam was Hood. One of his sons was Galon and the other was Khatan, the main son of Sheba. The Khatanis were the main inhabitants of Arabia. Saba (Sheba) spoke Yarib and became the first speaker of what we call Arabic. Saba's son was king. He had two sons, Hamden and Kahlan. The descendants of Hamden (the Hashed) were the Hamdens, the most civilized of all the tribes. The Khatalans protected them. There was jealousy among the Hamden and other tribes because they were closest to and got to Mecca first. All the roads of the Arabs came from Yemen.

There is no mention of Yemen in the Koran but twice it mentions Saba. Mohammad refers to them, he said, by her first son, Hamid. The Sheikh had nine brothers. He turned to politics, the other reason why I was here. The kings of the Gulf were afraid of the Arab Spring. They were afraid of their revolution, especially the Emirates and Saudi Arabia.[3] They wanted to try to stop it, to stop the people of the (Muslim) Brotherhood. (King) Abdullah, of Saudi Arabia, and Mohammad bin Zaid, Crown Prince of the Emirate of Abu Dhabi and the ruler of the UAE, were a team, and came up with a plan. They were the enemy but he didn't think that they would be as stupid as they were. First, they allowed el-Sisi[4] and his gang to come back to power, to imprison the president, Mohamed Morsi, and to shoot and kill a thousand members of the Muslim Brotherhood in the streets.

They allowed al-Houthi to attack Islah, the most powerful political party, founded in part by the Brotherhood, Zindani, and Ali Mohsen and the Al-Ahmar family, even his own home.[5] He meant, by the al-Ahmar family, his father Sheikh Abdullah, chief of the tribe, and attacked even my host's own compound. In August 2014, he had to take his elderly mother to the Czech Republic for physical therapy. Jane Marriott, the British ambassador, came and told him to leave immediately and not return. Al-Houthi would not stop at the border of Sana'a as he was ordered to do but would take the

---

[3] The United Arab Emirates

[4] Former General, and since 2014 President Abdel Fattah Saeed Hussein Khalil al-Sisi, of Egypt

[5] Al-Houthi is Abdul-Malik al-Houthi, leader of the Zaydi Shia cultural and military revivalist movement in Yemen; Abdul Majid Zindani was the most influential Wahhabi Muslim in Yemen, today in exile in Saudi Arabia.

whole city. Iran was not involved.

The Houthis took Sana'a on January 22, 2015.

"Abdullah and bin Zaid, who set this war up, thought that we, the Hashed, would fight al-Houthi." The Yemeni government had the support of the Gulf states to fight Islah and the Sheikh himself, and his side, meaning his men, and the Muslim Brotherhood, and get rid of them. They were revolutionaries after all. They decided not to fight. If Hadi fought al-Houthi, the Hashed would fight.

President Abdrabbuh Mansur Hadi, in power since 2015, was living in exile in Saudi Arabia.

"Mohammad bin Zaid, the leader of the coalition, kept pushing Saudi Arabia until the whole of Yemen fell. Abdullah was crown prince of Saudi Arabia for 20 years, but he was not a Sudari, not a full brother, not one of the Sudari Seven, and therefore wanted to stop his brothers so he could be king.[6] He formed a plan to attack Yemen and to be king. Luckily, he died."[7]

The Sudari Seven is a powerful alliance of brothers born to King Abdul Aziz, the founder of Saudi Arabia, and his wife, Hussa bint Ahmed al-Sudari, with whom he had the most sons, whose family, like his, came from the Nejd, in central Arabia. The royal family was close to and helped to finance Sheikh Hameed's clan. When his father, Abdullah ibn Husayn, Sheikh of the Sheikhs of the Hashed and President of the Yemeni Parliament, was in an automobile accident in Dakar, the Saudis sent a jet to bring him to a hospital in Riyadh.

"Their revolution," and by that he meant the Arab Spring in 2011, "took most of the strength from Ali Abdullah Saleh, who was president of Yemen for 33 years, until they forced him out. Saleh knew, and everyone knew, that the Houthis would kill him, and they did. Saleh controlled al-Qaeda, through his sons, from the beginning until he died. Al-Qaeda was losing at the moment, but Daesh was coming back, and would be a problem. The UAE controlled Daesh."[8]

---

[6] MEE Staff "King Salman Reasserts Sudairi Seven, Key Abdullah Advisor Removed." *Middle East Eye*, 13 Feb. 2015. https://www.middleeasteye.net/news/king-salman-reasserts-sudairi-seven-key-abdullah-advisor-removed.

[7] January 23, 2015.

[8] Al-Dawla al-Islamiyyah fil-Iraq wa al-sham, or The Islamic State in Iraq and Syria

Our ally, the United Arab Emirates, was behind ISIS?

He nodded. What he didn't say was that in 1978 his father, who my go-between called the most fearless and most honest man he ever met, told the Saudis to bring Saleh, an army colonel with a grade school education as well as a member of the Hashed with an encyclopedic knowledge of tribal politics, to power.

"The UAE and King Abdullah planned to invade Yemen. What they really wanted was to end the revolution and to bring Saleh back to power. He was close to Mohammad bin Zaid, who planned the invasion as a way to get rid of Hadi. Mutab, King Abdullah's son, wanted to be king of Saudi Arabia. He and bin Zaid wanted to get rid of Abdullah. Bin Zaid was not allowed to attend Abdullah's funeral because of this. He spread rumors that Crown Prince Salman had Alzheimer's. When Salman became king, he pushed bin Zaid out. Iran and national security entered the picture. He chose Mohammad bin Salam as crown prince. He and his father had no choice but to invade. Bin Zaid went to Obama and said he was out and needed to be in. The U.S. had a military base in the UAE, and it supplied the oil to the base. It became, for public purposes, a coalition to fight what they called 'terrorism,' controlled by the UAE."

What about al-Qaeda?

"Ali Abdullah Saleh used al-Qaeda to facilitate the UAE's entry into Yemen, so that the U.S. could tell Abdullah it was a war on terror. The UAE wanted a continued presence there. It was preparing Daesh for this purpose. We (the Hashed) watched as a UAE helicopter landed in an area where ISIS was living but we didn't know what they did. It was impossible for Daesh, so strong, so powerful, to rise from nothing. We know who created it."

"General Ali Mohsen al-Ahmar, Ali Abdullah Saleh's boyhood friend, and later enemy, today the vice president of Yemen, has good ties with al-Qaida. Today al-Qaeda and ISIS are fighting alongside the Saudis, the UAE,

---

(ISIS). *Dawla* means "to call," in Arabic, to call to Islam. Sham refers to Syria or Damascus. ISIS can therefore mean "The call to Islam in Iraq and Syria." Shams also means "sun," in Arabic. ISIS is opposed to the acronym, Daesh, because it sounds like *Dahes*, which means sows discord in Arabic, or *Daes*, crushes underfoot. The U.S., other nations and the U.N. say ISIL for the Islamic State in Iraq and the Levant. The word once meant east of the Mediterranean. Levant comes from the French, lever, to rise. The Levant is where the sun (ash-shams) rises, in the East.

and the government, against the Houthis, who are aligned with Iran. Every Yemeni knows this."

What did he know about the death of Jamal Khashoggi?

"It was a tragedy. It was a very stupid way to kill him. When God wanted something to happen it would happen. This death was a punishment from God to Mohammad bin Salam. It will be with him for the rest of his life. He committed that crime. It is not easy to kill a man." The Sheikh had a pained look. "He is a very arrogant man. He killed without even caring. This was not the Sahara. He was a part of civilization. Western intelligence agencies did far worse things, but they did them secretly. The Saudi Consul General could have prevented it, but he gave in to the Crown Prince. He was finished. Now, wherever he was posted people would remember."

Was Khashoggi worried?

"He went to the ambassador in Ankara, who was a friend of the Sheikh's, and said he didn't feel safe. It was a simple document he needed; all he had to do was sign it, and then they stamp it."

I thought of our lunch in Bahrain in 2014. He said he wished he had the courage to write about ISIS, what he called "raw Wahhabism." He was courageous. He walked through that door.

The Sheikh wasn't worried about a threat from Afghanistan.

Many Yemenis went there and stayed and brought their families. Maybe there were widows there and maybe Jalaluddin Haqqani married one. He didn't know about a possible marriage to a Yemeni in Yemen or in the Gulf. Bin Laden married a woman from Yemen. Marriage was important, politically, in the Arab world. There was a place near Aden where hundreds of men over the years became policemen and then went to Bahrain, the UAE, or elsewhere in the Gulf and joined the police or the security services. They wanted to attack him. He had one of his sons marry into the family of his enemies. Now, if someone wanted to attack him, others said, well, he's one of us now. So it would be for Jalaluddin Haqqani. It was networking. He smiled.

The Kajaki Larah

I flew to Ankara to see Abdul Rahim, the Afghan ambassador to Turkey, who, during the Afghan-Soviet war was the Mujahideen spokesman, often on American television. He met with Congressmen, especially Charlie Wilson of Texas. He was later ambassador to Washington. In December 2001, we met again, in Kabul. He was now Minister of Communications. His beard was long and his eyes were sad. They'd had over twenty years of war.

He smiled now, but said Russia and Iran were supporting the Taliban.

Pakistan told Iran and Russia that it would have the Taliban fight ISIS. Most of the suicide operations were done by the Haqqanis. The Quetta Shura (Taliban leadership council) did not have the ability to do this. After the Soviet War (1979-1989) they formed the Council of Afghan Mujahideen Commanders to have a common strategy to defeat Najibullah, the Soviet-backed president.[9] They met near Chitral on the Pakistani border. He was the translator. Ahmed Shah Massoud, the Tajik guerrilla leader,[10] proposed Jalaluddin Haqqani as President of the Council. He was eloquent and precise on how to proceed, but he didn't want to be President.

For ten years Rahim represented Jamiat-e-Islami, the Afghan political party, in Pakistan. All he did, he said, was work with American, British, French, and Saudi intelligence agencies. They gave him hundreds of visas, always at night. It seemed they went upstairs at each embassy as if it were a separate building. Everything was run today by the intelligence agencies.

I flew to Istanbul to catch the night flight on Turkish Airlines to Kabul. The agent said the flight was full. I sat next to an Afghan businessman. The plane was over half empty. We waited for twenty minutes. A swarm of young men came down the aisles talking loudly, with small bags or backpacks, and climbed into their seats, moving around restlessly. Who were these men? Soldiers maybe. They were Afghans, said the businessman. They were in prison here, and the government was sending them back. Every night it was the same. I looked at the boys, young men really. All that they

---

[9] Najibullah was the Communist President put in power by the Soviet Union.
[10] Ahmed Shah Massoud was killed by al-Qaida two days before 9/11.

had gone through, and now they were being sent back. Each boy's family paid $10,000 or more to smugglers to take the *Kajaki Larah* (the Black Way), one of the largest and longest smuggling operations in the world. They left their villages and went to safe houses in the Tribal Areas the size of Connecticut, off-limits to outsiders, in Pakistan and from there rode in minibuses down to Baluchistan province and crossed to Iran where smugglers took them to Turkey. If they were strong, and lucky, they made it to Britain and northern Europe, where there were good social benefits, where they worked to pay the money back, and were able to support their families. The Black Way was the result, like al-Qaeda, the Haqqani Network, the Taliban, and ISIS, of the Afghan-Soviet war. "Blowback" is what the CIA called it then. Be careful what you create, that it doesn't blow back to hit you. It did on 9/11.

In 2008 I was kidnapped by the Taliban and wrote a book about it.[11] In 2010, Paul Golob, my editor, asked, for my next book, drawing also on my youth when I was a runner, to write about pushing the limits of human possibilities. I researched ideas, talked with Jim Wickwire, a friend from Seattle and the first American to climb K-2, and with track friends. I wanted something political and physical. An Afghan-American, who translated for these boys for the British police, told me about the Black Way. I found boys working in outdoor markets in London, but they wouldn't talk. I found one in Birmingham who did. I wanted to travel with them, but publishers and CBS were afraid that I would get in trouble. I gave the story to *60 Minutes* and wrote an article about them.[12] Two weeks before, I flew from New York to London and met with men from the Middle East for this book. I had dinner with Jonathan Dove, an opera composer, and Alasdair Middleton, his librettist, who were writing a government-funded opera on the Black Way, drawn in part from my article. The British also sent boys back home. When we landed in Kabul the next morning, I watched them walk up the ramp, and stop, hiding their sorrow. They would try again, or, maybe, like others, they would join the Taliban.

---

[11] Jere Van Dyk, *Captive: My Time as a Prisoner of the Taliban*. (New York: Times Books, Henry Holt and Company), 2010
[12] Jere Van Dyk, "On the Black Way," *Foreign Affairs*, 30 Apr. 2015

The Tanga Khola
December 13, 2006

The snow got worse, but the mountain pass to Khost was closed. We stayed with a friend of Sultan's and the next day it opened. That evening we reached Khost, ten miles from the Pakistani border, ate on the floor in a guesthouse with 50 men, and found a place to sleep. Sultan was afraid that someone would see that I was a foreigner. Back outside, the street was empty. Men in a jeep with rifles stopped us and let us go.

We found another guesthouse, and the manager heard us speak English. Where was I from? America. He shook his finger, no. This was good. I could blend in. In April 2004, Pat Tillman, the professional football star who joined the Army, with his younger brother Kevin, and became a Ranger, and the most famous soldier in the Army, was killed in Afghanistan. I came here to look into this.

The next morning, the shining turquoise dome of Jalaluddin's mosque dominated the city. The Taliban were coming back. I didn't dare go to the mosque again. I sat with a U.S. Army report on Pat Tillman's death that his father gave me. Sultan and Zidran came with a sturdy man named Mansur, six feet, in his 50s, with a thick black beard and a black turban with silver stripes, a former army major. His ID said he was an S-2, an intelligence officer for the U.S. Army. He would take me to where the footballer was killed.

Was Haqqani around here?

He was stronger than ever. He was behind the attack. His people had killed 260-270 people for being U.S. spies. He was afraid and hadn't slept well for months. Those who worked for the U.S. were afraid, but there was no option. Because of corruption he couldn't get a job. The key was Pakistan. Hamid Gul, the former head of the ISI, was in charge of the Afghan cell.

What about bin Laden?

He was living in Miralee, in the Tribal Areas, between Bannu and Miram Shah, under the protection of Pakistani intelligence.

The next morning the sun was bright and the sky was blue with tuffs of white clouds. We walked to the edge of the city. Three armed turbaned men stood behind a dirt-crusted 4x4 by the road. We hugged one another gently. I could feel their rifles beneath their shawls. We climbed slowly into the hills, following a track, and passed two men standing by a stream. One was the Taliban commander from this area. If I wasn't here, Mansur explained, he would arrest him. I looked at the land, the trees and the drifts of snow. I knew this land. I had been here with Haqqani's men. We reached the canyon where Pat Tillman was killed. The 75th Ranger Regiment was ordered here to "disrupt the Haqqani Network" and "to kill or capture Osama bin Laden."[1] Mansour pointed east. Mullah Omar, and all the Taliban leaders, were there, in Pakistan. Everything—logistical support, landmines, weapons, and Taliban came across at night. It was because we did not recognize the Durand Line and Pakistan would not let it rest. They wanted to control Afghanistan and Central Asia.

How far were we from Shah-e-Khot, I asked one of my guards? I lived there with Haqqani. He looked back smiling, holding his rifle level. It was near here. We could go there if I wanted. His cousin was in a dispute with Haqqani over some timberland. Was he worried? Someone threw a grenade into his house because he worked with the Americans. He left his job and lived in Khost. We hiked up to the eastern ridgeline. Haqqani was just over there, Mansur whispered. He was being protected by the Frontier Scouts in Miram Shah. The Americans knew 100% where he was, but there was something going on between the Pakistani government and the Americans, and the Afghans were getting squeezed. Jalaluddin hated computers and technology. They took man away from God. During Jihad he said a Muslim could marry an American girl, but not a Russian. Today he said the Americans were worse than the Russians. They were the worst Crusaders. He didn't believe that America landed on the moon.

Only Arabs talked about the Crusades. It was the Arabization of the war. I thought of Rahman, the Egyptian, who had stayed with us for two weeks, the beginning, I felt, of what would become al-Qaida and other modern jihadi movements. I decided at that moment to return to the mountains, and to have the Taliban take me to Jalaluddin. He would know about bin Laden. I had a contract with the U.S. Army War College to write a monograph on Islamic Fundamentalism in South Asia. I returned to Kabul and began to do my research. I met with Burhanuddin Rabbani, the former Mujahideen president.[13] His beard was white now. He was more refined, but still as distant as he was years ago. "When Daoud came to power he wrote to him and said if he got rid of the communists they would accept him," he explained. "They saw that they had to flee. They set up a *shura* in Peshawar.[14] They were separate from Babar."[15]

The next night I walked down an icy dirt driveway to the office of Mohammad Eshaq, editor of *"Payan-e-Mujahed"* (Message of the Mujahideen). He sat under a single light. There were no ideological discussions on Islam in Afghanistan. Islam was intertwined with family and tribal codes. Fundamentalist Islam came from the outside. Kabul University was a hotbed of political activism in the 1970s. The constitution of 1964 allowed for political parties. The bureaucracy was corrupt and old fashioned. It did not know the arguments that the students were making. The Soviet-leaning PDPA—the communists—was on one side, the Islamic parties on the other. The public did not understand the anti-Islamic groups. There was a division between intellectuals and the common people. This battle continued, unnoticed by the international community.

---

[13] Steven Elliott, *War Story: Sometimes the Real Fight Starts after the Battle* (Carol Stream: Tyndale Momentum, 2019).

[14] Ash-Shura, from a verse in the Koran, where believers are praised for consulting with one another. Thomas Patrick Hughes, *Dictionary of Islam*, Rupa & Co., Calcutta, 1992.

[15] Pakistani army Major General Naseerullah Babar, 1928-2011

Dar-ul-Uloom
(The House of Knowledge)

I flew to Delhi. It was early spring and the morning was cool and misty. Two monkeys played in the trees outside my window. We drove through quiet streets and took a highway north. It narrowed to two lanes, and we passed villages and baked mud brick factories. There were trucks, cars, bicycles, and carts filled with sugar cane, pulled by water buffalo. Girls and women in bright-colored saris carried loads on their heads. Over 850 million Indians lived on $2 a day or less.[16] This would change,[17] but not by much.

We reached Deoband, a quiet town with a red sandstone mosque with a white dome, in the Moghul style, rising high over a row of one and two-story buildings. I walked through an open gate in a red brick wall, onto the campus of Dar-ul-Uloom, down a walkway through a wide trimmed lawn, and up a flight of stairs to a row of bearded men in bare feet sitting on the floor at their desks on a balcony. A man pointed to the far end. I sat next to a thin man with a white beard. Fans purred overhead. "Have you found any terrorists here yet?" asked Adil Siddiqui, the public relations officer. A man brought tea and cookies. This was a spiritual institution. This area, which encompassed about 50 miles between the Ganga and the Jamuna, was noted for its spiritual values and was important for Hindus and Muslims.[18] Muslims came here because this school provided shelter for them. Discrimination was natural in a caste-driven country like India.

In 2005, the government commissioned a report, the fourth since independence, on Muslims in India. In 2006, "*The Report of the Prime Minister's Committee on Social, Economic and Educational Status of the Muslim Community of India,*"[19] was tabled in Parliament. It stated: Over 60% of Muslims in rural areas did not own land. India ranked fourth in the world in the number of tractors, yet only 2.1% of Muslims had one. Only 1%

---

[16] *Time*, 26 Mar. 2007.
[17] Central Intelligence Agency, The World Factbook
[18] The Ganga is the Ganges River and the Jamuna is the Brahmaputra. Jere Van Dyk, "The Long Journey of the Brahmaputra," *National Geographic*, Oct. 1987.
[19] Sachar Report on Status of Indian Muslims

had a hand pump. Nearly 60 % of Muslims had never attended school; 3% went to madrasas; 3% were college graduates; 6 % were policemen; a low percentage worked in government bureaucracies. Banks refused to grant loans in some Muslim areas. Most Muslims lived in artisan, pre-industrial communities. They, like Christians, were outside the Hindu caste structure. In 2016,[20] Muslims ranked lower than the Scheduled Classes and the Tribes, the Untouchables.

Two days before, Gautam Navlakha, a Hindu, co-founder of the "People's Union for Democratic Rights," told me that Muslims in India were like African Americans. A high percentage was in prison. There was a sense of deprivation, of insecurity and sense that you would not receive justice if you were Muslim. He said there was a Hindu fascist element, referring to the Indian People's Party[21] (BJP), the National Volunteers Union[22] (RSS), and the Bajrang Dal, a youth organization that wanted to stop Christian missionaries from converting Hindus, Muslim population growth, and to find the "fundamentalists" hiding in India, all of which gave rise to Islamic fundamentalism. In December 1992,[23] thousands of Hindus, led by the World Hindu Council, part of the RSS, armed with hammers, went to Ayodhya, in central India, and urged on by the BJP, against a Supreme Court order, destroyed the Mosque of Babur. Hindus believe that Ayodhya was where Ram, the Hindu god, was born, became human and had his castle,[24] but that Babur destroyed it to build his mosque. Riots broke out. Over 1,000 were killed, mostly Muslims, in the worst religious violence since Partition. In February 2002, a trainload of Hindu pilgrims visited Ayodhya. As they returned home to Gujarat, near the Pakistani border, the train stopped at a town called Godhra. A fight started between Hindus and Muslims. A car caught fire and 59 people died. Narendra Modi, a member of the RSS, was Chief Minister of Gujarat. His aides called for a strike. Riots broke out.[25] A World Hindu Council leader urged the rioters on. Over 1,000 Muslims were killed. In 2005, the U.S. banned Modi from the U.S. because of his alleged complicity in the riots.

---

[20] Zeeshan Shaikh, "Ten Years after Sachar Report." *Indian Express*, 26 Dec. 2016.
[21] Bharatiya Janata Party.
[22] Rashtriya Swayamsevak.
[23] "Timeline of the Riots in Modi's Gujarat," *New York Times* 6 April 2014.
[24] Times of India+Economic and Political Weekly+19 April 2017.
[25] *Economic and Political Weekly*, 2 Mar. 2007.

In 2014, the RSS campaigned on a promise to rebuild the temple to Ram. Modi, who joined the RSS as a boy, became Prime Minister, and the U.S., drawing closer to India to surround China, invited him to Washington. M.J. Akbar, a Muslim journalist, told me in 2007 that America's revolt against the British was a jihad. He joined the BJP and became Minister of External Affairs. I went to see Ajai Sahni, editor of the *South Asian Intelligence Review*. Three riflemen patrolled outside his compound. He said the BJP reflected the same mind set of radical mullahs. Everyone felt discriminated against in India. There was a constant sense of loss. There was the golden age of Hinduism, and India was a land of milk and honey until the bloody Muslims came.

Once Indians never saw themselves as Hindu or Muslim. Once, the Indus River was called the Sindhus, the center of the Sindhu civilization. The Persians could not pronounce "S" and so it became Hind. The land east of the Sindhus was Hind. The people were called Hind, from which comes Hindu.[26] The British turned Hindu into India. People west of the Sindhus were Afghans.

My driver in Kabul, like many Afghans, called India "Hindustan."

Dr. Indu Ignihotsi, a former history professor at Delhi University, a senior fellow at the All-India Democratic Women's Association, explained that Afghanistan to India was one region. Long before the arrival of Islam people and tribes moved freely. The communalist view—that the state should be divided along ethnic or religious lines—was an attempt to interpret history from a religious viewpoint. The Deoband said there was one Muslim community, and the BJP and the RSS said there was one Hindu community. The British, who came to exploit them, unlike Mahmud,[27] who just came to plunder and then left, saw them through caste or religion, the only way they felt they could understand them to rule them. "Afghans regard every native of India with undisguised contempt," wrote Sir Mortimer Durand, while negotiating the Durand Line.[28] In 1919, male Hindus in Afghanistan had to wear yellow turbans, and women yellow dresses to

---

[26] Romila Thapar, *The Penguin History of Early India: From the Origins to A.D.1300*, Penguin Books, India, 2002
[27] Mahmud of Ghazni, A.D. 97-1030 was the first Afghan Muslim invader
[28] Louis Dupree, *Afghanistan*. (Princeton: Princeton University Press 1980)

identify and distinguish themselves from Muslims.[29] This maybe was where Hitler got his idea to force Jews to wear a yellow star. Islamic fundamentalism was only one of the fundamentalisms they were facing, Ignihotsi felt. They faced an aggressive Hindu fundamentalism also.

"There must be purpose in life," said Siddiqui. All five fingers were not equal. Everyone had his own way of thinking. There were 40 places in the Koran where they were told to use their minds and to follow their own thinking. People here had made it their aim to lead a religious life. It was Islam, wrote Hannah Arendt, which gave Afghans an interpretation of history from Adam to Judgment Day,[30] providing a way that would lead to redemption and eternal life. The Taliban, backed by Pakistan and Arab states, ignored Western condemnation and destroyed the Buddhist statues at Bamiyan, a symbol of Buddhism, an offshoot of Hinduism, which promised Nirvana but not Paradise, a symbol of idolatry to Wahhabis.

The Jamaat-e-Islami Hind (India) headquarters was in a poor, crowded area on a dirt road in Delhi. It had a madrasa for girls and one for boys, a mosque, and a publishing house. They opposed the founding of Pakistan and nationalism, said Dr. N.K. Afandi, a spokesman. Islam was an international faith. They wanted people to know that it is the best model to shape human society. He drew on his cigarette. Yes, people found it disgusting, but it was not banned in the Koran. We watched little girls dressed like nuns in white hijabs and long blue dresses, running in a field, laughing. Others preached about the rituals of Islam. Jamaat was different from traditionalist peoples.[31] He meant the Deobandi. The Jamaat were seen as closer to al-Qaida.[32]

Siqqiqui and I walked through the campus. Every year, 10,000 men from around India took a test to be admitted. Many from around the world wanted to study here but the government would not issue visas. They accepted 800 applicants a year. There were 3,500 students. Everything was free. Age was no barrier. A student could be 60 and his teacher 30. A student could have four or five children and two wives, and his teacher may not even

---

[29] A.C. Jewett and M.J. Bell, *An American Engineer in Afghanistan* (St. Paul: North Central Publishing Company, 1948), 6.

[30] Hannah Arendt, *"The Origins of Totalitarianism"* (Harcourt Brace & Co., New York, 1975).

[31] "Traditionalist" Islamic Activism: Social Science Research Council, New York.

[32] Anatol Lieven, *"Pakistan: A Hard Country"* (PublicAffairs, 2011), 154.

be married. I saw a man with a gray beard, lying on a rope cot, studying in the sun. Once, al-Andulus, Baghdad and Cairo were vibrant educational centers. In the tenth century there were 300 madrasas (maderis) attached to mosques in Baghdad.[33] A madrasa in Cairo had 6,500 books on architecture, astronomy, and philosophy.[34] The British built madrasas to educate a class of clerks and managers for the East India Company.[35] Muslims built more madrasas the more they felt that the British were destroying their culture.[36]

Deoband was supported by donations, said Siddiqui. It had never and would never accept money from any government. Students got a one-month holiday during Ramadan, when Muslims fasted from sunrise to sunset, to come closer to God, to know hunger, to understand the poor. The Saudis could give the money to someone working in Saudi Arabia, said Praveen Swami, a journalist in Delhi. He could bring it as a gift.[37] We walked past student rooms, one with a motorcycle poster on a wall. Students walked by carrying books. One stopped to practice his English. We walked under archways and down narrow lanes, cool in the afternoon heat. A woman passed us, her face covered by a black, diaphanous veil. This was how it should be, Siddiqui noted. Women here observed purdah so as not to tempt the students. All precautions should be taken to preserve morality.

Purdah comes from the Persian "curtain," adopted by the Arabs and brought to India where it is called the "burqa." The Greeks of Byzantium required women to be veiled. The Koran calls for some to be veiled. *"O Prophet! Tell thy wives and their daughters, as well as all (other) believing women, that they should draw over themselves some of their outer garments (when in public); this will be more conducive to their being recognized (as decent women) and not annoyed."*[38] The Bible says *"Women adorn themselves in modest apparel with shamefacedness and sobriety; not with*

---

[33] Gregorian, *"Islam a Mosaic, Not a Monolith,"* 30.
[34] M. Ahmed, "Islamic Education Prior to the Establishment of Madrasahs." *Journal of Islamic Studies*, 1987.
[35] Barbara D. Metcalf, "Traditionalist Islamic Activism: Deoband, Tablighis and Talibs." *Barbara Metcalf: Piety, Persuasion, and Politics: Deoband's Model of Islamic Activism* (University of California, Davis), Social Science Research Council.
[36] William Dalrymple, *"The Last Mughal,"*India: Penguin/Viking, 2006, 22.
[37] Author interview, March 2007, New Delhi.
[38] Al-Ahzab (The confederates) 59 (The Koran).

broided (braided) hair, or gold, or pearls, of costly array."[39]

We walked outside the campus and down a lane. A pretty woman, her face uncovered, in high heels wearing a jeweled anklet, walked by with a girlfriend. A student approached, glanced over, and turned away. She was the world in all its temptation. He had to study and focus on God. Each student was required to pray five times a day, Siddiqui continued. They rose at five, prayed, had breakfast and went to classes from 6:30 to 10:30 and from 2:30 to 4:30. They studied math, Arabic, Persian, Urdu, and English, science, geography and social studies. They become Qaris, experts in recitation of the Koran. They studied it, and the Hadith, the thousands of the written sayings of the Prophet, which were not in the Koran; they studied *fiqh*, or Islamic law and logic. They taught computer skills and journalism now. They had to adjust to the modern world.

I felt sorry for the student who glanced at the woman. Sex was sinful outside of marriage,[40] even, as Jimmy Carter said, to think about it. The Taliban were poor and couldn't afford to get married.

They got paid to fight. They, like the Mujahideen, burned girls' schools and forced women to cover up. They hated what they wanted and could not have. "We limit their (women's) roles in public," wrote a Saudi journalist, "ban them from public participation in decision making, we doubt them and confine them because we think they are the source of all seduction and evil in the world."[41] The word for woman in Arabic is "*hormah*," from "*haram*," (prohibited). Women are dangerous, they who bring life into the world, who create a home, what gives man comfort, and strength, what he needs to live on earth, but which is not his home.

We went to a guesthouse for lunch and as we ate a hearty soup, Siddiqui went to the heart of fundamentalism. "Every Muslim wants that all the comfort in life, all the facilities, should be removed so that they can be closer to God. All they want to do is to die. Some become suicide bombers. Islam is not in favor of life. This life is temporary. Only life after death is permanent. We must prepare for that life."

---

[39] 1 Timothy 2:9.
[40] Deuteronomy 22:22.
[41] Lawrence Wright, "The Kingdom of Silence." *New Yorker*, 5 Jan. 2004.

The 9/11 hijackers went to Las Vegas[42] where they drank and had women dance for them. They went to a night club in Florida. They, like Jimmy Swaggert, the televangelist who went with a prostitute, succumbed to the temptations of the world. Their martyrdom would wash away their sins. *"Indeed, those who surrender themselves to Allah and do good works shall be rewarded by the Lord: they shall have nothing to fear or regret."*[43] They would give their lives to God. The Bible says, *"...Know ye not that the friendship of the world is enmity with God? Whosoever therefore will be a friend of the world is the enemy of God."*[44] *"The unbelievers rejoice in this life: but brief indeed is the comfort of this life compared to the life to come."*[45] President Bush said soldiers who died in Iraq died a noble death. If a Muslim killed other Muslims, they went to Paradise. If he killed himself, it was suicide, forbidden in the Koran.

In 2004, Cardinal Joseph Ratzinger, later Pope Benedict XVI, wrote, commenting on secularism in Europe and the low birth. "The West reveals here a hatred of itself."[46] He suggested that European culture was dying and that "there is a strange lack of a desire for the future," while Islam, under pressure from the West, had become the fastest growing religion in the world. Muslims must be humble. *"Do not walk proudly on the earth. You cannot cleave the earth, nor can you rival the mountains in stature."*[47] They, like Christians, must follow God's will. *"There is no triumph except that given by Allah."*[48] *"You have no will except as Allah wills."*

"We support the education of women," said Siddiqui. "If a woman is taught, then the whole family learns. We oppose co-education. People will be tempted. This would put our morality in danger. Those who do not want education for girls are not following the teachings of Islam."

Often, men said this, afraid that the more women were exposed to the West, the less moral they would become. "Islam emphasized morality," Siddiqui added. They must not lose their character, the main pillar of Islam. The *maulavi* (graduate) must be a symbol of moral rectitude. Relations with

---

[42] "Home." *Daily Mail Online*, 8 Sept. 2011.
[43] Al-Baqarah/The Cow 111 (The Koran).
[44] James 4:4 (New Testament).
[45] Ra'd/The Thunder 26 (The Koran).
[46] *Avvenire*, April 15, 2004.
[47] Al-Isra/ The Night Journey 17:37 (The Koran).
[48] Al-Anfals/The Spoils 8: 10 (The Koran) 35 Ibid 76:30.

a woman outside of marriage were immoral and an injustice. They gave classes on the morality of men and women. Afghans talked of preserving a woman's "sexual honor." In ancient tribal culture it was crucial to control women because only a woman knew the father of her child. In rural Afghanistan when a girl reaches puberty she disappears into her village.

In Kashmir, I met with Hameeda Nayeem, a professor at the University of Kashmir. Her parents wanted her to get married, but she wanted an education first. They were upset, but her father knew the Koran. Part of the Prophet's mission was to free women. Where did it say in the Koran that anyone had the right to keep her down? Islam gave her freedom. It was the fanatics today who did the disservice to Islam. When you craved freedom for yourself and saw colonial powers destroying it, as she had seen India crushing hers since her childhood, then she had to act. Purdah was not part of Islam. You could not impose a code on anyone in Islam. If the Prophet was not given the authority to impose such a law, how could any petty person do this? "Democracy has been the inner logic of history," she wrote. "It is the will of the people and not their leaders or politicians that finally triumphs at the end of the day." "*And abide quietly in your homes and do not flaunt your charms as they used to flaunt them in the old days of pagan ignorance*," said the Koran.[49]

"The British hanged thousands of Muslims in Delhi in 1857," said Siddiqui. For Indian Muslims, it was jihad, a defensive war against the invader. It was nine years after the War of Independence that this institution was founded. It was for the revival of Islam.

Sometime after, according to legend, what the British call the Indian Mutiny of 1857, a young man called Mahmud journeyed to Deoband, where he met an older man also called Mahmud, who sat with him, said Saddique, in the Indian tradition, under a pomegranate tree and taught him, over ten years, the Koran. The British would not let him preach in India and so in 1915, Mahmud, the first Deobandi graduate, went to Afghanistan and preached that with God on their side they could defeat the British.

After World War I, the independence movement grew. Many Dar-ul Uloom graduates worked with Mahatma Gandhi, Saddique added. After driving the Britishers out the voice of Islam could be raised because of the

---

[49] Al-Ahzab/The Confederates 32:33.

meritorious service of those who came from this institution. Dar-ul Uloom opposed the creation of Pakistan.

It did not want to divide the Umma. Before Partition, students came here from around the world. They were internationalists, and that tradition continued. Their purpose was unchanged, to form religious citizens and to serve Islam, humanity, and the world. They formed and molded others in the same pattern. He took me to meet the vice chancellor, a lean, vigorous man in his 90s. They were not attached to any political party or to any political thought, he explained. Their principle was the same as it had always been: to serve humanity and bring a message of peace. The U.S.A. was against Islam. It was the biggest terrorist in the world. Each graduate had his own thoughts. Each madrasah followed the thinking of its founder.

Back outside Saddiqui pointed to a large gray mosque with cupolas and minarets, rising high over the campus. They were expanding it because they had more students. It was called the Taj Mahal of Deoband. He smiled. The Taj Mahal, built by Shah Jahan, a Mughal emperor, is a mausoleum in memory of his wife, Mumtaz Mahal. "Fundamentalism" was a misconception. Everyone was a fundamentalist. You needed to have certain principles. They were attached to those of their holy book, as one who was attached to the Holy Bible was a fundamentalist. To use the phrase Islamic fundamentalist was an attempt to defame Islam. Islam and Christianity had been at loggerheads—he smiled, he loved this word—from the beginning. After 9/11 Mr. Bush said this was a *salabi jang*, a crusade. Jihad means effort to, for example, make yourself better and seek a better job. It can mean to fight against those who are against us. We teach jihad in the true sense of the word. It is a weapon of self-defense.

The root in Arabic is *jhd*, to strive, to struggle. Jihad meant war, said M.J. Akbar. It was not evil. It was to fight against injustice. It was a matter of just war. Siddiqui took me to a small room with a low ceiling, overhead fans, a tiled minbar from which an imam delivered his sermon, simple carpets and straw mats to pray on. Students came close to us. Siddiqui pointed to a marble urn filled with dirt and sprouts of grass. It was where the pomegranate tree stood. Siddiqui stood silently in respect. This was Haqqani's heritage, the home of Deobandi Islam.

In May, as I was finishing my monograph in Pakistan, the editor of *Times Books* who I had met with before, sent an email. I returned to New York and we talked again about a book on the Tribal Areas, a blank space on a map, he called it. The CIA couldn't find bin Laden. I could find him, I felt, through Jalaluddin. I returned to Kabul and met with two tribal chiefs from the border region. One, named Azfar, said he would take me across the border. Not a hair on my head would be harmed. He drove with a pistol in his lap, his bodyguards behind us, passing, falling back, passing again. We stopped by a shop, near Khost city, where two boys were changing a tire in the dirt. He pointed at a narrow baked-mud house. It was Haqqani's first mosque. He was a *"Malang,"* a mystic living on alms, a holy beggar, a Sufi, a man who wore his hair long or in a bun, in Pakistan a *"be-shar,"* (an outlaw).[50] I had seen young mullahs standing by a road by a mosque with their hands out.[51] He was a *"kabarri,"* a scrap dealer, who bought materiel from Afghanistan's wars and sold it in Pakistan. His mother's name was Ladonna. No one knew his father's name. He was saying that Jalaluddin was a peasant. "The Indians…make numerous distinctions among humans," wrote Mohammad Abu Rayhan al-Bruni, a Persian linguist, the founder of Indology, who accompanied Mahmud on his raids into India.

"We differ from them in this, for we regard all men as equal except in piety. This is the greatest barrier between them and Islam." He believed, like Greek Christians, that man must believe in one god to achieve salvation.[52]

We reached Azfar's village and sat in the shade. He looked at the pictures in my book about my time with the Mujahideen.[53] "Haqqani, Gulbuddin Hekmatyar and Yunus Khalis were fighting for the CIA, British intelligence and Saudi Arabia," he said softly. It made him cry, all the destruction, all the deaths, just to satisfy the U.S., Britain and Saudi Arabia. "Who was Yunus Khalis?" a chief in Jalalabad shouted at me. "Who was his grandfather?" It is the most important question in Afghanistan. It is class warfare. It is the story of this book. The call came for evening prayers.

Azfar and the other chief didn't pray. They hadn't prayed all day. Al-Bruni said "common people" worshipped idols, but the Greek elite, like

---

[50] Lieven, *"Pakistan: A Hard Country,"* 154.
[51] From maula, meaning lord or master, but in general, a learned man.
[52] *Tahqiq ma la'l-Hind (History of India)*, Hyderabad, 1958, p.54.
[53] *In Afghanistan—An American Odyssey*, (Coward McCann) 1983.

Hindus worshipped only God. Night fell. Riflemen stood guard. Azfar said men from his tribe fought in Kashmir in 1947. During the Soviet war they went to General Gul[54] to ask for weapons.[55] They were dead because they remembered the Durand Line, he said. They wanted men who would burn Afghanistan.

I asked Gul how many Arabs, and other foreigners the U.S. and its allies brought to Afghanistan in the 1980s. "We brought 54,000 men from 38 countries to fight in Afghanistan and registered everyone. The CIA was very happy," he said proudly. The 9/11 Commission said after the Soviets left in 1989, and the U.S, that 10,000-20,000 Arabs trained in camps run by al-Qaida.

That night Azfar and I six other men sat on a cloth and ate a delicious feast, and then a curly haired man came to me. He remembered me from before. After 9/11 U.S. jets bombed them at night. Jalaluddin was buried in dirt and rubble up to this chest, but they pulled him out. How did the U.S. know where he was but couldn't find bin Laden?

The next day Arif's uncle, 6' 3," his green and black turban spiked high to show his status like a Comanche chief's war bonnet, arrived from Miram Shah with two guards. We walked in the desert away from the others. Men were on a *ghazi*, a holy mission, to kill tribal chiefs, he said softly. A ghazi was also one who fought the infidel invader. If they found me, they would behead me. I said, reluctantly, I wouldn't go with him. He thanked me. He would not have to try to protect me. We returned for lunch and then I sat with Haqqani's man under a tree. He pointed in my book to a picture of his bodyguard. He was killed two years ago. I remembered this thin smiling teenager in his Russian fur hat with a rifle standing by Jalaluddin's door. He guarded him for over 30 years.

---

[54] Lt. Gen. Hamid Gul (1936-2015), head of Military Intelligence (MI), later the Interservice Intelligence Directortate, (ISI), 1987-90.
[55] *"The 9/11 Commission Report,"* *W.W. Norton & Company, Inc.*, New York, 67.

The Rise of Christianity and Islam

In 45 A.D., Mark, who wrote quoting Jesus, *"Go ye into all the world and preach the gospel to every creature,"*[56] began to preach to the Copts, *"qubt"* in Arabic, in Greek, *"aigyptious,"* descendants of the ancient Egyptians,[57] bringing Christianity to Egypt. In 251 a boy, called Antony, was born into a peasant family. When he was about 18, a minister preached that he must sell all that he owned, give the money to the poor, and follow Jesus. He moved from his village by the Nile into the desert.[58] At 35, he went up into a mountain, and founded Christian monasticism.[59] In 312, Constantius I, seeking help before his battle with Maxentius at the Milvian Bridge on the Tiber, saw a vision of a burning cross on the sun and had it painted on his men's shields. They won in what is considered a turning point for Christianity, for some the First Crusade. Now emperor, Constantine saw himself as a servant of God. In 330, to create a new Rome, he moved the capital of the Empire to Byzantium,[60] at the juncture of Europe and Asia, called it Constantinople, and founded the Byzantine Christian Empire. Just as Christians would not serve in the Roman army, he felt that he could not be a Christian and be in politics. He was not baptized until he was dying.

In 350, Arsenius, a well-born highly educated tutor in the court of Emperor Theodosius, prayed to God to escape the need to conform to the world, to be a witness for and to discover the will of God, who told him to flee, to pray, and to be silent. He fled to Egypt and went into the desert, becoming one of the thousands of the Desert Fathers,[61] whose lives of mediation and prayer inspired poets in Arabia. There, between 567 and 573[62] Mohammad (The Praised One) ibn Abdallah, was born into the Hashem, the ruling clan of the Quraysh,[63] descended from Ishmael (he who

---

[56] Mark 16:15.
[57] *Encyclopedia Britannica* (1967 ed.), p. 477–478.
[58] Matthew 19:21.
[59] Henri J.M. Nouwen, *"The Way of the Heart,"* New York: Ballantine, 2003, 5.
[60] Founded by the mythical Byzias.
[61] Henri J.M. Nouwen, *The Way of the Heart*, 14.
[62] Maxime Rodinson, *"Muhammed,"(* New York: Pantheon Books, 1980), p.38.
[63] Ibid. It means "shark" in Arabic, although it is not clear where this comes from.

laughs) in Mecca, a pilgrimage site, caravansary, and trading center in a mountain gorge near the Red Sea, on the caravan route from al Yaman (the South) to Damascus and elsewhere in the Byzantine Empire. Some caravans, with goods from India, had 1000 camels. His father died before he was born. His mother died when he was six. All around Arab Christians, part of a community, the church, and Jews, part of the AM, in Hebrew "the people," worshipped "*al-Lah*" (the God). Other Arabs worshipped idols. He was brought up by his paternal grandfather, custodian of the Kaaba, the temple of the gods, and later by his uncle Abu Talib. Mohammad married at 25 to Khadija, about 40, a wealthy trader, twice married, widowed, with children. He was a good trader, husband, and father. But merchants were growing rich and no longer shared their wealth with their tribe weakening tribal solidarity.[64]

Mohammad, a seeker, like a Desert Father, went into the desert to Mt. Hira three miles away to meditate and pray in a cave.[65] One night when he was about 40, the archangel Gabriel (*Jibril*), or the Holy Spirit,[66] appeared and said "*qaraā*" (recite),[67] from which comes *al-Quran* (Koran), "The Recitation." He was the Messenger of God.[68] For 23 years he recited messages calling for moral reform and for all to surrender *(Islam)*, from *al-salam* (peace) to the one true God, and his will. At first, they had no name and called themselves the faithful (mu'min)[69] and only later did they call themselves *muslimun*, the singular of which is *Muslim.*[70] They were part of the "*Umma*" (community), from AM, a new tribe, of the poor, equal before God.

He was called a false prophet, and he and his followers fled 200 miles north to Medina. The Bedouin (desert Arabs) rejected them,[71] setting the precedent that Muslims must fight. They were poor but created a Muslim state,[72] took Mecca, and Mohammad rode at the head of an army making

---

[64] "*The Cambridge History of Islam: The Central Islamic Lands*" (Cambridge: Cambridge University Press, 1970) 10
[65] Rodinson, "*Muhammed*" 69
[66] Ruhu Al-Quddus
[67] Gregorian, "*Islam a Mosaic, Not a Monolith,*" 5
[68] Rodinson, "*Muhammed*" 69-71
[69] Ibid, p.129
[70] Ibid, p.188, 235
[71] Repentance 9:97, The Koran "The Desert Arabs surpass the town dwellers in unbelief and hypocrisy".
[72] S. Athar Husain, "*The Glorious Caliphate*" (Karachi: Hafiz & Sons, 2001), p.15.

treaties with Christian and Jewish communities. He sent missionaries to al Yaman, whose tribes opposed this religious invasion from the north. In 632, he sent his cousin, son-in-law, and most importantly, his adopted son, Ali ibn Abi Talib.[73] That June, Mohammad died. The Umma chose Abu Bakr, a merchant and early convert, to be the Khalifa, from *Khalif*, (*Caliph*, in English), a successor, he who led the daily prayers, their leader. He fought uniting most of Arabia and sent the believers to evangelize the world. Christian Medieval writers called them the Saracens[74] barbarian nomads of the desert, who conquered the Byzantine provinces of Egypt and Syria. Some tribes beat down by Greek or Persian rule welcomed them, but then, going against the Koran, they sought power, angering Mohammad's original followers. The Caliphate *(Khalifate)* moved from Medina to Kufa, in today's Iraq. Civil war erupted and the second and third Caliphs were murdered. Ali, the fourth, fought the governor of Syria, related to the third Caliph, but then agreed to talk. In 661, one of his men, angry that Ali, Mohammad's true successor, would, by debating this, go against the will of God, killed him with a poisoned sword while he prayed in a mosque in Kufa.

Ali became a *shaheed*, or witness, a martyr, from *martys* (witness) in Greek, a witness for God, and Islam divided into Shia and Sunni. Shia *(Shi'a)* means followers, the followers of Ali, because Arabs believed in the power of blood and that a man's virtues passed to his descendants, and that he was Mohammad's successor, murdered by Sunnis, who felt that Mohammad's companions, the virtuous rightly guided ones *(al-Rashidun)* were more qualified. Sunni means path. Sunnis are the "People of the Path," traditionalists who believe in the Koran and the Hadith, the codified sayings of Mohammad. While all Caliphs had to be of the Quraysh tribe, they did not have to be a direct descendent. In 661, Muyawiya, an Umayyad, a merchant clan of the Quraysh, became the Caliph, founding the Umayyad Caliphate, which he moved from Medina to Damascus, where he created a dynasty, putting itself above the Umma.

Muslims revered Jesus as a prophet, but Mohammad brought God's final message. Islam had to rule. In 674, a Muslim army and navy laid siege to Constantinople. After three years and 30,000 killed, they retreated. In 711,

---

[73] Ali, Muhammad's cousin, married his daughter, Fatima. They had two sons, Hassan and Hussein.

[74]"Saracen,"*Encyclopædia Britannica (1967), Vol 19*, Saracens.

the Muslim viceroy of Africa sent General Tariq bin Zayed, a former Berber slave, with 12,000 men across the Mediterranean to liberate Christian Spain. He landed at what became Jabal-ul-Tariq (Gibraltar), Tariq's rock, beginning what would become "*al-Andalus*," Muslim Spain. He ordered his men to burn their ships so that they could not retreat, and then offered a prayer, which is that of the Pakistani army.[75] That year Muhammad bin Qasim, with 12,000 Arabs, crossed the Arabian Sea to what is today the mouth of Indus River, at Karachi, the commercial center of Pakistan. In 732, Abd ar-Rahman, the Muslim governor of Cordoba, led a cavalry across the Pyrenees and on the Roman road at Tours met the cavalry of Charles Martel, the ruler of Francia, today France and Germany. For a week they faced one another and then ar-Rahman charged. Martel won, what western historians call a turning point in history, and Arabs, the Court of Martyrs. Had they left behind their tribal feuds and cared more about victory than booty, they might have won. The road to Britain was open.[76]

In 741, a clan, descended from Mohammad's uncle, Abbas, living in Syria, angry at the inequality of the Umma, and following a hadith which said an army would rise in Khorasan, the eastern province of Persia, and to follow the black flags of this army over ice, for it brought with it *al-Mahdi* (the messiah), sent Abu Muslim, a former Persian slave, part of an anti-Umayyad group, there, where he called for equality as it existed under Mohammad, raised an army and in 747 unfurled a black flag, and rode west. The army of the Umayyad Caliphate, raised a white flag, and rode east. In 750, they met in Iraq. The Abbasids killed almost the entire Umayyad dynasty, and created the Abbasid Caliphate, beginning the "Golden Age of Islam."[77]

In 780 Ahmad ibn Hanbal[78] was born in Baghdad. As a teenager he walked three times, over 1000 miles, to Mecca. He said the Koran had existed for all eternity, ignoring that Othman, the third Caliph, issued the first official Koran and had all others destroyed. He died in 855, an ascetic, and populist martyr, the father of fundamentalist Islam. In 800, in Persia, Shia Muslims from near the Caspian Sea, followers of Zayd ibn Ali, a

---

[75] "Motto of Pakistan Army." Pakistanarmy.gov.pk/motto.php
[76] "Charles Martel," *Catholic Encyclopedia*, http://www.newadvent.org/cathen/03629a.htm.
[77] Gregorian, "*Islam a Mosaic, Not a Monolith*" 200
[78] Ibn or Bin means "son of."

grandson of Mohammad's grandson, Hussein, led by a priestly class
(imams), who claimed descent from Mohammad, but did not believe that
imams were divinely inspired, or that leadership should pass from father to
son, calling themselves Zaydis, migrated to al-Yaman seeking religious
freedom.[79] In 860 they established an Imamate (priestly kingdom) which
lasted until 1962. Today they are called the Houthis. In Central Asia, the
Arabs built posts against the Turks, who, like traders along the Silk Road,
converted from Buddhism and Shamanism to Islam. From Gazni, today a
dusty town southeast of Kabul, Mahmud, a Turk and founder of the
Gaznivid dynasty, rode 17 times from 1001 to 1025 through the mountains
passes, [80]where the tribes resisted before joining him. They invaded
Hindustan, looting temples, destroying idols, razing towns and villages,[81]
killing Shia,[82] bringing Sunni Islam to northern India, and assuring that it
would be dominant in Afghanistan.

Constantinople was now the most powerful Christian city in the world.[83]
The Benedictines, the most powerful monastic order in Europe, led by its
monastery in Cluny, wanted to reunite it with Rome.[84] This led to more
pilgrimages to the Holy Land and the will to reconquer Spain. In 1071 the
Ottoman (Osman) Turks conquered Baghdad, a vibrant educational center
with 300 madrasas attached to mosques,[85] like al-Andalus and Cairo.[86]

As Muslims they were faithful to the Abbasid Caliphate.[87] In 1076 they
took Damascus, home of Syriac Christianity, whose liturgy is in a dialect of

---

[79] Albert Hourani, *"A History of the Arab Peoples"* (London: Faber and Faber, 2013, 221

[80] Charles Allen, *"God's Terrorists: The Wahhabi Cult and the Hidden Roots of Modern Jihad."* (London: Da Capo Press, 2006) 7-9.

[81] H.W. Bellew, *"Races of Afghanistan,"* Thacker, Spink, and Co., Calcutta, 1880, 73.

[82] Thapar, *"The Penguin History of Early India,"*419 According to Thapar, Mahmoud may have also conquered Indian cities to reduce the import of Arab horses. The most profitable business for Ghazni traders was exporting horses to northern India, 425-434, 438-39.

[83] George T. Dennis, "1054 The East-West Schism," *Christian History*, Oct. 1, 1990, www.christianitytoday.com/history/issues/issue-28/1054-east-west-schism.html.

[84] *Encyclopedia Britannica*, Vol. 23, 1967 ed. 11

[85] Gregorian, *"Islam a Mosaic, Not a Monolith,"* 24

[86] M. Ahmed, "Islamic Education Prior to the Establishment of Madrasahs," *Islamic Studies*, vol. 26, no. 4 (1987).

[87] Gregorian, *"Islam a Mosaic, Not a Monolith"* 26

Aramaic, which Jesus spoke, once the *linqua franca* of the Middle East.[88] From Constantinople to Rome the call came for a Crusade, from the Spanish *"cruzada,"*[89] to retake Asia Minor and the Holy Land. In 1099, Christians retook Jerusalem. Eleanor of Aquitaine and other women became Crusaders. Then Genghis Khan (1155-1227) came, along with Christians, followers of Shamanism, and nature religions,[90] off the Asian steppe, creating the largest empire in history, and captured the Abbasid Caliphate.[91] In Damascus, Taqi ad-Din Ahmed ibn Taymiyyah (1263-1328), a jurist and follower of Hanbal, angry at the destruction of the great Mesopotamian cities and their irrigation systems, which in the 1930s had not been repaired,[92] said the Mongols conquered them because they had become weak and enamored of Greek philosophy. They had to return to the Koran, to the Hadith, and to the sayings of the Rashidun. He was the first *"Salafi,"* one opposed to any change in Islam, the first to call for war to restore Islam to power. He and his followers were the *salafiyya*, "followers of the forefathers."

In 1362, the Turks took Constantinople, called it Istanbul, founding a new Caliphate, the first political and military capital of the Muslim world in a non-Arab city and colonized the Middle East.[93] Timor I Lung (the lame Timor), Tamerlane, born in 1336 near Samarkand, took Delhi, and two years later Aleppo and Baghdad. In 1492, Christians retook the Iberian Peninsula. Christopher Columbus, of Genova, left on his voyage, the beginning of the Spanish Christian Empire.

In 1498, Vasco da Gama of Portugal, charged to open the trade routes to India, and still angry over Muslim rule, sailed east with four ships and 170 men and Augustinian monks but with no goods to trade with the Arabs, beginning the European conquest of India. On the East Africa coast, he forced a sultan to give him a navigator, who followed the monsoonal winds to India. The Augustinians founded a mission in Zanzibar.[94] On his next trip, da Gama stopped a pilgrim ship returning from Mecca, robbed the pilgrims,

---

[88] Robert L. Wilken, "Christianity Face to Face with Islam." *First Things*, 2009.
[89] "Marked with a cross."
[90] Author: Sheila, "The Birch Tree." *Notes from a Russian Garden*, 24 Oct. 2013, https://notesfromarussiangarden.wordpress.com/2013/09/17/the-birch-tree/.
[91] Gregorian, *"Islam a Mosaic, Not a Monolith"* 26-35.
[92] Robert Byron, *"Road to Oxiana."* Oxford: Oxford University Press, 1982, 46.
[93] Eis-tin-polin (Istanbul), meaning "in the city," in Greek.
[94] "Home," *AUGNET*. http://www.augnet.org/?ipageid=2131.

locked them in the holds, and against the pleas of his crew burned to death over four days all 350 men, women and children,[95] one of the worst maritime massacres in history.

---

[95] Gary Paul Nabhan. *"Cumin, Camels, and Caravans: A Spice Odyssey."* (Berkeley: University of California Press, 2014) 231-239.

The Birth of the Modern Mujahideen

In 1525, Babur, of today's Uzbekistan, a Turk who claimed descent from Genghis Khan, and Tamerlane, moved to Kabul from which he invaded northern India and routed its ruling Afghan tribal chiefs, founding the Mughal (Mongol) Empire,[96] whose revenues at its height were more than the Ottoman and Persian empires combined.[97] North was the Hindu principality of Jammu, and the larger Buddhist kingdom of Kashmir, until the 13th Century, when the Sufis[98] inspired by Christian monasticism came and Kashmir became mostly Muslim and part of the Mughal Empire.[99] In 1600, a group of London businessmen, anxious to take the spice trade from the Dutch, who had taken it from the Portuguese, founded the East India Company. In 1602, the Dutch founded the Dutch East India Company, the largest corporation in recorded history. In 1604, the French created an East India company. American colonies traded with Europe, the Ottoman Empire, and North Africa. People were curious about Islam and the Koran sold well in bookstores. Thomas Jefferson had a Koran in his library.[100]

In Arabia in 1703, Muhammad ibn Ab al-Wahhab was born into a family of jurists in the poor Beni Temin tribe in Uyainah, an emirate in the Nejd, a rocky scrubland, a rolling desert, and Bedouin who fought over grassland and oases.[101] He studied in Medina, where some teachers taught the theology of Hanbal and Taymiyyah. In 1730, Shah Waliullah, an Indian mullah went on Haj to Mecca[102] and studied in Medina.[103] Seven years later,

---

[96] Mogul or Mughal is Arabic for Mongol, but Babur, Zahir Ud-Din Mohammad (1483-1530), was a Turk. The Moghul Empire should therefore be called a Timurid or Turki empire.

[97] Dalrymple, "*The Last Mughal*"

[98] Sufi, or those who profess the mystic principles of the tassawwuf.

[99] Hourani. "*A History of the Arab Peoples*," 72-75.

[100] John B. Boles, "*Jefferson: Architect of American Liberty*" (New York: Basic Books,) 2017, 85.

[101] David Dean Commins, "*The Wahhabi Mission and Saudi Arabia*", (London, I.B. Tauris) 7

[102] Hajj means "setting out," or pilgrimage to Mecca, one of the five pillars of Islam, required of all Muslims.

[103] Allen, "*God's Terrorists*," 48-49.

Nadir Shah, a Turkish soldier of fortune who became king of Persia, raided Kandahar, from *Gandhara*, of the Gandharan Buddhist civilization of what is today eastern Afghanistan and western Pakistan, the earliest records of which are from the time of King Darius of Persia, Fifth century, B.C. He pressed men into his army, including Ahmed Shah Abdali, about 22, a Pashtun chief, with 20 thousand horsemen. Nadir Shah took Kabul from the Mughals, rode east into the mountains, where again the tribes made him pay a toll, then joined him, and they conquered northern India. Ten years later he retreated, but was beheaded in his tent on the frontier. In the chaos, Ahmed Shah, a commander in his cavalry, stole his treasury, split his men into two sections, to confuse his enemies, and rode to Kandahar. The Pashtuns held a tribal council, like that of Athenian democracy, where only male leaders could vote. Ahmed Shah remained silent and was chosen chief of the Pashtuns. He became Ahmed Shah Durrani (Pearl), for the pearl he wore in his ear.[104]

Al-Wahhab returned home and became a revivalist preacher calling for all to believe in the one true god, to fight the apostates, the unbelievers, the blasphemers, and the Turks. Shah Waliullah returned, angry at the British occupiers, that the Mughal Empire, weakened by Nadir Shah, accepted Sufis, and that its princes married Hindus, and like al-Wahhab wanted his fellow Muslims to live simply and truthfully as they did during the time of Mohammad. In 1744, al-Wahhab allied himself with Mohammad ibn Saud, a minor, charismatic chief, and married into his clan. They rode from oasis to oasis killing and plundering, calling on men to believe in the one true god, and to join them. God would protect them and they would enjoy the camaraderie and love of other believers. If they were killed, they would go to Paradise. The Turks called them Wahhabis, and likened them to the Kharajites,[105] early Muslims who separated from society to follow the true Islam, who felt that a man's virtue, not his lineage, was important, and that only he who did not seek power could be the Khalifa.[106]

In India, the British defeated the Dutch and the French and began to

---

[104] Sir Olaf Kirkpatrick Caroe, *"The Pathans"* (Oxford: Oxford University Press, 1958), 249- 257

[105] "Those who revolt, or "those who went out," in Arabic.

[106] "Verily I have set thee (Abraham) as an Imam (leader) for mankind," Surah ii, the Koran.

destroy the Moghul Empire. In 1747, Shah Waliullah called upon Durrani to revive it.[107] Durrani defeated the Moghuls, but as a Muslim did not place himself over them. He, like Mahmud, returned to refill his treasury, to protect the Empire, creating his own Empire, which included Kashmir, part of Persia and Central Asia, the largest after the Ottoman Empire in the second half of the 18th Century,[108] and founded modern Afghanistan. In Kashmir, a series of warlords ruled until the Hindu maharaja of Jammu created the state of Jammu and Kashmir.

In 1776, Americans founded the United States, which led, in France, because of poverty,[109] a selfish aristocracy, and the Catholic Church[110] in 1789 to the French Revolution, which led to the Terror,[111] and to Napoleon.[112] "In Britain, there were fears of invasion, rumors of war, famine, and pestilence," wrote a Christian author.[113] Men's hearts were failing them because of fear. "The study of the Holy Scriptures was stimulated and the spiritual life of the people was deeply stirred." In 1795, Christians, drawing on the power of the East India Company, created the London Missionary Society, the British and Foreign Bible Society and other groups to preach the gospel in India, which led in 1857 to the Indian Mutiny, in truth a religious war.[114] "The highest task, the task without precedent is that which awaits the (Dutch) East Indian Civil Service official…it should be considered as the highest honor to serve in its ranks…the select body which fulfills the mission of Holland overseas." In 1805, the British reached Delhi, disbanded the Mughal army and began replacing Muslim leaders with Hindus. Shah Waliullah's son issued a "*fatwa*" that Delhi had become enslaved by infidels[115] and must return to Islam.[116] Muslim traders financed

---

[107] Allen, "*God's Terrorists*," 31
[108] Thomas Barfield, "*Afghanistan: A Cultural and Political History*" (Princeton Univ. Press, 2012), 97-105.
[109] Boles, *Jefferson: "Architect of American Liberty*," 126.
[110] Ibid. p.198-199.
[111] Clery et al, "*A Journal of the Terror: Being an Account of the Occurrences in the Temple during the Confinement of Louis XVI*" (Cambridge: Folio Society, Cambridge University Press), 1955.
[112] Thomas Stewart Veitch, "*The Story of the Brethren Movement*" (Glasgow: Pickering & Inglis, 1934), p.11.
[113] Ibid, p.12.
[114] Hannah Arendt, "*The Origins of Totalitarianism. New Ed. with Added Prefaces New York*" (Harcourt Brace Jovanovich, 1973,)
[115] Kafir or kufr or "That which covers the truth;" i.e., denying the existence of God,

madrasas preaching jihad.[117] Waliullah's followers, whom the British called Hindustani fanatics, led the first Wahhabi jihad against the West.[118]

In 1808, the East India Company, wary of Napoleon allied with Persia or Russia, sent Mountstuart Elphinstone, a Scottish diplomat, to explore trade routes to Central Asia, to gather intelligence, and to negotiate an alliance with the Emir of Afghanistan. He was the first Westerner to cross the Indus[119] considered at different times, the border of Persia and India, into the land of the Pashtuns, what Herodotus called Pactiya,[120] arriving in Peshawar February 25, 1809, where the "*Kingdom of Caubul*," gave him a splendid reception. He was struck by the verdant beauty and vitality of what tribesmen today call Pekhawar, the Afghan winter capital, before the mountains, where Mahmud, Shah and Durrani used the tribes as an advance force and reservoir of soldiers who brought back spoils of war and tied their economy to India.[121] In 1824, Wahhabi missionaries reached Peshawar, called the second Arab invasion of Afghanistan.

In 1830, France invaded Algeria. In Delhi, the British abolished the Moghul court of Bahadar Shah II,[122] closed madrasas and substituted English for Persian, the language of the court. In 1837, British Royal Marines took Aden, population 500, in The Yemen, to use as a coaling station. In 1850 in Kashmir, Britain pursuing its "Forward Policy," Kipling's "Game Great"[123] against the Czarist Russian Orthodox Christian Empire, for control of Afghanistan, and Central Asia, created the Dogra dynasty, a buffer against Russia.[124] In Delhi, British officials planned to abolish the Mughal Court, to introduce British laws, and Christianity. Once, British

---

infidelity, not believing the Koran or any of the tents of Islam.
[116] Charles Allen, "The Hidden Roots of Wahhabism in British India," *World Policy Journal*, XXII, Summer (2005).
[117] Dalrymple, "*The Last Mughal*" 83
[118] Allen, "The Hidden Roots of Wahhabism in British India"
[119] "Journey to Caboul" recounts Elphinstone's journey of January 7 to June 27, 1809.
[120] Caroe, "*The Pathans*," 441.
[121] Gregorian, "*The Emergence of Modern Afghanistan*"10-15.
[122] Dalrymple, "*The Last Mughal*" 73
[123] Karl E. Meyer and Shareen Blair Brysac, "*Tournament of Shadows: The Great Game and Race for Empire in Central Asia*," (New York: Basic Books, 1999) 382
[124] Praveen Swami, "*India, Pakistan and the Secret Jihad: The Covert War in Kashmir, 1947-2004*," (Abingdon: Routledge, 2007), 1-25

citizens intermarried with Hindus and Muslims when they were drawn to Indian culture, but now, it seems, they saw Indians more as heathens and pagans.[125] In 1857, 64 regiments of the East India Company's Bengal Army[126] rebelled[127] igniting the Indian revolution. Lower class Muslims, calling themselves the Mujahideen,[128] and jihadis, those who die in defense of the faith, and the British *Nasrani* (Christians), fought to expel evil from Muslim land, as required in the Koran, killed Indian Christians, and saved British Muslims. The British brutally put down the rebellion.[129] Britain disbanded the East India Company and made India part of the Empire.[130] Muslim rule,[131] which began in 711 in the south ended in 1858. Muslims, 20% of the population, had ruled a thousand years.

In 1866, Mahmud made his way to Deoband. Today Dar ul Uloom's website says, "Political decline had reduced Muslims to a state of helplessness and misery, distraction and anxiety; by the establishment of Darul Uloom Deoband, they received equanimity, composure, and stability." Mahmud brought anti-colonial Deobandi Islam to the Pashtuns.

---

[125] Dalrymple, "*The Last Mughal*" 10

[126] Ibid

[127] Lieven, "*Pakistan: A Hard Country*" 48-52

[128] Azim Nanji and Razia Nanji, "*The Penguin Dictionary of Islam*," (New York: Penguin, 2008) 243 and 418

[129] "Indian Mutiny," *Encyclopædia Britannica,*

[130] *Encyclopedia Britannica,* vol. 23, 1967 ed. 456

[131] *Indian History - Muslim Period in India,* http://www.gatewayforindia.com/history /muslim_history.htm.

The Birth of the Haqqanis

In 1869, France and Egypt finished building the Suez Canal. In 1881 the French invaded Tunisia. Russia, to protect the Eastern Orthodox Church and the Serbs, opposed the Ottomans. In 1882, the British again invaded Egypt. In 1893, Mortimer Durand, foreign secretary of British India, journeyed to Kabul, where he was given a grand reception and where he negotiated, in Persian,[132] the French of Asia, a treaty, but with vague threats a delimitation of the frontier with India, with Abdur Rahman, the Emir of Afghanistan.[133] Twice Britain fought Afghanistan, and twice they lost, weakening Afghanistan.[134] The British were now at the Hindu Kush, a new buffer against Russia. Rahman, who needed arms and money to fight his internal enemies, signed the Durand Line Accord,[135] giving away for 100 years part of Afghanistan, dividing Pashtun tribes, and creating what the British called the Tribal Areas of India, a second buffer against Russia. In 1897, Rahman, was able, finally, to bring most of the tribes to heal and disarmed the population.

In India in 1903, Abul ala Maududi was born into a religious family in Hyderabad, and homeschooled to assure a proper Muslim education. He rebelled, wore western clothes and played cricket. In 1914, war broke out in Europe. The Ottoman Empire allied with Germany against Britain and France. The Sultan—only an Arab could be a Caliph—declared jihad against the British Empire. In 1916, Britain and France, with the assent of Russia, drew up the secret Sykes-Picot-Sazanov Agreement to divide up the Ottoman Empire. In 1917, Turkey lay in defeat. The Soviet Union was formed. Maududi's father died and he had to work. He became a journalist and the intellectual and political descendent of Shah Waliullah.

In Afghanistan, in 1923, King Amanullah, who had abolished slavery, banned madrasas, provided education for women, tried to lift the veil and curtail polygamy and child marriage, called for jihad against the British. In

---

[132] Caroe, "*The Pathans*," 388
[133] Dupree, "*Afghanistan*," 425-28
[134] Wars of 1839-42 and 1880-90.
[135] Dupree, "*Afghanistan*," 427

1924, the Mangal, a subtribe of the Zadran and other tribes, manipulated by British intelligence, revolted against him and the Kabul elite.[136] Britain recognized Afghanistan, but stopped subsidizing Amanullah or allowing him to import arms from India. He established diplomatic relations with the Soviet Union, raising his and Afghanistan's stature for standing up to the West. In 1924 the Ottoman Caliphate fell.

In 1928, Hassan al-Banna, 22, an Egyptian school teacher and Muslim activist whose father was a watch repairman and who worked in a mosque, upset at the way that the British treated workers in the Canal Zone, founded *"al-Ikhwan al-Muslimun,"* the Society of Muslims Brothers, the Muslim Brotherhood.[137] He, like the Benedictines, like al-Taymiyyah, Martin Luther, al- Wahhab, the Deobandi, and Maududi, called for a return to their faith to give them strength. In 1929, Amanullah abdicated, and the tribes felt powerful. In 1931 in Kashmir, a Muslim peasant led a revolt against the Hindu maharaja who had taxed them into poverty. In 1932 Kabul University was founded.[138] In 1941, Maududi, inspired by al-Banna, and the Bolsheviks, founded Jamaat-i-Islami (The Islamic Society) to rebuild India.[139]

In 1943, the first of four sons was born in a baked mud house, with a dirt floor, no electricity or running water, in Saran, a small village among pine trees and rocky hills in the foothills of the Suleiman Mountains of Paktia Province. He was named Jalaluddin: Jalal, or loftiness, sublime, splendor, or glory, in Pashto, and Arabic; and din: belief, creed or faith. Jalaluddin means "greatness of faith." A man, they say, becomes his name. As a child, he rose, like his parents, before dawn, had breakfast of hot unleavened bread, baked in a village tandoor, and yogurt from their goats, sometimes watered down. Tea was expensive, a close friend told me. When he was old enough, he went to the mosque with his father for morning prayers. Sometimes they had potlucks, where a man brought a portion of meat, or bread, or a vegetable and men and boys ate together. Women and their daughters ate separately, cooked, cleaned, brought water from a stream

---

[136] Swami, *India*, *"Pakistan and the Secret Jihad,"* 7
[137] Thomas Ruttig, "The Loya Paktia's Insurgency," *Decoding the New Taliban*, ed. Antonio Giustozzi (London: Hurst, 2012) 58
[138] Gregorian, *"The Emergence of Modern Afghanistan,"* 309
[139] Sayyid Abul A'La Mawdudi, *"Come Let Us Change This World,"* Markazi Maktaba Islami, Delhi, 1991.

or from a well, took care of their children and worked in the fields. They stopped at prayer times, performed their ablutions with sand if there was no water nearby, and prayed towards Mecca.

In 1944, the government opened a school in Kabul to teach Shari'ah, or Islamic law. There were no public schools or madrasas in the mountains. They, like most Pashtuns in eastern Afghanistan and of the Tribal Areas, were poor but not ignorant or indifferent. As Britain prepared to divide the British Raj into India and Pakistan, Jawaharlal Nehru, who would become India's first prime minister, came to the Tribal Areas to convince the tribesmen to join India, but they, whose ancestors had fought with Mahmud and Durrani were not interested. They would be a part of Sunni Pakistan. On August 14th, 1947, India was divided into the Dominion of India and the Dominion of Pakistan, within the British Commonwealth. In India, the princely states were bound, legally and morally, to choose between India and Pakistan.[140] In Kashmir, Gulab Singh, the maharaja, was wary of Nehru's socialism, and how he, a Hindu, would fare in Pakistan. Hindus backed by the state, attacked Muslims, killing thousands. India sent forces to pressure Singh. Pakistan was determined that Jammu and mostly Muslim Kashmir would be part of Pakistan. But its army had only three generals. The British refused after the war of 1857 to raise a Muslim brigade. Pakistan hired nearly 500 British officers, two of whom commanded.[141] They raised the Irregulars, a Pashtun militia from the Tribal Areas. They swept north towards Srinagar. Singh panicked. India would help, but only if Jammu and Kashmir became part of India. He signed the papers of succession and fled to Bombay.

But the Irregulars, who Margaret Bourke-White[142] called "savage nomads," like the Arabs at Tours in 732, did not see a difference between conquest and pillage. For three days, she wrote, they terrorized Hindu, Sikh and Muslim alike,[143] giving India time to land enough troops to stop them. Pakistani officers called for jihad. Religious scholars issued fatwas. The Pakistani commander took the nom de guerre, Tariq, after the Berber general

---

[140] Hassan Abbas and Jessica Stern, *"Pakistan's Drift into Extremism Allah, the Army, and America's War on Terror"* (Abingdon: Routledge, 2005) 17
[141] Stephen P. Cohen, *The Pakistan Army*, Oxford: Oxford University Press, 1998 17.
[142] The first American female war photojournalist (1904-1971)
[143] Swami, (*India, Pakistan and the Secret Jihad,*) 21-22

of North Africa, and the Irregulars became the Mujahideen.[144] Pakistan wanted to send "a liberation army to Palestine to help the Arabs free the Holy Land from the Jews," wrote Bourke-White. In 1948, *Dawn*, the English-language newspaper and voice of the government, condemned the founding of Israel, and called for a united front of Muslim nations to fight for the "salvation of Islam."[145] The Pakistani army would be the defender of the Umma.

That same year, Sayyid Qutb, born, like Maudidi, into a religious family, who memorized the Koran as a boy, taught school and became a novelist, literary critic, and bureaucrat in the Ministry of Education, received a grant to study education systems in America. He studied in Washington D.C. and earned a master's degree at what is now the University of Northern Colorado.[146] There is a photograph of him laughing with the president. He studied at Stanford. He admired America's economic success and technology, but not what he called its violent culture, and racism, its materialism and loose moral conduct. He was horrified to see a dance in a church. "In the United States," he wrote, "a man is valued by the size of his bank account." He called America's God money, and democracy a Western religion.[147] In America, it appears, he returned to Islam. He was a Puritan. It was bred into him as a boy, as water feeds a plant. When he returned to Egypt he wrote, "In the Shade of the Koran," which influenced bin Laden. He explained, in *Milestones*, his theory of "*jahiliyya*" a time of darkness, meaning the Western order, led by America and Europe, was in spiritual decline and decadence. Al-Qaida, the Taliban and ISIS call democracy a Western religion.

In 1950, the school of Islamic law became the Faculty of Theology and Islamic Law at Kabul University.[148] In 1953, Daoud Khan, like his first cousin, Shah, a descendent of Ahmed Shah Durrani, became prime minister. The U.S., in the Cold War, approached India, seeking an ally, but it wanted

---

[144] Hussein Haqqani, "*Pakistan: Between Mosque and Military*" (Washington: Carnegie Endowment for International Peace, 2005, 28-29.
[145] Margaret Bourke-White, "*Halfway to Freedom*," (New York: Simon and Schuster, 1949), 93-94
[146] Steven A. Cook, "*The Struggle for Egypt: From Nasser to Tahrir Square*" (Oxford: Oxford University Press, 2013), 85
[147] Sayyid Qutb, "*In the Shade of the Koran*," (London: MWH Publishers, 1979), 53
[148] Gregorian, "*The Emergence of Modern Afghanistan*," 309

to lead an unaligned movement.[149] In 1954, the U.S. signed a mutual defense agreement with Pakistan, to contain the Soviet Union, and as an ally in the Middle East, the beginning of the U.S.-Pakistan military alignment.[150] "The basic relationship with India was intellectual," said Secretary of State John Foster Dulles, who called India's neutrality, "immoral,"[151] in contrast to its relationship with Pakistan, "which came from the heart."[152] France, after eight years fighting Vietnamese communist and nationalist forces, with financial help from the U.S., lost the battle of Dien Bien Phu, and French Indochina. The U.S., in part to keep India from becoming communist, took its place.[153] Algeria began its fight for independence. Daoud asked for more U.S. aid, but like previous leaders wanted to remain nonaligned. The U.S. said no. Going against the advice that Abdur Rahman gave his son on his deathbed to never trust the Russians, Daoud asked the Soviet Union.

In 1960, Daoud, to reunite the Pashtuns along the Durand Line, sent soldiers, in mufti, into the Tribal Areas. The tribe wanted to be left alone and pushed them back. In 1961, he invaded with a larger force, and the tribes, and Pakistan's F-86 fighter jets, repelled them. In Kabul, the People's Democratic (Communist) Party of Afghanistan (PDPA), close to the Soviet Union, became active.[154] In 1962, the Algerians overthrew the French, the first Muslim victory over a western nation, exciting the Muslim world. The U.S. war in Vietnam grew. Students from Berkeley to Berlin to Tokyo debated the merits of capitalism and communism. In1966, in Kabul, Ghulam Mohammad Nazi, and Burhanuddin Rabbani, on the Faculty of Theology and Islamic Law, went to al-Azar University in Cairo, where they joined the Muslim Brotherhood.

In 1970, Jalaluddin, 22, who was in Kabul during this time, went down to Pakistan to Akora Kethak, a settlement of one story nondescript concrete and wood buildings and on the crowded dusty road between Peshawar and

---

[149] Marvi Sermed, "What Pakistani National Interest Is Served by the Presence of the Haqqani Network on Our Soil?" *Daily Times*, 28 Jan. 2018,
[150] Stephen Cohen, "*India and America: An Emerging Relationship*," The Brookings Institution Press.
[151] Ibid.
[152] Ibid, p.95
[153] Ibid, p.4
[154] David B. Edwards, "*Before Taliban: Genealogies of the Afghan Jihad*," (Berkeley: University of California Press, 2002) 25

Islamabad to Dar'ul Uloom Haqqania, the Haqqani House of Learning, a one-year Deobandi seminary of stark white buildings in the Mughal style, surrounded by a high black wrought iron fence, founded in 1947 by Maulana Abdul Haq who had studied at Deoband. In 1971, he finished his studies of the Sunna—the Hadith and the Koran, changed his name, as Afghan men do, to Jalaluddin Haqqani. In 1972, Nazi and Rabbani, with students, founded the Muslim Youth Organization (MYO), which debated and fought the Marxists on campus. Nazi went to India, where he was murdered, possibly by Zahir Shah. When his body was returned the road was packed from the airport to the university.

In 1973, Daoud Khan, who hated the MYO, aided by leftist military officers, and communists, overthrew Zahir Shah in a palace coup and became President, establishing a republic, ending the Durrani dynasty. Rabbani, and MYO students, who called him "the Red Prince," changed the MYO to Jamaat-i-Islami (the Islamic Society). After Daoud killed some students, Gulbuddin Hekmatyar and Ahmed Shah Massoud in the engineering faculty and others fled to Peshawar. That same year Zulfikar Ali Bhutto, a Shi'a aristocrat became Prime Minister of Pakistan.

There were long camel caravans in the streets of Kabul then, the "*kuchi*" (nomad) women unveiled, the only sound that of bells tinkling around a camel's necks. School girls wore short skirts and long socks, and laughed holding their books. Some women were veiled but most dressed like women in the West. The U.S. Embassy gates were open. Peace Corps volunteers played the Marine Corps guards in flag football at Thanksgiving, and people watched from the bleachers. There were over 5000 hippies in Kabul, and the sound of the Jefferson Airplane and the Rolling Stones mixed with the smell of hashish and the call to prayer. The hippies brought Afghanistan into the international drug trafficking networks.[155]

Daoud met with the Shah of Iran and twice with Bhutto. In 1977 Zia ul-Haq overthrew Bhutto and imprisoned him. April 1977, Daoud, who got rid of the communists around him after he came to power, went to Moscow for three days. He met with Brezhnev who said they were trying to bring the communist factions together. Daoud said Afghanistan would always be independent and walked out of the room. On April 29, 1978, Afghan

---

[155] Dupree, "*Afghanistan*" 755

communists, with the KGB, killed Daoud and his family in the Arg Palace and installed a new government.

In February 1979, the Atyollah Imam Ruhollah Khomeini flew from France, where he had been living, escorted by Mirage jets, to Tehran, and implemented his philosophy of *"vilayat-i-faqth;"* that the Shi'a clergy were the guardians not just of the faithful but of the state, and overthrew the Shah of Iran, the first Muslim fundamentalist victory over Westernization in history. In March, Egyptian President Anwar Sadat signed a peace treaty with Israel. In April, General Zia ul Haq hanged Bhutto. In November, Wahhabi revolutionaries took over the Grand Mosque in Mecca, quoting Khomeini, who quoted Qutb, who quoted Shah Waliullah, calling for "an end to corruption, ostentation, and mindless imitation of the West" and to return to Islam. On December, 24th the Soviet Union, worried about the revolt, the revolution in Iran, by its failure over 150 years to eradicate Islam in Central Asia,[156] about the Mujahideen, that the Soviet Union would soon become majority Muslim, that its satellite government in Kabul, and its leader, Hafizullah Amin, who attended Columbia University, were too close to America, invaded Afghanistan.

That same year, Jerry Falwell, a Southern Baptist minister, whose church had 22,000 members and an audience of millions on radio and television, an unofficial leader of what President Richard Nixon called the "silent majority," those who supported him and the war in Vietnam, referring to Roe vs. Wade, the Supreme Court decision regarding abortion, asked what had happened to this great republic. Oh God, he prayed, save our nation. Oh God, give us a revival. He, like Qutb, felt America was in moral and spiritual decline. Political operatives saw a voting bloc. Billy Graham said: "I don't want to see religious bigotry in any form. It would disturb me if there was a wedding between the religious fundamentalists and the political right. The hard right has no interest in religion accept to manipulate it."[157] A political religious movement had begun.

On October 6, 1981, President Sadat was assassinated while watching a military parade in Cairo. The BBC announced in its Arabic broadcast that *"Usuleyyoun al-Muslemoun"* (Muslim fundamentalists) killed him, the first

---

[156] Gregorian, *"Islam a Mosaic, Not a Monolith,"* 84
[157] *Christianity Today*, 2005

time these words were used. *"Usual,"* means roots, the roots of Islam: the Koran, the Hadith, the *"Ijma,"* and *"Qiyas."* The Koran was the word of God; the Hadith were the codified thoughts of Mohammad; the Ijma, the consent of the *"Mujtahidun,"* the wise scholars; Qiyas was the truth, arrived at by them. That evening I flew to Pakistan, a fledgling reporter for the *New York Times.* A week later I took the train from Rawalpindi up to Peshawar. We walked at sunset from the station down a wide empty road with the smell of flowers in the air.

"Here then," wrote Sir Olaf Caroe, the last British governor of the Northwest Frontier Province of India, "with a shadowy ancestry and a foundling sire are grouped together these illustrious tribes whose names resound through the pages of 150 years of English writing, names synonymous with wild deeds of daring, famed for their strange mingling of loyalties with impatience of control."[158]

I stayed at Deans, once a British hotel, with hardwood walls, linen tablecloths, heavy cutlery, and waiters in frayed starched white jackets. I found a driver, Munchi (secretary), who took me to the seven Mujahideen military-political parties, authorized by Pakistan, fighting the Soviets. Gulbuddin Hekmatyar, a small, cold, soft-spoken man, said they would win because they had God. Burhanuddin Rabbani, with a thick black beard, slouched in his chair, like a king on a throne. Russia was the first enemy he said, and America the second. Munchi took me to see Yunus Khalis, of Hezb- i-Islami Khalis (the Khalis Islamic Party). He had a barrel chest, a deep voice, a bandoleer, and a pistol. He was sitting on the wood floor, drinking green tea, talking with two men. I joined them. A man brought me a glass of tea. A man smiled and asked how could they help me? I wanted to live with the Mujahideen.

A few days later I rode with four men, one of whom was bandaged, down a narrow paved road through checkpoints into the Tribal Areas, a land of baked mud homes, camels, donkeys, women with jugs of water on their heads, men with rifles, dun-colored old British forts, with pathways lined with white painted stones, and Pakistani flags hanging in the sun, to Miram Shah, the fly and mosquito invested capital of North Waziristan. I hiked with a relay of guides up into the mountains. The air was brisk and the sky a

---

[158] Caroe, *"The Pathans,"* 21

shimmering blue. We walked across a high plain, and down into a valley through a bombed village to a compound, the doors ten feet high, to a small room overlooking the interior, where bearded men knelt on the floor over a map. One shook my hand, welcomed me with a deep voice and said we would talk later. It was Jalaluddin. A man gave me a small plate of honey to go with my tea. A shiny rust-red Kalashnikov, with a scope, superfluous on an assault rifle, leaned against a wall.

We were at *"Shah-e-Khot"* (the King's place). We were 18 men,[159] a British photographer, Ken Guest, a former Royal Marine, and me. Each man carried a six-shot Lee-Enfield, the same rifle we used in the Civil War. We sat around campfires and lived on gritty rice, bread, and tea. MI-24 helicopter gunships like giant gray caterpillars, came slowly, or hovered, over us. Five times a day, Jalaluddin stood on the roof of his room, and called his men to prayer. They placed their rifles in front of them, and bowed in the dirt, the rain, and the snow. Men put their hands over their hearts and bowed their heads wishing me peace. When we hiked, they said *"estale mache,"* may you not be tired. One day a big-boned man came on a donkey with a guide. His name was Rashid Abd al-Rahman. He was an Egyptian army major. Haqqani put him with Ken and me. We had a small fire in our room and slept on a sandy floor. Rahman didn't like me, an American. Did I have any news about President Sadat? I said he was killed a month ago, and Rahman was happy. Haqqani, I felt, was part of something larger than here. We had three Sam-7 anti-aircraft missiles. Rahman insisted on firing one. Jalaluddin let him. He fired at a helicopter, and "killed many rocks," said Mallem (teacher) my interpreter, ruefully. The Russians now knew who, and where, we were.

One night as we walked back from attacking an army fort with a mortar, the men were laughing and talking, like athletes after a victory. An artillery shell landed a few yards away, a dud. Jalaluddin and his men kept talking. I walked alone. These men were happy and strong, fighting for their faith and the only life they knew. One morning, an MI-24 hovered above us. I watched a man looking up, as we hid in a room with weapons and stacks of pine boxes stenciled, with the type of ammunition, in English, shivering with fear. When I left, half of them led me slowly, single file as dusk approached

---

[159] Anthony Rogers et al. *"Flashpoint! At the Front Line of Today's Wars,"* (London: Arms and Armour, 1994), 9-37

through a mine field, with two camels in the lead as mine sweepers. Both of them stepped on mines and screamed in the dark as a man cut their throats. We reached a ridge, and the men prayed. They would die to protect me. I hiked sadly backed down to Pakistan and to a compound where other Haqqani men welcomed me.

"You Are Like Our Founding Fathers"

On May 5, 1982, President Reagan, at a speech at Eureka College, his alma mater, declared that America would fight the Soviet Union by supporting anti-communist groups seeking their freedom, wherever they were.[160] In June 1983, I wrote an op-ed in the *Times*, passing on the plea of the Afghans to provide something to shoot down the helicopters. I felt that if the U.S. did this that the Soviets would respond with greater force. One day after doing an interview in a radio studio about a book I wrote on my time with the Mujahideen, a man interviewed before me came over. His name was Zalmay Khalilzad, an assistant professor at Columbia and consultant to the State Department on Afghanistan. He wanted to start an organization to help the Afghans, and to promote the Mujahideen. I was upset at what I had written and wanted to help women and children. He brought a group of men together at Columbia. A gray-haired man in a blue suit took notes. I became the executive director of "Friends of Afghanistan, Inc." We had lunch in the White House with an intense man on the National Security Council, after which he gave me booklets with CIA stamped on them. Zbignew Brzezinski, President Carter's National Security Advisor, was head of the board of directors. We provided a grant to a university to create a news bureau in Peshawar where Afghans would learn to be print and video journalists, and to send their reports to the Middle East to show what the Soviets were doing in Afghanistan. It became the *"Media Information Department of The Islamic Afghanistan,"* the news agency of the Pakistani-controlled Mujahideen Government-in-Exile. Abdul Rahim, the Mujahideen spokesman, later ambassador to the U.S., was the director. He said it was "a reliable news agency," supported by the U.S. Embassy in Islamabad.

Zalmay and I met with former Secretary of State William Rogers at his law office in New York, where he said the Mujahideen were freedom fighters, like our Founding fathers. No, I thought, they were not like George Washington and Thomas Jefferson. Then I realized that they were like us, men with rifles fighting for what they believed in. On March 21, Afghan

---

[160] Robert Michael Gates, *"From the Shadows: The Ultimate Insider's Story of Five Presidents and How They Won the Cold War,"* (New York: Touchstone, 1996), 256

New Year, 1984, I saw Rogers in the White House where in the East Room President Reagan put his arm around an Afghan-American girl in a colorful Kuchi dress, and said, as the cameras rolled, "We are with you. You are freedom fighters. You are like our founding fathers." The U.S. had moved its war against communism to Afghanistan and the Mujahideen were its proxy army.[161]

The U.S. invited the Mujahideen government-in-exile, comprised of a representative from each of the seven Mujahideen political parties, to New York to present its credentials to the United Nations, and to meet with President Reagan in Washington. I organized an evening at the U.N. Plaza Hotel, where they would meet U.N. delegates. I stood at the door welcoming everyone. Din Mohammad, who was with Yunus Khalis when I met him, arrived and asked when I was returning. Warmth swept over me. Gulbuddin, the rotating president, and a Sunni, huddled with the Iranian Shia delegation. The next day I took him to the U.N. where he humbly presented his government's credentials at a police box, then gave a speech to a small crowd of Afghans. We went to a press conference that we hosted. That night I sat in his room as he lay on the bed in the Roosevelt Hotel, owned by Pakistani International Airways. A man from the State Department called to confirm his meeting with the President. I told Hekmatyar. No, he couldn't do that, he replied, in his soft feline way. I told the official. "Who did he think he was?" he shouted. He knew very well who he was, an ambitious, ruthless, deracinated, anti-American Afghan, from Kunduz in the north, a member of the Muslim Brotherhood, with no tribal backing. The next night, he sat against a wall at the home of the Pakistani ambassador to the U.N. and dominated the room with his personality. The Mujahideen returned to Peshawar where he gave a speech condemning the U.S., which was supplying his political party with millions of dollars in materiel, making him wealthy. His party issued a statement threatening me. Khalilzad traveled to Saudi Arabia, which was matching the U. S. support for the war. China, NATO allies, and Arab nations supported the Mujahideen.

In 1989, the Soviet Union left Afghanistan, al-Qaeda rose, the Mujahideen took power and Hekmatyar became Prime Minister, briefly. Civil war broke out. He earned the name, "the Butcher of Kabul" for sending thousands of rockers supplied by Pakistan into Kabul. He became close to

---

[161] Ibid, 425

bin Laden. In 1994, the Taliban rose in Kandahar to cleanse the land. Twice they failed to take Kabul. Jalaluddin instructed them how to attack from the north and they took the city. In February 23, 1998, bin Laden, Ayman al-Zawahiri, of Egyptian Islamic Jihad, the leaders of al-Gamaá al-Islamiyya, and Jamiat-ul-Ulema in Pakistan, and the Jihadist movement in Bangladesh, announced at a press conference, in Khost Province, Haqqani territory, the formation of the World Islamic Front for Jihad against Jews and Crusaders. On August 7th, al-Qaeda attacked the U.S. Embassies in Nairobi, and Dar-es Salaam. In response, the U.S. fired 75 cruise missiles into their training camps in Khost Province and at a pharmaceutical drug factory in Khartoum.

On September 11, 2001, I took the subway to Wall Street where I worked at a private investigative firm. It was quiet and I saw the flames rippling across the World Trade Center. I walked over and looked up at a woman with long curly black hair looking down from an open window. The building began to crumble and people screamed, and we ran. A giant black ball four stories high came down Broadway and another came up Rector Street. I ducked into a restaurant and followed others to the basement. We waited, and I walked up the street through the ashes to where I worked. Soon, the second building crumbled and the sky was black. A friend and I walked up Broadway through the ashes, thicker now, and it was silent and the wind blew. There were broken windows, buildings covered with soot, a crushed police car, men walking in a daze and smoke rising from a large pile of rubble.

That evening a friend at CBS Radio came up to me on the street and said "Afghanistan." Could I come in tomorrow? Yes, it came from there, my small country. Until then I had only thought of the tragedy.

In October, the U.S. invaded Afghanistan. That November, Franklin Graham, Billy Graham's son, said he believed that Islam was an evil and wicked religion.[162] I saw the beginning of a religious war. On December 24th, I stood on the tarmac at Bagram Air Base, built by the Russians, 35 miles north of Kabul, and looked up at a ridge. I wondered how different the Taliban were from the Mujahideen. I walked through Kabul, silent and empty, past piles of debris, and destruction. In February 2002, Daniel Pearl went missing in Karachi. I took a CBS camera crew and went there. We

---

[162] NBC News 11/16/01.

learned that he had been kidnapped and slaughtered, and that the ISI, which grew in power in the Afghan-Soviet war, held Omar Saeed Sheikh, an Englishman of Pakistani heritage, for a week, and then gave him to the police. Secretary of State Colin Powell said the ISI was not involved in Pearl's kidnapping.[163]

On March 2, the U.S. Army announced that it had launched Operation Anaconda, its largest ground offensive since Vietnam, at Shah-e-Khot, where al-Qaeda and the Taliban were making a final stand. I thought of the Haqqanis and the men there, of Rahman, the Egyptian, and what I had heard about the Haqqanis' ties to al-Qaeda. I returned to Afghanistan and stood in a field and watched sadly as a B-52 bombed Shah-e-Khot. My driver, fixer, and I drove east past blackened villages in the hills. I had walked in those hills. We reached the top of a mountain pass and I stood in the snow and the wind blew. Jalaluddin was nearby. I was the enemy now, but I wanted to talk to him. We drove down the icy dirt road and across the windy plain, between jagged snowy mountains. In the distance, I saw a gleaming white mosque with twin turquoise and dark wood minarets, looming over the land. It was Haqqani's mosque, said my driver. He was married to a wealthy Arab. I felt that he had sold his soul. It was like a giant cathedral overlooking a town in France or Spain. In Khost, I walked through the high black wrought iron gates onto a campus. Boys carried books or sat in the sun talking. Men stood outside the mosque and across the way was a new madrasa. I gave my card to a man. He hadn't seen Jalaluddin recently.

I learned that Yunus Khalis was alive and we drove from Kabul to Jalalabad, found a guide, and drove into the foothills of Tora Bora to his compound. It took over an hour, but finally men let me see him. We entered the compound and walked past children's plastic toys, took off our shoes and walked up a few steps into his home, and to his room. He lay on his bed on his side. He was thin and wore a prayer cap. His face was gaunt and his beard was trimmed. I shook his hand gently. It was warm and soft. It had been callused before. He thanked me for coming. A small boy was sitting with him. A little girl, in a dress, climbed onto the bed. He picked her up and kissed her on the check. He had married a 20-year-old woman, his second wife. I thought of her in the kitchen crying, her life destroyed. Her family arranged the marriage. He was famous, and a great mujahid. I talked about

---

[163]"Tariq Ali: Who Really Killed Daniel Pearl?" *Guardian*, 5 Apr. 2002

our meeting and that he sent me to live with Jalaluddin. He was grateful that I and others came to help them during Jihad. He was sick, his leg was broken, and he hurt all over. He took my hand and clasped it over his eyes. He wanted to see a doctor in India. The man next to me refused to let me talk about bin Laden. Did he have a good life? "Oh yes," he replied, softly. The man said we had to go. He had been saying it for ten minutes. I kept trying to talk about Jalaluddin and bin Laden, but the men stopped me. I sat on the bed, took his hand and said goodbye. We walked outside. The men kept telling me how lucky I was. Journalists came here all the time, but no one saw him. We drove back up through the canyon where in 1842 Pashtuns slaughtered a British expeditionary force, the worst defeat of the British Empire. I now had to find Jalaluddin.

Major General
Naseerallah Babar

It was April and steaming hot in Peshawar. We passed identical red brick houses with front lawns surrounded by a cyclone fence. I saw a large white Buddhist statue on the roof of one house and told the driver to stop. Retired Major General Naseerallah Babar, a burly man in a brown shalwar (long shirt) kameez (baggy pants) showed me his artifacts, swords, and statuary. He collected Gandharan art. He wore a small diamond ring on his left hand. We sat on sofas and he adjusted his shalwar over his knees. A servant brought samosas and tea. I was told that he created the Mujahideen and rode with the Taliban into Kabul.

He did his bit for Pakistan. In 1973, the world was changing. Mao[164] was getting old, and they were afraid that Brezhnev was going to try to fulfill Peter the Great's wish to reach the warm waters of the Indian Ocean.[165] In Afghanistan, Daoud launched his coup, became president and set off bombs in Pakistan. Prime Minister Bhutto created the secret Afghanistan cell.[166] In 1960 and 61, as prime minister, Daoud sent troops to attack them over the Pashtunistan issue. Afghanistan was the only nation to vote against Pakistan's admission to the U.N., in 1947, because of the Durand Line, he reminded me. Yunus Khalis, Hekmatyar and Massoud and some of their compatriots, angry at Daoud's ties to the communists, came to see him. He was Inspector General of the Frontier Corps, the Pashtun paramilitary created by the British. He gave them passports, code names, and put them in the army. He called Hekmatyar 'the electrician' and Massoud 'the plumber.' He was building a house and a nucleus in Afghanistan. If they were to succeed, they needed a leader. Hekmatyar was clearly the most capable, but they needed a spiritual leader and brought over Rabbani. He called him the 'mason.' He went to the U.S. Embassy for funding. They knew nothing about weaponry. In 1897, Abdur Rahman

---

[164] Mao Tse-Tung, founder of the People's Republic of China, died in 1976 at 82.
[165] Leonid Brezhnev, General Secretary of the Central Committee of the Communist Party, USSR, 1964 - 1982.
[166] Hussein Haqqani, *Pakistan: Between Mosque and Military*," 102

disarmed the population. They had to train them in ambushes and operations. Three people knew: Bhutto, the chief of Army Staff, and the Foreign Minister.[167] The Afghan cell was at work.[168]

It was clear that when Daoud and Bhutto were meeting that he and Babar were implementing Bhutto's "Forward Policy" to rule Afghanistan and Central Asia.[169] In 1993, the Durand Line Accord was to expire. The Haqqanis were not part of his project. In August 1975, the Afghans finished training and took the name "Mujahideen." He took the leaders to meet the CIA in Islamabad. He gave them rifles that Pakistan captured in the 1965 and 1970 wars with India. They, except Hekmatyar, who stayed behind, attacked government sites in Afghanistan. Afghan forces captured or killed 80 men, most of them, but he called the attacks successful. More men joined them. Bhutto, under pressure from Jamaat-i-Islami, created to be a like a Bolshevik vanguard, tied to the ISI, banned alcohol and gambling, declared Friday a day of rest and Islam the state religion.[170] He appointed Zia ul-Haq, a small man from the lower middle class, who he called "a dog," and his "monkey general," who acted humbly, avoiding alcohol, while other officers drank, and prayed while others did not, to be chief of army staff.[171] In July 1977, Zia overthrew Bhutto and declared Pakistan an Islamic state. Babar, close to Bhutto, stopped training the Afghans. In April 1979, Zia hanged Bhutto. Robert Gates, former Director of the CIA, wrote that the U.S. began to support the Mujahideen in July and elsewhere wrote "long before" the Soviet invasion, and that Brzezinski, the National Security Advisor, "complained over and over" that the CIA was not doing enough to help them.[172] In 1988, Benazir Bhutto became Prime Minister,[173] and again in 1993.

In 1996, Babar, now Interior Minister, helped bring the Taliban to power. In November 1998, Brzezinski, said in an interview the U.S hoped to lure the Soviet Union into Afghanistan in revenge for helping North

---

[167] Ibid 102

[168] Ibid 175

[169] Shakil Durrani, "General Naseerallah Babar - A Legend of a Man." *Express Tribune*, 15 Feb. 2011.

[170] Lieven, "*Pakistan: A Hard Country,*"153

[171] Syeda Hameed, "An Excerpt from Syeda Hameed's Biography of Zulfikar Ali Bhutto." *India Today*, 11 Feb. 2018.

[172] Gates, "*From The Shadows,*" 149

[173] Benazir Bhutto was Prime Minister from 1988 – 1900 and from 1993-1996.

Vietnam, to create for Russia its own Vietnam.[174]

In 1999, in his book, *A Charge to Keep*, George W. Bush wrote about Billy Graham and becoming a Christian.[175] In October 2002, Jerry Falwell called Mohammed a terrorist. In March 2003, the U.S. invaded Iraq. President Bush said, "Bring 'em on." American Christians, now a political force, supported the war overwhelmingly.[176]

In October 2005, I had dinner with a small group of Pakistani journalists in Islamabad, two of whom said in February 1998 Pakistani officials drove them in cars with ISI license plates into Afghanistan to the press conference where bin Laden and al-Zawahiri announced the formation of the *International Islamic Front for Jihad against Jews and Crusaders*. The next day one of the journalists named Bashir and I drove to Peshawar, where I visited the U.S. Consulate. A Pakistani aide asked who I was working with. I said Bashir and he asked that I send his regards. I met a man called Sultan through him. He warned me about him. He had been imprisoned by the ISI. That night, a man followed Bashir, Sultan, and me on our way to dinner. They wouldn't discuss it. That weekend was *"Eid al-Adha,"* the Sacrifice Feast, when Muslims celebrate the story of Ibrahim,[177] who was willing to follow the will of God and kill his son, Ishmael, like the Biblical story of Abraham and Isaac.[178] Bashir took me to his village where boys and girls watched a man slaughter a water buffalo and took platters of the meat to the poor.[179]

The U.S. fired missiles at Damadola a town in the Tribal Areas to kill al-Zawahiri, there supposedly for an Eid dinner, but hit a madrasa. Pakistan called the strike an infringement of its sovereignty.[180] Hayatullah Khan, a photojournalist, published a photograph of a missile fragment with U.S. markings, and disappeared. Six months later he was found dead, in military handcuffs, by a road. I had to cover an anti-American demonstration by an

---

[174] David Gibbs, "Brzezinski Interview," The University of Arizona, *"Le Nouvel Observateur"*

[175] Bush, *"A Charge to Keep,"*

[176] Charles Marsh, "Wayward Christian Soldiers," *New York Times*, 20 Jan. 2006

[177] Assaffat 100-111.

[178] Genesis 22: 1-18.

[179] Ibid.

[180] Declan Walsh, "Exclusive Interview: General Pervez Musharraf, President of Pakistan."*Guardian* 28 Apr. 2006.

alliance of political-religious parties,[181] after which Sultan took me to a mall to use the internet. A group of madrasa students in white clothes and prayer caps—"Wear white for it is a most pleasing color," said Mohammad—were there, one of whom showed me a magazine, *"Manba al-jihad,"* The Fountainhead of Jihad, with a photo of Jalaluddin, his eyes hard, his beard wild and gray, on the cover. Gone was the warmth I remembered. It was a fund-raising magazine for the Middle East, available in the bazaar.

That April, 2006, back in New York, I read an interview in the *New York Times* with Pat Tillman's father. I felt that the truth had not come out. I would go to where he was killed and talk to the Afghans, the only possibly disinterested people who were there. That July, I became an advisor to the movie *Charlie Wilson's War*, about the colorful Texas Congressman and the Afghan-Soviet war. Milt Bearden, the CIA station chief in Pakistan from 1987-89, was the CIA advisor. I asked him over breakfast in Los Angeles about Haqqani. He put his head down. He wished he had come over. In 2002, he wrote an op-ed: "When I was running the CIA's covert action in Afghanistan, Jalaluddin Haqqani, the legendary commander of Paktia Province, was shot in the knee during a Soviet assault. Urgently, he asked if I could do something. I sent a portable x-ray machine, and the bullet was located. But it was Ramadan and Haqqani refused to break the fast with anesthesia. Instead, he put a stick between his teeth and told his medic to go after the bullet with a knife. The operation was a success and Mr. Haqqani and I, in the Pashtun tradition, would be friends for life. Of that I was assured."[182] He never met him, but he admired him.

That November, on the movie set in Morocco, Charlie Wilson and I talked about Afghanistan. He called Haqqani "a great warrior," and "goodness personified." The 9/11 Commission Report ignored Haqqani. I felt it was because men in Washington called him a low-hanging fruit. He was ripe to come over. I returned to Afghanistan. I had my contract from the U.S. Army War College to write, and I wanted to go to where Tillman was killed. I needed a guide. I was wary of Sultan, but he was a Pashtun. Tillman was killed in Pashtun territory. I was trying to find Mallem, my interpreter with Haqqani. He brought a man named Mallem Jan, a swarthy man, in his

---

[181] Muttahida Malis-e-Amal (United Action Front).
[182] Milton A. Bearden, "War of Secrets; When Playing the Field, the Game gets Rough," *The New York Times*, 9/8/2002.

40s, who had defected to the NDS.[183] He hugged me but I didn't know him. There was an albino, with white curly hair, and a man with a shaved head with one hand in his coat pocket with him. Mallem Jan used to be with Haqqani.

He was married and had children now. He called Sirajuddin and said he needed more money.

Sirajuddin said they needed younger men. The albino said he went with Haqqani to the U.S. Embassy in Islamabad after 9/11. I heard and read that the U.S. asked him to come over, but he said he would return to the mountains and fight America.

Sultan went to Khost. Three days later he returned. The next morning it began to snow. We drove south, and picked up a guide named Zadran by the road. The Haqqanis were Zadran.

---

[183] National Directorate of Security, or Afghan intelligence

Din Mohammad
January 14, 2008

That August I returned to the mountains and met with the Taliban hoping to find Jalaluddin. I returned periodically to Kabul. It was Friday, the Muslim Sabbath, late afternoon, a cold, quiet gray day. I was in my room at the Gandamack Lodge. The window was open. There was a loud explosion. A man shouted, "They hit the Serena." It was a suicide bomber. I heard automatic gunfire and sirens. I went outside, opened the metal door, and went out to the street. I started to run to the hotel and realized that it was dangerous. The sirens kept wailing. That evening I heard that the Taliban infiltrated Chechens into Kabul, then that the Haqqani Network hit the hotel. I was angry and in despair. How could they kill civilians?

The Serena was owned by the Agha Khan Development Network. The Aga Khan, a multibillionaire descended from Ali, son-in-law to Mohammad, was the 49th hereditary Imam, or spiritual leader, of the Ismaili Shia, the Fatimid dynasty of North Africa, Egypt, and Sicily. In America they were called the Episcopalians of Islam. Al-Qaeda, ISIS and the Taliban did not consider them Muslims. The war that began with the death of Ali, killed as he prayed in a mosque by a man who felt that he wasn't following the will of God, continued.

A week passed. It was snowing and windy. I sat with one of my mountain guides, called Shahwali, on a mezza, a small wood platform six inches off the floor, in the cold in a café. We were going to an interview that he arranged. He had a book with him, in Pashto: *The Life Story of Yunus Khalis*. I looked at the author's picture. It was Din Mohammad. I had been trying to find him. It was he who sent me, with Yunus Khalis, to live with Jalaluddin. Din Mohammed was the right hand to Yunus Khalis, said Shahwali. He talked about his brothers, Abdul Haq and Abdul Qadir, famous Mujahideen leaders, that Qadir worked for the ISI, but clashed with them, and they killed him, a vice president of Afghanistan. It was outside the governor's compound in Jalalabad. Everyone knew this story. I thought back to my time with the Mujahideen. Abdul Haq ran anti-Soviet operations in

Kabul, establishing a network that I felt the Haqqanis adopted. He lost a foot stepping on a mine. After the Soviets left, he moved to Dubai and went into business. After 9/11, he returned to Afghanistan with a small group to rally tribesmen against the Taliban, but his enemies alerted the ISI and it sent the Taliban, who surrounded him. Die like a man, he said to those with him. He faced his killers. I didn't know, as we sat there, half the story.

We took a taxi to the office of the governor of Kabul, with high sloping thick walls. People hunched over in the wind. Two guards huddled at the entrance. We had to wait, but when we entered the governor and I looked at one another and smiled. "As soon you walked in, I knew that I knew you." he said. It was 1985. "No," he replied, "1984." He motioned for me to sit next to him. I remembered sitting with Gulbuddin in his hotel room. I asked how their meeting went with Reagan. They didn't meet with him. Gulbuddin was president of the Mujahideen government in exile and because he refused to see Reagan they had to return to Peshawar. Din Mohammad later met President Reagan three times. He smiled ruefully. "You called us freedom fighters then. Now you call us warlords." When they met General Walters at the U.N., he saluted all seven of them individually. "I salute all of you," he said.[184]

They met President Bush Senior in 1989. He had won the election and wanted to take a vacation, and asked if they could meet in ten days? They were returning to Peshawar, and once there would not be able to come back. He gave them a half hour. His first question was if Benazir would help them. She had just become Prime Minister. "We thought she would." Bush said they would give them political support and ammunition. He paused. I had a girlfriend then. I was trying to decide if I should marry her. I told her that Hekmatyar, standing with the Iranians, who were Shia, was the President. They leaned forward, smiling, and shook hands.

For years I thought that he threatened to kill me because I forced him to shake hands with a woman in public. In 2007 I went to the Pakistani embassy in Kabul to apply for a visa. I told the acting ambassador about my time with Hekmatyar hoping that it would help. He took me to lunch and assured me that he didn't care about shaking hands with a woman in public.

---

[184] Retired Lt. General Vernon Walters was UN ambassador from 1985-89.

He told me, as if I was a spy, to find out about Khalilzad,[185] and his alleged
tie to the Azizi bank in Kabul. I didn't get a visa, one reason why I crossed
the mountains into Pakistan. I wanted the adventure.

It was a different world now. He agreed. Before, Reagan said "You are
helping us." Now the Americans thought they were helping the Afghans.
There was a lot of money here for the police and for reconstruction. It would
be much better if the Americans would go to the villages and learn about the
culture of Afghanistan. The U.S. should show the Afghans how to stand on
their own feet, not try to carry them on their shoulders. The international
community said it had spent billions of dollars here. This money may have
come here, but it may have gone back to America under the name of
commissions, implementation, running costs, advisors, consultants, all these
names. "We were cows drinking our own milk," Afghans said.

When he was governor of Nangahar Province, the U.S. said it wanted to
spend a great deal of money to get rid of the poppies. He said form a
committee of government people and farmers.

He would have them agree to (1) stop growing poppies, and (2) create a
new livelihood. Sit on the ground and talk to them. He eradicated 96% of the
poppies. The U.S. wanted to use force. If they did this the people would
grow it in their homes. They needed money. Poppies would end, but the
people would not be happy. The enemy would benefit. The people needed
peace, security, jobs, and to live in dignity. They were afraid of U.S. and
NATO soldiers. The international community only consulted with Afghans
who lived in America and Europe. They wanted to hurt the Mujahideen. He
meant the U.S., like the Russians, only wanted to work with secular people
who could afford to flee, not the poor religious men who fought.

They said they would make Afghanistan like a Western country in a few
months. The people loved their culture and it was confusing for them to
change. Afghanistan was a junction. So many civilizations had passed
through here. Pakistan wanted to use them to get to Central Asia. Al-Qaeda
was here. Palestine and Iraq had become issues here. The U.S. and NATO
were here. China, Iran, Pakistan, and Russia were afraid. The Arabs came
here because there was no place for them in their own countries. If the U.S.
put pressure on Iran, it put pressure here. Iran and Pakistan were like two big

---

[185] U.S. Ambassador to the United Nations, 2007 – 2008.

trees. If you grew a little tree in between them, it was difficult for the big trees to accept this. If the Taliban remained in the mountains, it would be a problem. If they brought them in, there would be no one that others could use against the government. He meant other countries. When the U.S. came it only waged war against the Pashtuns. It targeted schools. If he wore a turban and had a beard, the Americans thought he was al-Qaeda.

Who killed Abdul Haq? He sighed. He came back to try to talk with the Taliban and with tribal leaders, to bring everyone together. The Taliban didn't say he was their enemy. They didn't give him a chance to talk to them. His son, Hazitullah, who was 21, was with him. We were silent. He lost his son and his brother that day. Many people, including those who were Taliban, said they would help him. He came with only a few men to talk with elders, and the Taliban, and to convince them to stop the bloodshed. Some in Washington backed him, he didn't know who. After his brother was killed the U.S. picked Hamid Karzai to be president.

His other brother was Vice President Abdul Qadir, assassinated in 2002. Someone killed Abdul Haq's wife and son. What was he going to do? He could sit and cry, but that was not a solution. He could pick up his rifle, but neither was that. His grandfathers died for this country. If they didn't find a solution, then thousands of people would be killed. An aide stood at the door. There was a room full of people waiting. Had he seen Jalaluddin? Not in ten years. We agreed to meet again. He knew how to reach him. That night I met with President Karzai, and his national security advisor. I asked him about Haqqani. He said he had a stroke and died.

The next day I walked through the snow to see Maulvi Mohaiuddin Baluch, his religious advisor. He sat at his desk, stacked with books, in a small wood house. A fire crackled in a Bokhara, like a Franklin stove. Outside the snow blew sideways. Afghanistan was part of Khorasan, the ancient name for this whole region. He fingered his prayer beads. Islam was not just a religion, but the basis of Afghan culture. The British and the Soviets were defeated on the basis of religion. Islam was deep in the Afghan soul. They were religious because of their geographic position and because people lived in small, isolated villages. Afghanistan had been attacked many times and always defended by religion and now that religion was Islam. Kings had ruled here without religion, but as soon as someone wanted to take it away, they had trouble. Zahir Shah and Daoud did not touch Islam.[186] Fundamentalism, like pornography and movies, came from outside Afghanistan. He quoted the hadith that said if you saw the black banners coming from Khorasan join that army even if you had to crawl over ice. No power would be able to stop it and it would finally reach the Dome of the Rock, where they would erect their flags.[187]

On February 16, Shahwali betrayed me, and I was kidnapped in the Tribal Areas, the next American journalist taken after Daniel Pearl. After I was released, CBS said I could no longer travel east of Turkey. I realized that to cease being a victim and to stay relevant, I had to change my focus to the Middle East. On July 8th, the Taliban launched a suicide attack on the Indian embassy in Kabul, killing 58. The U.S. blamed the Haqqani Network.[188]

---

[186] Zahir Shah was king from 1954-73.
[187] Ali H. Soufan, "*The Black Banners*," (W.W. Norton, New York, 2011) xv
[188] https://www.dni.gov/nctc/groups/haqqani_network.html.

Al-Sharq al-Awsat
The Middle East

In November 2010, a policewoman in Sidi Bouzid, a town in central Tunisia, confiscated the wood cart and produce belonging to Mohammad Bouazizi, 26, a vegetable seller. His father had died eight years before and he was supporting his family of eight. He didn't have a license. He tried to pay a fine, but the policewoman wouldn't accept it, and according to reports, spat on him, slapped him, and insulted his father. Humiliated, he went to officials to complain and to recover his cart. They refused to see him. In despair, he set himself on fire.[189] His mother said he died for the sake of his dignity. He became a martyr for the poor, and started a revolution that swept, like a brush fire, through what the West called Arab Asia, until the British and the French in World War II began to call it the Middle East.[190]

In May 2011, Navy SEALS killed bin Laden in Abbottabad, a city east of the Tribal Areas. Americans cheered in the streets. I would go to the Middle East, write a monograph on Islamic fundamentalism for the Army War College, as I had on South Asia, and combine the two into a book. The War College gave me a contract, but it did not provide funding. I contacted Richard Perle, a friend from Senator Jackson's office, former director of policy planning at the Pentagon, who had helped when I was kidnapped. He introduced me to the director of a foreign policy foundation. He was interested in part of my proposal: "The Haqqani Network in the greater Middle East." Board members questioned my thesis. I read what others wrote. Most felt that they were focused on their region. The foundation gave me funding and I got a book contract. The editor's assistant walked me to the door. If I met Jalaluddin Haqqani, what would I ask him? I was taken aback. "Why did he use suicide bombers? Why had they changed?" She pressed the elevator button and wished me well.

---

[189] Rania Abouzeid, "Bouazizi: The Man Who Set Himself and Tunisia on Fire," *Time* 21 Jan. 2011.
[190] Raphael Patai, "*The Arab Mind*," (New York: Charles Scribner's Sons) 1973, p. 12

Liverpool

I flew to London and took the train to Liverpool, walked out down Lime Street, past the India House and the West Africa House, built when Great Britain ruled much of the world. Why was I going there, a man asked? The Beatles weren't there anymore. I laughed. They were gone, like the Empire, but not the Islamic movements that it inspired. I found Victoria Street, in honor of Queen Victoria,[191] who presided over the Empire, and the Millennium Building, smaller, less confident.

Tahir Qassim, born in Yemen, slim, with short gray hair, took me to a café. Beatles music was playing. He talked about Yemen and al-Qaeda. All the complexity of the Middle East was there. I wanted to start there; it was more dangerous, more unknown, like Afghanistan.

---

[191] Kirsty Oram, "Victoria (r. 1837-1901)," *Royal Family* 3 Feb. 2021, https://www.royal.uk/victoria-r-1837-1901.

The Algerian

It was cool and windy. I sat on a bench outside a hotel next to a motorcycle repair shop, and watched guests enter and leave. A man with a trimmed gray- black beard dark hair wearing dark slacks and a tweed sport coat looked over. This was the man. I joined him inside. His name was Abdullah Anas, the nom de guerre of Boudjema Bounoua, the son-in-law of Abdullah Azzam, the "Emir of Jihad," once the most famous jihadist in the world. We sat in the coffee shop. He told me to go first. "I went to Afghanistan in 1981," I said. "I lived with Jalaluddin Haqqani." He went in 1983, and lived with Massoud. He was Tajik, I was Pashtun, he said. Ahmed Shah Massoud was the most famous guerrilla leader, a handsome, pious man who spoke French, and read Persian poetry. Azzam compared him to Napoleon. Peter Tomsen, U.S. envoy to the Afghan Resistance, said he fought the Russians better than Napoleon.[192]

Anas went to public school in Algeria until the 6th grade and then to a madrasa. He heeded the call of Azzam and went to Afghanistan. He was 24 and innocent. He wanted to make a better world, and then it became severe. He clenched his fist. They believed in a cause, but that did not mean that there were not crazy people, a Yousef who wanted to blow up a bus to get rid of all these spoiled people. He helped Azzam run the Services Bureau,[193] which he set up in Peshawar, to help the Arabs who came to wage jihad. Bin Laden later financed it, and with funds he raised in Saudi Arabia. Jalaluddin raised funds when he went there on Haj.[194] Bin Laden was a nice man, polite, shy, and quiet. In 1988, he said they should start a universal jihad. What did he mean? He wanted to continue their jihad in other counties. How? There were Muslims in Europe, America, North Africa, and Malaysia. Again, he asked, how? Bin Laden was lost. Then, he said with disdain, the Egyptians, led by Ayman al-Zawahiri, with their superior ways, took over.

He, a physician from a distinguished family, came to Peshawar in

---

[192] Peter Tomsen, *"The Wars of Afghanistan: Messianic Terrorism, Tribal Conflicts, and the Failures of Great Powers,"* (New York: Public Affairs, 2011,) xiii
[193] Mustafa Hamid and Leah Farrall, *"The Arabs at War in Afghanistan,"* (New York: Hurst, 2015), 65-87
[194] Ibid 66

1980,[195] worked in a medical clinic, left, returned, ingratiated himself with
bin Laden, mocked Azzam, and melded his group, Islamic Jihad, with al-
Qaeda. In 1989 Azzam and two of his sons were killed on their way to
Friday prayers in Peshawar, the first remote-controlled strike in Afghanistan
and Pakistan. Who killed him? He didn't know. Azzam wanted to help form
an Islamic government in Afghanistan. Al-Zawahiri wanted to take jihad to
other countries. They were all Afghans, Anas told Massoud. He was Afghan
in his heart. He was Tajik, I was Pashtun. Twice he said it. After the Soviets
left, in 1989, Afghanistan fell into civil war. He did not come to help
Afghans fight one another. He saluted Massoud and said goodbye. He could
never forget that time. Afghanistan was the heart of his life. He showed me
on his phone part of a documentary.[196] He was laughing, with a bushy beard.
I thought of walking with Haqqani's men, drinking tea in a roadhouse, in the
winter, the warmth of that, and moving on.

He married Azzam's daughter, returned to Algeria, bringing jihad,
which he said was peaceful, and joined the Islamic Salvation Front (FIS),
founded in 1989,[197] to form an Islamic government governed by Sharia.[198]
In 1991, the FIS won local elections and a majority in the national assembly
in the first round, in the first free elections in Algeria in 130 years. "The
outcome was more a no-confidence vote against a corrupt, incompetent and
self-satisfied establishment than an endorsement of an Islamic republic,"
wrote Jonathan Randall.[199] The government cancelled the election and put
6,000 members in camps in the Sahara. The army launched a coup, and with
the security apparatus, a terror campaign. Members of the FIS created the
Armed Islamic Group. (GIA)[200] In 1998, the GIA renounced killing civilians
and created al-Qaeda in the Islamic Maghreb.[201] Over 250,000 people died
when the army stole their election, Anas explained. Life, he learned in
Afghanistan, was not black and white. Jihad was over.

Were the Haqqanis in the Middle East? He paused. He was with the

---

[195] Lawrence Wright, "The Man behind Bin Laden," *New Yorker* 12 Sept. 2002.
[196] "Frontline," WGBH, Boston, 2006.
[197] "Islamic Salvation Front" *Oxford Islamic Studies Online*.
[198] Sharia only appears once in the Koran.
[199] Jonathan C. Randal, *"Osama: The Making of a Terrorist"* (New York: Vintage,
2005), 65-67
[200] Groupe Islamic Armee (GIA).
[201] Maghreb means the West in Arabic.

Mujahedeen in the North. As they walked through the hills they chanted, "Once they finished here, they would cross the Amu Darya.[202] They would free the Muslims in Central Asia who were then under Communist rule." Everyone was like that except Haqqani's men. They said, "After Afghanistan, then India." He looked away in disgust. The Pakistani army was fixated on India.[203] It controlled the Haqqanis.[204] [205]

---

[202] Mazir-i-Sharif is the largest city in northern Afghanistan.
[203] C. Christine Fair, "*Fighting to the End: The Pakistan Army's Way of War*" (Oxford: Oxford University Press, 2014), 99- 201
[204] Ibid. 79
[205] Al Yamen, the name, maybe given by Muslim geographers, meaning right hand side, or the south, of Mecca.

Al Yaman

Dawn came and the light was bright and there were endless waves of sand in a vast brown sea. It gave way to sheer gray mountains jutting up, treeless, stark and empty. Then a large flat plain appeared, and a settlement with straight roads, empty in the morning sun, and then the land widened into a vast dun-colored city, Sana'a, 7,400 feet high, 2,500 years old, capital of *al Yaman*, the southwest corner of the Arabian Peninsula.

Arabia Felix, or Happy Arabia, the ancients called it, Arabia Odorifera,[206] fragrant Arabia, Paris of the ancient world, romantic, luxurious Arabia, a blessed, fertile land of gold, frankincense, and myrrh, rain-fed Arabia, unlike Arabia Deserta in the northern desert interior. A thousand years before Islam, they worshipped the sun (Shams) the Star god, Athtar, and Ilmaqah, the Moon, and buried their dead in caves.[207] The earliest writings on Yemen focus on the Sabeans, of Saba (Sheba) their queen, and King Solomon. They were Semites, but not Arabs, who came from the north, although their languages were similar. The Sabeans spoke Sabaic, a lost language. Yemen comes from a Sabaic word meaning the south. It was the Sabeans who harnessed the camel, created a high-level sematic culture, and who traded with Somalia and India. They were protected by the desert to the north and rough seas. The Arabs were desert dwellers, who traced their lineage to Ishmael,[208] son of Abram, whose brother was Isaac. Isaiah refers to the Arab pitching his tent in the desert.[209] In 600 BC, Jeremiah wrote, "Like an Arab in the desert."[210] They, too, were cameleers, but they bred a new animal, the horse, and by the second century began to move into the south, becoming the enemy, and an ally.

The Abyssinian (Ethiopian) Christian Empire,[211] founded by Christian

---

[206] Eudaemon Arabia.
[207] Khadija Al-Salami and Charles Hoots, *"Tears of Sheba,"* (Hoboken: John Wiley & Sons, 2003), 318
[208] *Encyclopedia Britannica*, 1967, vol. 2, 171
[209] Isaiah 13:20
[210] Jeremiah 3:2.
[211] Hourani, *"A History of the Arab Peoples,"* 10.

missionaries from Egypt, or, by Matthew[212] or maybe by Greco-Roman traders along the Red Sea,[213] invaded Yemen in the 4th Century, until the 5th Century when Judaism ruled, which led the Abyssinian Christians to return.[214] In 25 B.C. Aelius Gallus, the Roman governor of Egypt under the Emperor Augustus, led 10,000 soldiers down the Red Sea coast to subdue its tribes, but guerrillas, deceitful guides, and malaria forced him to turn back. Rome wanted to control *"Bab al-Mandab,"*[215] the southern entry to the Red Sea, as the U.S. Navy does today, and the route to India. They never again marched deep into the Arabian Peninsula.[216]

Minarets rose, like rockets on their platforms, a stadium appeared, a few multiple story buildings, and rows of dusky houses. A half dozen fighter jets sat under a row of canopies. The plane stopped in front of a one-story corrugated steel building. I was 2,000 miles from the Tribal Areas, a long way from the Haqqani Network. The terminal was small, dark, with leather ammunition belts hanging from a metal stand. A man stamped my passport, checked my bag, smiled, and waved me on. The baggage carousel started, like an old engine. The ATM machine didn't work. Outside, a man in western clothes, late thirties, came forward. His name was Khalid al-Hammadi. A journalist in London told me to call him. He got worried last night and felt he should meet my plane. I was grateful. We passed a checkpoint, reached a crowded street and stopped at another one and two soldiers looked us over. It was hot and dusty and old cars and trucks moved slowly. There were no stop lights. This was old Arabia. Khalid started the Freedom Foundation, which promoted freedom of the press, and received funding from the U.S. Embassy. I had come at a difficult time. I must not walk in the streets. An American was kidnapped on the street last week, but they were keeping it quiet to keep the ransom demand low. We came to a hotel. There was a Toyota pickup out front with a machine gun in the back, and wiry soldiers with hard eyes and rifles. An Ethiopian at the counter said not to leave the hotel grounds. Khalid said there were secret police in the lobby.

---

[212] Tom Bissell, *"Apostle"* (New York: Pantheon Books, 2016), 338
[213] *Encyclopedia Britannica*, vol 8. 1967, 783
[214] Hourani, *"A History of the Arab Peoples"* 10
[215] "The Gate of Tears."
[216] Bernard Lewis, *"The Middle East,"* (London: Weidenfeld & Nicholson, 2000), 39

I called the U.S. Embassy to register. A man told me to go to the website. I called the military attaché's office. A man said an American had been kidnapped and I had to leave immediately. I called the political officer, and a secretary took a message. I walked around the hotel grounds wondering if men could scale the high walls. Two days later, a German guard at the German embassy was shot and killed in the same parking lot where the American was kidnapped. A U.N. employee was kidnapped off the streets. I had dinner with a German aid worker who said there were at least six foreigners being held in Yemen. The embassies were on lockdown.

In November 2008, al-Zawahiri[217] said Nasir al-Wuhayshi, a Yemeni and former aide to bin Laden, was to be the head of al-Qaeda in Yemen. In December, suicide bombers struck the U.S. Embassy killing 17 civilians and guards. In January 2009, al-Wuhayshi announced that he was head of al-Qaeda in the Arabian Peninsula (AQAP), comprised of Yemenis and Saudis. That Christmas, Amur Farouk Abdulmutallab, a Nigerian student here, lit a bomb in his underwear as his flight descended into Detroit. Two months ago, al-Zawahiri announced that al-Wuhayshi was "general manager" of al-Qaeda, a position bin Laden outlined in a 2010 letter found in Abbottabad extending al-Qaeda's core to Yemen. On August 4th, the U.S., after intercepting a phone call between al-Zawahiri and al-Wuhayshi closed 21 embassies and consulates in the Middle East.

On Friday, Dahan al-Najjar, one of Tahir's contacts, came to my hotel. He wore a white thobe, and a jambiya, a curved dagger in a sheath. He was from Taiz, in the South, when Yemen was divided between North Yemen and the Democratic People's Republic of South Yemen, where the Soviet Union stationed 450 tanks and 300 armored personnel carriers.[218] Dahan lived in Dearborn, Michigan, heart of the Arab community in America. He had a Bachelor's and PhD from Kiev State University when the Soviets gave scholarships to qualified South Yemenis.

He drove a new SUV up Zubairy Avenue. Traffic stopped. A man was beating a drum, and people were chanting. Yemen, the poorest country in the

---

[217] Gregory D. Johnson, *"The Last Refuge,"* (London: W. W. Norton & Company, 2012), 48-49

[218] Victoria Clark, *"Yemen: Dancing on the Heads of Snakes"* (New Haven: Yale University Press, 2010), 53 Paul Dresch, *"History of Modern Yemen,"* (Cambridge: Cambridge University Press, 2000), 53

Arab world, was the only democracy on the Arabian Peninsula.[219] Many Yemeni soldiers and students studied in the Soviet Union. Dahan spoke Arabic, English, and Russian, which he taught at Wayne State University, and Ukrainian. Here there was no difference between al-Qaeda and the fundamentalists. People, especially the uneducated, felt that they were the representatives of God. The fundamentalists—the Muslim Brotherhood, the "*Ikhwan*," "The Brothers"—controlled the Ministry of Education, the schools and universities. In 1937, Ahmad Noman, from a landowning family in Taiz, went to Cairo, the intellectual capital of the Arab world, to study, where he and Muhammad al-Zubairy, after whom the avenue was named, joined the Ikhwan.[220] Noman finished his studies and returned to Aden. The Ikhwan looked warmly to Yemen, more isolated and less corrupted by the West,[221] hoping to make it more religious, equal, better educated, and prosperous. Al-Zubairy returned home. In 1947, an Ikhwan emissary from Cairo joined them. In January 1948, Imam Yaha, the Zaydi emir, was riding in a convoy through a mountain pass when Ikhwan gunmen killed him. Yaha's son rallied Zaydi tribal leaders and the kingdom survived. The Ikhwan were allied with tribal sheikhs, supported by Saudi Arabia, and army generals. The Ikhwan believed in the Caliphate.[222] He shook his head, reflecting the religious-secular divide. A boy with a crippled arm came by begging, then a man leading a blind man. Children pounded on the windows. Saudi Arabia, the enemy, supported the Ikhwan in Syria and Libya but not in Egypt. When Abdul Aziz was uniting Saudi Arabia in 1934, he took three of their provinces—Asir, Najran and Jazen.[223]

Asir was once a small independent domain on the Red Sea, which Harry St. John Philby, a British Arabist, saw, as he mapped it for Abdul Aziz, was a Garden of Eden, with men in loin clothes and unveiled women, misty mountains, and juniper forests.[224]

This fight over land was part of the ancient hatred between Yemeni

---

[219] Helen Lackner, *Why Yemen Matters: A Society in Transition* London: Saqi, 2014, p. 2, 35. Dresch, "*History of Modern Yemen*," 186-87

[220] Dresch, "*History of Modern Yemen*," 51-54

[221] Ibid, 141

[222] Hourani, "*A History of the Arab Peoples*," 22, 346-347

[223] A. Vasiliev, "*The History of Saudi Arabia*," (London: Saqi Books, 2000), 283-86

[224] Robert Lacey, "*The Kingdom: Arabia & the House of Sa'ud*," (New York: Avon, 1983), 165

tribes and those of the northern desert, between the Himyarites, the descendants of Himyar, son of Qahtan, the pure Arab, *al-Arab al-Arabiya*, who conquered the Sabeans, whose merchant ships sailed to India, the better camel breeder, the great caravan nomads, the true desert dweller, the *bedu*, the plural of which was Bedouin, the better warrior, against the sons of Ishmael.[225] The transfer of power began with the Kaaba, 500 miles north on the caravan route. Saudi Arabia and every state in the Gulf—Bahrain, Kuwait, Oman, Qatar and the United Arab Emirates—was a kingdom.

He turned down a side street, drove past baked mud buildings, women in abayas, dogs, cats, cars on blocks, and garbage. At an intersection, a policeman, in a black beret stood on a platform, whistled and cars, mini-buses, pedestrians, and motorcycles converged on one another. People smiled, chatted, shouted, and pushed forward. A boy in jeans, holding an elderly woman's hand, escorted her through traffic. There was order in the chaos, reflective of Yemeni culture, which was stronger than the state. The regime of former President Saleh,[226] wanted to make life hard for everyone so that people would want him to return. There were 100 dialects of Arabic. He learned in the Soviet Union that people wanted freedom. He would rather be free than have food. He paused. But then he had enough to eat every day. According to the World Food Program[227] almost half of Yemen's population went to bed hungry. Yemen had the third highest rate of child malnutrition in the world.[228] Over 80% of the poor lived in rural areas,[229] where al-Qaeda was strong. Over 70% of Yemenis were under 25. The biggest employer was the state, mainly the military and the security apparatus. 70% of the population was rural. Al-Qaeda lived in the mountains, where it recruited and formed alliances with the tribes. In 2011, it was the urban youth, in the

---

[225] *"The Cambridge History of Islam,"* Cambridge: Cambridge University Press, 2000 6; see also Encyclopedia Britannica (1967 ed.), under Arab, and Yemen.

[226] Salah was president of North Yemen from 1978 – 1990, and after unification between North and South in 1990 of the Republic of Yemen. After the Arab Spring demonstrations of 2011, which Saleh tried to crush violently, the Gulf Cooperation Council, led by Saudi Arabia, brokered his resignation.

[227] "Millions are facing food crisis in Yemen, U.N. Agency says," *Reuters/New York Times*, 9/30/12.

[228] Lackner, *"Why Yemen Matters,"* 15, Lackner stated that child malnutrition was the second worst in the world, led only by Afghanistan.

[229] Ibid, 14-15

Arab Spring, who called[230] for real democracy, freedom, and an end to corruption.

We came to the Yemeni Center for Research and Studies, a brick building with no electricity. Men talked in the dim light. Women wore abayas. A white- haired man from Aden drank tea with condensed milk, cardamom, and sugar. Was he a Marxist? He wished, but socialism didn't work. This was the first center for the studies of humanities in the Arabian Peninsula. The Arab world was over 2,000 years old, and there had been few changes in the last 50 years, one the discovery of oil.[231] In the 1960s, Aden was the most modern city in the Arabian Peninsula. Abu-Dhabi and Dubai were villages. In 2010, Qatar's per capita income was $86,440,[232] the UAE's $47,890.[233] In 2011, Yemen's was $2,170, Afghanistan's under $700.[234] Another change was South Yemen became Marxist. The humanities meant the study of man. The Koran was the word of God.

Most of the men were smoking. The Arabs were first to distill *al-khol*, forbidden in the Koran. A woman, her faced uncovered, showed me a theater where they put on plays. We drove to a gas station and waited 20 minutes as men shouted over a cacophony of horns and generators, which provided power to pump the fuel. Gas was 50 cents a gallon. Oil was Yemen's main export, and 70% of the state's income, most of which went to the military and the security apparatus. Plus, militants destroyed the pipelines. Yemen produced 200,000 barrels a day. Saudi Arabia produced nine million barrels.[235] The U.N. ranked Yemen 140th out of 180 in its Human Development Index. More than half of Yemenis live on less than $2 per day. Only 15% had access to electricity. Less than two percent of the land was arable and most of the ground water was used for farming gat (*Catha edulis*),[236] a leafy shrub, and narcotic, banned in the U.S., the demand for

---

[230] Stephen W. Day, *"Regionalism and Rebellion in Yemen,"* (Cambridge: Cambridge University Press, 2012), 276

[231] Lackner, *"Why Yemen Matters,"* 305; Victoria Clark, *Yemen: "Dancing on the Heads of Snakes"* (New Haven: Yale University Press, 2010), p. 6-7, 131-132; *IMF Country Report*, No. 09/100, March 2009, p.12.

[232] The International Monetary Fund estimated it would soon be nearly $110,000.00.

[233] Lackner, *"Why Yemen Matters,"* 15.

[234] *Afghanistan - GDP per Capita*, http://www.indexmundi.com/facts/afghanistan/gdp-per-capita.

[235] Ibid.16

[236] Lackner, *"Why Yemen Matters,"* 16-17

which was so great that the World Bank, and the World Health Organization, estimated that Yemen would soon face a water crisis.[237]

A woman in an abaya looked over, her eyes sparkling. The founder of the Follies Bergere said the most important part of a woman, what men looked at after a while, was her eyes. We passed a construction site where the Chinese were building a library. There was no university in Yemen until 1970. We drove into the mountains that surrounded Sana'a, like in Kabul. There were no trees, only adobe and cement block houses. We came to a park with flower bushes, families, children playing, and a tower honoring the 10,000 Egyptian soldiers who died in the revolution of 1962-1965.[238]

In 1962 Sana'a was a walled city, when Imam Ahmed, the Zaydi Emir, with bullets in him from an assassination attempt in 1961, died in his sleep.[239] His son, Mohammad al-Badr, took his place. A week later, a group of junior army officers, followers of the Pan-Arab socialist, President

Gamal Nasser, one of the "Free Officers" who seized power in Cairo in 1952, overthrew him and established the Yemen Arab Republic. Egypt maybe instigated the coup.[240] Saudi Arabia, Britain and the U.S. backed the royalists.

Egypt sent 70,000 soldiers here, nearly half its army, and the tribes fought a guerrilla war. The Egyptians, who called Yemen primitive[241] barely got out of Sana'a.[242] Half of the Egyptian army was mired in Yemen during the 1967 Arab-Israeli war.[243] Nasser called it his Vietnam. "Islam is the answer," shouted the Ikhwan in the streets of Cairo.

We drove higher into the mountains to a park with a column with a pagoda top with Chinese characters, in honor of the Chinese who died building the first paved road in Yemen. Ahmed established diplomatic relations with the Soviet Union and China. Both supported South Yemen.[244]

---

[237] Poverty in Yemen, *World Bank* 18 June 2012, http://www.worldbank.org/en/news/feature/2010/01/20/poverty-in-yemen.
[238] Ibid. 124 Clark, "*Yemen: Dancing on the Heads of Snakes,*" 90-100.
[239] Today called "Old Sana'a," a UNESCO world heritage site.
[240] Betty S. Anderson, "*A History of the Modern Middle East: Rulers, Rebels, and Rogues,*" (Stanford: Stanford University Press, 2020), 282-85
[241] Dresch, "*History of Modern Yemen,*" 93
[242] Eugene Rogan, *The Arabs: A History,*New York: Penguin Books, 2009, 416-418
[243] Clark, "*Yemen: Dancing on the Heads of Snakes,*" 95
[244] Interview with Hassan Noman, General Secretary, Yemeni Socialist Party.

Chinese influence dated to the Tang Dynasty (618-917)[245] China had been providing aid since the 1950s. The largest Arab population in China was Yemeni. In 2013, China imported nine percent of its oil from Yemen.[246]

Below was the city, covered with a haze of pollution, and a dun-colored mosque with six minarets. Saleh took the land, had other men invest, and built the Saleh Mosque to show that he was a good Muslim, Dahan explained. It could hold 44,000 people.[247] His men kept weapons in the basement. A boy about five ran by in the field wearing a small jambiya. Why did they wear them today? It was cultural. This belonged to his father, Dahan replied, touching his. He said on his deathbed that it must go to him. I thought of a rifle that a chief in the Tribal Areas showed me. His ancestor had used it to defeat the British. He would give it to his son.

Yemen sent many men to Afghanistan to fight the Soviets. When they returned, they had no jobs. Selah used these men to fight the South, which was Communist, had more oil than the North, and more water. He brought Somalis, Egyptians, Arabs, and Algerians and made bases for them. Some became military officers, others policemen, imams and teachers. A small cadre went to Afghanistan and started al-Qaeda in the Arabian Peninsula.[248] A few days ago al-Qaeda attacked an army base on the Gulf of Aden. Newspapers said they wore military uniforms and drove army trucks. Dahan said they were backed by generals. We drove up to a ridge where there were two cars and boys selling boiled eggs. One had two birds on his wrists. We were at 9,000 feet. Men could hide in the mountains here, said Dahan softly. Yemen would become the next Afghanistan.

---

[245] Ibid., p. 305.
[246] Ibid., p. 311.
[247] *National Geographic*, https://www.nationalgeographic.com/ photography/.
[248] Johnson, "*The Last Refuge*," xiii

The Zaidi Prince

The lobby was quiet. I looked up and saw a woman in an abaya, her black gloved hands on her knees, sitting across from me, her back straight, staring. Did she work for the government? I went back to my book. I looked up again and she was gone.

Ali Hamid, of medium height, with gray hair, in a gray pinstripe suit, white shirt, tie and cufflinks, came through the hotel screener. He was in a meeting and came to say hello. Did I need anything immediately? He was in a rush, but would return tomorrow. The next evening, he wore khakis, a sport jacket, and boat shoes. He pointed to a photo on the front page of a newspaper. This was who I needed to see. It was a turbaned man with an orange beard, Sheikh Abdul Majeed Zindani. The U.S. called him a "specially designated terrorist."[249] Ali pointed to the wall behind him. Once, this was a discothèque. No more; fundamentalism. Outside he took my hand, and we walked into traffic, and cars stopped, or swerved, and we reached the other side. He took me to a kiosk where I could buy newspapers, to a store to get a cell phone, to a small shop where I bought a map. The city was alive with merchants, shoppers and goods on the sidewalk. We walked down a side street to a burned, boarded-up building, once a cinema, and to a street where men were selling gold jewelry to women in abayas. "*Janga Zargaree*," a jewelry war, Afghans called the war America was fighting, but not really, against the Taliban. Women here, like in Afghanistan, carried their wealth in gold and jewelry.

We came to a stone mosque. His great, great, great grandfather built it 350 years ago. It was the Al Mahdi Mosque.[250] His name was Hassan al-Mahdi. He was the Imam of Yemen. Ali, a former ambassador to the Arab League and to India, was descended from the Emir of Yemen. It didn't matter. It wasn't like England or Egypt where they called you prince this or that. We walked to Tahreer, or Spark Square, where students sparked the 2011 revolution. Men huddled in the dark. An Austrian couple was

---

[249] *U.S. Department of the Treasury*, http://www.treasury.gov/press-center/press-releases/Pages/js1190.aspx.The press release misses Zindani's age by at least 10 years.

[250] Al Mahdi means "the rightly guided one." It can also mean "the messiah."

kidnapped here three months ago.

The next day we took a taxi to a compound with ivy growing over the sides. A small sign said, "The Sanaá Institute for Arabic language study." Inside, a sullen long-haired man ignored my questions and directed Ali to a room where a woman in an abaya directed us to a large *mafraj*, lined with cushioned seats. Mohammad Ainsi, in his 40s, rushed in. He once had hundreds of students from the West, but he wouldn't take any now, especially Americans, only Malaysians or Singaporeans. It was too dangerous. I had to leave before people found out I was here. One of his students was Omar Farouk Abdulmutallab. He was a normal student, then he met some people from outside, and kept to himself. One day he was gone. He told me to leave quickly. Anwar alWalki, the Yemeni American al-Qaeda leader, mentored Abdulmutallab. Zindani mentored alWaliki. John Walker Lindh, called the American Taliban, studied here. He gave away money in the streets, fought in Kashmir, joined the Taliban, was captured by the U.S., and imprisoned for twenty years.

We took a taxi to "*al-Qadamah*," the Old City, before Sanaá outgrew its walled borders, a world of pathways, tower houses, and Moorish windows. We followed a stone path. It grew wider and Ali stopped at a small sign, "*The Center for Arabic Language and Eastern Studies*," and knocked on a rickety wood door. A man, about 30, in a keffiyeh, an Arab headdress, protection, like an Afghan turban, against the sun, dust and sand, and a mahwaz—the skirt that men wear—, and sandals led us up the stone steps to the second floor. A man, about 40, wiry, in pants and a sports coat, sat at a wood desk. The room was cool. There were filing cabinets, a book case, a table, and windows. They had only a few students and would take me. Ali left and I walked out to the main city, bought a keffiyeh, went to a café, had tea, thought of the kidnapped victim, and returned to the hotel.

That night Russian Television (RT) in Moscow emailed and asked if I would comment on events in Afghanistan. I could do this on any network if it didn't compete with CBS. RT was the government, but each time a producer said they would promote "*Captive*," and they did. I rode through Sanaá nervously. A man at the studio said he worked on a project for CBS. The next day I went to CALES and registered. My room had a single bed, an armoire, two windows, a desk, a whiteboard, and a chair. The next morning, I walked around the corner to a bakery, where two boys kneaded dough and an older boy, about 12, pushed a wood platter into a tandoor. I bought two loaves and went upstairs to the kitchen, ate and had tea and went to class. My teacher, Karim, a thin man, wore a suit, and carried a briefcase. I studied, met students from Europe and Malaysia, bought food in the souk, a mahwaz, and sandals, and explored Sanaá, checking to see if I was being followed.

The Old City, Houthis, and the Rise of al-Qaeda

All around, there were green, red and white signs, the color of the Iranian flag, on the stone walls, or white banners overhead that said, "Death to America," "America the incubator of al-Qaeda," or "America, supporter of al-Qaeda and Israel" in Arabic and English. Yet people were friendly. In the evenings, the cacophony of the muezzins' calls to prayer, swept over us. Al-Qademah was a village, the safest place in Sanaá. On Friday the souk was quiet. Mohammad, from my RT interview, came with his daughter Malik (angel) in a pink dress and we sat in the courtyard at CALES and discussed my project. Then he drove through the souk, Malak leaning over the seat, listening. I felt a presence, and saw a woman in the back, in black, holding a child. We crossed the city, with potholes and children in bare feet, one a girl with dark skin, from the coast, he said, across from Djibouti, Somaliland and Ethiopia, looking through garbage. We passed half a dozen men in thobes, sandals, blue sport coats, with AK-47s, stopped in front of his in-law's house, and the backseat emptied. He drove up to the men. They got in a fight with the police, who called them al-Qaeda. Muhammad introduced me. Where was I from? Canada.

Everyone said I must never say America. "Invite him to come see us," the man said. We drove away. Some of the Hashed got in a small traffic accident with a car with a police officer in it, and his bodyguards were in a car behind him. They thought he was being targeted. No one was hurt, but the police burned the car, and one man called them al-Qaeda. His life was over, Mohammad said softly. Why? They were the Hashed. They would kill him for that? It was a matter of honor.

"We went to a restaurant, up a flight of stairs and sat behind a curtain so no one would see me. We had delicious grilled fish from the Red Sea. Muslims, Christians and Jews were the same," he preached. "If you believed in God, in the afterlife, and the importance of good works, then you were fine." He was Zaydi, but not Shia. They were all Muslims, not divided by sect. The Houthis were extremists. The Saudis planted Wahhabis among them. Now Iran was backing them against the Saudis. I was safe at CALES, which was part of the Ikhwan. The next day he drove me to an interview. "There were numbers in the Koran which explained the end times to come in about 50 years. The Prophet believed that Judgment Day would come soon." *"When the Trumpet sounds a single blast; when earth with all its mountains is raised high and with one mighty crash is shattered into dust on that day the Dread Event will come to past. On that day you will be displayed before Him, and all your secrets shall be brought to light."*[251]

At a checkpoint, a soldier opened his door, and frisked him. Was this related to the attempted al-Qaeda prison break that I had heard about? He nodded. They were ordered out to frighten us. I thought of the color-coded system during the Bush Administration warning Americans which days were more dangerous.[252] We came to the al-Saleh Mosque, as large as a stadium and drove on to Hadda. It came from the Himyarite era when the shadow of the palace, said to be 20 stories high, fell over this area, hence the name, Hadda, or shadow. We parked on a dirt street, climbed up steps in the dark and knocked on a heavy wood door.

Abdul Ghani al-Eryani, a prominent political analyst, invited us in. He was just watching that supermodel, Christine, she said at 60 she forgot things. Christine Brinkley... Yes, she said age was a state of mind. I pondered that he was watching a U.S. fashion model on television, the power of America. We sat on the floor, and he served coffee from their family farm in Eryani. In the 17th Century, British, Dutch, and later American ships loaded coffee from Mocha.[253] Today they exported terrorists, weapons, immigrants, and gat to Saudi Arabia. He didn't like the term Islamic fundamentalism. Islam was a secondary identity here, which showed how foolish U.S. policy was. There were two great tribal competitors. The Madhaj, who invited in the Abyssinians, the regional clients of Rome, and the Kahlan, who invited in the Persians. They rebelled against Mohammad. Islam came in the 1960s in the back of a Toyota pickup. He meant young, bearded men with rifles and rocket-propelled grenade launchers, like the Taliban.

Once, it didn't matter whether you were Shi'a or Sunni. Your identity

---

[251] Al-Haqqah (The Inevitable), The Koran, 69:17-18

[252] David Kravets, "Color-Coded Threat Level Advisory under Attack," *Wired* 16 Sept. 2009, https://www.wired.com/2009/09/threatleveladvisory/.

[253] Clark, *"Yemen: Dancing on the Heads of Snakes,"* 20

was your tribe. The Kahlan, the tribe of the Queen of Sheba, was as powerful as the chief's ability to rally his men.

Each was concerned about his honor, and survival. The Bedouin were indifferent to religion. When the Yemenis, called Afghan-Arabs, who fought in Afghanistan in the 1980s, returned, they were socialists. They called themselves The Abyan Army. Abyan was a Governorate, like a province, in the south on the Gulf of Aden.

When the government defeated them, they became the Islamic Army of Aden. In 1998, they kidnapped 16 westerners who they wanted to exchange for their comrades in prison. Yemen tried a rescue attempt, but two kidnappers and four hostages were killed. Western intelligence agencies knew that Yemen and, more ominously, its institutions, were filled with Afghan-Arabs sympathetic to al-Qaeda.[254] The Islamic Army praised al-Qaeda's 1998 attack on the U.S. embassies in Nairobi and Tanzania, and joined its attack on the USS Cole. Al-Qaeda was Yemenis born and raised in Saudi Arabia, 60-80% of the leadership. The Wahhabi tradition, from Saudi Arabia, was Hanbali-Wahabbi Islam. He went with his wife, who was from Abyan, to see her family. He met with the al-Qaeda leader who complained that his men kept missing prayers. They fought for one another, or for money.

A Taliban commander in the Tribal Areas, recovering from battle wounds, said they got paid for every American they killed.

Yemen was facing an economic disaster. Gat farming had all but depleted the water table. Every afternoon, half the male population, it seemed, rushed to a gat market, where men sold gat, which looked like spinach, or to a man sitting with a burlap bag under a tree. Young men could either join the army or al-Qaeda which remained economically viable through money from extortion, kidnappings and from the millions it received from rogue princes in Saudi Arabia, who helped them escape from prison. Former president Saleh, and his former ally, distant cousin and now enemy, Ali Mohsen al-Ahmar, commander of the northwest military sector of the country, which includes Sana'a, paid al-Qaeda a salary, and provided houses in Hadda.

It was here, an enclave of wide streets, and compounds, where parents threw birthday parties for their children in a land, like Afghanistan, where

---

[254] Soufan, "*The Black Banners*,"154

only the upper class knew when they were born.

In 2008 or 2009, the U.S. gave the addresses of al-Qaeda to the government, which denied knowing where they were. They arrested 30 suspected members in one day. Saleh used them to destabilize the system so that people would want him to return to power. He and General Ali Mohsen funded al-Qaeda in the Arabian Peninsula. Each controlled a faction of the franchise.

Was the underwear bomber working for al-Qaeda, or the government, or was there a difference?

There were 85 assassinations last year and al-Saleh had a hand in most. The underwear bomber was working for al-Qaeda. The U.S. didn't care about Yemen because it didn't have oil, until the Afghan-Arabs returned. The White House declared that Yemen was al-Qaeda central. It wasn't, but the U.S. was trying to make it so. It worked with the security apparatus, and pursued its own assassination program, ignoring the fact that the terrorists were the end product of a long line of decisions that the U.S. made. America's approach was to develop large projects that didn't work, integrated with security. Why didn't we copy al-Qaeda? Go into an area, identify the biggest problem, say, that the people needed a $25,000 water pump, buy it, and put it to work.

In 2006 I sat with a group of men in Lower Swat, near the Tribal Areas, below a line of jagged mountains sparkling in the rising sun. Could bin Laden hide up there? Yes, an old man, replied, but he would need permission from the tribal leader. It was the same here.

The founding leader of al-Qaeda, close to bin Laden, was arrested with $100,000 on him. He was the son of a sheikh who received a subsidy from the state. Saleh operated like a feudal lord dispensing government money. The huge deployment of police I saw this morning was because the power centers were fighting one another. The "Death to America" signs in al-Qadeemah began to appear in 1979 when Khomeini came to power in Iran. Hussein Badreddin al-Houthi was an imam (preacher) and an ambitious, charismatic Zaydi Parliamentarian from Sa'dah, a governorate on the Saudi border. In 1993 he went a pilgrimage to Qom, where Khomeini lived, stayed a year, and brought this message back. The phrases increased xenophobia. Iranian intervention was growing.

There was a picture in the newspapers[255] of a ship stopped off the coast carrying rifles and surface to air missiles. The Houthis were Zaydis who wanted to recreate their former kingdom, as Pakistan wanted to recreate the Moghul Empire, "an Islamic bloc from the Arabian Sea to the Urals,"[256] the reason it backed the Taliban and the Haqqani Network. Iran wanted to retake Khorasan, as the Pashtuns wanted their land back in Pakistan.

The Zaydis lived in the north and were a quarter of Yemen's 30 million people.[257] They had been going to Qom since 1947. When Houthi returned in 1994, he started the Believing Youth Forum, which became the Supporters of God (*Ansar Allah*) and in 2004 evolved into a fight against corruption under the rule of President Saleh. In 2004, his forces killed al-Houthi. His followers became known as Houthis. The Old City was their enclave. After Operation Desert Storm, the 1990-1991 war to oust Saddam Hussein from Kuwait, and to protect Saudi Arabia, the Saudis let U.S. troops stay, against the Koran, one reason why bin Laden created al-Qaeda. "*Believers, know that the idolaters are unclean. Let them not come near to the Sacred Mosque.*"[258] Until then, Saudi Arabia financed the Wahhabis here as they did in Afghanistan and Pakistan but now afraid of militant Islam on its southern border, asked the Ikhwan for help. The Saudis financed the chief of the Hashed to form a coalition of tribal clients, Wahhabis, businessmen and the Ikhwan to create *Islah*, the most powerful political party here. The Saudi clan used militant Islam since the 18th century to gain and keep power over the tribes of Yemen. They had a long-standing strategic goal to maintain access to the sea. The U.S., and its allies, because of oil, the U.S. treaty and Saudi wealth, which it used to purchase billions of dollars in arms, supported the Saudis.

What about the telephone conversation between al-Zawahiri and al-Wuhayshi, which forced the U.S. to close 21 embassies and consulates? It was in major U.S. newspapers.

El-Iryani smiled. Al-Zawahiri and al-Wuhayshi wanted publicity. It was a successful al-Qaeda operation. The U.S. publicized this, and al-Qaeda

---

[255] Yemen Observer 11/19/13.
[256] Kamal Davar, "*Tryst with Perfidy: The Deep State of Pakistan*" (New Delhi: Rupa, 2017), 40
[257] *CIA World Fact Book*, 2020
[258] Repentance (Al-Tawba), The Koran, 9:28

recruited. Everyone won. The old power elite were using al-Qaeda against the new government, and in negotiations with the security apparatus. The first suicide attack in Yemen was the USS Cole in 2000. In 2010, a security officer told him he could turn a poor young boy into a suicide bomber in one week. There were 13 al-Qaeda training camps here in the 1990s to early 2000. In 2010 Yemeni cargo planes were transporting sheep from here to Somaliland. They offloaded the sheep, loaded men and weapons and flew to Yemen. The sheep were a cover to bring in militants who had made their way to Somaliland, an autonomous region in Somalia, home of al-Shabab (the boys), the al-Qaeda affiliate. The Saudis were countering Iran. It was now a Sunni- Shia war.

The next afternoon Mohammad and I walked into a marble foyer and down a hallway to a wood paneled room with a green marble coffee table and a desk with a Yemeni flag carved in the front.

A man brought lemonade and tea. A man in a pale green suit joined us. He was advisor to President Hadi for Strategic Studies, and Scientific Research, a dual portfolio. Did I want to chew gat? It was their think tank, he smiled. There was extremism here, but the Islamophobia in the West was unjust. There were Islamists, but before they went to Afghanistan they were not allowed to be here, officially. Egypt was the hub of Islamic extremism. Yemeni students went there and came back filled with the spirit of extremism. He meant filled with the idealism of the Ikhwan, when in 1948 they tried to overthrow the Zaydi Imamate.

A one-eyed man the Imam had jailed years before, put 150 bullets into him. The Ikhwan kept their activities secret until 1978 when Saleh came to power. It became their golden age. The Sunni Ikhwan and Saleh, a Zaydi Shia, worked together. In 1979, after Khomeini came to power and the Soviet Union invaded Afghanistan, the Ikhwan, backed by the Saudis, the Egyptians, the U.S., and Pakistan, recruited people here to go to Afghanistan. Zindani was in charge.

The U.S. and its allies in 1979 recruited Yemenis to go to Afghanistan? This was not in the 9/11 Commission Report.

In 1988 the Yemenis began to return and were treated poorly. They decided to continue here what they were doing in Afghanistan. Bin Laden organized al-Qaeda. In 1994, they were invited here. In 1998 the Islamic

Army of Abyan appeared, and then al-Qaeda. In October 2000, they bombed the USS Cole and in October 2002 the French ship the Limburg.[259] In 2002, the U.S. drone war began. He stood up, his lecture over, and left.

The next day Mohammad and I walked up marble stairs to in an apartment building to the office of Dr. Saeed Ali Obaid, in a yellow shirt, and dark pants. His desk was empty and the walls were bare. He was the author of *The al-Qaeda Organization: the establishment, the ideology, background, and the extension*, published in Cairo in 2008. All 3,000 copies sold out in a month. The second edition, published here, was titled *Al-Qaeda in Yemen*. Mohammad said he was the foremost scholar on al-Qaeda in Yemen.

He spoke softly. Al-Qaeda began after 1990 when, after the Afghan war, it recruited, mainly from the tribes. In 1992, the strong members, who came from Afghanistan, attacked U.S. forces on their way to Somalia. There were two branches: a Yemeni branch and a Saudi branch, formed in Saudi Arabia in 2000. Al-Qaeda from Afghanistan and Pakistan was part of the USS Cole attack. From 2002-2009 they built a foundation. In 2006, al-Qaeda launched its first suicide attack. A large group was captured. Then 23 members, including the emir and the military commander, dug a tunnel, dropping the dirt in the sewer, for a month, came up and saw that they were still inside the prison, kept digging and came up near a mosque. Some escaped and others stayed back giving them time to spread out, and then they escaped.

In 2008, the Saudis started to come here, individually or two men together, to help build their website. In January 2009, al-Qaeda officially declared itself and the U.S. created the name "al-Qaeda in the Arabian Peninsula." The Saudis defeated al-Qaeda in Saudi Arabia in 2009. The remaining members fled here. They engaged in the vicious attacks which were the hallmark of al-Qaeda. They had ties to the political security apparatus, and to the tribes. Since 2009, as al-Qaeda became stronger, it fought the Americans and the government.

But I was being told that Saleh, and parts of the military, backed al-Qaeda. He put his hands, prayer-like, to his lips. It was true. I had to realize that these people were young and had a deep faith in God, which enabled them to overcome obstacles. After 2009, their strength was the union of Saudis and Yemenis. Now they had Egyptians, Libyans, Pakistanis, and

---

[259] http://news.bbc.co.uk/2/hi/middle_east/2324431.stm

Somalis. Al-Qaeda began with the Salafis,[260] who followed the Koran, and the words of Mohammad's companions the *"salaf al-saleh."*[261] They did not chew gat and sought purity to be worthy of God. They ran the farms where boys started as students and were nurtured to become terrorists.

Obaid said the al-Qaeda movement really began, long before, with a man called Muqbil al-Wada'I,[262] a Shia Muslim born in Dimmaj, a Zaydi enclave north of Sana'a, into a lower-class family. He went to Saudi Arabia to study where he discovered errors in Zaydi teaching, graduated from two universities, wrote books on Islam, and returned home to further his studies. He found that in spite of his accomplishments Zaydi aristocrats, because he was low class, still looked down on him. Scholars pressured him to accept Zaydi teaching. He declined and returned to Saudi Arabia. The Ikhwan asked him to join them but they were too materialistic. He met Muhammad al-Qahtani,[263] a preacher who called himself the Mahdi and joined his "Movement of the Muslim Revolutionaries of the Arabian Peninsula."[264] Again that word, *"al-Mahdi,"* the Messiah.

On November 20, 1979, al-Qahtani, with men from secret cells in the Saudi army, and weapons they had smuggled in, with foreigners, mainly Yemenis backed by Saudi princes, and led by Juhaiman al-Ataiba,[265] their political leader, who blamed the West for destroying the values of Saudi society, seized the Grand Mosque in Mecca. Al-Qahtani called for the purification of Islam, and for a return to the early "Golden Age," a time of justice and equality. In the 18th Century, the Qahtan tribe, with 50,000 warriors, agreed to join the Saudis, but only if they could continue raiding Yemen.[266] The Saudis agreed, but now al-Qahtani, was determined, it seemed under the banner of Islam, to fight them. Al-Ataiba denounced the government, which talked about religion but was corrupt and oppressive. He called Saudi princes "drunkards" who lived dissolute lives in luxurious

---

[260] Salafiyun, or ahl al-sunna wa al-jamaa, the people of the traditions and of the book.

[261] Laurent Bonnefoy, *"Salafism in Yemen,"* (New York: Hearst & Company, Ltd, 2011), 42

[262] Ibid p.200 See also Dresch, *"History of Modern Yemen,"* 200

[263] Commins, *"The Wahhabi Mission and Saudi Arabia,"* 167-170

[264] Vasiliev, *The History of Saudi Arabia*

[265] Commins, *"The Wahhabi Mission and Saudi Arabia,"* 206 - 207

[266] Ibid 39

palaces, and for Muslims to live simply, under the Mahdi, as they had during the time of the Prophet.[267]

Khomeini used the same words in February 1979, like Qutb, and Shah Wailullah before him.

They fought government forces for two weeks, with thousands of pilgrims trapped in the mosque. Hundreds were killed. The government called in French Special Forces. The attack influenced a teenage bin Laden[268] and frightened the Saudi royal family to its core. Al-Qahtani and al-Ataiba were executed. Al-Waidi was imprisoned for six months and expelled.[269] He returned to Dimmaj, and founded a school, Dar al-Hadith.[270] The tribes around him, most of which were Shia, were opposed. He had 300 boys and no electricity, but he persevered and founded the Sunni Salafi movement in Yemen. The Sheikh was critical of the Saudi royal family, but later seduced by money said they should obey their rulers, but then he said they were corrupt, and they had to fight them. This changed during the Afghan war when the Egyptians came and said these people or those people were not good Muslims.

He meant al-Zawahiri and his followers and the concept of "*takfiri*," that a Muslim, because of mistakes in his acts or thinking, had become an apostate. This began with Sayyid Qutb who saw Nasser torture Muslims. How could a Muslim torture another Muslim and be Muslim? "*A Muslim was one who avoids harming Muslims with his tongue and hands.*"[271] Takfiri grew in importance in Saudi Arabia when men went to Afghanistan, and to Bosnia, and returned to find a corrupt society, and U.S. soldiers. They attacked the state, which tortured them, which led them to join al-Qaeda.[272] Al-Waidi had tens of thousands of students in the U.S., the U.K., and Europe. He went to Germany and to the U.S. for medical treatment. He died there in 2002.

---

[267] Vasiliev, "*The History of Saudi Arabia*" 396
[268] "1979: Remembering 'the Siege of Mecca.'" NPR, 20 Aug. 2009, https://www.npr.org/templates/story/story.php?storyId=112051155
[269] *The Cambridge History of Islam* 495
[270] "House of Tradition, or "Traditions of the Prophet Mohammad"
[271] https://versebyversequranacademy.wordpress.com/.
[272] Thomas Hegghammer, "*Jihad in Saudi Arabia*" (Cambridge: Cambridge University Press, 2010), 74-75.

How could al-Waidi, after 9/11, be allowed into the U.S., unless the Saudis, maybe, opened the door?

What about his own life? Obaid smiled gently. He was born in Aden into a religious family, went to Aden University, but South Yemen was Marxist and there were no Islamic studies offered. He came north to Sana'a University where he met the Ikhwan who told him about a Salafi school in Sa'dah. He went there and went now on holidays. He taught Arabic in public schools. There were two types of schools. Those funded by the Ministry of Education, and "Scientific Institutes" funded by the Ikhwan, like CALES. He met al-Waidí, sitting under a tree, studying by a canal. He had found the true Islam. He was not interested in politics or economics only to live a life of religious perfection. He was fluent in classical Arabic in its most complex form. If you saw him today, you would not recognize him, a poor person walking in the street.

After President Saleh was forced to resign in the Arab Spring, soldiers were told to leave their camps, and their weapons. Al-Qaeda took them. Saleh gave foreigner fighters ID cards and passports. It was his pride, his need for revenge, and to return to power. Al-Qaeda was trying to stamp out corruption in the oil industry where men were skimming oil and selling it on the open market in Dubai. It had more influence in some areas than the government. It liked the Human Rights Watch report[273] which was critical of the U.S. It would not leave Pakistan, but its future was here. If I knew the true Islam, I would know al-Qaeda and not be affected. It wanted to establish the Caliphate and to get rid of the Crusaders. Al-Qaeda had given birth to a new al-Qaeda, and it was in Yemen. To find it I had to go to Aden, but with a bodyguard.

---

[273] "Between a Drone and Al-Qaeda," *Human Rights Watch*, 17 Nov. 2020, https://www.hrw.org/report/2013/10/22/between-drone-and-al-qaeda/civilian-cost-us-targeted-killings-yemen.

What is Shari'ah?

Mahmud, a friend of Karim's, less conspicuous in his old Toyota, than Mohammad's new SUV, stopped at a large stone house, with a flower garden in the front. A man, medium height, in a brown cardigan sweater, white shirt and khakis, led me on hand-woven carpets past modern furniture into his *mafraj*, of gray cushioned seats, books in Arabic and English, paintings, and photographs of his father, and of himself. An Ethiopian maid brought a thermos of *kisst*, made from the shell of coffee beans, and cookies.

His name was Mansur and he was an advisor to the Ministry of Culture, a judge, a lawyer, a poet, a professor of Arabic at Sana'a University, and a specialist in Shari'ah. With the photographs and paintings, he was clearly secular. He studied in a mosque with a mufti when he was 16, then law at Cairo University and at College University in London. For 30 years he was legal advisor to Yemeni Airlines, and to UNICEF. He wrote the Rights of Children in Yemen in 1993.

"*Shar*" means law in Arabic, "*sharia*" means path, which a camel takes in the desert to water, like the Koran, the source of life. "*Shari'ah*"[274] is divine law for Muslims. It came from God, he said loudly. Legal law was from human beings. The basis of all law in Yemen was "*Sharia*." There were many schools of thought. Its essence was justice, and said no one could come between God and man. Did it come from God? Mansur shook his head. He was never a strong believer. He loved studying, loved to learn and to gather knowledge. In his 20s, he studied Marxism and read *Das Capital*. He studied European philosophers and immersed himself in the pursuit of knowledge. He didn't believe in religion, only in man. It was his problem. He was imprisoned seven times. The first time for three years, the second time for one year, the third time for three months. He was 67 now. Every president of Yemen had put him in prison because he felt that he was dangerous, not to Yemen, but to him.

Did being in prison make him angry? Yes, of course. His eyes went

---

[274] While Shar-e-ah is the correct pronunciation I have chosen, for simplicity, to write Sharia.

hard, and then softened. He shrugged. He went on. He was a young officer fighting the royalists. They knew he was well-educated and studying Sharia. They hurt others, but not him.

He was what Graham Greene[275] called "the untorturable," those too educated, too upper class to torture. There are many types of torture. Terry Waite, assistant to the archbishop of Canterbury, who was held by Hezbollah in solitary confinement for four years, wanted to talk when we met about mock executions. Mansur wrote poetry in prison. He translated *"The Wasteland"* and Goethe. He left and returned with books of poetry, on literature and philosophy, magazine articles published in Beirut, Kuwait, and the UAE. There was a difference between the people and the government. If you were a good man, well-educated, the government did not want you. The people loved you and respected you more if you had been in prison. All these dictatorships—he waved his hand. Religious men came to him. They knew that he was not with them, but they respected his knowledge. He didn't believe that Sharia was always good law. It came from political people. If man accepted this, it would be better. He hid himself, to study more and to be even better educated. Education was a form of protection. The government, the secret police, and the Ikhwan were against him, but the Ikhwan talked to him about Sharia. He said what it said and what he thought. He was a mufti, a Muslim jurist who gave legal opinions, fatwas, and expounded on the law.

Did he believe in God? He hesitated. "No." Did that make him afraid, or sad? He was quite happy with his beliefs. As a young man he wondered. He went to Friday prayers once a year for social reasons.

What role did Pakistan play here? He didn't think it did, maybe with Saudi Arabia. Why had Islam become stronger? It was because there was no development. His voice grew louder. Western countries, beginning with the Portuguese, the British, the Dutch, the French, and then the Americans, came to Arab lands, took their oil, and didn't develop anything. There were no schools, no roads, children without shoes, people without food, near where the British were, and they did nothing. This was why the people became Marxist. The Islamists saw that the people had little. The difference between the West and here was that the rich always got theirs, and here no

---

[275] Graham Greene, *"Our Man in Havana"* (London: Oberon Books, 2015).

one got anything. The Americans, through their war, made bin Laden, and a Yemeni-Saudi alliance made al-Qaeda. In the 1970s, this alliance, with oil money, preached in the mosques to give money to fight the Russians, and to go to Afghanistan. The Russians did not believe in God, they said. America sent Yemenis there and used them. 9/11 was payback by those who were used. Everyone in America should know what war was like. We are all on the same earth. Saleh and Ali-Mohsen were together for 33 years. They, like Mubarak,[276] used the Islamists. Everyone had his own al-Qaeda. It was the daughter of the Ikhwan relationship with the government, which gave arms and money to al-Qaeda to hurt Western people, who gave money to us to fight al-Qaeda. Everybody, including America, was playing this game.

The 9/11 Commission[277] blamed Arab nations for sending Arabs to Afghanistan. It said neither President Clinton, or George W. Bush, or Donald Rumsfeld, or his deputy Paul Wolfowitz, wanted to attack al-Qaeda for the attack on the USS Cole.

Saudi Arabia was responsible for all the problems in Yemen. Pakistan did not deal directly with Yemen, but only through Saudi Arabia, maybe on behalf of al-Qaeda. Abdul Aziz said to his sons, "*All good things and all bad things came from Yemen. Keep your eyes on Yemen.*" They wanted their land back he said referring to Asir, Najran, and Jazen. They were first of all Arabs, and then they were Yemenis, like the Anglo-Saxons, a tribal federation. It was a question of blood and place. The Saudis gave money to the Houthis and to the Salafis to weaken Yemen.

Iran was a religious government. It said it was for the people, but it was Shia and against Sunnis. Saudi Arabia was playing the same game against Iran as the Americans.

---

[276] Mohammad Hosni Mubarak, President of Egypt from 1981 – 2011.
[277] *The 9/11 Commission Report, Authorized Edition, W.W. Norton & Company, Inc.* 202

The Religious Wars

The next day, after class Muhammed drove me up into the hills to his large gray stone house overlooking the city. We sat in his *mafraj* watching American cartoons in Arabic on television. His father, Ali, came home and we went to a small room for a feast of lamb, rice and vegetable dishes in small stone pots. All his sons and their families lived here. We moved to the mafraj to eat fruit and drink tea.

On television an imam in a white turban and gray robe, sat at a podium and preached with his hand out to a man in his 20s, with a beatific smile, sitting close and to a crowd sitting on the floor. There were large lighted columns, and a reflecting pool, a scene of beauty and peace, but the sermon was on Al-Anwar (The Lights), against the Sunni worship of the Companions of the Prophet, elevating them to the status of gods, and idols. "There should only be one God," Muhammad reminded me, as he picked a leaf of gat. Sunnis say the same thing.

His partner, in their production company, about 25, in a thobe, gray sport coat, and scarf, picked up my book which I had brought for Ali at his request. Was this a dictionary? I explained what it was. He was quiet. Did the Taliban harm me? Was this book in Arabic? What would people think if they read it? Was it anti-Muslim? I called Islam "tyranny." They were forcing me to convert. I told them I would write the truth. What did I think of the Taliban and al-Qaeda? I had lived with the Mujahideen, and the Haqqanis. One of my captors said Pakistan used the Taliban for regional purposes and al-Qaeda internationally.

He could take me to meet jihadis, to men who recruited children and who taught them to become suicide bombers. There was no such thing as al-Qaeda. They were mercenaries. They were used by higher-ups to fight. But they were religious. They believed in a cause. The young did, he replied, but they were being used by their leaders. This was a business. How would I be safe? He came from a big tribe. We would negotiate. They were professionals. They would want to show me their work. How did he become a journalist? He went to university and there decided he wanted to work in radio and television. He wanted to do something noble, and with dignity, and he wanted to be famous. I liked him, but it was too dangerous.

On the television a man looked down, opened the Koran, and preached. He finished, and a man in a white gown chanted deeply about the last sermon of the Prophet where he called upon Ali to be his representative. For over a thousand years Shias and Sunnis had been arguing and killing one another over this sermon. The chanting was hypnotic, and the crowd quiet. Mohammad said it was an Iraqi Shia channel. There were now Shia channels and Sunni channels preaching that the other was wrong. They had the Koran, but nobody followed it, Karim lamented. All the Arabs did was fight.

The Rival to Mecca

The Great Mosque made of gray stone, from the 8th Century, the center of al-Qademah, was fifty yards from CALES. On Fridays, it was full, and men and boys sat outside. The imam's sermon was carried on a loudspeaker. The mosque was destroyed by floods and rebuilt from the great 6th Century Axumite (Ethiopian) Christian Church, al-Qualis, from the Greek *ekklesia* (assembly).

There was a beggar sitting by a door. Inside there were thick wood beams, carpets, a few men reading the Koran and small groups talking. A non-believer was not to enter a mosque. I left and walked past a woodworking shop, clothing shops, a spice market, a knife shop, a tailor, kept asking for directions and finally I came to a small quiet plaza with a round high stone wall twelve feet across in the center, with a small, rusted fence on top, dusty bushes, small trees, pieces of paper, and plastic sacks, where al-Qualis once stood.

The Sabaeans, who maybe looked to Abraham as the founder of their faith, and some claim to be Sabaeans in Iraq,[278] created the caravan, brought frankincense, which the Romans, according to Thesiger, the English desert explorer, were looking for in 24 B.C., and myrrh to the Fertile Crescent, and ruled southern Arabia for over 1300 years.[279] Around the 1st[st] century BC, a Himyarite tribal federation, conquered them. It became the Kingdom of Himyar. Its last king, Dhu Nuwas, converted to Judaism, and fought the Christians of Ethiopia and Byzantium in Najran.[280] The king of Axum, the Ethiopian Christian Empire,[281] allied with Egyptian Christians, invaded again. They, with the help of Emperor Justin, built al-Qualis to draw pilgrims from the Kaabah. The Christian-Muslim war started here.

---

[278] "*The Sabean Religion,*"http://www.webpal.org/SAFE/ aaarenewal/revelation/x1sabean.htm.
[279] Wilfred Thesiger, "*Arabian Sands,*" New York: Penguin Books, 1964, 44
[280] Sura 85, 4-8
[281] Rodinson, "*Muhammed,*" 29

Luke Somers

That evening, Ahmed, our guard at CALES made sure that my turban was tied properly. I walked past the bakery, under the banner that said "Death to America," past shops built into tower houses, down a cobblestone street, across the stone bridge over a paved *wadi*, into the main city. I had learned that the American kidnapped was Luke Somers, a photojournalist. We reached the city center with banks and building with multiple stories, and finally an empty parking lot with room for three or four cars across and two deep. He was kidnapped here. Were they waiting for a Westerner, and saw him, with his haircut shaved on the side and open American smile, and forced him into a car? Someone, probably many people, saw them. The German was killed here. Inside, we walked down the aisles, the shelves filled with European, American and Yemeni food. Maybe they saw Luke here and waited outside. Kidnappings in Afghanistan took weeks to plan. They probably sold him to al-Qaeda. Kidnappers brought hostages to the Haqqanis. I stood there, thinking of Luke. We walked back by a different route fast in the night.

A Former Prime Minister

An armed guard led me past a carport, a lush green lawn, into a large modern home to a stairway. At the bottom, a short man in a white thobe and sandals stood with his arms out. It was Friday and he dressed casually, said Dr. Abdul Karim al-Eryani, former foreign minister, and prime minister, under President Saleh. He sat by his large dark wood desk. There was a sword on the wall, a television, paintings, and walls of books in Arabic and English. A Malaysian maid brought glasses of fresh orange juice.

After the Free Officers, led by Nasser, overthrew King Farouk in 1952, in Egypt, the Imam of Yemen would not allow anyone to go there to study. A year later, Eryani sneaked across the border to South Yemen, and took an Antonin Besse vessel from Aden, and 21 days later arrived in Cairo. "Antonin Besse was the greatest company on the Arabian Peninsula," he said. Besse, a Frenchman, with little education, borrowed money as a young man from a brother-in-law and sailed from Marseille, made a fortune selling coffee, and endowed St. Anthony's College, Oxford. In 1957, al-Eryani finished high school in Cairo. There were two scholarships available, under a State Department program, for Yemenis to study in the U.S. He went to the U.S. Embassy, which was open, like walking into a cafeteria. He took the required English test. When he finished the ambassador came out and said, "One is a cook, not a cooker." It was the only mistake he made.

In 1958 he went to South West Texas State College to study agriculture. Lyndon Johnson went there. He was an extension officer, someone who took what he learned to local farmers. The first semester was hard, but after that it got easier. His advisor helped him transfer to Oklahoma State in Stillwater. He loved campus life…until winter. He wanted to study how to grow vegetables and in 1960 went to Georgia. It was Kennedy vs. Nixon. He bought a '57 Chevrolet for $300. It was the only car with a JFK sticker on it. I imagined him, about 5'2" trying to see over the dashboard. It was the time of sit-ins, violence and forced integration. He watched Charlayne Hunter become the first Black woman to integrate the University of Georgia. He finally met her when he was foreign minister.

He was brought up in a village in Eryan, in the central highlands, in a family that had been in politics for 700 years. His ancestors were judges.[282] His family was involved in the 1948 revolution, when the Ikhwan tried to overthrow the Imamate. He was 14, and soldiers came and looted everything, but they recovered. In 1962, the Imamate was overthrown and Egypt, a socialist country under the Free Officers, invaded. His brother was accused of being a Ba'ath and with his uncle was on the run.

The Ba'ath (Resurrection) ideology rose in the 1950s in Syria, a call for Arabs to unite to be free and one people. Mohammad brought Arabs together into one society. Now it needed to be expanded to include all Arabs, secular, Christian and Muslim to love and understand one another, and to create a socialist nation. His uncle, Abdul-Rahman,[283] and his brother, were captured and his uncle sentenced to death. He wrote a letter to Abdul Karim from prison. An old education would not work anymore. It was now his time. But it was too dangerous. He got a master's degree in plant breeding. His uncle became president of North Yemen. He went to Yale, and got a PhD in chemical genetics in 1968. The Egyptians finally left and he left the U.S., and its luxury, and worked on a U.N. irrigation project in Yemen. After the coup in 1962 *Time* wrote that Yemen was rushing toward the 13th Century, a land of nomads and families living in brushwood huts, stone houses, and castles.[284] As a boy his teacher made him read Jalaladin al-Afghani, an Iranian, one of the first to propose Islamic modernism, the notion that Islam was compatible with reason and progress, not opposed to science. No girl in his village wore a veil. In the 1920s, women in Cairo demonstrated against the hijab. It was the Wahhabis—those who studied in Saudi Arabia—who changed everything. Wahhabi was Salafi, and vice versa, a religious response to being conquered. Ba'athism was a secular response. In 1952, when Nasser was establishing his revolutionary council, he had two Ikhwan members, but they had no power. In the early 1960s he was in conflict with the Ikhwan. El Mehsud, the spiritual leader, had one request: Impose a decree requiring women to wear a hijab.

He paused. Did I want coffee? He was a coffee addict. He picked up the

---

[282] Eva Sohlman, "Abdul Karim Al-Eryani, 81, Dies; Yemeni Politician Brokered Arab Spring Peace," *New York Times* 13 Nov. 2015
[283] https://www.nytimes.com/ 1998/03/17/world/abdul-rahman-al-iryani-ex-yemen-president-89.html.
[284] *Encyclopedia Britannica*, vol. 32,1967 ed. 888.

phone. His maid brought a bronze coffee urn, cups and saucers. Nasser told a joke. How did he buy one or two million hijabs? The Ikhwan were less rigid than the Salafis. There was no conflict between the two today. Oppressive regimes allowed them to expand. So they could say they didn't oppose this Muslim ruler. It gave Saleh religious credibility. The war between the Salafis and the Houthis at Dimmaj, began with a Salafi madrasa complex created by Saudi Arabia. He was referring to al-Waidi. The pact between the Saud family and the Wahhab family said the Saud family ran the state and the Wahhab family ran religious affairs. That changed after the Israeli victories. Neither nationalism nor socialism helped the Arabs. The cradle of Palestinian support was nationalism. They were nationalists and qualified to recapture Palestine. Today it was the Islamic movements.

"Do what you may, there is no true power among men except in the free union of their will; and patriotism or religion, are the only two motives in the world which can long urge all the people toward the same end," wrote de Tocqueville.[285]

In June 1967, Israel, which Arabs saw as a Western colonial outpost, defeated Egypt, Jordan, and Syria. Before then, they would never have talked of two states. The Islamists felt if they were in power that the economy would recover and that Israel, and its backers, would go away. Leaders have had to think how they could live with Israel. Today, the game was being played by Israel, not by Arabs. Israel rose as a secular state. Ben Gurion[286] would cry at what it had become. The synagogues in Sanaá were empty. A shopkeeper showed me a piece of silver jewelry made, he said, by Jewish artisans.

Many Saudi policies developed against the will of religious leaders, so the Salafis rose saying they were non-political, but they became political. Saleh used the Salafi movement that alWadi'í started.[287] He recruited the support of the Ikhwan. The spearhead of al-Qaeda was his boyhood friend, General Ali Mohsen. He and Saleh used the Mujahideen in 1994 after they returned from Afghanistan to fight the Marxists in the South, and discarded them. Al-Qaeda started with Yemenis born and raised in Saudi Arabia. They

---

[285] "First Things," January 2019, p.64.
[286] David Ben Guerin, born in Poland in 1886, was in 1948 the founding father and first prime minister of Israel.
[287] Laurent Bonnefoy, "*Salafism in Yemen*" (New York: Hearst & Company, 2011 5

started with the USS Cole in 2000. They studied in madrasas in the tribal zones of Pakistan. The Soviet invasion gave the Salafis and the Wahhabis their opportunity. The Yemenis were Wahhabi Mujahideen, like the Taliban.

A week passed. His office was dark. A guard turned on the lights. He came in, and sat quietly. His servant brought fresh orange juice, and a pot of coffee. He had promised to tell me the story of Abdul Majeed Zindani, the most powerful jihadi in Yemen.

He was a pharmacology student at Cairo University, and he failed, he said loudly. He did not finish. He returned to Yemen after the socialist revolution of 1962 and attached himself to Mohamed Zubairy, the most prominent opposition republican leader, an orphan, Abu al-Ahar, "father of the free," the unofficial poet laurate of Yemen, who went to Cairo with Ahmad Noman in 1937. "A kingdom with its grotesque roots was destroyed by a pen," Zubairy wrote after the Imamate fell. The pen was his weapon, the Ikhwan his tribe.

"Zindani was driven from Cairo because he joined the Ikhwan." He allied himself with Zubairy, who opposed Egyptian rule. The Saudis supported the Imam. The republicans controlled Sana'a, the royalists, backed by the British, held the southwest. Zubairy escaped to Pakistan after the coup in 1948. There the Syrian ambassador,[288] a member of the Ikhwan, took him in. In 1952, after Nasser and his men overthrew King Farouk, he became ambassador to Egypt, and Zubairy went with him to Cairo. In the 1960s, still attached to Zubairy, Zindani began talking about scientific miracles in the Koran. He worked with Zaydi tribes north of Sana'a. They formed Hezbollah (Party of God). It was such a strange name. Al-Eryani shook his head. He was at Yale and wrote to his uncle, Abdul Rahim al-Eryani, who was close to Zubairy. Egypt was dangerous, and the West would look warily on a party named Hezbollah. From 1967-1974, al-Eryani's uncle was head of the presidential council, as close to a president as Yemen had. Zandani, no longer able to hide behind Zubairy found another route to power. He had or developed superstitious explanations to many statements in the Koran. He said he could prove scientifically that God revealed the Koran to Muhammed. There was a verse: *"They will lose their breath as if flying to Heaven."* Here the Korean revealed the existence of oxygen. By making statements like this, he attracted many people to him.

---

[288] Umar-Baha al-Amiri.

Al-Eryani returned to Yemen. Here he had to reveal a personal family tie to Zindani. His uncle was a judge in the central highlands. He married a woman from the Zindani family. In 1956, when he sneaked over the border and down to Aden, he stayed with Zindani's father, Aziz. They often talked. In the late 1960s, Zindani joined with the Ikhwan who escaped Nasser and went to Saudi Arabia. There he became a Wahhabi, and a preacher, a good one, too, preaching on the miraculous Koran. During the 1970s, he came the tutor of Osama bin Laden. He became afraid, and still was, that the U.S. wanted to kidnap him. He said he could convince the world that the Koran was scientifically accurate. In the 1970s and 80s Zindani and bin Laden recruited Saudis and Yemenis to go to Afghanistan. Zindani and his entourage went from mosque to mosque recruiting young men. The Saudis supported Bin Laden and him.

In Islam, the most rigid of the four schools was Hanbali which was Wahhabi, and the cradle of both was Saudi Arabia. Salafis said they were Hanbali-Salafi. The main school of Sunni Islam in Yemen was Shafi, founded by Muhammad ibn Idris Shafi (767-820), born in Gaza, tied through his mother to Yemen. He said the Koran was the Word of God. A Muslim must practice the "sunna" of Mohammad, the Perfect Man, as recorded in the hadith, the manifestations of God's will, equal to what was revealed in the Koran. Each hadith had to be traced to Mohammad, in Arabic. Hanbalis believed the only thing that counted was the Koran and what the *Rashidun*, Mohammad's companions, said was true. To understand Yemen, its anger, fear, and love of Saudi Arabia, I had to understand Shafi, and Hanbali Islam. The nucleus for al-Qaeda started with the invasion of Afghanistan. The whole war was under the influence of the Hanbali-Wahhabi ideology. The Wahhabis built hundreds of madrasas in Pakistan. Western, Saudi and Pakistani interests coalesced to turn the Northwest Frontier Province of Pakistan into a Wahhabi enclave. The original support for Pakistan against India came from Saudi Arabia. Pakistan would not have a nuclear bomb without Saudi money. Zindani preached in Afghanistan in the 1980s. There he developed his tie to Jalaluddin Haqqani. Many recruits to Afghanistan, thanks to Zindani, were Yemeni. Al-Eryani told a story. It was November 30, 1996, Yemeni Independence Day, when the British left South Yemen. Guests from Fatah[289] were there. He was sitting next to Zindani at dinner.

---

[289] Fatah ("Victory") the political and military organization founded in 1958 by

He said the Soviets had drilled into the ground in Siberia, deeper and deeper, until they heard moans and cries and screaming. He was serious. The Palestinian next to al-Eryani was laughing. I was to go to any music shop or where they sold religious books and ask for the lectures of Abdul Majeed. He laughed at them. In the 1960s and 1970s, Zindani wrote books for primary, middle, and secondary schools, called "Tawhid Books." It was basic Hanbali thought—the oneness of God. The Ministry of Education placed them in the schools. Unfortunately for Zindani, in 1976, he became Minister of Education and cut all the nonsense. When he left in 1978, Zindani's books came back. Zindani respected him and called him a Darwinian, which was true. He studied the genetic control of aromatic amino acids. One could not be a geneticist without believing in Darwin. Zindani, like many Wahhabis, believed in a Western conspiracy against Islam. He was the father of extremism in Yemen. He mentored Anwar al-Awalaki. Most of al-Qaeda considered him their spiritual father. If I listened to the interrogation tapes I would see. He was a witch doctor. He said in studying the Koran he found that by using certain herbs, honey and grains he found a cure for AIDS, cancer, and hepatitis. He treated people and they died.

The 2006 election campaign was close and Saleh needed Zindani's support. He arranged a campaign event for Saleh at Eman (Faith) University, invited the diplomatic corps and declared that he had discovered the cure for AIDS. The ambassadors smiled amongst themselves. He said if a drug company knew his secrets it would steal them and make billions. To see him, I was to say I was interested in his medical discoveries. He was a very strange, complex personality who he knew so well. He put his medicine in empty water bottles. There was supposedly a big bottle that all students had to drink from when they went to the university. The Libyans believed his stories and sent people here to be cured. They found that he was a fraud. He was one of the richest men in Yemen. He was religious, unless he was Rasputin.

Yassir Arafat to establish a Palestinian state.

A few days later, Mahmoud drove through the dusty rolling hills of west Sanaá and came to a guard post, the entrance to Eman University. He stopped. We needed permission. He was afraid to go in. Zindani founded the university in 1993 with financing from Saudi Arabia. It was where he mentored al-Waliki, who mentored Omar Farouk Abdulmutallab, who studied there. Zindani connected, through Saleh, with Ali Mohsen in 1994. Zindani celebrated 9/11. The three most powerful men in Yemen used al-Qaeda as a tool to maintain power, and to become wealthy. They got money from Gulf countries and from ransom money. Saudi Arabia was the driving force promoting Wahhabi-Hanbali-Salafi Islam since 1974, when it became enormously wealthy after the Arab oil embargo following the 1973 Arab-Israeli war. Eman University's graduates were sent as missionaries around the world.

Professor Bakeel Zindani

The horns, motorcycles, vans and trucks were loud and men waved and wormed their way through traffic. There were 55,000 police in Sanaá, more than in New York,[290] Dahan said, and they never caught a motorcycle assassin. Mahmud gave his ID card to the guard, in a yellow and black leopard uniform, and drove onto the campus of Sana'a University. The ground was brown, like the buildings. Male students wore jeans, polo shirts, t-shirts and sports jackets, and women wore abayas. Bakeel Zindani in a blue blazer, jeans, a plaid shirt, sat by his desk, with four women in jeans and boots sticking out from their abayas across from him. He got a scholarship to go to America to get a master's degree. He went to Long Island University, then to Louisiana State to get a PhD. Katrina hit and he went to the University of Nebraska. After 9/11 he was afraid, but people gave him their phone numbers and said if he had any trouble to call.

Iran was supporting the Houthis and Saudi Arabia the Salafis. The Gulf States backed al-Qaeda.

Yemen was a good place for the monarchies to practice what they believed in, and attack Western interests, especially America. One reason why al-Qaeda was here was because of the U.S. presence. The U.S. supported dictatorships, and controlled Yemeni sovereignty, they said. Over 65% of Yemenis were not educated and believed them. There were no jobs for so many youths to be a part of society, or for them to support their families, and which was a victory for Iran, al-Qaeda, and Saudi Arabia, all of which wanted to control Yemen. Each member of the political elite was connected to another country, or outside organization. The U.S. and other countries gave money to these people to work for them. Who were these elites serving, Yemen or the countries that supported them? The U.S. was undermining democracy to influence leaders, 95% of whom received foreign support. He told his students to think beyond this and that they could do anything and be part of the future, but people were worried about getting enough to eat, and staying alive. Iran and Saudi Arabia wanted Yemen to be

---

[290] "New York City Police Department," *Wikipedia* 5 May 2022, https://en.wikipedia.org/wiki/New_York_City_Police_Department.

sick, but not to die. Hezbollah in Lebanon helped the Houthis. Iran and Saudi Arabia sent money to al-Qaeda and said fight the West. When a father supported his son, he had a goal in mind. The U.S. supported the military and the intelligence agencies, and they supported U.S. policies.

"We are obviously concerned about stability in Yemen," said Secretary of Defense Robert Gates[291] in 2011 during the Arab Spring.

Zindani pointed at "Bab el Mandeb," the strait, 12 miles wide, separating Yemen from Eritrea and Djibouti,[292] on a map on a wall. The U.S. Navy patrolled it to assure that oil moved through the Suez Canal, and watched for refugees from Africa, human trafficking to Europe. Thousands stayed; others crossed into Saudi Arabia. No one knew who might be dangerous.

Al-Anad, the air base, was here, where the U.S. kept most of its drones, and had its counterterrorism headquarters. It hired people to find al-Qaeda. Saleh supported the jihadi groups. It was a game. The West gave him money to fight them, but he had to show that these groups were a danger to the West, so he created the danger, and the money came. This was why the U.S. now fought these groups directly, with drones. He didn't know about the Haqqanis, but all Arab al-Qaeda members were linked. They crossed from Somalia to Yemen. Saleh was behind them. Students stood listening. Yemen was a training ground for foreigners. In 1994, Ali Mohsen received 3,000 Mujahideen who returned from Afghanistan. They used them to fight the Communists in the South. Was he related to Abdul Majeed Zindani? He had been waiting for me to ask this. Al-Eryani's uncle married his grandmother. They did not have children. Al-Eryani was the master of Yemeni foreign affairs, close to the U.S., but the Saudis opposed him.

That evening Mahmud drove me across the city. We passed a crowded outdoor café. Two bombs went off in the past few months at trash cans here. We drove down a quiet street. A brick walled compound appeared, the American Institute of Yemeni Studies. I came here when I arrived. There was a deep green lawn, rooms for scholars, a kitchen and a library. Americans in dark suits, foreign journalists and Yemenis sat in rows of

---

[291] Cynthia Johnston and Mohamed Sudam, "Yemen President Warns of Civil War, U.S. Concerned." *Reuters* 22 Mar. 2011
[292] The Gate of Tears.

chairs. A man with the Foreign Ministry presented a paper that he and a scholar from Stanford had written on security. We talked afterwards and agreed to meet. An American asked why I was there. I told him. It was better, if we talked in the bubble, meaning the embassy. I sent him a note. He copied me on an email to others asking that a man arrange a meeting. I never heard back.

When I was in Dr. al-Eryani's office, I saw a book, *Tears of Sheba*, by Khadija al-Salomi. He gave me her phone number. She was in Yemen making a movie, but agreed to meet at Café Mocha, inside a compound. She wore a pale green shirt that came to her knees, khaki pants, sunglasses, and a black scarf. She had been here for two months and was returning to Paris that night. The main problem was getting the actors, who were Egyptian, to work. If she brought in Europeans, they were fascinated by the country and the people and were excited to be here. The Egyptians were fat and lazy and overacted. She hired security, but when they went to villages to shoot, people in other villages demanded money or they would cause problems. Once an old man came to watch, stood on a roof and fell and died, and she had to pay money for that.

She grew up in Old Sanaá. Outside the gates there was nothing but fields. It was so nice then. They closed the gates at night. They were a normal family, but she wondered why her brothers had more rights than she did, and why her mother and grandmother were treated so badly. She got up with her grandmother at 4 a.m. to pray. She said a woman was born to marry or to be in the grave. It was bad to study, except to learn the prayers, otherwise, a girl would write letters to someone she loved, and bring dishonor on the family. When she was 11, she was married off to a man in his 40s. Her grandfathers, and uncles, and her father had all the power. She was terrified by all that was around her, and by the way that men treated women. I guess it was natural, she said softly. Men were stronger, and wanted power. She hated the injustice around her mother. After three weeks, she sued for divorce. Otherwise, she would have killed herself. She got a job on a children's program on television and used that money to support herself and her mother. She married an American and moved to the U.S. There she learned about freedom. But she wanted to help women, and became a documentary filmmaker. She moved to Paris and got a job in the Yemeni embassy. She returned and lived in a woman's prison for a week with a woman accused of killing her husband. She thought she did it because she wanted to kill her husband. She made a film about her. Selah came to Paris. She had made another film about a girl who refused to wear a hijab. She reminded her of herself. Salah watched it and liked it. She confronted him about the woman in prison. He signed her death sentence. He paid the blood money to the family, and she was freed.

Where did she get her courage? It went back to her childhood. She felt sorry for the women in prison. Some didn't do anything. If you were seen with a man who wasn't your husband it was assumed that you were committing adultery. Her friends, who were educated told her not to make the film. Why were educated people afraid? You couldn't change things if you worried about what people thought. Her first marriage was a matter of honor, but she thought it was to protect her. It was the worst thing because your family did it. It was poverty and arranged rape.

She didn't understand why they distinguished between men and women. If God created them, they were equal. She asked in school and people said it was forbidden to ask such questions. Men used religion to demean women, because if you were dealing with religion you were dealing with God. Religion was the easiest way to decrease the value of women.

Education was her way out. She had a foundation and supported 500 girls in Sana'a. She sold Yemeni products in Paris with a friend to raise money. She did a documentary titled *I Am a Star* about child marriage. She never heard about Sunni or Shia until she went to Paris. People didn't brag about going to the mosque. Everything changed after the Mujahideen returned from Afghanistan. Why was I in Yemen? I told her. She took a French woman to see her daughter in Dammaj. It was filled with foreigners. There was sewage everywhere and everyone was in Salafi dress. A Frenchman and his wife were upset that she wasn't covered. It was haram. Everything was haram. After a few days the French woman wanted to leave. She understood that her daughter, who needed what that place gave her, was happy there. A German wanted to leave, but the police brought him back. There were 6,000 foreigners there. It was all supported by the Saudis. Al-Qaeda was different. Those boys were neglected and lost, with no job, and older men said to them, "This life was short and no good and so it was better to make something for eternity."

They were so fragile and vulnerable. Older ones told them, "America is the enemy of Islam." Saleh, Ali-Mohsen, and Zindani nourished this. They never used their own sons, only the poor.

Zindani's son had an advertising agency and production company in Sana'a. She asked him his name and he was afraid to give her his full name. He knew that she knew.

She had a flight to catch to Paris. She was Yemeni. She only had a Yemeni passport. Yemenis were spontaneous, but their leaders kept them down. They had given up. That was why they chewed gat all day, trying to forget. She paused. She knew someone who could help me. She picked up her phone. He had connections to al-Qaeda.

The Sword

The ministry was in the hills behind a high dun-colored wall, octagonal, with blue tinted windows. A soldier with curly hair, in desert camouflage, smoking, waved us through the gate. We entered a large office, overlooking the scrubland. A man in a brown sport jacket and tie said I needed an exit visa if I wanted to leave the country. As I said I wanted to stay, a man in his 30s, clean-shaven, in a sweater, came in with a document, glanced at me, and left. The man asked Karim to write a letter confirming that he was my teacher. He would ask the deputy minister. I was to come back tomorrow; it would be ready, Insha'Allah (God willing).

Norman Cousins wrote that "Mohammad dreamed of a universal religion based on the noblest of ethics and taught that conversion by the sword was no conversion at all." The idea of universal brotherhood, like that of communism, failed because Mohammad's "followers ignored this and built an empire largely at the point of a sword."[293] I had to find men of the sword.

That night I called the number that Khadija gave me. A man said we would talk tomorrow. My Arabic wasn't good enough to do this alone. The next morning Karim and I sat in the kitchen drinking tea before class. I had called someone who may be tied to al-Qaida. Would he call him for me? He asked who gave me the number. Someone I met. He called. It was my al-Qaeda contact, he whispered. He would take care of everything. He was there yesterday. Where we were? We returned to the ministry. The deputy minister refused to extend my visa. Karim took my phone and went behind a glass partition and made a call.

I called Marwan, who I met at the American Institute. He would meet me at Café Mocha. I asked about Zindani. In the 1980s he went all over Sanaa from one mosque to the next, with bodyguards to show off, raising money for the war in Afghanistan and calling on young men to join the Mujahideen. There were those today who felt that Zindani was and is America's man here. When the Afghan-Arabs returned from Afghanistan

---

[293] Norman Cousins, *Human Options*, New York: W.W. Norton & Co., 1981 44.

Ali Mohsen and Saleh recruited them into the Central Security Organization, the only intelligence agency they had then. Ali Mohsen married Tariq al-Fadhli's sister. He could not have done this without Saleh's approval.

He and Saleh created the Aden-Abyan Islamic Army (AAIA), made up of Mujahideen, to fight the Socialists in the South, and a hadith to justify it.[294] "*Out of Aden-Abyan will come 12,000 giving victory (to the religion of) Allah and His Messenger. They are the best between me and them.*" Abu al-Hasan al-Mohdhar, close to bin Laden, was the leader. In 1998, they kidnapped 16 Western tourists, and four were killed in a rescue attempt.

What about Luke Somers? A Dutch couple was kidnapped in June on the street he lived on.[295] Men from the security apparatus rented a safe house there two months before. Their captors released a video in which the couple said if their demands were not met in ten days they would be executed.[296] They were released after six months. The woman said they were treated well, kidnapped probably by tribal people.[297] It was a tradition for tribes to kidnap people to put pressure on the government to build a new road, or to bring electricity to their area. They treated them as guests, they went hunting.

Last May, unknown men kidnapped Pierre Korkie, a South African teacher, and track coach, and his wife, Yolande, a relief worker. Mrs. Korkie was released. Her husband was still being held.

Saleh[298] had camps of thugs with arms and ammunition which the U.S. provided, and what they bought with U.S. aid. During the Arab Spring, Saleh used these weapons on civilians. Doctors had never seen tear gas before and brought the canisters to him. They didn't know what it was or how to treat it. He couldn't read the company name, but it was in Chicago. He wrote an email to President Obama and said what he had given them to fight terrorism Saleh was using on his own people. He resigned. I thought of an edgy, wiry man, about 40, with a creased face, in jeans and a t-shirt, who lived near CALES who asked me to come to his house for tea. A man saw us

---

[294] https://www.islamweb. net/en/fatwa/364714/site-does-not-answer-hypothetical-questions.
[295] "Dutch Journalist Kidnapped in Yemen," *Guardian* 2 July 2013
[296] "Dutch Couple Held Hostage Released," *Al Jazeera* 10 December 2013
[297] "Dutch Hostages 'Treated Very Well' by Yemen Kidnappers." *BBC* 11 Dec. 2013
[298] Bashar al-Asad, President of Syria since 2000.

talking, and said he was one of Saleh's men, and a sniper during the Arab Spring.

Marwan talked about Yemen's ghost army, a way to get money from the West. The U.S. was focused on al-Qaeda.[299] Saleh and Ali Mohsen were behind al-Qaeda. They absorbed some of the AAIA into the Yemeni army and gave others civilian posts. Saleh financed the Houthis, let them go to Iran for training, and used them against the Salafis and the Saudis. The Salafis were Yemeni Wahhabis financed by the Saudis to stop the Zaydis. No one knew who al-Qaeda was. Where were the families, except Anwar al-Walaki's family, who had come forward after their sons were killed? No one filed a claim, or complained, or said he wanted to sue.

Nasser al-Awlaki, educated in America on a Fulbright Scholarship, former president of Sana'a University, called President Obama "a child killer" for killing his son, and his teenage grandson. Navy SEALS would kill his eight-year-old granddaughter.[300] In 2009, al-Wahayshi wrote an open letter, calling the noble and defiant tribes of the Yemen to be like their defiant brothers of the Pashtun and Baluch tribes, who, aiding God, and his messenger Mohammad, made America and the Crusaders dizzy in Afghanistan and Pakistan. He called on them not to help Saleh, agent of the Crusaders, but to help the Mujahideen. *The Echo of Epic Battles*,[301] the al-Qaeda magazine, asked sheikhs to give sanctuary to the Mujahideen as tribes in the north gave sanctuary to Mohammad.[302]

Marwan said the USS Cole was Saleh's creation to convince the U.S. that al-Qaida could strike anywhere, and a way to get money from the Saudis. The U.S. would not freeze Saleh's overseas bank accounts. The next morning, there was new sign on the wall, with red and green paint dripping, next to the bakery. "Al-Qaida is the industry of America." Karim said the al-Qaeda man would procure a visa.

---

[299] Cynthia Johnston and Mohamed Sudam. "Yemen President Warns of Civil War, U.S. Concerned," *Reuters* 22 Mar. 2011
[300] "Seal, American Girl Die in First Trump-Era U.S. Military Raid," *NBCNews.com* 31 Jan. 2017
[301] Sada al-Malahim.
[302] Ibid.81

The Massacre

It was Friday, sunny and quiet. A loud bomb shook the windows. I waited for men to run up the stairs with rifles. I ran up to the roof and sat with my back to the low brick wall that surrounded it. I saw black smoke rising 100 yards away. I heard heavy rifle fire and crawled to another part of the wall and ran back down to my room. If they came in I would have to jump to the other house, across the pathway, and run. "They hit the Defense Ministry," a student shouted. I went outside. People were talking, and shopping in the souk. Some blamed Ali Mohsen, others Saleh. The rifle fire continued. That night we learned that a truck blew open the gate of the Defense Ministry, next to the Old City, then a 4x4 behind it, with men in army uniforms came and stalked the military hospital, killing doctors, nurses, and patients. There was CCTV footage on television. That night, a large light hovered over us. Rifle fire echoed around us.

The next morning, Karim said the Houthis attacked the Ministry of Defense. It took all night for the army to find them all. They were allied with someone, maybe Saleh. Over 75% of Yemen was Sunni. The Houthis, who were Shia, couldn't take over alone. They needed an ally. It may have been a coup attempt. Al-Qaida took credit for the attack, but it didn't want to, not after all those doctors, nurses, and patients were killed.

That evening I went, as planned, to meet a woman, a friend of Ali Hamid's, at a café, to learn about the South. I sat in the courtyard, looking at the high walls, wondering, if we were attacked, how to escape. Alia Faisal al- Shaabi, in a dark dress, black scarf, and a dark coat, came with her son, about twenty. She was from Aden. Her father,[303] a revolutionary, disappeared when she was a girl. He was vice president and prime minister of South Yemen, a member of the "Fedayeen." An *a fida'i* was one who sacrificed himself. In Iran they were the "Fedayeen al-Islam," the martyrs of Islam.

After finishing his studies in Cairo, her father met with George Habash, the Greek Orthodox Palestinian, of the Popular Front for the Liberation of

---

[303] Abdul Latif al-Shaabi.

Palestine (PFLP), in Beirut and then helped to create the Movement of Arab Nationalism[304] to fight Western-backed Arab governments. In Yemen he created the Movement of Patriots[305] to free the South from the British. In 1970 the Marxists tortured and killed him. She wanted his body, a proper funeral, and an apology. She wanted justice. It was the essence of Islam.

In 1986 they were sending young men to fight in Afghanistan, and people were following the war. When the men returned, powerful men used them to fight the South. Before, women could do as they pleased. That all changed.

Did she know Tariq al-Fadhli? Yes, his father was a sultan, and because of this, was forced out of the South. Tariq fought in Afghanistan. He wanted to be a sultan, to create an army and establish sharia. He was used to plant al-Qaeda in Yemen. He knew bin Laden. Ali Mohsen, who married his sister, and Zindani made Islam all about blood, power, money, and expanding their families.

A few days later, I met a doctor at Café Mocha. She wanted to sit inside in a corner where it was safer and no one could hear us. She, too, was from the South and went to school with girls and boys. She, too, learned about Islam in school, and prayed, but it was not important in their lives. The South was a Marxist state and she won a scholarship to go to Moscow. She was excited to go to another country and to meet new people. She went to a school to learn Russian, and then to the university.

When she was a girl, her older brother was in the army and at the university at the same time, agitating for human rights, and better health care. They took him away. She looked down at the table. The government came 18 months ago, and they went to a prison to see five men, but they had gone mad with dementia. She didn't know if one was her brother. Her eyes grew moist. She, like Alia, wanted my help. When I was a boy, we were always visiting the sick and elderly. You could not wash away your upbringing. That was why the Soviets took Afghan children to the Soviet Union to study, why they sent the Doctor, why the Ikhwan focused on education, and why the Wahhabis built madrasas.

When she returned from Moscow, she found that Saleh put her name on

---

[304] Harakat al-Qawmeyon al-Arab.
[305] Harakat al-Oawmen.

a black list. She cried and was afraid. She went to Aden to see her family and returned to Moscow. She returned five years later, as a physician, but they fingerprinted and interrogated her. The Ministry of Health sent her back to Moscow for more training. She returned in 1998 with a PhD in Hematology, but had to work two years without pay while going through a criminal investigation, because of her brother. During the war in Afghanistan, they, as women, began to feel that they were "haram." In 1994, after the Mujahideen returned, adults began to tell children to throw rocks at her because she did not wear a long black coat. She was not afraid of those boys. Today, for her daughters there was more religion than math or physics in school. Women were the problem. She sent her daughters to Germany to study. Women covered themselves out of fear. During the revolution she and other doctors created a field hospital and gave lectures on how to administer first aid. In 1998 she created and became the director of the National Blood Transfusion and Research Center. In 2010, the Saleh government, the prime minister, and the Ministry of Health, called her a communist. Zindani sent boys to Afghanistan, and now he was involved with al-Qaeda. What was she? She was a mother, a doctor, and a revolutionary, she replied.

A Soldier of the Left

The next day a white-haired man stood alone on the sidewalk of a busy street. Mohammad parked his SUV and we crossed through traffic. As we approached the sidewalk, the man turned towards a walkway, took a few steps, and turned back. We took the walkway to the back of an apartment house and climbed in the dark up wood stairs to a landing. A door was open. We entered an apartment, took off our shoes, and entered a small room. The man was picking up papers from the carpet. A little girl entered with a tray of tea and cookies, and he took it. We shook hands, but he didn't smile. We sat on the carpet.

In 1962, he, a young soldier, joined the revolt with the Egyptian army against the Imam. He later studied military society, in Egypt, and here, and its role in fostering social change. He was a retired major general.

In 1894, a French, Jewish artillery officer, Captain Alfred Dreyfus, was charged and convicted in a closed court in Paris of passing military secrets to Germany and sentenced to life in prison on Devil's Island in French Guiana. In 1896 an investigator found new information proving that Dreyfus was innocent. French officials covered this up. There was another trial and again he was convicted, and finally he was freed. The "Dreyfus Affair" divided France, with a pro-Army pro-Catholic faction on one side, and secular France on the other, exposing anti-Semitism in France and Europe. In response, Theodore Herzl, a Viennese Jewish journalist living in Paris wrote *The Jewish State*, a book calling for the creation of a Jewish nation, a refuge for Jews, and a solution to anti-Semitism. It was part of a Zionist political movement. Zion referred to Jerusalem, to the Promised Land, for Christians Zion was Heaven, God's dwelling place.

At the time, the Ottoman Turks ruled Palestine.[306] Jews were a minority. The Turks opposed more migration, afraid of political turmoil. In 1917, Britain, at war with Turkey, issued the Balfour Declaration[307] promising to help establish a homeland for Jews in Palestine, one reason for which was to protect British interests in Egypt, particularly the Suez Canal, and the route to India.

---

[306] Palestine comes from "land of the Philistines." Genesis 21:32
[307] Isaac Watts, "We're Marching to Zion,"

In 1922, after World War I the League of Nations gave Britain, which had ruled Egypt as a colony since 1882, Palestine as a mandate. The Ikhwan fought the idea of Israel, which it called a Western outpost in the Muslim world. In 1948 the British left and Israel was founded. The combined forces of Egypt, Iraq, Jordan, Lebanon and Syria invaded, but the Israelis fought back and increased the size of Israel. In January 1949, an armistice was declared. The Muslim world was in shock. In 1952, six Egyptian army officers, angry at Egypt's defeat, and who called themselves the Free Officers, led by Lt. Col. Gamal Nasser, a socialist, born into a working-class family, mounted a bloodless coup against King Farouk, the first military coup in Arab history, electrifying a defeated Arab world. A tall, commanding revolutionary since he was a boy, Nasser called for pan-Arab-socialist unity. Upset at U.S. support of Israel, he turned to the Soviet Union.

In 1955, the U.S., to try to contain the Soviet Union, in the Cold War, helped to create, with Britain, Iran, Iraq and Pakistan, but did not join, the Central Treaty Organization. In 1958, Egypt and Syria formed the United Arab Republic. It died in 1961. But Nasser was determined to lead the Arab world and to break the hold of its European masters. On September 6, 1962 Sanaá was still a walled city, when Imam Ahmed, whose father was killed by the Ikhwan in 1947, and who escaped assassination in 1961 died, and his son, Mohammad al-Badr, took his place. A week later, a cadre of junior military officers, some tied to the Ikhwan, but more to Nasser, who backed them, overthrew al-Badr and established the Yemen Arab Republic. Britain, Saudi Arabia and the U.S., backed the royalists, who in the future would be called Houthis.

The Yemeni army was like the CIA in Chile overthrowing its elected leader, the general continued, referring to the 1973 military coup against the Marxist-Socialist, Salvador Allende. There had been coups here from the right and the left. Saudi Arabia was behind all of them. In the 1973 Arab-Israel war, the U.S. airlifted arms to Israel. In response, OAPEC[308] reduced oil production to put pressure on the U.S., and its allies. The price of oil, and the income of Saudi Arabia, increased fivefold.[309] Wahhabis moved out

---

[308] Organization of Arab Petroleum Exporting Countries.
[309] Vasiliev, *"The History of Saudi Arabia,"* 393

more into the Muslim world.[310] In 1974, Lt. Col. Ibrahim Al-Hamdi, a member of the *gadhi* (judges) upper class, who, since the time of Mohammad, ruled to establish justice, mounted a coup, and became president. There were three good years of rainfall. Yemenis, working in Saudi Arabia, were sending money home. The Saudis began to build madrasas and Scientific Institutes.[311] Al-Hamdi appointed al-Zindani to be Yemen's first "Spiritual Guide," assuring the rise of Wahhabism.

In 1977 on the eve of a visit to the South, which frightened Saudi Arabia, afraid of Socialism and unification, al-Hamdi was killed, along with his brother, and successor.[312] Sheikh al-Ahmar, of the Hashed, backed Saleh, 32, to be president. He opened the gates for the Afghan-Arabs, and, backed by the U.S., the U.K., France, and China, to fight the Soviets in South Yemen. Everyone had his own al-Qaida, the daughter of the Ikhwan relationship with the government, which gave arms and money to al-Qaeda to hurt Westerners who gave money to Yemen to fight al-Qaeda. After the bombings of the U.S. embassies in Kenya and Tanzania in 1999, the U.S. called al-Qaeda a terrorist organization.[313] The Arab regimes called the Afghan-Arabs terrorists. The U.S. backed these regimes for their oil and natural gas. The regimes looted their wealth, destroying the middle class. The people were beaten down. Tribesmen once enforced a tribal culture. You could have a good conversation with a tribal woman. Now Wahhabi culture ruled, and women could no longer talk to another man.

The rich had power and the poor joined al-Qaeda because they were poor, and there was no justice. The regimes used the Islamists to force on young men the idea that everything was haram, creating the view that there was nothing worthwhile in life. Those who controlled the suicide bombers lived luxurious lives.

Was there a link here among the Islamists to the Tribal Areas of Pakistan? He gave me the name of a man. He warned me not to leave Sanaá, and to see public people only.

The next day I met with yet a man who worked for an international organization but which I could not identify. The U.S. Navy was patrolling

---

[310] Commins, "*The Wahhabi Mission and Saudi Arabia*" 152, 158
[311] Dresch, "*History of Modern Yemen*," 142
[312] Lackner, "*Why Yemen Matters: A Society in Transition* 107-08).
[313] "Foreign Terrorist Organizations - United States Department of State"

the Gulf of Aden. There were refugees coming in, mostly from Somalia and Ethiopia, human trafficking heading toward Europe. Thousands stayed here, others crossed into Saudi Arabia, stayed or went north. No one knew how many among them were militant.

The National Security Council

Zarb (sword) and I met and shook hands on a quiet street. He, Karim and I climbed the stairs to an apartment and entered a room with pale blue diaphanous drapes, and cushions. I heard a baby cry. A man about 35, in jeans and a leather jacket, on the National Security Council, came in.

The Islamic movements began with the Muslim Brotherhood movement in Egypt in 1928, he began. They later merged with the Salafi and Wahhabi movements in Saudi Arabia. The Khomeini revolution contributed to this movement. The Mujahideen came back from the Afghan war bringing an ideology that began with Ibn Hanbal and became an opposition movement against the Mongols in Baghdad in the 12th Century, against the Ottoman Turks in the 17th Century, the British in the 19th and 20th centuries, and now against America. The Ikhwan movement had two parts. The first believed, like al-Banna, in democracy, and played a role in the Arab Spring.[314] The second was part of the Salafi-Wahhabi movement. Zindani was the leader of this level. You could not separate al-Qaeda from the politicians. They started and used today al-Qaida to fight their battles. The three powers: the tribes, religious figures, and the politicians all fought one another. This helped al-Qaeda's strategy to control military bases and towns, to find places to hide, and to work with the tribes. After the revolution, they made it easy for al-Qaeda to get weapons.

Saudi Arabia was behind the attack on the hospital. It was afraid that it would lose Yemen as its backyard. The government knew that Saudi Arabia had controlled the leaders of al-Qaida since 2002. After 9/11, it wanted the world to focus on Yemen, not Saudi Arabia. After all, 18 of the plane hijackers were from there. Since then, they had tried to make Yemen the center of al- Qaeda.

The Saudis did not control all of al-Qaeda but could when necessary. The U.S. was allied with Saudi Arabia, needed its oil, as did its allies, and was afraid to expose the truth. Saudi intelligence planted people in al-Qaeda, Yemeni intelligence probably also, and maybe the Americans. The spies were loyal to al-Qaeda and moved up within the hierarchy.

---

[314] Hassan al-Banna, Egyptian, founded the Muslim Brotherhood, 1928.

The royal family remembered that Abdul Aziz, said, "Beware of the Yemen" before he died. Bin Laden's bodyguards were almost all Yemenis because of their culture of revenge.[315] After the Afghan war, Egyptian intelligence officers came here, afraid of the Mujahideen. Seven of the hospital attackers were Saudis. They may have entered Yemen when the Saudis expelled thousands of Yemenis in 1990 after Saleh supported Saddam Hussein in the Gulf War or in 2011 after the Arab Spring when they were afraid that by relying upon cheap foreign labor, they were depriving young Saudis of jobs and who might rise in anger. In 2013 it changed its labor laws and expelled more Yemenis, including extremists. The proof was the Saudis were involved.

Ayman al-Zawahiri was last here in the 1990s to help the Egyptians move from Afghanistan. The tribes hid them. Selah used them to play with America. Bin Laden chose the Yemeni leaders, wrote to them, and controlled them, as well as his men in Saudi Arabia. Al-Zawahiri let local leaders make decisions because they knew the terrain. There were conflicts between Saudi al-Qaeda and Egyptian members. Pakistanis trained the bomb makers. Al-Qaeda sent men to Iraq and Syria. It was at war with America, the head of the devil, which controlled the Arab dictatorships, and Israel. Drones killed members of al-Qaeda, but too many innocent people, angering villagers who supported them more. U.S. officials worked in Djibouti, Bahrain, Saudi Arabia, and here. Two years ago, there were Afghans, Pakistanis, Somalis, Iranians, at least 12 nationalities of al-Qaeda here, thousands of them. They sold qat, honey, drugs, and weapons in Saudi Arabia, which supported them. They made more from kidnappings and robbing banks. Prince Bandar, head of Saudi intelligence was close to all the Islamic groups. Everything was to preserve the Saudi kingdom.

Prince Bandar al-Sultan, a former fighter pilot, was ambassador to the U.S. from 1983-2005, famous for his lavish parties at his homes in Aspen and Washington. After 9/11 a photo of him appeared looking down at President George W. Bush at his ranch in Texas.

I wanted to meet with Zindani. I called his brother who worked at Islah. He was polite, but neither of them would be available. I had to see the political director. Islah had a brand new multi-storied building, with guards

---

[315] Soufan, (*Anatomy of Terror*) 76

out front in blue shirts and bullet-proof vests and rifles. As we walked upstairs, I glanced in a room on each floor, with industrial carpeting, shoes at each door, the walls bare. *"The angels do not enter a house where there are pictures,"* said Mohammad.[316] Man must not try to imitate what God has created.[317] The Taliban destroyed the Buddhist statues at Bamyan, every head on every sculpture, every human image, these false gods, in the Kabul Museum. Nothing could come between God, and sinful man. *"He is the mighty one, the merciful...He first created man from clay, then bred his offspring from a drop of paltry fluid. He molded him and breathed into him of his spirit. He gave you eyes and ears and hearts: yet you are seldom thankful."*[318]

Saeed Shamson, in a light gray suit, sat against the wall. Islah, which meant reform, included academics, young people, women, soldiers, anyone could join. He did not say that it once refused to develop the port of Aden, afraid that it would open the door to infidels.[319] The Arab-Afghans fought under Saleh and were probably with him in his palace. He told al-Qaeda he was their emir. His nephew supervised them. There was a group called al-Qaeda for Ali Abdullah Saleh. The U.S. drone campaign was making them sympathetic. Islah met with U.S., U.N, and European delegations, but he didn't know what America wanted. The Islamists won in Algeria in 1992 but we refused to support them. Twice Hamas[320] won in Palestine, but we objected. In 2012, the Ikhwan won the election in Egypt. Then the army killed thousands and put more in prison. They believed in democracy but were afraid the U.S. would betray them.

How was Shari'ah compatible with democracy?

Sharia and democracy were mechanisms to protect humanity, to mind your money, to protect women from violence, he replied. God created these rights. The Koran existed to protect them, and to honor them.

That evening Muhammed called. He talked to the man the general said I

---

[316] "Pictures - Halal or Haram?" *Just Ask Islam*, http://www.justaskislam.com/184/pictures-halal-or-haram/.
[317] "Why Are Muslims Not Allowed to Hang Photos of Their Family on the Walls of Their Houses?" *Islam Stack Exchange* 1 Oct. 1963.
[318] As-Sajdah (Prostration) 8 (The Koran).
[319] Clark, *"Yemen: Dancing on the Heads of Snakes,"* 271
[320] Harakat al-Mugawamah al-Islamiyyah (Islamic Resistance Movement)

needed to reach who could introduce me to the al-Qaida man. His father read in an Islah newspaper that I was in Yemen studying al-Qaida. I thought of Daniel Pearl. *Jang* (war), a Pakistani newspaper ran an article saying he was Jewish; a message to his captors.

An Al-Qaeda Messenger

I asked Karim, through Zarb, to arrange a meeting with Abdarazk al-Jamal, a journalist, and al-Qaida spokesman. The general recommend him. It had to be public. I wore, at his insistence, a mahwaz, sandals, and a headdress. Karim rushed ahead, nervously, through the Old City. I had to hurry; we were late. We went to the main city and walked down a dead-end street and entered a plaza filled with tables, and men eating, or drinking tea.

Al-Jamal, medium height, in a white thobe, turquoise sports jacket, white shawl folded over his shoulder, sunglasses back on his forehead, and I shook hands. He had a bright silver wedding band. He was the most beautifully dressed man I had seen here. He asked what I wanted. I was studying Islamic fundamentalism and wanted to talk with people he knew about their beliefs and goals, my way of asking al-Qaeda not to harm me.

He said there were two groups: the Mujahideen who returned from Afghanistan, and al-Qaeda. The Mujahideen were angry that al-Qaida had stolen their fame. There was a new al-Qaida today. It was the new Mujahideen, unique, separate, and did not work with anyone. The Salafis, Islah, and the Tablighli worked with foreign powers. Al-Qaeda did not work with anyone, nor could I meet them. I could meet with the old Mujahideen but no one knew the new. Be careful, almost all researchers who wrote about al-Qaeda worked with the police and the security apparatus. The U.S. was on one side and the police and army were on the other. I looked at the men around us, plates of grilled fish, of chicken and rice, at a man next to him. Who was the security apparatus? Could he take my picture? He took them of all foreign journalists he met. I knew they already knew me. He took a picture and paid for our tea. We left and he walked slowly behind us. Karim walked fast through the street. He didn't want to do this. He was scared. Jamal was from Abyan. He saw al-Qaida in his eyes. I thought of the courtroom in Karachi when the police brought in Daniel Pearl's kidnappers and sat them on the wood floor in the back under a blanket, protecting their identity. It would be like that here.

I studied all day, worried about the article about me, and al-Jamal. The director thought I was being set up. I asked Marwan what he could find out about Mohammad's father. He told me to be careful.

That evening I went to the souk. Children were playing, and motorcycles, the Old City's taxis, roared by. I passed skinny cats foraging in a pile of garbage, carts and wheelbarrows from which boys and men sold clothes, and shampoo, past the fruit seller, the man reading a newspaper who sold vegetables. Yemen ranked fifth on the illiteracy rate in Middle East.[321] The rate was rising, but not for women.[322] I came to an ATM. During the Arab Spring, a crowd destroyed this symbol of the West. A mini bus stood nearby. The driver asked if I was going to Hadramout. Bin Laden's father was from there, now al-Qaeda territory. I withdrew money, and bought food to cook. The next morning, Karim took out a sack with a bottle of half a kilo of number two grade.

Yemeni honey, $40 a pound. There were honey stores throughout Sanaá where thin, quiet Salafis, who controlled the honey business, stood behind buckets of honey, from different regions, what the Koran called a gift from God,[323] what a friend in the White House said the Haqqanis were selling in the Middle East.

Hassan Noman, general secretary of the Socialist Party of Yemen, placed a tray with two cups of thick milk tea on a low glass table in a small glass-enclosed porch. Nearby was a book on nation building and income inequality. The Socialist party, he began, was the result of British colonialism where people saw that they lived well, and Yemenis had little. Islam was not opposed to wealth, but carried a message of equality.

There was a knock at the door. He opened it and someone handed him a tray of two cups of thick Adense tea. He placed it on the table. It was the best thing that British gave them, he said smiling. In the early 1960s, in Aden, political and religious groups and trade unions, working with parties from the north, formed a national front for the liberation of the South. The British left in 1967. In 1969, the party took on a leftist ideology. They needed economic assistance and turned to the British, and Saudi Arabia, but they said no. They asked China and the Soviet Union which agreed to help. In 1970, the South became a Marxist-Leninist state. He did not say that in

---

[321] https://www.thoughtco.com /adult-illiteracy-rates-middle-east-2353335.
[322] "Yemen Adult Literacy Rate, 1960-2021." *Knoema*, https://knoema.com/atlas/ Yemen/topics/Education/Literacy/Adult-literacy-rate.
[323] The Koran Surah xvi (An-Nuhl/The Bee) 70.

1979, the South, maybe coordinating with the Soviet Union, Cuba and Ethiopia, attacked the North hoping to launch a revolution on the Peninsula. The U.S. put an aircraft carrier off the coast,[324] and gave Saudis tanks and anti-tank missiles[325] for North Yemen.

In 1990, Saddam Hussein invaded Iraq and Saleh supported him. On May 22, bin Laden, the Mujahideen, Saleh and Ali Mohsen began an assassination campaign against the South. In November, Saleh, Ali Mohsen, Zindani and the Ikhwan created Islah. In 1992, they exploded bombs in two hotels where U.S. soldiers were staying. They shot a rocket at his house. They called them Communists. Today, the Islamists were powerful. Al-Banna was not radical, but Sayed Qutb changed the direction of the Ikhwan. It competed with Nasser and had to flee to Saudi Arabia. There, with the Wahhabis, they created a severe Islam. The Pakistanis were the most extremist. The eastern part of Afghanistan and into Pakistan was the worst place.

This was Haqqani territory.

Everything came from one head—Pakistan. There was a meeting in Peshawar among all the groups from Palestine, Egypt, elsewhere. Zia ul Haq gave a speech. They didn't need them to liberate Afghanistan. Why didn't they go back to their own countries and liberate them from these corrupt regimes? Bin Laden said he would start his work in Sudan.

After 1994, Noman taught at a university in the UAE where he read the story about Zia ul Haq. They talked about surrounding the oil-producing countries, starting with Yemen. When they returned, Saudi Arabia, Selah, and Abdul Salam el-Halal convinced more than 5,000 Mujahideen to leave. El-Halal took 3,500 and went to Somalia, Sudan and East Africa. He was in Guantanamo, and urged me to see his family.

The National Security Force, the security apparatus, worked with them today. They worked with Saleh and Ali Mohsen. They worked underground and were not well known. He talked proudly about a fishing collective that he created and still existed on the Red Sea. What about the assassination attempt against him the week before? He said his driver backed out onto the street. A bullet hit the roof, just above the window. His driver got away. The

---

[324] Gates, *"From The Shadows,"* 149-150
[325] Dresch, *"History of Modern Yemen"* 149-150.

man used a silencer. He was a professional. He fired from the minaret. They didn't know who was behind it. It was Friday, and I could hear the footsteps of men walking to the mosque, forty yards away.

The Salafis

Karim sat at my desk in my room with a dictionary and paper going over my questions. Zarb had arranged a meeting with the Salafis. A Finnish scholar, doing his PhD on their movement, met with them, and they kidnapped him. We drove to an area of narrow streets, and garbage, of barefoot boys playing soccer, and stopped. A burly man in a mustard-colored thobe that ended above his ankles, his headdress hanging loosely— the Salafi uniform—stood in the street. He would take us to the Sheikh. We walked to a small car. Mahmud, my driver, said he would follow us. I got in the back seat next to the Salafi. Zarb appeared, and climbed in the driver's seat. Karim sat up front. We drove down two streets, and parked. Mahmud parked behind us. We walked up the street. Zarb stopped. Be sure to touch them and talk to them to show that we were friends.

I followed him up a dirt path to an open door. We took off our shoes. The Sheikh, about 6'3" 200 pounds, in a white thobe, with a thick sandy beard, white headdress, held his hand out, smiling. We entered a small dark *mahraj*. I shook hands with a boy about seven and asked his name. The Sheikh urged him to answer. Our guide told me to sit next to him. Karim sat next to me, and Zarb sat across the floor. The Sheikh sat on a cushion. A laptop lay open on a low table in front of him, a smart phone beside it. I thanked him for agreeing to meet. I had come to learn from him. He thanked me for coming. I was their guest. What did Salafi mean?

He prayed, thanking God, and the Prophet Mohammad, for this opportunity to spread his word.

Salafi meant to come to Islam. It meant calling people, with mercy. Salafi came from Moes (Moses) and from Ibrahim. It meant not calling someone to violence. No one knew of Salafis ever making bombs any place in the world. They didn't want to kill anyone who came to them with a passport. Salafi was to call people, not to force them. The Koran said, *"There shall be no compulsion in religion."*[326] No one asked the victims of 9/11 to become Muslim, I said. The Sheikh smiled gently. He invited me to come to Islam. They had to invite you to Islam before they killed you. Salafi

---

[326] The Koran (The Cow) Chapter 2, verse 256.

began with the teachings of Mohammad. It was their foundation. The Prophet, peace be unto him, said the best people were the Salafis. If you followed them, you were following him. The Sheikh, quoting a hadith, said only the Salifis would not burn in Hell.

They knew the true path.[327] "Issa" (Jesus) and Moes, like Mohammad, presented this path, for they were true prophets.

Salafi was a group, not a party. You could not join the Salafi as you could the Ikhwan. They should begin in the mosque to teach people the Koran and the Sunna. In the past Allah sent a messenger. They were part of that message. I saw a skinny curly headed boy, about 13, sitting half up under a thick blanket. I wondered for a split second if he was being trained as a suicide bomber. They lived simply, like Mohammad.[328] A person's manners explained himself in society. But they were at war with the Houthis, no? God said they were allowed to defend themselves. The Wahhabis used war to win converts. Wahhab was a famous person in the Salafi movement but only Mohammad was their leader, he replied. They supported the president, and advised and taught him how to live, and to govern properly. They opposed the Arab Spring. They supported the president, no matter how bad. A revolution was worse.

I lived with the Haqqanis in Afghanistan years ago and understood Islam a bit. "The Mujahideen in Afghanistan were stupid." "They fought the Russians so the Americans and the British and French wouldn't have to. Haqqani was used by America. They were all stupid." There was a knock on the door and the Sheikh went out and returned with a thermos and glasses. He poured coffee for me. Why was America against Islam? We had been coming to their lands to fight for centuries. But al-Qaeda attacked America. Yes, but from the beginning everyone said al-Qaeda was bad. He leaned closer. They called people to Islam. What about women? Americans felt that they treated them unfairly. He shook his head. Women were responsible and superlative. In the West they treated women like tools, to sell things in bad ways. He was right. Could a woman be a politician? We were six here. If we were here, why should a woman be a politician, no, she could not. Did he have a daughter? He did. What if she wanted to be a doctor or a business

---

[327] *Islamhelpline*, http://www.islamhelpline.net/node/3389.
[328] *The Oxford English Dictionary*, vol. 2 453

person? They supported education for women, and that which kept their manners. If his daughter wanted to be any of these things that was good, but she had to remain separate from men. It was to protect her.

I was to tell the American people not to harm the Yemenis, and don't treat them like they were all terrorists. They were talking with me because Mohammad dealt with Christians and Jews.

Their mother, Saffiyah, was Jewish, the daughter of the chief of a large, powerful tribe—Yes, Mohammad saw her—and she was beautiful, and also married. But then her husband was killed in battle, and Mohammad married her.[329] It was like the story of King David who wanted Bathsheba.[330] The sheikh refilled our glasses and then his own. He leaned forward inviting me to Islam.

---

[329] *Muhammad's Marriage to Safiyyah*, https://answering-islam.org/Responses/Osama/zawadi_safiyyah.htm.
[330] 2nd Samuel 11.

Guantanamo

We sat in a car just outside the Old City. A man in a dark red mahwaz and a headdress came toward us carrying a cell phone and a can of Pepsi. We shook hands and followed him around to the back of a large stone house and we climbed in the dark up the stairs, took off our shoes, and entered a *mahraj* that could seat at least 60, with rich blue and gold silk cushions. There was a picture of a man on the wall, and three small ones of children.

They had lost hope, said Nabil Ali, older brother to Abdul Salem Ali al-Helal. If there was a judicial system in the U.S., why didn't they try him? They were four brothers and three sisters. Abdul Salem's two sons died three years ago. There was a storage place here, but they found a way to open the box and were looking through their father's things, found a grenade and were playing with it, and it went off. Omar was 12 and Yousef was nine. He pointed to the photographs. I put my pencil down. His daughter was in the other room.

In 2002, the Egyptians invited him to a conference in Cairo. He was in his hotel and they arrested him. He was 37, a businessman, and a colonel in the army. They didn't hear anything for two years. He was an intelligence officer who worked in political security. The U.S. Embassy called. He went there. A Yemeni-American said if he gave them his information they would give him $2 million. It included all who Saleh and Ali Mohsen used in 1994 to fight the Socialists. They wanted to know where he sent 3,000 men in Africa. He refused. Everything was related to the Mujahideen and al-Qaeda, Ali Mohsen said. The U.S. oversaw everything. A former prisoner told him in 2010 a group of U.S. Army officers came to see his brother. They would give him $5 million if he testified against Saleh and Ali Mohsen, and a new life in America. He said no. The U.S. tortured people. Yemeni intelligence worked with them. If they let him, he would get this information from his brother. He was afraid that the Americans, or their agents, would kill him. He had all his documents. They could have them. He was shouting now.

Yemenis gave money in the mosques to help pay for the Mujahideen to fight the Russians. It was a matter of protecting Islam. For the Americans it was for their interests. Yemen welcomed the Mujahideen when they returned, but the government was afraid, and deported them. His brother was in charge of this. He didn't know what to do. He would sell this house. He would kidnap me. He would do it. He stared at me. He wouldn't do anything wrong. If he did, they would be returning to the jungle. His voice was softer now. Two hours passed. He thanked me for coming. As I write this, in July 2022, his brother is still there. He has, it appears, given up his life to protect the Afghan-Arabs in his care.

Is This How Al-Qaeda Really Began?

The hotel was between small shops on a dusty road. Was this place safe? There was a gunman at the door, and a man with a clipboard. He led me down a winding hallway to restaurant. Marwan in a suede jacket and a brown thobe waved me over to his table. He was with Abdul Bari Taher, in a mahwaz, sweater, sport coat, and a wool cap, a journalist, a writer, head of the Public Book Authority, the national library, book publisher and buyer, Yemen's Library of Congress. He came from a religious family and studied in Mecca in the 1950s. He returned to Yemen in 1960 and became a teacher. After the revolution of 1962, he taught and wrote on literary criticism and philosophy.

The start of the Islamic movements began with Abdul Hakim al-Badeen, who in the 1940s was the head of the Ikhwan in Yemen, and the founder of Islah. He took part in the 1948 revolution.[331] The Ikhwan discreetly became powerful, as Mohammad worked discreetly for 15 years before becoming influential. They began preaching in 1928 and then in 1948 assassinated the Imam. The Ikhwan felt that a re-awakening of the faith would begin here from which they could evangelize the world. In their oath, they must go to Yemen. He quoted the Koran: *"Faith is Yemeni and Wisdom is Yemeni."*[332] Yemen was backward, tribal and illiterate, which provided good soil for their ideas.

In the 1950s, Saudi Arabia founded the Islamic Movement University at al-Dawa University, in Medina, for foreigners: Afghans, Bangladeshis, Pakistanis, Somalis, Yemenis—where we found all the problems today. Saudis were not allowed on campus. It was not a real university, but focused on Wahhabism and jihad, so that its graduates would teach Wahhabi Islam in their own countries. In the 1960s, a graduate received a salary of 3,000 Saudi riyals.[333] Most Yemeni graduates joined Islah. In the 1970s, Zindani established The Islamic Science Society, under which he then created 150 "Scientific" institutions, financed by Saudi Arabia, which paid all their

---

[331] Dresch, *"History of Modern Yemen,"* 56
[332] Clark, *"Yemen: Dancing on the Heads of Snakes"* 12
[333] 3000 riyals in 1965 equalled nearly $5400.00 in 2018, in 2022 about $800.

salaries, even in the Foreign Ministry. The institutions gave children military training. All the books in the Ministry of Education were financed and printed by Saudi Arabia. The Saudis oversaw the syllabus. They couldn't live without Saudi money.

The Ikhwan controlled the Ministry of Education and Islah. After the Soviet invasion of Afghanistan, the Saudis built hospitality houses, in reality training camps, for the Mujahideen. Many Yemenis were sent there, and then shipped to Afghanistan. The Saudis paid $14,000 a head. Zindani collected donations in mosques, but it was a cover. The Saudis told him to keep the money. They gave each Mujahid $7,000 and a one-way ticket to Pakistan. Thousands went from here. The Saudis planted the seeds of al-Qaida. South Yemen was Marxist. Rich families sent their children to school in Saudi Arabia: Ramzi bin al-Shabeeb, Tariq al-Fadhli, and bin Laden, among others, although the bin Laden family had become Saudi by then. The Yemenis, not the Egyptians, were at the beginning.

In the 1970s, the Soviet Union established the National Front in the South to fight the north. The Saudis, in turn, created the Islamic Front which led to war on the southern plateau. Taher joined them. In 1994, Saleh and Ali Mohsen created the Aden-Abyan Army to fight the South. The Mujahideen were the core component, a continuation of the war in Afghanistan. Bin Laden and the Mujahideen wanted to take over the South. Saudi Arabia paid for every bomb and bullet. The Saudis, while opposed to communism, opposed unification. The U.S., wary of succession movements since the Civil War, wanted unification.[334] Saudi Arabia created al-Qaeda.

After the war some joined Ali Mohsen's First Armored Division. Others were distributed among the Republican Guard and other forces. Some were given positions in the bureaucracy. Ali Mohsen and Saleh divided up what they had inherited into private armies. The Mujahideen competed for power, and Selah used them to terrify neighboring countries to show that Yemen was confronting an insurrection and needed money to contain it. Al-Qaida and the Mujahideen were under his control. In 1992, he used them to threaten U.S. soldiers who were staying in Yemen on their way to Somalia. In 2000, they mounted the U.S.S. Cole operation.

---

[334] *The Yemeni War of 1992*, The Emirates Center for Strategic Studies and Research, 1995.

If so, it was the government that attacked the U.S.S. Cole. He nodded.

The massacre at the Defense Ministry was a strange and terrifying incident. Many parties could be involved. They were trying to bring Saleh and Mohsen back together. The target, and the victim, was President Hadi. They controlled al-Qaida, and were against the Defense Ministry. A split in the Saudi royal family could affect them here, Marwan added. King Abdullah wanted a successful transition of power here. Prince Bandar could be supporting other militants. If one was going to take military action, look for another conflict. One followed the other. Both parties were at war with one another. If one party made a plan, like the bombing, to take power, the other party may let it go, and then will come in and take over, the Houthis, for example. Two men in ill-fitting suits walked in and sat at the table behind me, and began writing.

Other countries may be involved. If Ali Mohsen and Saleh controlled al-Qaeda, did Anwar al-Walaki and Umar Farouk Abdulmutallab, the Nigerian, work for them? It was clear that Saleh controlled al-Walaki and the Nigerian. He had been giving bad information to the Americans who killed the wrong people with their drones. He wanted to entangle you here, and then you needed him to eradicate al-Qaeda. America knew this game but kept quiet. If Saleh controlled al-Walaki and the Nigerian, he was directly targeting America. There were warlords here with experience in the Balkans, and in Waziristan. They used this war to recruit poor people to join al-Qaeda to create suicide bombers. They could train them in the army. By saying Waziristan, he meant the Tribal Areas of Pakistan

The two men behind me got up. One shook my hand, and they walked away. Marwan said al-Qaida financed a chain of date, fruit and vegetable shops, and furniture stores. Another thing was honey. The shops claimed that it was Yemeni honey, but it was coming from Pakistan.

The Tablighi

"No desire is more natural than the desire for knowledge," wrote Aristotle. We were never satisfied in our search. Nature did not do anything without a reason. There must therefore be life after this life, where our desire becomes satisfied. Montaigne agreed but felt that we had to study ourselves to find out what we needed, and to instruct ourselves.[335]

Tablighi Jamaat (The Missionary Society) was founded in India in 1929,[336] a revivalist Muslim movement, centered in Pakistan, linked to the Deobandi[337] the largest missionary movement in the world.[338] My jailer's father was with the Tablighi. My fixer, Shahwali Hazrat, said his mother made him join them, to repent he hinted, for betraying me in a phone call months later.

It was evening and the wind blew the dust, a plastic sack and a piece of paper in the air, the detritus of the modern world. Karim was talking on his phone. Men and boys walked into a single-story concrete mosque twenty yards away. It was time to go in. We joined a group of men in simple clothes sitting on the floor in a circle. They nodded smiling. I thanked them for letting us join them. We were silent. What did Tablighi mean? A man with a henna beard asked if I wanted tea. A man came with a tray, a teapot, and glasses of milk tea. A man put a glass in front of me; another opened a box of cookies. I could not understand the Tablighi unless I spent three days with them. They didn't have a leader. Everyone was equal, as they as Muslims were equal before God. They were different from other organizations because they believed in the Holy Koran and the Hadith, together called the Sunna. If I believed in God, and that everything came from him, I would find happiness. God created all that was good, the stars, the sky, the mountains. He pointed to a wall. You needed pillars to hold up the ceiling.

---

[335] Michael de. Montaigne "*The Essays*," (New York: Penguin Classics, 1993), xix-xx.
[336] *Thenews* 13 Aug. 2018, https://www.thenews.com.pk/latest/ 354706-tablighi-jamaat-in-britain-splits-sharply-in-two-factions.
[337] "Tablighi Jamaat: An Indirect Line to Terrorism," *Stratfor*, https://worldview. stratfor.com/article/tablighi-jamaat-indirect-line-terrorism.
[338] Lieven, "*Pakistan: A Hard Country*"129

Who held up the sky? Only God did. The goal of man was to know God and to pray to him. The men nodded. Outside the wind blew and the dust swirled. There were bedrolls and mattresses against the wall. There was kindness in their eyes. But I heard that they were training suicide bombers. I remembered the three Tablighli striding happily down a mountain in Kunar Province, Afghanistan. They were traveling from village to village preaching, living in mosques, taking food for payment.

Tablighi meant to call, to call men to Islam, and to God. The Umma was one nation, and they should call this nation to God. He called me now to Islam. The Prophet Mohammad began their movement. All a man had to do was to accept God into his life. The Tablighi were the same everywhere, said a thin man with a wispy beard. He had traveled to nine countries. He saved his money, left his family and went to preach the gospel. How were they different from the Salafis? They focused on the Koran and the hadith. The Tablighli only needed one hadith, the message from God. Tablighi meant mercy. A younger man invited me to Islam. Politics were not allowed in their work. Problems came because people did not know God or Mohammed. They prayed for them to change their ways. They lived for God, and to go to Paradise.

The definition of jihad was to call you to Al-Lah. They never fought? Finally, a man leaned forward. If they were attacked, they fought. They asked us to eat with them. They would kill a sheep in my honor. Karim shook his head. I thanked them but we had to go. We had been there for two hours. As we left, I saw *miswak*,[339] a branch the size of a pencil, next to a bedroll. Mohammad used it and Muslims used it as a toothbrush, the first part of their ablutions before praying. I carried it when I was trying to pass as a Pashtun. The Babylonians used it, and civilizations before them. It was recommended by the World Health Organization. It had fluoride in it.

We drove slowly. There was a man next to Karim who kept asking if I had permission to be there. He thought he was intelligence. The Tablighi were kind men, but poor. They didn't answer my questions about Afghanistan. They were afraid, Karim replied, looking out the window. They felt I wanted to link them to the Taliban. When I asked what jihad meant, the man next to him said, ah, I had come to ask that question.

---

[339] Salvadora Indica.

The next morning the sky was a bright clear blue and the air was brisk. We entered a modern office building, took an elevator, the first I had seen in Yemen, to the office of Media Freedom, Rights and Development. Khaled al- Hammadi, was at his desk. I thanked him for picking me up at the airport and apologized for not calling him. Manners are more important than laws, said Edmund Burke.

Al-Qaeda was involved in the attack on the Defense Ministry, with the Houthis. Selah provided the logistics, uniforms, vehicles and maybe weapons. Officials visited the site before the attack.

They wanted to make the country unstable to help Selah come back to power. The Saudis gave Saleh $300 million to mount the attack. They want to stop the revolution from succeeding because they could be next. Prince Bander oversaw it. There was oil on the border, and the Saudis bribed Saleh, like every president, not to dig. He signed, like every president, the three provinces over to Saudi Arabia, which paid him and tribesmen a monthly sum to attack the regime. There were many foreigners in al-Qaida in Saudi Arabia. If something happened to a foreigner, it was to send a message to his government.

This meant that Luke Somers was being held by Saleh. Karim had another class and would take a taxi. Zarb came in a small car with a female interpreter. She wore a colorful scarf, and her abaya had bead work, like pin-striping on a car. Her name was Naseem. She learned English at Sana'a University and worked at a newspaper. I said almost all women here were in a full hijab, and niktab, meaning with only their eyes showing. It depended upon your family, she replied. If you were educated, you had more freedom.

They didn't know that I had met Dr. Obaid and we returned to his office. I said I had seen the Salafis. He wanted to be sure that I understood that they appeared 900 years before the Wahhabis, who were strictly Saudi Arabia. Since the Afghan-Soviet war they had spread through eastern Afghanistan and western Pakistan building madrasas, training boys to wage jihad, to bring people, by violence if necessary, back to God. To become a Salafi, you needed to be very conservative; you stayed there or continued until you reached al-Qaeda. A democratically elected leader was illegal in Islam. The Ikhwan took part in the Revolution. "It was a revolution led by the young," inserted Naseem. The adults stole it. The Salafis were afraid, said Obaid. If they took part in politics, they might not go to Heaven.

Al-Qaida was behind the attack on the hospital. Saleh provided the weapons and helped them move through Sana'a. They kidnapped infidels, took money and released them. Al-Qaeda and the Pakistani bomb makers were linked. The Egyptians planned the attacks. The U.S. took some of that anger away by bombing a wedding party killing 17, and not apologizing. There were two evils: U.S. drones, and al-Qaeda.

That evening, I went to the bakery and a boy, about 12, was sitting by the counter reading a book. Always, the boys were covered with flour, but he wore a white headdress, a jacket, a thobe, and sandals. He looked almost angelic. It was the first time I had seen a boy in Sana'a reading. What was it? He held the book up. It was the Koran. I thought of a video of Mullah Dadullah, a vicious Taliban leader, gruffly signing a piece of paper for an angelic looking boy in white clothes. It was the boy's father's name, and his grandfather's name, his ticket to Paradise. Another boy sat next to him. Dadullah quickly signed his paper. I gave the boy money for three loaves, about $.30. He dropped it in a drawer and picked up four loaves from the stack by the oven, smiling. We were becoming friends. I would pay him more next time. I wanted to take him away, afraid that he was going to kill himself.

Al-Qaeda

It was dark as the plane flew over the desert. Aden, at night, like Miami, was warm, and steamy, but with no pollution. I stood on the sidewalk. Three men with rifles watched me. A man in a mahwaz and keffiyeh stood alone by a 1960s red and white Ford. I was told never to take a taxi alone. He had a warm glint in his eye, and I liked his car. It rattled, and the music, a' rote, between a banjo and a guitar, sharper, brittle, was fast, secular Yemen. A sea breeze flowed over me. We came to the hotel. It was 2000 riyals, $10. He raised the price three dollars. He put his head down smiling. I paid him.

The next morning, one of four sons who owned *Al-Ayyam* (*The Days*), the mostly widely read newspaper in South Yemen, and I sat in the hotel café. He ran the National Democratic Institute in South Yemen, funded by the U.S., helping young men and women to promote democracy. In 2009, Selah sent a man to his father with a blank check and said put down a number and he would get it, plus cars, land, houses—only don't publish what people said. His father said no. He put him in jail for four months. They needed to take him to Germany, but Saleh refused to give him a passport. He died. Saleh killed him. His nephew came with tear gas, a machine gun, RPGs, rifles, and attacked them. It was impossible to live with the North, a tribal society.

But the South had five million people, the North over 22 million. Yes, but until 1994 they had the strongest army on the Arabian Peninsula, with the best equipment, provided by the Soviet Union.

He drove along the water, past a fortress, whose origins were unknown, on top of Sira Island, from which the British fired in 1839, and took Aden, which came from *Janat Aden* in the Koran, or beautiful gardens. It was the best time, being a colony. He went to school in England.

Their compound was at the top of a hill. Bashra, with short gray dark hair, a moustache, and glasses, in a mahwaz, sat at his cluttered desk. He ran the newspaper. He went to the University of Alabama. It was the best time he ever had. After he graduated, in computer science, he went to Drexel, and got an MBA. Tea? He picked up the phone. A black man brought two cups of thick Adenese tea.

People over 70, if they spoke English, had an English accent. They were a different society from the North. There used to be a beer factory here, and it made the finest beer. They said it was not Islamic, and destroyed it. They were barbarians. You were free here. You could drink a beer or go to the mosque to pray. Selah was stronger than the government. He controlled al-Qaeda, his tool. The strongest army here was the Republican Guard. His son was in charge. Mubarak, in Egypt, was a good soldier for the U.S. and they let him go. Selah knew how to play the game.

Everyone called it a game, the killings, and deaths upon deaths, like in Afghanistan.

He learned in the U.S. that to find the root of the problem to trace the money. Saudi Arabia brought Selah to power. Prince Sultan[340] created the "Special Commission," through which he controlled 32,000 Yemeni sheiks on his payroll. Saudi Arabia was opposed, at all costs, to unity. He talked about the oil fields which spread from Saudi Arabia into Yemen. A civil war was coming, and another revolution. They saw the helicopters dropping al-Qaida operatives in Abyan and alerted the U.S. Embassy. And? He shrugged. The Americans received but they never answered. The families of al-Qaeda killed by drones, or in battles, showed him their sons' ID cards. They all said "Bureau of National Security." When the army took over Abyan, a general handed over all the bases to al-Qaeda.

Why didn't the U.S. force Saleh, Ali Mohsen and Zindani to put an end to al-Qaeda? He shrugged. They, Hadi, sheikhs, and private militias controlled al-Qaeda. The Ministry of Defense statement put out within 12 hours of the attack on the hospital that said all or most of the attackers were Saudis. The National Security Bureau had lists and photographs of all Saudis linked to terrorist groups. They knew the attack was coming, but not where or when. The number of hardcore ideologues in the Middle East was very few. It came from the Wahhabis, who controlled the mosques, and preached an ideology of hate. His family saw its role to try to prevent extremism.

Was al-Qaida selling honey?

---

[340] Sultan bin Abdul Aziz al Saud, former Saudi Defense Minister and Crown Prince, died in 2011.

His eyes brightened. When you wired money to a farmer to buy his honey it disappeared. He didn't keep records. There was honey here from Pakistan, and passed off as Yemeni whose honey, mentioned in the Koran, was the best in the world.[341]

Once there were Parsis[342] here, Jews, Hindus. Aden was part of the West. Now it was all the purification of life. Outside, he pointed to a wall, 12 feet high and a foot thick. In the 1980s, it was a few feet high. Then Saleh's nephew came. In 1992, the first thing Islah banned was Christmas and New Year's. You could be arrested for carrying a cake.

Yassin, a thin man with dark hair, in western clothes, holding a cigarette, and I sat in the cafe. All around men, mostly in jeans and polo shirts, were smoking, secular Yemen. A dark-skinned man in a white turban, mahwaz, sandals, black and white sport jacket, a red scarf folded over his shoulder, and a beard, entered. I walked up to the front and we shook hands. His name was Ali al-Kurdi. He smiled coldly and we walked to the back. He sat across from me, his back straight, Yassin between us. I thanked him for coming. He nodded, solid, like a prize fighter. He looked at me like he wanted to fight. Zarb arranged this.

He was in Afghanistan from 1990 to 1992. The Russians were gone. They were fighting the Communist government. Why did he go? They had a Marxist government here. Because of the hardships people faced, they wanted to pray. The government harassed them. He looked for a place to fight jihad. The United States and Saudi Arabia made it easy to go to Afghanistan. He went to Sana'a, got a visa for Pakistan, flew to Karachi and then to Peshawar. He stayed in the Bait al-Ansar.[343] He was al-Qaida.

How did he know to go to Sana'a? How did he get there? He paid his own way. The political security agency, the tribes, and religious people all had offices to send men to Afghanistan. They arranged everything. Did he meet other men and feel a sense of camaraderie that they were engaged in a great cause? He met men at the airport. He had heard of the massacres, and the rapes. He wanted to help Muslims. He spent three years in the army. He was in prison for six months for going to the mosque. He was transferred

---

[341] https://www.alaraby.co.uk/english/features/2015/1/28/honey-fraud-in-yemen-leaves
-bitter-taste
[342] Parsis are Persians who fled to India during the Muslim conquest of Persia.
[343] "The Services Bureau," started by Abdullah Azzam.

from every regiment for doing this, but every time he had a chance to learn how to use new weapons. Did he grow up in a religious family? No, he was a rover, a nothing, suffering on his own but then he went to the mosque, and his life changed. *"When a man is brought to Islam and he performs it well, God covers all his former sins."*[344] When he died, he would go to Paradise. *"God has promised the believers, both men and women, gardens through which running waters flow, therein to abide and goodly dwellings in gardens of perpetual bliss."*[345]

In 1984, the government told women to take off the veil. He was a socialist, but the government was fighting Islam. He wanted to fight back, but he had no power. In Peshawar, after a month of physical training, they sent him to other camps where the instructors saw that he knew all about the weapons they were using and they moved him to camps where he learned about explosives, and how to detonate them using a cell phone. His instructors were Egyptians and Saudis. He had a friend they sent to Tajikistan and on to Chechnya. They would go wherever Muslims needed help. He learned how to operate a tank. There were Americans, Burmese, Pakistanis, from everywhere. The sent them to the battlefields in Nangahar, Paktia, Khost and Logar, and up to Kabul.[346] He fought with Hekmatyar, with Yunus Khalis, and Rahbani.

If he was with Khalis, he fought with Haqqani.

Those first two and half years were the best part of his life. He was young and he was defending Islam. Every day, at any moment, they could be killed. He didn't think of money, or marriage. He would die for God. It would be an honor. At the beginning Afghans and Arabs were together, but then the intelligence agencies came and separated them to keep track of their people. Spies could not go on the battlefield. He leaned back in disdain. When they fought it was as if they were born from the same belly. When they were in camps, the spies watched them. The Algerians and Egyptians were worried that they would be executed when they returned.

In the 1980s, conservatives said the CIA was too liberal. It created "Team B," a competitive analysis assessment conducted outside the CIA to

---

[344] Mishkat 10:3, the Hadith.
[345] Al-Tawbah (Repentance) 72.
[346] Nangarhar, Paktia, Khost, and Logar are southeast Afghan provinces.

study Soviet intentions in the Cold War, forcing the CIA to be more aggressive in Afghanistan. The CIA became more Populist. After 9/11, it tortured men in jails from Poland to Thailand. It was the "browning" of the CIA, Milt Bearden said. The what? "The brown shirts," he replied. He meant Hitler's men.

Governments were sending men to die. Did this anger him? No. When he went, he didn't think he would come back. He went to fight the injustices against Muslims. He would become a martyr for Islam. One of their instructors was Thor. He smiled. They called him "the black." He was from Somalia. Most of their teachers were PhD s, doctors and managers. In addition to military training, they taught them about Islam. They fought Communist Afghans, and other Communists, even female Indians flying MIGs. They shot some down and captured the pilots.

Caste-ridden India had a large communist party, seeking equality.

He met twice with bin Laden, first in Hyderabad—an upscale area of Peshawar—where they discussed fighting the communists in Aden. After Kabul fell, Southerners came to see bin Laden to sell him weapons. If he and other Mujahideen wanted to study he would pay their expenses. Jihad, for them, in Afghanistan, was over. When they returned, they held a reception for them, they were heroes. When he arrived in Aden, they harassed him. He wanted to get married and settle down, but he was accused of firing on the Gold Mohur Night Club and went to prison. He was referring to 1992.

During the Cold War, the U.S. had a listening post in Ethiopia. The Soviets backed Somalia which in 1977 started a war with Ethiopia, which, coupled with a drought, led to famine, clan warfare, and starvation. In 1992, the U.N., and the U.S. provided relief. The U.S. launched Operation Hope to end the starvation, and bring peace. The Marine Corps stayed in hotels in Aden before going into Somalia. When al-Kurdi fired at the night club, the U.S. was gone.

The ICRC[347] and Amnesty International visited al-Kurdi. The government sent him from the Central Prison to al-Fatah, the political security prison, to be executed. There were 15 of them. They took all the bearded men, including Northerners, put them on ships and sent them to Socotra, an island in the Gulf of Aden. When Aden fell, the prison gates opened. He went back to prison in December 1992 to July 1994. They beat him. They put people in acid.

---

[347] The International Red Cross.

"They also buried people alive in containers," Yassin said. It was a Marxist government, al-Kurdi reminded me. They put him in prison for the attack on the U.S.S. Cole. It was as easy to be charged for anything in Yemen as changing your shirt. Yassin nodded. He was discharged and then put back in prison for seven months, and discharged again. In 2005, they put him in prison for a year. He did not see sunlight, his family or his parents. They were put on trial in a cage with 23 others charged with creating an armed group to kill Americans. This was a specially knitted shirt, he smiled. No one knew one another, but they called them "The Zarqawi Cell," after the al-Qaeda founder in Iraq. The judge found them innocent. He was sent to another governorate.[348]

Their case went to an appeal's court and they were freed. But Salch put him in prison for two years until 2007. They beat everyone, accusing them of being al-Qaeda.

The U.S. and the security apparatus were running Yemen, Al-Kurdi said. He expected to be detained again. He was classified as a terrorist one of the victims of America's Global War on Terror. He made less than $100/month as a technician at a private school. He rented out part of his house. He bought things on credit. He started a human rights organization. The government was hunting for the foreign fighters, and he wanted to help them. They were in Chechnya, Bosnia, and Iraq. He was referring to those Col. al-Helal had taken to Africa.

I showed him my book with a picture of Haqqani on the cover. He checked his watch. It was time for prayers. He put his jacket next to me and left. Yassin lit a cigarette. Was he okay? Yes, but he had never translated anything like this. He worried about my security. I didn't know what to make of al-Kurdi. He said he was poor but he dressed beautifully. He moved around in what he said, said Yassin. I had to be careful. He could be working for the government. A small man came and sat where al-Kurdi was sitting. There were not many foreigners here, he said. It was not safe to be in Aden. The hotel security chief, in a blue shirt and tie, joined him. I asked the short man where he learned English. He worked for oil companies. He brought foreigners and Yemenis looking for opportunities together. Was I a journalist? What was I? Why was I here?

---

[348] There are 21 governorates in Yemen, below them districts, sub-districts, villages and sub-villages.

I was a researcher studying Islamic movements. Al-Kurdi returned, unrolling his sleeves. I handed him his jacket. He shook hands with the security chief, and the small man. They both left. He wanted to help Muslims. He and other Afghan-Arabs were used as a trade item between countries. He was still here, like a rock. He didn't regret anything in Afghanistan. Jesus and Moses suffered a lot because of religion. They were better than he was in the eyes of God. If you were going to fight for your religion you must be ready for all kinds of suffering. During the time of the Koran, Christians and Jews were burned in trenches. He meant the Battle of the Trench, when Mohammad's forces defeated a larger army of Queryish in Medina.[349]

During the Communist rule, people suffered. He was more fortunate than those who were put in acid or buried alive in containers. Yassin nodded. No wonder he went to Afghanistan. He was proud that he was not a thief, a killer, or a beggar, proud that he had been in prison for political reasons. I heard that there was a Selah al-Qaeda, an Ali Mohsen al-Qaeda, a Saudi al-Qaeda. If you were a tool, you would get everything, he replied. The Saudis wanted to sabotage Yemen. Al-Qaeda was their tool. If the government wanted to assassinate someone, they sent an al-Qaeda person. The Arabs and the Americans were suffering because of U.S. policies. It sent troops to Arab countries. It was natural that they would defend themselves, and their wealth, and so Americans were dying. It was unjust. The Arabs would die defending their land, and go to Paradise, but the U.S soldier did not know why he was killed.

The Taliban, in their suicide recruitment tapes, chanted about their land. "Today is a good day to die," said Crazy Horse, rallying his men against the invaders.

If he died fighting in Chechnya, he would be happy, but if an American mother lost her son, it would be unjust. Soldiers and their families were of no value to American politicians. He would be happy if his children became martyrs. He would go to Chechnya. It was a man's duty, whether young or old, American or Yemeni, to die for Islam. It was the duty of all to sacrifice their lives for Christians living in Muslim countries. This was the true Islam, even to protect the Jews in Muslim countries.

---

[349] https://en.wikipedia.org/wiki/ Battle_of_the_Trench.

Were there foreigners coming here to train for jihad? Al-Kurdi looked at me and at Yassin. People used to come here to study the hadith, and now so many, Pakistanis, Somalis, Afghans, had left to go to Syria, and to fight the Houthis. "What about Haqqani? Was he sending people?" His face went cold. He had no idea. His look had told me the truth. He was still tied to these people. He wanted to mediate between them and the government. If I had questions for al-Qaeda, could I give them to him? Did I mean that I wanted to go to al-Qaeda? He had a sinister smile. Going in was easy but coming back was hard.

Did he regret any part of his life? No, he had sought the truth. His only regret would be not going to Paradise. A new generation was looking for jihad as a badge of honor and it make its mark.

Once it was Kalashnikov against Kalashnikov. Now it was dynamite. Once it was face to face. Now America fought from the skies. This war needed suicide bombers.

I walked him to the door, feeling uncomfortable. I sat with Yassin. Al-Kurdi felt like a time bomb. He never talked with anyone like him. I didn't want him to continue and get hurt. No, it was very interesting. He was 60, old now. He had his house, and his children were grown. He and his wife were in good health. Al-Kurdi seemed a little crazy. Yemen was a dangerous place, he added. He left. The small man was sitting at a table drinking tea. I went to him. Why did he come and ask what I was doing? I went up to my room, and came back. He was walking out of the small gift shop. I understood, I said, it was dangerous here. "People talk, they like to talk, but they say nothing," he said. We shook hands. Al-Kurdi dressed like al-Jamal. He loved beauty and smiled when I took his picture, yet he wished for martyrdom. I went swimming in the pool. Twenty yards away waves splashed against the rocks. I felt darkness around me.

In the evening, a man named Adel called, a friend of Zarb's. We met in the café. He wore blue framed glasses, and western clothes. He'd stopped being a journalist. Islah threatened him. They said he was writing too much about al-Qaeda. He was married, and had a son. He showed me a picture on his phone of a cute little boy. "What did Islah say exactly?" They sent a text message warning him. That was enough. People were afraid of journalists. They had power. He asked why I was here. I was looking at the links between here and Waziristan. This was new. He could translate, but no journalism. He was 28 and wanted to live a good life with his family. A stocky man, in dark pants and a black shirt, came and spoke to Adel. He wanted to join us. Who was he? Adel said he was with the security forces. I told him to take a seat. He had a hard look about him.

Who did I talk to here yesterday? Who have I met? I brought a man in here who scared everyone. How long had I been here?

I told him. He punched in his number on his phone. How did I meet al-Kurdi? I gave him Zarb's name. I wondered if I was putting him at risk, or myself, then realized that I had met Adel through Zarb. The security man gave me his phone and Zarb tried to explain to me who he was. Karim called. Haider was Zarb's friend. But Zarb introduced me to al-Qaeda. Haider would protect me. I was to give him 10,000 riyals. Haider told me not to leave the hotel. I was to tell him everyone I talked to. It was for my own protection. He was not hotel security. He was the security apparatus. He asked for my phone number and gave me his. He was on the phone again.

He would be around. I was not to trust anyone, said Adel. I didn't know who was watching. There may be war soon and people were poor and looking out for themselves.

CNN was on the television by a coffee stand, clips of football games, golf matches, the soft life of America. Adel taught Arabic and would introduce me to a fixer. He had two British students and found it rewarding. He wanted to go to Malaysia and to open an Arabic language school. I knew a Malaysian at CALES who wanted to start a series of schools. I would find his number for him. He wanted to meet again. I must be careful, he repeated, very careful. It was evening, and the waves came crashing in, and the palm trees blew back and forth. It was snowing in New York. Haider and a man were sitting at a table, a pile of gat between them. A guard walked by. They watched for men coming in from the Gulf, or over the walls. I imagined a small boat landing and al-Qaeda running toward the hotel. I walked back to Haider. He was alone. I gave him 10000 riyals, about $50. He told me to take some. I said no and walked along the water. Karim called. Fawaz was trying to come to see me, but al-Harek, the Southern Separatist Movement, attacked police headquarters, killing a man and blocked the road.

Later that night, Fawaz, about 35, came to the cafe. Two women in abayas, with only their eyes showing, with big fancy purses, sat at the next table. One took out her phone. Fawaz called his interpreter. It was a woman. Did I care? Nasrin, of Indian heritage, in a burqa, Hindi for abaya, her face uncovered, met us outside. She was Muslim. Her family lived in Aden long before the British arrived. She worked for SABA, the government news agency. I explained my goals. Fawaz listed the people we could see. Haider came over. Fawaz gave him his phone number and he punched it in. He was upset that I had talked to a man. Fawaz asked who. I told him. He knew al-Kurdi. He followed bin Laden. He married a Pakistani. He had two wives, the other was Yemeni. He blew up the hotels where the Americans were staying in 1992. They were going to execute him, but he now worked for Selah's security apparatus.

If he married a Pakistani, and was with bin Laden, who did not speak Pashto, he was tied in some way to the Haqqanis. I mentioned the honey business. Al- Qaeda had businesses, and was involved in the honey trade, Fawaz said. In Abyan when the army entered, there was no gas, yet al-Qaida had gas. It now owned gas stations. When Abdul Latif's brother died, there was a funeral and al-Qaeda put bombs in the water coolers and 50 people were killed; everyone except Abdul Latif. Who was Abdul Latif? No one answered. No one knew about the honey business.

Al-Qaida was friends with Saleh's chief of intelligence. Nasrin was an interpreter for al-Kurdi. When he learned that she needed a job he had people in the government write a letter for her. He called her all the time. "How are you, sister?" he asked. Al-Kurdi lived for two years in Pakistan after fighting in Afghanistan, said Fawaz. In 1994, Saleh gave the Afghan-Arabs good jobs and kept them in the South. When al-Qaeda came from Afghanistan, following the call of Osama bin Laden, Saleh moved al-Qaida here. What about Tariq al-Fadhli? Nasrin knew him. He brought al-Qaida from Afghanistan. In 2011, he had three sons with al-Qaida.

Fawaz arrived late the next morning. A suicide bomber killed an army officer on the road near here. Al-Qaida was distributing leaflets in La-Haj. It was 20 miles away. He would take me to al-Qaida. That evening I put on Yemeni clothes and sat by the door. Was I really going to do this? I imagined walking into a room and being trapped. Fawaz pulled up outside. We shouldn't do this. We could invite Abdul Latif to come here. I wondered if he had saved my life.

The Story of Maher

Three men entered the room, Ahmed, about 35, computer technician, part-time journalist and photographer, six feet, in a gray tee shirt, Bermuda shorts, and sunglasses; Maher, small, thin, about 18, in a mahwaz, pale yellow shirt, blue jacket, sandals, a towel for a headdress; Wahid, psychologist, wiry, 5'8" with a smart phone, and a pack of cigarettes. They lived in Ja'ar, a town in Abýan. In 2007, there was no government. Al-Qaeda came, gathered the people and said it would establish an Islamic government. That was how it started.

No, said Wahid, it was when Ali Mohsen and Selah began to pay salaries to young, unemployed, uneducated men to prepare them to fight for them. They stirred things up. They were doing this elsewhere but mainly in Abyan, said Ahmed. Nasrin said they were in Aden, too. Selah told the boys it was God's will that he gave them 70 virgins in Paradise and he would give them ten more. Ahmed agreed. The illiterate boys believed him, at least some did. The government said to do what they wanted. It got worse during the Arab Spring. Saleh warned if he had to resign it would lead to civil war.

Fawaz laughed. He knew an Arab-Afghan, a friend of al-Kurdi, who had a militia. He called him one night. He was at the home of head of the Political Security Organization, the main intelligence service.

Wahid continued. If the boys didn't get paid they attacked soldiers at checkpoints. Saleh and Ali Mohsen would tell them to stop. This time the attacks began as talks stalled over Saleh's resignation. On March 10, 2011, at 5:30 a.m., a large group appeared at the October 7th Munitions Factory. There were only a few people there, and the night manager. Al-Qaeda said to go in peace. People came and looted the factory. The workers wore plastic shoes, necessary there, but al-Qaida didn't know, and set off an explosion killing 250 people.[350] The government blamed the Aden-Abyan Army. One report said the blast occurred after Islamic militants drove out forces loyal to Saleh. CNN quoted Secretary of Defense Gates: "The U.S. had a good

---

[350] "Accidental Explosion at Yemen Arms Factory Kills 100," *Independent* 28 Mar. 2011

relationship with President Saleh. He was an important ally in the counterterrorism arena."

The groups were not getting paid, and refused to allow officials in. Saleh's men and Ali Mohsen's men were facing one another. After al-Qaeda left, Wahid and others found the minutes of their meetings and read that Selah and Ali Mohsen were supporting them. The day after the explosion, for the first time they saw army jeeps and cars enter their area with the white flag of *Ansar al-Sharia*, in black.[351] They were Yemenis, Afghans, Iraqis, Pakistanis, Chechens, Syrians, and Afghan women, too. Zinjabar, the capital of Abyan, was under al-Qaeda control. The rebels and the foreigners knew that people were afraid of al-Qaeda. That's why they became *Ansar-al-Sharia*. The government financed them. They had no allegiance to anyone or faith in anything.

One was Abdul Latif. They robbed the central bank of $10 million and wanted to go to their leaders in the central mountains, but Latif said no. He took 10-15 riflemen, machine guns, ammunition, and the money. He had a friend who knew the former chief of police of Aden, and they went to him. He called the Minister of Defense and said Latif left al-Qaeda. They could use him. He helped the army, like no one else, to get rid of al-Qaeda in Abyan, Ahmed said. Al-Qaeda told Latif if he didn't agree with their concepts to go, but if he did to keep quiet, and he could stay. They were young men with nothing to do. They had families. Al-Qaeda was paying them. They were not more than 300 or 400. They lived in the mountains.

I asked Maher where was he from, and how old was he. He shifted in his seat and looked at Ahmed. He and Wahid urged him to talk. He was from Ja'ar and was 20 or 21. He spoke softly. What did he do for a living? He was a handyman. What did his father do? He was old, he waved his hand dismissively. He went to school until the fifth grade and then he, as the oldest, had to support his family. He had two sisters and four brothers. Were they religious? They went to the mosque; they were a normal family. He was a laborer, and carried things for shopkeepers. What happened to him? There was a school, a police station, and a qat market next to one another. A plane bombed the police station. I didn't understand. Ahmed smiled. Al-Qaeda controlled the city, and the air force was bombing them. There were electric

---

[351] Supporters of Sharia.

wires lying around, and people took them to sell. Maher was sitting with two friends and al-Qaeda asked them who took the wires. He didn't know. They took them to a house and beat them for three days, and asked if they knew certain people. They said no. They kept beating them with sticks and whipping them with the wires. He had to confess to all that he had done since he was a boy. They put something in juice and gave it to him to drink. They kept looking smaller.

He fell into a coma, woke up and they gave him more juice. They did this for three or four days. He was in a coma, and they took him and the other boys to the market. They cut off his hand and showed it to everyone. The room was silent. Fawaz moved his chair back away from me. Ahmed moved his chair away from Maher. "They picked it up," Ahmed showed, holding his hand high. They walked through the market shouting "*Allah-oh-Akbar.*" Who were these men? What did they use to cut him? They used a medical instrument, said Ahmed. He watched them. When Maher awoke, his hand was bandaged. It was about three days later. It was at night and they were there. There was a bag overhead and a needle in his arm. The next afternoon, he woke up and there was no one there and he ran and found a friend, and called his family. They went to the hospital in Aden. They gave him painkillers and bandaged his hand again. For seven to eight months, he went back and forth. What happened to the others? They cut off their hands.

Nasrin had her hand on her mouth. "One was older, married and had children," said Ahmed, putting his head down. How could he support his family? "I was supporting my family," said Maher softly. What about the future? What did he want to do? He had no future. We were silent. Did he want to get married, and have a family? How could he find a wife? How was he going to earn a living, I wondered? If it was written by God, it would happen. It was God's will, Maher replied. All he thought about every day was how could he support his family.

Wahid was a psychologist dealing with depression, and tension. In Islam, if you had your hand cut, people thought you are a thief. But everyone knew what happened. No, people thought he was a thief. They only know that this happened. When Maher walked in the market, he hid his hand. At Ahmed's urging he brought his hand out from his jacket pocket and pulled back the sleeve. Again, I asked if he was religious. He went to the mosque every day. What did he think of al-Qaeda? They were the most criminal people, he said loudly. Everyone thought they were, said Ahmed. Why did they have power? He laughed. It was propaganda. They had little power, but they were terrorists. They thought they could talk with them, but now they wanted to kill them. If he saw them, he would kill them, Maher added.

Wahid said he knew the man who cut him. They studied together in Russia. The room was silent. Maher stared across the table. He thought he was Chechen. Where was he now? We didn't talk about this, Wahid replied. Where was he, asked Maher louder? We were not here to talk about the sorrow, we were telling a story, Wahid insisted. We were not talking about the sorrow, Nasrin, pleaded. No, we were talking about it. We had to push through this. We were silent, horrified at the cruelty done to this boy. They were in sympathy, said Nasrin quietly. I asked Maher if this was helping or hurting him. It was normal. It was a crime that happened.

What did the people of Abyan feel? They felt that the regime left them. The schools were closed. They needed drinking water. A group of doctors and nurses opened a field hospital. They contacted the French doctors.[352] The man who cut Maher was a doctor. He was part of al-Qaeda.

After they took over the hospital, they asked them for the records of the patients with TB and diabetes, and the mental patients, so they could treat them. Finally, they did. They called the Red Crescent for water and started their own schools. Al-Qaeda was upset because they were teaching that the earth was round. It was oval. They said there was no revolution in 1967 against the British. Finally, for peace, they asked them to supervise the schools. They separated boys from girls. People gave money to keep girls in school and al-Qaeda got mad. The government said the children could take their exams. Al-Qaeda wanted to enter the school with weapons. They didn't feel that this was good for the children. Some were from Afghanistan and Pakistan.

Could they forgive al-Qaeda? To forgive was personal, said Ahmed. What they did in Abyan called for justice. The only one who could forgive was the person harmed. If you killed, you had to face justice. Ahmed became a journalist because they were afraid to come to Abyan. He had a camera, and he had to take pictures. Al-Qaeda crucified a man. He was

---

[352] Medecins sans Frontieres (Doctors Without Borders) won the Nobel Peace Prize in 1999.

looking at him and a man tapped him on the shoulder. He was next. Al-Qaeda was strong among weak people Maher said. It was a dark, terrorist power. Al-Qaeda convinced boys the U.S. was anti-Muslim, and came to kill them, so they must kill Americans. It was hard to convince people that al-Qaeda was wrong.

The Renegade

A dusty, beige SUV with tinted windows raced into the parking lot and parked facing the exit. Fawaz's phone rang and he went outside. A lean man in a dark mahwaz, sandals, a black shirt, sunglasses, black kefiyyah, with a shorter man holding a sack, walked slowly, with a confident, athletic gait. Fawaz walked with him, smiling and gesturing. They entered the room. Abdul Latif wore a 9mm pistol on his left side with the handle in front. He was slightly cross-eyed and had a limp handshake. He sat and put two phones in front of him. His bodyguard sat next to him. Latif's left hand and wrist were black, like they were charred, and oily. He put his sunglasses back on. I thanked him for coming. He was pleased to be here. I wanted to hear his story. In the name of God, the most merciful, he prayed. His name was Abdul Latif Muhammed Hussein Fadel. In 2011, al-Qaeda appeared in Abyan. There was a lot of injustice because the Yemeni government didn't help the people.

What about him? He paused. He was born in 1981. He finished secondary school when he was about 19 or 20. Before 1990, all young men in South Yemen, after finishing school, were sent to camps for two years of military training. They were not in the regular army, but toughening them in camps to prepare them if the government needed them. After this, some joined the army, or the police; others went back to school, or tried to find a job, or went to college. Most city men didn't like these camps. I kept thinking that the hotel guards let him carry a 9mm pistol in here. Once, he didn't have a job, and he joined a gang, and Selah and Ali Mohsen paid him a salary, preparing him and his men and other gangs for when they would use them to create chaos, to assure that more money came from America to fight al-Qaeda. When he and his men didn't receive their salaries, they attacked soldiers.

Al-Qaeda started to appear in Ja'ar in March 2011. They talked with them about their goals, which was to return their rights to them to help them against the government and to spread the will of God. They had other goals which were to kill people who didn't follow God's will. But they called for justice. What did he think of them? He leaned back. He was not 35, and had been fighting for 15 years. How many men had he killed? Who didn't like justice, he smiled, slowly picking leaves of gat and chewing them. Fawaz brought him a bag. Later, these men appeared in Zinjibar, and began killing soldiers, looting, and destroying houses. They, about 300, would come and then disappear into the mountains. They were in small groups. One group did not know what the other was doing. If you were arrested and knew, if the government tortured you, you could talk. He talked as if he had all the time in the world. He kept us waiting for six hours, and didn't apologize.

The group of 300 dominated, and then other men came. He and his men, about 15, didn't know where they came from. They were killing soldiers. He felt useless. He and his men had no power. They stole from him and from the people. One was from the Philippines, another from Australia. There were many Saudis. He didn't see any Afghans or Pakistanis. They made a big mistake by working with them. Who was backing them, Saleh and Ali Mohsen? I didn't know this? He laughed. He had a slight lisp, maybe from the RPG. How could he survive being hit by a rocket propelled grenade? Every few minutes his phones pinged. He put his glasses on his forehead and looked at his phone and kept talking. He rallied the people. They trusted him. He and his men were sorry that they had been with al-Qaida. The gangs and al-Qaeda joined forces. They stole $10 million from a bank, and there was a stand-off between the two groups. He took 60 machine guns, not rifles, one of which cost two million riyals, said Fawaz.

Al-Qaeda had wives and small children even foreign wives. It was dangerous. They rented houses, but they never gave their nationalities. They called themselves the Aden-Abyan Army. The people were afraid of them and so they used this name. It came from the hadith that Saleh and Ali Mohsen made up. Was al-Qaeda growing or losing power? It was growing. They, in the People's Committees, made 30,000 riyals a month. America and Saudi Arabia gave money to the government, but it kept stealing it, looting the country. They fought these people for their dignity, he said. The government before the 2011 revolution and the new one were the same. There were five murder cases and he and his men found the killers. The government couldn't find them. The Yemeni army was an agent of America, and he didn't know what America wanted. There were 4,000 in the Peoples' Committees, and 2,500 under him fighting al-Qaeda. The government had no control in Abyan, so he set up his own government. This gunslinger, this guerrilla leader, maybe this Robin Hood, was the Sultan of Abyan.

Al-Qaeda was an organization of foreigners and Yemenis. They took over two schools in Abyan and taught children how to make bombs. They said the Yemeni army was an agent of America and they had to fight them. Everyone hated America, Nasrin said. It interfered in their internal affairs, and it backed Selah. Latif saw U.S. soldiers in Abyan, but America was not serious about fighting. He and his men filled the vacuum. There was an All-Arab sports festival in Yemen in 2010, and the country was open and he heard that many foreigners, a number of them Somalis, came then. Their first battle, on the 15th of Ramadan 2011, went from 2:00 in the morning until six the next evening. They fought in close quarters and lost three men. If they fought in an open space, al-Qaeda would know that there were only a few of them.

This was an Islamic battle trick, Nasrin added. The Prophet Mohammed used this tactic.

After the battle, the Minister of Defense contacted Latif and offered him five million riyals ($20,000) and ten crates of ammunition. He was afraid that Latif was still with al-Qaeda. Nasrin smiled. The Minister of Defense was afraid of one man up in the mountains? The chief of security gave them money and supplies. They used the money to buy weapons at an arms market. They bought food, arms and ammunition on credit and paid their debts when the government paid them. They were considered the most effective force against al-Qaeda. There were about 11,000 in al-Qaeda, many in the government. They came in small groups and dispersed. Latif held six districts. He had many suicide attacks against him. One was a car filled with explosives.

Why didn't the Americans want to fight? He laughed. I came from them. Why was I asking him?

He had at least eleven attacks against him. He took off his glasses to show his eyes, and his hand. He'd lost three brothers and many relatives. Seven times they had put bombs in his path. He seemed calm. He waved his hand. It was destiny if he was killed. It was God's will. It was now a war of aggression, and vengeance, and would never end. Nasrin said it would take a hundred years to resolve. What kind of man would fight al-Qaeda? He laughed again. All Yemenis were armed and knew how to fight. He used guns as a boy.

There was no direct state support of al-Qaeda, but indirectly it came from Saleh and Ali-Mohsen, and other men. Was there a tie between al-Qaida here and in Pakistan? He didn't know, but Ayman al-Zawahiri came to see Tariq al-Fadhli in 1992. Latif got support from every corner of Abyan. He loved the Salifis. They supported him against al-Qaeda. Foreigners came to their centers, especially to the House of the Hadith, at Dammaj, from Somalia, Europe, and America. Saudi businessmen and charities, linked to the government, paid for everything. Al-Eryani said it was a good business. Al-Qaeda said it was fighting the Salafis, but the real Salafis were pacifists.

Al-Qaida wanted to fight with the Salafis against the Houthis, but the Salafis in Dammaj said no. They were Wahhabis, controlled by Saudi Arabia.[353]

The fighters had families. They needed food, rifles, bombs, and machine guns. They got funds from Saudi Arabia. He had two wives. Life and death were in the hands of God. He and his men could not run. The people and the army supported him. What about the Taliban? Al-Qaeda and the Taliban were the same. That was his information.

Latif left as calmly as he came. He walked slowly across the parking lot. His SUV raced to the entrance, waited, then headed into traffic toward Abyan.

---

[353] Bonnefoy, *"Salafism in Yemen,"* 57-60

Tariq al-Fadhli

How could we get to Tariq al-Fadhli? He was a brave man, said Nasrin. He had much information. He knew how al-Qaeda started in Yemen. It would be dangerous, but Fawaz could take me.

The next day Karim called. If Haider appeared I was to say that I was going to take my lunch with Fawaz. The spy was in the lobby drinking tea. Fawaz came up to me. Haider appeared and told me not to go anywhere. Fawaz and I walked to the door. He had tinted windows. I was to stay out of sight until he brought the car around. I stood outside in an alcove. An SUV pulled up and Haider came up behind me. He talked to Fawaz, who told me to get in the back. Haider looked at me and walked back inside. We raced through a checkpoint and the men put out their hands in disbelief, drove down a narrow street, and waited. Nasrin appeared and joined us. We passed a park, with a statue of Queen Victoria, and drove for half an hour along the water, past the home of the Saudi consul, kidnapped months ago by al-Qaeda. Saudi Arabia arrested al-Qaeda women who were raising money in mosques there, and al-Qieda took the consul.

Half a dozen men stood outside a compound. I entered a courtyard and walked up the stone stairs into a house. Tariq al-Fadhli, medium height, short hair, large piercing eyes, in a pressed royal blue shirt, light blue and white mahwaz, sandals, and a cigarette, welcomed me. Nine men were sitting against the wall. We shook hands. It might be harder to harm me if I was friendly. I sat next to al-Fadhli. Fawaz said I had been in Afghanistan during the Soviet time. Al-Fadhli smiled broadly. He was a treasure of information.

He went in 1986 to Peshawar to see Abdullah Azzam who gave the Arabs lectures and led them in prayers. He divided men and sent them to Massoud, to Hekmatyar, to Yunus Khalis, to Sayyaf. He brought supplies from the Red Crescent and other groups. Osama was independent. They passed through Miram Shah. There was an emir for each region. Here it was Yunus Khalis. The Afghans respected the Arabs who they felt were tied to the Prophet.

Al-Fadhli stroked my arm gently, to show how men touched them. They spoke the language of the Koran. They were sitting in Haqqani's hospitality house having tea. An Afghan came over. Al-Fadhli said he was a communist from South Yemen. The Afghan pointed his rifle at him. It was close. He shook his head. He made jihad with Osama. In 1990, he and five or six Yemenis talked about transferring the spirit of jihad to the South. The north would be like Pakistan and supply them with weapons. The sheikh of the north should be like Haqqani, who everyone liked, and respected. He would have training camps, provide weapons, and operate on both sides of the border.

They went to Osama and said jihad was finished, let us go to South Yemen. A few months later they flew to Sana'a. They met with tribal leaders who talked about unification. The Afghan Arabs talked about jihad. They wanted to take their views to the people. They mounted a coup, but Saleh backed the Socialists, and they failed. Everyone went to his own region and started his own group. Osama was in Jeddah but focused on Yemen. He gave millions of dollars to sheikhs until 1993 when they left him. Al-Fadhli lit another cigarette, disgusted. His right cheek, filled with qat, bulged like a balloon. Saudi princes were borrowing money from bin Laden. His family was building palaces for them. He never worked with the U.S. If he needed weapons, he presented a demand to Prince Sultan, who gave it to the U.S., who sent it to Pakistan.

From 1993-1996 Osama was a refugee in Sudan. He created an Advisory Board to oppose the Saudi regime, made cassettes, printed leaflets, and recruited law students, lawyers and religious figures to talk about the unjust laws in Saudi Arabia. The Saudis asked the Sudanese to make him be quiet. They said he could stay, but no jihad. He ignored them. The Saudis went to Bakar, his oldest brother, and told him to stop Osama, or they would freeze his money, end ties to the royal family, and confiscate their land. King Fahd sent Bakar to Khartoum to tell Osama to come back and they would make him the king's envoy for Islamic World Affairs—a new position.

For Osama it was not the life he was born to live. He was like a brother, quiet, humble and polite. His guards lived better than he did. He didn't have a refrigerator. He gave out money without counting it. He formed an Advisory Board in Saudi Arabia and sent a man from there to Yemen. He started a youth organization that was behind the Khobar Towers explosion.

In 2015, the U.S. and Saudi Arabia would announce the arrest of Ahmed al-Mughassil, tied to Hezbollah, as the mastermind. Al-Fadhli said al-Qaeda in Saudi Arabia was behind the attack.[354]

Osama had good relations with the Arab intelligence services, and with the Europeans, until he decided to fight on his own, then the Europeans left. He shook his head in disgust.

How did he and bin Laden become friends? When Osama's father went, as a young man, from Hadramaut to Saudi Arabia he took a boat along the coast. They reached Shuqrah, where his uncle, Saleh al-Fadhli, was in charge. They had to pay a fee of two qersh to pass. It was nothing, but bin Laden had no money. He said let us go and they would send him the money. His uncle said no. Bin Laden's friend returned to get the money and bin Laden stayed for two days with al-Fadhli, who lavished his hospitality on him. The man returned with the money and they left.

After many years bin Laden became rich. Al-Fadhli's father and brothers went to Saudi Arabia. Bin Laden's father and other wealthy Yemenis invited them to lunch. Where was this man who stopped him for two qersh, bin Laden asked? Al Fadhli's father pointed to his brother. Bin Laden went over and hugged him. "Osama said to everyone, they must never treat Tariq al-Fadhli badly. Even if he drank and smoked, they were to treat him well. It was in his will," Nasrin said.

Eleven men now, their mouths filled with qat, like cows chewing their cud, listened. Why did he go to Afghanistan? There was a picture on the wall of him in shalwar kameez holding a rifle. He went from Saudi Arabia to fight jihad. The Saudis were, even today, the biggest suppliers of mujahideen in the world. The government recruited them through the mosques. He spent three years in Khost, first at Jihadwal,[355] run by Haqqani, the sheikh on both sides of the border. Everyone liked him. It was where Osama and his men separated from others, and where al-Qaeda was born. Wahhabis from Saudi Arabia taught them. The first group would go to South Yemen.

---

[354] "Saudi Arabia Said to Arrest Suspect in 1996 Khobar Towers Bombing," *New York Times*, 26 Aug., 2015
[355] Hamid and Farrall, *"The Arabs at War in Afghanistan,"* 134

They trained in Haqqani's camp but Abdullah Azzam was in charge. Osama became the main supplier of money, and arms. When they left, in 1990, Osama went to Saudi Arabia, and then to Sudan. Omar Bashir[356] was in power. U.S. Forces were in Saudi Arabia. The Saudis invited infidel troops into the land of the two holy cities, against the Koran. Osama was angry. The Mujahideen, in every country, who went to Afghanistan, became then the enemy of Saudi Arabia. It was destroying all they fought for. It was enemy number one today. Yes, he said, lighting another cigarette. In 1992, U.S. Forces came to Aden to go to Somalia. The rumor was the U.S. would transfer its base in the Philippines to here. The Mujahideen were going to attack their hotels and their planes at the airport. The U.S. got word and left three hours before. They hit the Gold Mohur hotel. He was with al-Kurdi. It was the first Mujahideen operation in Yemen. He was in prison in 1993 and 1994 for this attack, and for attacking the Socialists.

Al-Fadhli put his hand on my shoulder. Osama's plan was to fight the communist and socialist forces of South Yemen, then the Imperialists, and then the Zionists. He would use Sudan as his base, but the Saudis, and the Americans, put pressure on the government. In 1996, he tried to create a new group with Jalaluddin, who was in Sudan, with Omar Abdur Rahman of the Islamic Somali Union. He, al-Fadhli was there. Osama was planning to bring weapons from Somalia, whose army then was supplied by the Soviet Union, to Yemen.[357] Al-Fadhli, Haqqani and bin Laden had dinner. The Taliban were about to take Kabul. Osama did not know them and he asked Haqqani who were these people. If they were good then they should ask them to join them. He asked Haqqani to go talk to Mullah Omar, and to give him a report. He sent an envoy with Haqqani to say that he would return to Afghanistan, but they had to protect him. He could help them get rid of Ahmed Shah Massoud who was working with French intelligence.

Jalaluddin returned to Afghanistan and met with Mullah Omar. He sent a message to Osama. If he returned, they would protect him and fight for him as if they were fighting for their women and children. The Sudanese government was coming under more pressure from the Americans and the Saudis to arrest them. Bin Laden flew from Khartoum to Qatar, if he remembered correctly, and then to Kandahar.

---

[356] "Omar Al-Bashir: Sudan's Ousted President," *BBC News*, 14 Aug. 2019
[357] Hamid and Farrall, *"The Arabs at War in Afghanistan,"*187

I heard that he flew to Jalalabad and stayed near Yunus Khalis. Ah, al-Fadhli smiled. Yunus Khalis was a good man. At the beginning al-Qaeda was small, a simple people's movement. Ayman al-Zawahiri was the leader now. Al-Fadhli looked at me hard. He never met him but he didn't like him. The Egyptians surrounded Osama and kept others away. The Egyptians were good talkers. In 1994, there was a war between North and South and he joined Selah.

He didn't say that Saleh freed him from prison, coopting the heir to the Fadhli Sultanate,[358] as he did al-Kurdi.

Yes, they called his father the Sultan. His family ruled for, oh, 700 years or more, he waved his arm back. It was not good to say Sultan in the 1990s. Communists, socialists, and Islamists were fighting for power. The communists and the socialists confiscated his land. He wanted to fight them in Afghanistan and here. The British exiled his grandfather to India, and his uncle to Tanzania. He liked the name Zanzibar and named a town Zinjubar in Abyan.

From 1990-1994 Abyan was under al-Fadhli's control. He, meaning al-Qaeda, joined Saleh to fight the Socialist South. The civil war ended. The government created groups of men to fight. They wanted to fight Christians, but there were no Christians, Abu Ali al-Harethi represented Osama here. He took part in the U.S.S. Cole operation. In 1997, Abu Hassin al-Mihdar created the Army of Abyan,[359] and demanded that all foreigners leave the Arabian Peninsula. Al-Fadhli was the mediator between Hassin and Selah. Christmas 1998 Hassin kidnapped 16 tourists. The Yemeni Army attacked him too soon. Four tourists were killed. Selah asked al-Fadhli to ask al-Qaeda to stop all attacks, but the new generation of al-Qaeda wouldn't listen to him.

Abu Hassin al-Mihdar, the nom de guerre of Zain Abdain al-Mihdar, also fought in Afghanistan. The tourists were killed in the crossfire when the army tried to rescue them. Saleh, supposedly, executed him in 1999. A year later, almost to the day, the Aden-Abyan Islamic Army attacked the U.S.S. Cole.[360] When Osama returned to Afghanistan in 1996, he had a worldwide

---

[358] https://en.wikipedia.org/ wiki/ Fadhli_Sultanate
[359] Aden-Abyan Islamic Army.
[360] "War to Crush Terrorist Group May Have Set Stage for Cole Attack," *Los*

organization. Al-Fadhli knew this organization, but who knew the new one? He returned to Afghanistan to see Osama to clear up some matters. Osama's most important contribution to the Taliban was giving $3 million to a commander to open the southern route to Kabul. There was an alliance between him and Mullah Omar. Jalaluddin engineered their relationship.

What led him to Afghanistan? Was it because the Communists took his land, or Zindani's speeches? He shook his head. His brother was in the U.S. studying in Texas and went to meetings at the Islamic Youth Union. Their family was living in Jeddah, and his brother came home to visit. They lived there since 1967 after the Marxists came to power in the South. They weren't religious, but his brother was. He was planning to go to Cypress on vacation, and his brother asked why didn't he go to Afghanistan? He felt something.

He was standing when he said this and moved his body. He went to mosques and listened to sermons and lectures. He went to a shop to buy a cassette of a lecture and saw a sign. "We can give you free tickets to Afghanistan and $200-$300 expense money to go to the Arab Services Bureau, run by Abdullah Azzam." It was signed by Prince Salman, the Crown Prince. He decided to go. There was a movement for Jihad all around the world. The office in Saudi Arabia that sent men was the same one that sent men to Chechnya, to Bosnia, to Iraq, and now to Syria. The Mujahideen always came from Saudi Arabia. Today there was an air bridge from Yemen to Turkey to Syria. A Turkish Airlines flight left every morning at 2:30 for Istanbul. The Mujahideen had no borders. Already 350 had taken smuggling routes or waterways from here to Eritrea, to Ethiopia across Africa to Mali.

I saw the departure time, when I arrived, listed at the airport.

Was there a route from Afghanistan and Pakistan? Were al-Zawahiri and Haqqani involved? They came by boat. Osama paid for this before. Now funds came from women in Saudi Arabia who collected "*zakat.*" It was a 10% tax on earnings that Muslims were to set aside once a year to help the poor. People gave donations in mosques. Al-Qaeda made money from kidnappings and robbing banks. Dr. Al-Eryani told me that they had $35 million from kidnappings. Al-Fadhli was the mediator between al-Qaeda and the Saudis for the eleven al-Qaida women in a Saudi prison. Luke Somers, I felt, would survive.

The mosques arranged the travel for the Mujahideen, even in America. If he wanted to go, and had no money, they could provide the documents. There were many involved, Sufis, Salafis, Tablighlis. Al-Qaeda was the main party. How could this land bridge exist? He put one hand over one eye. Governments turned a blind eye. It was a way for them to get money from America. This had been the plan since the time of Osama. Saleh, Ali Mohsen, al- Hamdi[361] all closed one eye. Who was al-Qaeda? They knew all of them. They kept them for the future. In 1996, Osama told Selah he wanted to open a front along the Saudi border and to put a radio station there. He would pay the entire Yemeni budget for three years. Selah panicked. Saudi Arabia had spies in the government. The Mujahideen come from Pakistan through Eritrea. This fit with al-Eryani's story about the sheep. The government gave them papers.

America's big mistake, to the benefit of Jalaluddin, was to leave everything in place in Pakistan.

After jihad, the Algerians and the Egyptians could not go home. Some went to Bosnia. Peace in Pakistan meant peace in the Arab world. The Pakistani army was close to the Saudi army. He put his fingers of his two hands together. Saudi Arabia was considered the bomb maker of Pakistan. If Iran developed a nuclear bomb, Pakistan would help Saudi Arabia build one.

Al-Qaeda was growing. The headquarters were on the border of Shabwah and Abyan governorates. In one place there were only ten meters between al- Qaeda and the People's Committee. If they wanted onions, they had to go from one side to the next. Ahmed, Maher and Wahid said this. Al-Fahdli was under house arrest. He refused to fight *Ansar-al-Sharia.*[362] He would not fight his own tribe, he said sternly. He meant al-Qaeda.

We left at night, the warm night air caressing and the moon bright on the water. Three days later, we returned. The room was filled with men chewing gat, smoking, and laughing. His wife had a baby. He had twenty children now, 11 sons and nine daughters. He named his son Athoa Khattab, after a

[361]Clark, "*Yemen: Dancing on the Heads of Snakes,*"104-08
[362] Murad Batal al-Shishani, "Profile: Yemen's Ansar al-Sharia." *BBC News* 18 Mar. 2012

Saudi friend, a member of al-Qaeda killed in Chechnya.[363] Al-Fadhli's
father had 37 children. He had 17 to go. His eldest child was maybe 24,
studying business administration at American University in Beirut. He
wanted her to be a diplomat and a politician, and to teach him about politics.
He would have her marry an American.

We rode along the water, placid like a lake. I thought of what al-Fadhli
said about men travelling from Pakistan to Eritrea and across Africa. When I
was beginning this project, I called a Pashtun I knew in the West. I will
call him Yasir. I asked him to find a man who would know about such
routes. He knew someone. I sent him a note asking him to meet me in one
week in Dubai.

I saw al-Kurdi again. He gave me a letter, with a stamp, thanking me for
my interest. It was too dangerous to work with him. The next night, I went to
the airport. The 2:30 a.m. Turkish Airlines flight was the only one listed
after mine. Karim and a friend of his met me at the airport in Sanaá.

---

[363] *Wikipedia* 23 May 2022, https://en.wikipedia.org/wiki/Ibn_al-Khattab.

The Foreign Minister

It was a cold winter morning. Abu Bark al-Qirbi, the foreign minister, wore a gray thobe, with cufflinks, and sandals, a large ring on his left hand and a big black watch with a thick tan leather band. His office in back of his compound was cold. A servant poured tea from a thermos.

What created an image of a country, he asked? What was portrayed abroad was different from the reality. Even before al-Qaida there were elements of this image because of Osama bin Laden. He lived in Saudi Arabia, but the origins of his family were here. Therefore, Yemen came to be seen as where al-Qaeda originated. The Western media, because it did not or had not investigated this faithfully, perpetuated this myth.

I had read many times that al-Qaeda began in Peshawar as the Soviet war ended. Al-Fadhli said Wahhabis taught them near Miram Shah, which meant the Tribal Areas, where the Political Officer, a position created by the British, for each Area knew everything that happened. My jailer told me that the political officer had come to see him, meaning that Pakistan knew about my kidnapping. I kept thinking that General Zia told the Arab Afghans to fight in their own countries. Taher said al-Qaeda began in Saudi Arabia. Al-Fadhli said Pakistan and Saudi Arabia were as close as two fingers together.

If a terrorist undertook an attack the worst thing to say was that all Yemenis were like this, said al-Qirbi. This provoked people and they sympathized with the people because they'd been accused wrongly. Bin Laden was reported to have said that Yemen could be their haven. Elements of al-Qaeda did come here because of the conflicts, the instability, the lawlessness, and the poverty. The Arab Spring led to the rise of al-Qaeda. It gained power because of the U.S. invasion of Iraq against Saddam Hussein and the West's actions against Col. Muammar Gaddafi in Libya. Al-Qaeda was a movement that was against U.S. hegemony, and Israel, and it wanted Sharia. Many people supported them because of this, especially in the rural more religious areas. Yemen had not developed an effective counterstrategy, but saw them as outlaws, and had not looked hard at their ideology. The drones and collateral damage were helping them. Other countries in the region, because of poverty, poor governance and corruption helped al-Qaeda recruitment. The Arab Spring occurred but the economic situation was worse here than before, as elsewhere. Look at Egypt, or the military budgets of the U.S., Europe and the Gulf countries. They didn't invest in schools or hospitals here. The Shia-Sunni conflict, which began with the U.S. occupation of Iraq, would get worse.

A wall was filled with photographs of him with Arab leaders, George W. Bush, and Pope John Paul. There was a prayer mat by the door.

Al-Qaeda thought it was autonomous, but its communications were under constant surveillance. It was only one group of many, which were linked. Al- Qaeda wanted to show that it existed, period. If oil companies stopped drilling, or if visas became hard to get, they considered this a success. It was sad that a Yemeni businessman or student was deprived of a visa somewhere because of something al-Qaeda did. Yes, refugees were coming from the Horn of Africa, and there were fighters among them. Yemen had a 1,600-kilometer (1000-mile) border from Bab al Mandab to Oman. There were good trade relations between Yemen and Pakistan. Yemen exported most of its honey to the Gulf, so it was possible that honey came in from Pakistan.

In 1994 when the Mujahideen were coming back from Afghanistan these elements had a dialogue with the government, and some were rehabilitated. There were ties between Ali Mohsen and Tariq al-Fadhli. They maintained them in order to keep track of al-Qaida, and to try to contain it. Mohsen subsequently married al-Fadhli's sister. Since 2009, the government was more occupied with internal politics and al-Qaeda was able to regroup. I was wrong to say that the previous regime-controlled al-Qaeda. As for the attack on the hospital at the Ministry of Defense, until they had finished their investigation and had the DNA results, they could not rely upon ID cards to say who was responsible. The militants coming in were Pakistanis and Saudis in al-Qaida, but the total number was a few thousand. Yemen was located at the door to the Red Sea along oil shipping lanes. It was an uphill battle to improve its image. If Yemen's partners could reverse the policies on travel visas and investment, it would help. I had traveled the country, he said, and knew that it was not as bad as it was portrayed.

I made numerous calls to Ghaleb Saeed al-Adoofi, a recent ambassador to Pakistan, number two in the Foreign Ministry. Finally, he agreed to see me. Zarb gave me Zindani's number. I called him many times. An assistant said he would see me if he could send a message to the West. I would write what he said. That afternoon the CALES accountant said I was late in paying him. I paid him the next morning, but he was surly. The director came to my room and again said I was drawing attention here.

Zindani asked me to send a list of questions. I sent them, related to his interest in medicine and scientific proofs in Islam, said I had seen Yunus Khalis, the only Westerner to see him. He had fought the good fight and his jihad was over. Did he feel that he had fought the good fight for Islam, or was there more work to do? He agreed to see me. Al-Adoofi's assistant called to say that he couldn't see me now. I persisted and he arranged another time. I bought a plane ticket to Dubai. As soon I met with him and Zindani I would leave. I did not try to reach Saleh or Ali Mohsen. An Irish journalist was in a taxi when a motorcyclist shot at her but missed.

That evening, al-Adoofi's assistant cancelled our meeting. The next day Zindani's assistant called to say that he was sick. Karim said something was up. Ahmed, a driver, and I left before dawn. As we passed the bakery, I looked for the boy but he wasn't there. At the airport, an official saw my new visa. Why was I leaving?

Dubai

The next morning, I waited in a hotel lobby in Dubai, filled with Arabs, Europeans, and Russians on vacation. Yasir arrived with Hassan, a short, pudgy man with a moustache and gray black hair. We sat in a corner. Yasir wanted to take care of money. Hassan said he was afraid of me. Hassan opened a notebook to a photograph of Masood Azhar, the head of *Jaish-e-Mohammad* (Mohammad's Army), a Pakistani jihadi group, in a black turban, wire-rimmed glasses, and a black beard. He showed photos of other men, a map of the Tribal Areas, a stone house, a white car, and motorcycles outside.

A page was titled: "Rout map of Al-Qaeda fighters come and go from Waziristan to Syria and Egypt." It was a list of links among the jihadi groups of Pakistan with those in the Middle East, and the routes that Al-Qaeda, the Taliban and these groups took from the Tribal Areas abroad, and back. He showed base camps, training camps, hideouts, safe houses, and the routes men took to Islamabad and Karachi, where men received them and sent them on. Was this all true? Wasn't it dangerous to gather this? He, unlike Yasir, didn't want money, only his plane fare. He was a researcher. The groups he profiled were run, worldwide, from eight divisions of the ISI, each run by a major general. Another general controlled the Haqqanis, who were separate. He showed where the core al-Qaeda lived,[364] south of Peshawar, in the Frontier Regions, between the Tribal Areas, and Pakistan proper.

They went to Rawalpindi and to Islamabad to the Khalid bin Waleed seminary in Ghorhra Mor, run by Maulana Khalil Fazal-Rahman Khalil, founder of *Ansar-ul-Ummah* (Supporters of the Ummah). He was the main fundraiser for Al-Qaeda and the Taliban in the Middle East, especially in Saudi Arabia. He worked with Nasiruddin Haqqani, the main Haqqani fundraiser.

---

[364] In 2017, the government of Pakistan would merge these areas into Khyber Paktunkhawa, what the British called the Northwest Frontier Province, today officially part of Pakistan.

Three months before, Nasiruddin, Jalaluddin's eldest son,[365] was shot leaving a bakery in Islamabad. A jeep drove up and took him away. Either the NDS,[366] the ISI, or the CIA killed him, but he didn't know why.

The second route was from Kohat to Dera Ismail Khan via Lakki Marwat, near Peshawar, to the Settled Areas and on to the Punjab, Pakistani's largest province. There they met the jihadi groups and the leaders of *Sipah-e-Sahaba Pakistan*, (SSP)[187] an anti-Shia group formed in the 1980s to oppose wealthy Shia landlords and to counter rising Iranian influence.[367] Lashkar-Jhangvi (Jhangvi's militia) was a splinter group. Jaish-e-Mohammad provided logistical support and sent men to Karachi. The Shia were working with Sunnis while Iran and Saudi Arabia were trying to use and divide them in Iraq and Syria. Ansar-ul-Ummah headquarters was in the SITE area, Karachi.[368] Jaish-e-Mohammad and Arab intelligence agencies provided travel expenses, documents and guidance. One page listed hideouts in Karachi—in a Pashtun area controlled by drug and land mafias, arms smugglers, and the Teerek-e-Taliban (TTP), the Taliban movement of Pakistan.[369] The list went on detail.

Routes went from Jani Khel, Mirali and the Shawal valley, in North Waziristan, south to Baluchistan, the province below Afghanistan. He listed where the hideouts were. He showed the routes from Karachi to Quetta and across Baluchistan to Iran. The groups provided travel documents and paid the human smugglers. They crossed the Iranian border at Tafton and Mashkel and went by car, bus, and on foot, staying in safe houses, across Iran to Turkey, to safe houses, from which they went to Iraq, Syria and Egypt. One page, titled "Afghanistan and Pakistan to al-Qaeda in the Sinai Peninsula and the Maghreb (North Africa)," listed routes under the direction of Ayman al-Zawahiri that went to his brother, Mohammad in prison in Egypt. Another showed the link among the TTP, Lashkar Jhangvi International, the Muslim Brotherhood, and al-Shabab in Somalia. A listing,

---

[365] M. Ilyas Khan, "Nasiruddin Haqqani: Who Shot the Militant at the Bakery?" *BBC News* 12 Nov. 2013

[366] National Directorate of Security, Afghanistan's intelligence agency.

[367] Army of the Companions of the Holy Prophet.

[368] https://wordpress.com/id/. Sindh Industrial Trading Estate, built in 1947, after partition, to create an industrial base in Pakistan.

[369] The Tahreek-e-Taliban (Taliban Movement of Pakistan) kidnapped the author in 2008.

"Pakistan to Syria to the Sinai Peninsula," was the link between al-Qaeda followers of bin Laden, and the Islamic Front and al-Nusra in Iraq. A fourth listing was a link among the TTP and ISIS. A fifth showed the link among Pakistani jihadi groups the Abdullah Azzam Shaheed (Martyrs) Brigade in Syria. The final alliance was among the Punjabi Taliban, Jaesh-e-Mohammad, and numerous other groups in the Middle East.

London

Abdullah Anas wore dark slacks, a gray cashmere sweater, and a dark tweed sport coat. The restaurant was empty, except for one table with four people. We sat in a corner. I said I had been in Yemen. I met a man, Tariq al-Fadhli, who said he knew him.

Was he Yemeni? His eyes were bright. Where did they meet, in Peshawar with Abdullah Azzam, or in Afghanistan? I didn't know. He founded al-Qaeda in Yemen. Did I have a picture? No, but one of my fixers did. He didn't trust anyone who was there after the Soviets left. Those who came later weren't waging real jihad. He said he was with bin Laden in Sudan. Abdullah asked if he knew him there. I didn't know that Anas was there also. There was another man, I added, Ali al-Kurdi, involved in the attacks in Aden in 1992, and on the USS Cole. He was al-Qaeda and worked with Ali Abdullah Saleh. I met him a second time and we talked about Abdul Latif and the People's Committees. He said he could make one call and Latif would be dead.

Anas turned his head in dismay. Was this jihad? No, it was gang warfare. Did he know anyone in Egypt? No, everything was ruined. The Ikhwan were destroyed.

Egypt

We came down over the desert, and the wind buffeted us, and then lights appeared in a haze. The dust cleared and Cairo, a vast lighted oasis, the cultural and intellectual capital of the Arab world, appeared.

The next morning, I walked along the Nile and watched two women, in hijabs, rowing in a skull. Then four women came, in hijabs. Garbage pushed up against the land. I was in Zamalek, an upscale island, and diplomatic enclave. I passed garbage, cats foraging for food, women in black tights and hijabs, and men in jeans and t-shirts. I ate in a café where men and women smoked shishas. Men in sunglasses walked with women in tight jeans like couples in Paris.

At my hotel I asked a clerk for my key, in Arabic. He said I must learn Egyptian. A Malaysian at CALES said what he learned here in school and heard on the streets were different languages.

There were large pictures in store windows of a young General Abdul Fattah el-Sisi. In 2012, Mohamed Morsi, of the Ikhwan, was elected President. He appointed el-Sisi, who portrayed himself as religious, like Zia ul-Haq, in Pakistan, to be commander-in-chief of the armed forces. In 2013, el-Sisi, like Zia, mounted a coup against the man who appointed him, and threw him in prison.

The muezzin's call to Maghrib, the sunset prayer, came, a sacred sound over a world of black tights and cigarettes. That night I talked with an American journalist. He warned me that it was a crime to talk to an Islamist. He had seen the Al Jazeera journalists in prison.[370] I didn't want to go there, he said. The Bush Administration sent Muslim captives to Egyptian prisons. Later, I stood outside my hotel. At 10 p.m., an hour late, a pretty woman in a gray skirt, black stocking, gray cape, a large diamond ring, approached. Her name was Sara. We walked down the street and then a path to a large white tent. Inside was a restaurant with waiters in dark suits, and a man in a tuxedo at a white grand piano. She took off her coat. She wore a sleeveless dress.

---

[370] "2013–2015 Detention of Al Jazeera Journalists by Egypt," *Wikipedia* 13 May 2022, Jazeera_journalists_by_Egypt.

Nearby were two Western men in suits, a blond-haired woman in a short, black leather skirt, and two bottles of whiskey on the table. At 10:30 a woman joined us, and at 11 p.m. another, wearing a necklace with a cross. It was Thursday and people stayed up late, said Sara, a friend of a friend in London. One woman was born in Baghdad of a Spanish mother and Egyptian father and brought up Catholic. Her husband died and she ran his company. The third woman was an artist.

Sara was born in the U.S. to an Egyptian father, pursuing a PhD in marine biology, and an American mother. They went to Washington, D.C., to the only mosque in America, to be married. Maybe one percent of the population drank, she said. There were no gangs, no drugs, and no pornography here. As a result, there was little crime. She felt safer here than in L.A. What about the coup against Morsi? It wasn't a coup, she said sharply. They hated the Ikhwan. The dinner went downhill from there. The next night I opened a heavy wood door to a small restaurant. The bartender asked who I was meeting. I said the artist's name. He checked a clipboard and found her name. I could stay. I ordered 7-Up. A man next to me was drinking Sangria. She was 90 minutes late. The traffic was terrible. She said there were other places like this where Christians could meet in safety. When I returned to my hotel there was a note from Abdullah, with the Foreign Ministry, in Sanaá.

Regarding the Haqqanis, they had found that honey dealers were driving expensive new Toyotas and changing them frequently. Since 2011, there were more car dealerships, an indication of a new money-laundering track.

Cairo had over 20 million people, the third largest Muslim city in the world. People came here to get away from their tribes and villages.[371] The next day I followed a street to a dirt alley, passed cars on cement blocks, garbage, and skinny cats. Two men sat in the shade drinking tea. An imam was chanting on a radio. I followed the path deeper into a labyrinth, past small posters of Mohamed Morsi on the walls. Two boys played with a ragged soccer ball. I reached a dead end and a woman in an abaya smiled and told me which way to go. I crossed through traffic to the Egyptian Museum, surrounded by barbwire. Two men with German shepherds rushed

---

[371] "Cairo Population 2022" (*Demographics, Maps, Graphs*), https://worldpopulation review.com/world-cities/cairo-population

over. A man took my pen and studied it. Another frisked me. I passed a row of armored personnel carriers and soldiers behind machine guns, black buses, and men in black boots, stood in a line and went through a scanning machine. A guard frisked me. I bought a ticket, walked through a metal detector, and another guard frisked me.

The Egyptian Museum was dimly lit, dusty, filled with statues, intricately crafted jewelry, a gold painted chariot, coffins and sarcophagi, a memorial to the preparations for the afterlife. A man shined a light on a mummy, and children crowded around. Ancient Egyptians believed in Ra, the Sun God. They lived for 35 years on average, and then there was eternity. Soon ISIS would behead 21 Egyptian laborers on a beach in Libya because they were Christians. Both Christians and Muslims believed in Heaven and Hell and hated one another. How familiar the face looked of a woman on a coffin with a modern haircut, and light brown eyes.

The Iranian Connection

The next day my taxi stopped at a building near Tahrir (Liberty) Square where in 2011 students and graduates began the Arab Spring. The drive turned the meter off before I could look at it. I took out money and he tried to grab a bill. Inside, the lobby was dark, and a guard refused to let me go upstairs. I called and handed him the phone. He mumbled and pounded on the elevator buttons. We creaked upwards. A woman in a hijab took me to an office overlooking the Nile. He wore a gray suit, dark tie, a pink shirt with monographed cufflinks. There were bookshelves, and a map of Israel on the wall. His card said al-Ahram.[372]

He worked for the government paper, and for the Iranian channel?

He was a journalist. His job was to transfer the truth to the people. If some said there was a revolution, he passed it on, or if it was a coup. Egypt was suffering from a crisis, political and economic. He said on television they must solve this in a political way, not by tanks. The military was the political authority now, and they only followed one way. There were demonstrations. Some were the Ikhwan, some were opposed to them, and some were afraid of the army. I thought of my dinner with the upscale women. "Hysteria," the American called it. "The rich were happy to see Mubarak fall, gleefully watched the Brotherhood get gunned down in the streets, and now they supported a military government. Liberals," he said with disgust, drawing on a cigarette.

Half the population supported the army and the other half supported the Ikhwan. More than half were against the coup. After the military took over people thought the problems would be solved. Since then, many had been arrested, and killed. There was anger here, fear, and danger. The two powers were the military, and the Islamic movement. Neither side could destroy the other. Saudi Arabia and the Gulf states supported the military against the republican populism of the Ikhwan. They had no moral authority, only the power of money, which was considerable. If Morsi had more time the Ikhwan would have succeeded. The army realized this. He made mistakes,

---

[372] "The Pyramids," founded in 1875.

but he compromised, and kept ties with Israel. When it attacked Hamas[373] he sent his prime minister to Gaza, contacted U.S. officials, and solved everything in three days. He wanted to do what was best for Egypt, and to avoid another war between Hamas and Israel, which was afraid of Islamic movements. The Western media did not understand the Ikhwan. The West was against Islam.

I looked at the map of Israel. There women wore bikinis, and others covered their heads.

The difference between al-Qaeda and the Ikhwan was that the Ikhwan was a major political party opposed to violence. The Western media put all the Islamic groups into one package. But Morsi appointed as the governor of Luxor the man who was responsible for the 1997 attack on the tourists, I said, referring to The Islamic Group[374] and al-Zawahiri's Egyptian Islamic Jihad. They killed 57 people including an eight-year-old boy. All of them were against terrorism now, he replied. It was perverse to put a mass murderer in charge of a world-famous tourist site. The Western media never called a Western military attack a Christian attack or an Israeli attack a Jewish attack, but here they did, he replied again.

He was involved, I heard, in bringing Iran and Egypt together. Yes, Morsi reached out to have normal, not special, ties. He supported the Syrian people against Assad. Iranian tourists came here and Egypt traded with Iran. Now, under the military, that had stopped. But Egypt was Sunni and Iran was Shia. He agreed, but the Ikhwan did not have any problems with the Shia. The Saudis did because scholars and sheikhs there issued fatwas[375] saying the Shia were not Muslims. The Saudis supported the Ikhwan in Syria and opposed them here.

---

[373] Hamas ("zeal" in Arabic) acronym for Harakut al-Muqawamah al Islamiyyah (Islamic Resistance Movement).
[374] Al Gamm'a-al-Islamiyya
[375] A written religious or judicial sentence pronounced by the Caliph, a mufti, or a qazi (judge).

The House of Knowledge

The Nile was low in early March. I sat in a waiting room and watched it flow by. According to the Egyptian Gazette, founded in 1880, Egypt was running out of water because the Nile was so polluted. There was photograph of a man standing in the river gathering water in a jug next to a dead donkey. Over 85% of the water was used for agriculture. An air-conditioner purred loudly, like an old car engine. It said "Power USA." It was the real power here, people said.

Two young men sat at metal desks staring at their computers. I sat next to a man in a blue blazer, slacks, shirt, and tie, who had come before me. Forty minutes later a man walked by. The young men stood and said I could go in. It was the power of the West. I walked through two rooms, past a large table filled with books to the office of Dr. Hassan Abu Taleb a thin gray-haired man in a dark suit, and suspenders. He was chairman of the board of the House of Knowledge,[376] one of the oldest printing houses in the Arab world. 2021 would be their 110th year. Yes, Cairo was the intellectual center of the Arab world. He placed his hand on his chest. It was the heart of it. When the people rose up against the Ikhwan this spilled over into the rest of the Arab world. It was a model of peaceful change drawing on the diversity and energy of the masses hoping for a new outlook and a new symbol of Egypt. If you asked the poor who represented Egypt, they said Nasser or Sadat. Nasser took care of the poor, and the middle class. Even Sadat, with his win in 1973 over Israel, was loved.

On Yom Kippur, the Day of Atonement, the holiest day in Judaism, Egypt attacked Israel, and broke through its defenses, but Israel fought back and surrounded the Egyptian First Army. The U.S. intervened and prevented the army from being crushed.

The common people looked to el-Sisi, who loved Egypt, to protect them, said Taleb. Morsi said the Ikhwan was his family, and his tribe. Yes, Nasser imprisoned, tortured, and killed them giving rise to a hardened, survivor, mentality, but Morsi chose the Ikhwan over the people.

---

[376] Dar al-Marrif.

Ibn Khaldun[377] (1332-1406), an historian, wrote that *asabiyya*, (family spirit), which Mohammad opposed because the Umma was more important than the family, was the fundamental bond of human society.[378] The preferred marriage in Arab culture was that between cousins because it meant all the children were of the same family, which made it larger, more powerful, more prestigious, and more honorable. Al-Qaeda was a family. So were the Haqqanis. Taleb was saying that the Ikhwan were not part of Egypt. When the French and the British ruled here, they looked down on the Egyptian elite, which looked down on the masses.[379] The elite knew that it had to learn from Europe. The masses saw the Europeans as modern Crusaders.

"From the time of the Prophet," wrote Bernard Lewis, "in the Muslim world, the definition of the Other, the alien, the presumptive enemy, was the *kafir*,"[380] the unbeliever.

The Ikhwan were trying to establish the Iranian model here. The real decision maker, like Khamenei in Iran, was the Supreme Guide. They used Molotov cocktails and shot officers of the police. What about the snipers shooting demonstrators, and the bodies which journalists found in hospital morgues? The army didn't kill anyone, Taleb insisted. Journalists lied. The Ikhwan were violent and the army had to defend itself. He was emotional, and his voice was loud.

The Egyptian National Human Rights Committee issued a report on Rab'a, a mosque where the Ikhwan gathered during the uprising, stating that the army was trapped inside, and that the Ikhwan fired on them. How many were killed? "561," Taleb replied, "Ikhwan? 336." He spoke softly. He needed to rest from shouting. He had many friends who were with the Ikhwan. He wanted them all to reconsider.

In August 2014, Human Rights Watch issued a report[381] stating that army and security forces systematically killed 1,150 people at Rabá.

---

[377] Hourani, *A History of the Arab Peoples*, 1-4
[378] Raphael Patai, "*The Arab Mind*" (New York: Charles Scribner's Sons, 1973), p. 92-93
[379] Ibid. 272-273
[380] Lewis, Bernard. "*The Political Language of Islam*" (The University of Chicago Press 2017 4-5
[381] "All According to Plan," *Human Rights Watch*, 24 May 2021, https://www.hrw. org/report/2014/08/12/all-according-plan/raba-massacre-and-mass-killings-protesters -egypt.

Al-Qaeda was in the Sinai, 23,500 square miles, a desert bordered on one side by the Suez Canal, on the other by the Red Sea, because of Morsi. They came in under him from Syria, Gaza, Afghanistan and Pakistan. They smuggled weapons from Libya, Iran and Sudan, but they were stopping them now. The Afghans and Pakistanis reflected the international slogan of al-Qaeda, which, like Hamas, considered Egypt the enemy, an extension of the West. Al-Qaeda came through the Sinai and the Ikhwan gave them money and visas. Al-Zawahiri wanted to create a caliphate here. When Morsi was in Pakistan he met with a representative of al-Zawahiri and invited him to return. He did not know there was a deep state, a strong media, a civil society. Western journalists looked at a lot of data, but it was like America collecting data about the Shah of Iran and not being able to see Khomeini coming.

Egypt worked with America in the 1980s sending men to Afghanistan, which led to al-Qaeda.

No, it was America, Pakistan, and Saudi Arabia. President Sadat knew these young men, after learning to fight, could cause trouble here. He would fight the Soviet Union diplomatically, he said. Under Mubarak, they banned travel to Afghanistan. Egypt backed the U.S. and some who went were Ikhwan. When they returned, they put 7,000 in prison. He helped to rehabilitate them. Some were involved in the plot to kill Sadat, others in the attack on the Swiss tourists. Assad, in Syria, used these men against the Americans in Iraq, and now he fought them in Syria. They would fight in Riyadh, Berlin, Paris and Doha. No one would know who the enemy was.

Egyptian Intelligence

Khalid Aharon, a retired two-star general, with the Mukhabarat, in a tailored gray suit, came quickly from behind his desk, stacked with papers. Two aides hovered. I was interested in Islamic fundamentalism, and how Egypt was coping. I meant radicalism, he said sharply. He would give me twenty minutes.

The West had abandoned them. The U.S. and the Europeans were not giving them the resources they needed to stamp it out. They didn't understand how important the battle was with the Ikhwan who had been killing them, and their youth, in the streets. They were fighting them in the Sinai. Egypt had purchased 21 Apache helicopters, but they were in the U.S. for maintenance. They were fighting the Ikhwan, the Pentagon said. U.S. Senators came to see him and people from the U.S. Embassy. The White House was against you they explained.

In 2012, when the Ikhwan won in a free election, I read that President Obama chose to work with them. Morsi gave 58 speeches the year he was in office and went on 18 trips abroad, he responded. Eighteen! Could I imagine? He made an agreement with the U.S. to protect Israel. The general rubbed his hand over his head and sighed.

The agreement was part of the 1978 Camp David Accords overseen by President Carter and signed by President Sadat and Israeli Prime Minister Menachem Begin.

Morsi was in power one year and three days.[382] He didn't run the whole country. In 2011, when Mubarak left office and before the Ikhwan came to power, the trans-Sahara pipeline that sent natural gas to Israel exploded 15 times. Egypt sold gas to Israel at a steep discount. He sighed. When Morsi was in power there was not one gas pipeline explosion. He left office on the 3rd of July. The next day, the pipeline exploded. He wanted to show the U.S. that once he was gone Israel would not be safe. When he was in office there was not a single missile attack from the Sinai or Gaza into Israel. He forced Hamas to sign an agreement to stop fighting, and Israel signed it. Morsi

---

[382] 6/30/12 – 7/3/13.

proved that he was working in America's interests. On July 5th, three missiles were launched from the Sinai into Israel. The message to the U.S. was "Please put us back into power." The pipeline exploded six more times. Israel took Egypt to court, in Geneva, because they signed a contract to provide natural gas and were not doing it. They gave it to Israel at $3 a barrel. It was $12 on the open market. He rubbed his head. It was part of the peace treaty.

Was al-Qaeda or the Taliban, here? There were three sectors: The first were those who fought in Afghanistan with the Taliban and who lived in the Peshawar area and were banned from returning. They were sentenced in court to prison. When Morsi came to power, he freed them. Egypt sent these men. An Egyptian businessman told me that planes were waiting at the airport to take them. No, they went to wage jihad on their own, poor men, or al-Qaeda, not the men who went in the 1980s. When they returned, they wanted to carry on their fight here, but Egypt didn't want that.

They went to the Sinai. There were about 3,500 who returned from fighting with the Taliban.

During the Arab Spring, Hamas and the Ikhwan went to the eight jails where these men were kept and freed 20,640 prisoners. The military put many back in prison, and some came on their own in exchange for a reduced sentence, but thousands were in hiding. There was another group, with men like Mohammed al-Zawahiri, Ayman's brother, who Morsi released from prison. After taking office, Rafaa el-Tahtawi, Morsi's chief of staff, asked him to sign a decree to free him. He signed it within an hour. El-Tahtawi called the prison director, asked for his fax number and sent him the decree. The director said he couldn't release him. El-Tahtawi sent a car to the prison and brought him to his office. They had tea then he took him down the hall to see the president. The army recorded everything.

Dr. Taleb said when Morsi was in Pakistan he talked to a representative of al-Zawahiri.

He smiled. Dr. Taleb was his friend. Egyptian intelligence monitored all al-Zawahiri's calls.

Ayman told Morsi he had to create a revolutionary guard like Iran and must use men from Afghanistan, Yemen, Somalia, Pakistan, and Palestine and to do this quickly. He needed an army that was loyal to him. Otherwise, the Egyptian army would go against him. Could I imagine, creating your own army? The military monitored Morsi's secret emails to the headquarters of the Muslim Brotherhood, in Germany. Yes, it was there. They monitored his communications with Iran, and Hamas. They gathered intelligence against Iran, and Ikhwan headquarters.

If Pakistan knew Morsi was talking with al-Zawahiri, then Pakistan was supporting al-Qaeda.

"Where did they find bin Laden?" he replied. Was Pakistan his enemy? It was not working for the interests of Egypt, or for others. They gave all this information to the C.I.A. The U.S. wanted to protect Israel above all. He and his colleagues felt it was the main reason it supported the Ikhwan, and to control Egypt. I asked about the Egyptian army major. It probably wasn't his real name. He would not be surprised to see the Taliban here. The radicals went to Sudan and from there crossed the border by camel. They smuggled arms in from Libya.

Al-Azhar and Walid of the Ikhwan

Al-Azhar,[383] founded in 975 as a Shia (Ismaili) seminary, became in the 12th Century, under Saladin, the chivalrous, religious Kurd, who defeated the Crusaders, the center of Islamic learning.[384]

The lobby of the administrative center with small with carved wood chairs, a dome ceiling and narrow bronze chandeliers, bare walls and a velvet rope attached to shining brass stands leading to an auditorium. There was to be no sign of any human form, no music, no liturgy in a mosque, only calligraphy, the art form of sacred texts, in Islam. A man with sandy hair in a gray suit came from behind the ropes. I explained why I was here and wanted to see the Grand Mufti.[385] He read my card. Someone would contact me.

I walked back down the hill, past dormitories, and students in white skull caps to Old Cairo, and its ancient mosques. A hustler, about 40, approached, spoke in Arabic, switched to English and pointed to a stand with small boxes and trinkets. They were not good quality. I waited, tired of being told that it was Obama's fault that the Ikhwan came to power, and that the tourists no longer came. Secular Cairo could not accept that the Ikhwan gained seats in the 2005 parliamentary elections,[386] or that Morsi was elected.[387] We walked down winding dirt allies to his shop where he made real boxes everything natural. Two boys, about 14, with chisels stood at a work bench. One showed me a small box inlaid with Mother of Pearl, and other boxes. The man asked if I wanted tea.

A man in his late 30s with a shaved head in a light gray suit came and stood eating spaghetti from a plastic container. I should talk to him, said the owner. He was Ikhwan. Was the army looking for him? Yes, but he wasn't

---

[383] "Al Azhar University," *Al-Azhar University*, http://www.azhar.edu.eg/en/
[384] *The Cambridge History of Islam: the Central Islamic Lands* (205) states that it started in 971. The Al Azhar website says 975.
[385] "Hadd," *Oxford Islamic Studies Online*, http://www.oxfordislamicstudies.com/article/opr/t125/e757.
[386] "Muslim Brotherhood and Egypt's Parliamentary Elections," *Council on Foreign Relations*
[387] *Final Report of the Carter Center Mission to Witness the 2011–2012*

afraid. His name was Walid. He quit his job teaching. They took the money and changed the management. It was a well-known school, owned by the Ikhwan. He found a new place to live. He expected to be arrested at any moment. He looked down the alley. He had a wife, two girls and a boy. They were with his family. He would stay and keep fighting for legitimacy. They were trying to improve the country. President Morsi said if they wanted Egypt to become important, they had to produce their own food, medicine and arms. Since the time of Nasser, Egypt had failed at everything, even football.

There were paintings of boys playing with a ball in Pharaonic times.

Egypt was supposed to be an agricultural country yet they couldn't produce enough food. They couldn't make a single tractor. Why was I here? I was at Al-Azhar. I had to be careful, they twisted their words. Morsi had problems because they, and the military, the security people, and businesses, were against him. Hassan al-Banna tried to work with al-Azhar but got nowhere.

The Ikhwan drew their strength, and the army recruited, from villages along the Nile. Herodotus called Egypt "the gift of the Nile." It was over 3000 miles long and brought rich silt down from equatorial Africa through the desert. It was Egypt's mother (masra), its life's blood, like the Indus in Pakistan. Taxi drivers said I was in "*um al-duniya*," the mother of the world. Walid finished eating and leaned against the wall. There were one million members of the Ikhwan and two to three million behind them. It took six to seven years to become a member. He joined because al-Banna had a vision to teach the world about Islam and to fix humans, not by war, not by beating people, but through a relationship between the people and God. They wanted to make the land fertile. The Koran said we were in the desert, and we must build a good building. He went to the mosque and men talked to him about brotherhood where you were more than friends. They were a family. They helped one another, and they loved Egypt. They were ready to die for the ideas of Hassan al-Banna, who said their goal was God, their leader was Mohammed, and the Koran was their way. It was their constitution. Their way was legal jihad, defense, and to die for God. That was the most beautiful thing that he could think of. He dreamed to die for God. He was ready to become a martyr.

Was he afraid? Yes, but he went here, he went there, he lived his life. If he wasn't afraid, he wouldn't be human.

There were over 20,000 people in detention centers and prisons in Egypt. The cells were filled with students who called for revolution, like students in Yemen in 2011, in Paris in 1968, and some in America. When Thomas Jefferson arrived in France in 1784, he was surprised at the poverty.[388] Modern terrorism began in the French Revolution. *"Oh pleasant experience of hope and joy! / For great were the auxiliars which then stood? / Upon our side we were strong in love/Bliss was it in that dawn to be alive / But to be young was very heaven,"* wrote Wordsworth. Byron, Shelly, Beethoven, and Goethe were there in spirit.[389] It led to the Terror of 1793-94,[390] to Danton, and Saint Just, who, like al-Wahhab, wanted a perfect state, like the Taliban, to Robespierre, and the other 17,000 killed by La Guillotine, La Razor.[391]

Hassan al-Banna's dream was to conquer the world. If Islam ruled it would be a world of peace and brotherhood. Jews, Christians, Muslims would live together. What was he going to do now? He had found another job. He lived underground. Corruption was the problem, and it would make the country fail. The army was filled with thieves[392] interested in themselves. Since 2014, when el-Sisi took power, with 97% of the vote, Egypt had gone from 94th to 117th out of 175 countries in its level of corruption,[393] rampant in the Arab world.[394]

In 2018, el-Sisi ran again for president and again received 97 percent of the vote.[395] The former head of Egypt's anti-corruption agency was jailed for five years by a military court for insulting the armed forces,[396] and

---

[388] Bois, *"Jefferson: "Architect of American Liberty,"* 126
[389] Alan Woods, "British Poets and the French Revolution," *In Defence of Marxism* 23 July 2003, http://www.marxist.com/british-poets-french-revolution-1.htm
[390] "The Unfolding of Language by Guy Deutscher," *The Guardian,* 2 July 2005
[391] Charles Dickens, *"A Tale of Two Cities"*(London: Puffin, 2016)
[392] Zvi Bar'el, *The Egyptian Army Is Making a Fortune in Sinai,* Haaretz, 20 Sept. 2019.
[393] *"Egypt Corruption Rank - 2021 Data - 2022 Forecast - 1996-2020 Historical - Chart,* https://tradingeconomics.com/egypt/corruption-rank.
[394]https://knowledgehub.transparency.org/helpdesk/egypt-overview-of-corruption-and-anti-corruption.
[395] John Davison and Ahmed Tolba, "Egypt's Sisi Wins 97 Percent in Election with No Real Opposition." *Reuters* 2 Apr. 2018
[396] Heba Saleh, "Egypt's Former Anti-Corruption Chief Jailed for 5 Years." *Financial Times* 24 Apr. 2018

mocked by the media, controlled by the government.

It was getting late. Walid said not to worry, we were safe here. This was not Chicago. Its gangland reputation still existed. He had a degree in Arabic from Cairo University, but where he truly learned was in the mosque. When he was young, he played football and the Ikhwan had a team. They put on plays and they sang. They were not terrorists. Bit by bit he became Ikhwan and part of a brotherhood. The military had ruled Egypt since Nasser. Under Morsi for the first time, it was a democracy. But democracy meant the rule of man, not God. If we agreed, Walid countered, if we were good people, like the three of us, we would live in a good country. The Koran talked of general things. The rules were to be made by man. No one could say he was acting on behalf of God. Again, he said to be careful at al-Azhar. In 1961 Nasser brought it under state control. Hassan al-Banna, saw in 1922 that they were weak.

The boys kept working. Evening came. What did he think of al-Qaeda? He didn't know much about it, but Hamas had the right to their land, even if you shot rockets at them, it was their land. Al-Taleb talked about the land. In Taliban suicide tapes they sang of their land.

In 1954 when Nasser arrested and tortured the Ikhwan people said they had to fight, but al-Banna said the Muslim Brothers were preachers, not judges, said Walid. Some wanted to carry a gun, but he refused. Some wanted to fight in Chechnya, and Afghanistan.

A man with a barrel chest joined us. He hated the Ikhwan, he said in a loud, grating voice. He was in the tourism business and thanks to the Ikhwan his business was ruined. They voted for Morsi because he said he knew God, but he knew nothing. He shouldn't mix politics and Islam.

The owner urged me to go with the man with the loud voice. We walked down allies and climbed up the dusty steps of an old mosque onto the roof, looked over the city filled with minarets, listening to the calls to prayer. There was an American journalist, Daniel. He brought him here. He worked for the Wall Street Journal. He took him to a special shop for papyrus. We followed pathways to a shop. A woman let us in to a room filled with papyrus drawings. I saw Daniel Pearl's card under her glass desktop. A man brought tea. I said Daniel Pearl was slaughtered by al-Qaeda. They were silent.

Two days later I returned to al-Azhar. A man escorted me into a large office. A man with a *zebibah* (raison) a prayer bump, on his forehead, like Sadat and al-Zawahiri, a sign of piety, and the Mufti, a tall, dour man in a white prayer cap, joined us. He left and we sat at a table. He was the spokesman for the Mufti, said Dr. Ibrahim Negm. He gave me a booklet, "The Future of the Religious Field in Egypt: The Danger of Extremism and al-Azhar as an Authentic Alternative." He wrote it and thought it might be of interest in light of our talk on the phone. He met with intellectuals and politicians, including U.S. Senators, part of their effort to broaden the discourse among Muslims and Christians, and others. There were rival religious authorities.

Like the Deobandi? He nodded, looking at me. They wanted to be the authoritative voice for Islamic interpretation. Deoband was a code of thought, but it lacked a proper understanding of the lived realities in the modern world. Their approach took them to the past without building bridges to the present. Al-Azar was interested in traditional legacies. The modern world meant the concept of IT and globalization. There was no longer the land of Islam (*Dar al Islam)* and the house of war (*Dar al Arb*). For al-Qaeda, the West was the far enemy, land of the *Kaffir*. They had to live in the modern world. This had a bearing on fatwas and how they understood Islam.

But Islam was the submission of man to God, was it not, and democracy was the rule of man? It was religious pluralism, the issue of dealing with man as a Muslim. In the past, it was all based upon religion. Today, it was based upon citizenship and the modern concept of law which meant equal rights under the law. Substantiation was found in the Prophet's example. The life of the Prophet, Peace be unto Him, was found in four paradigms.

Walid said Al-Azhar was made up of worldly men working for the military.

Al-Azhar was an ancient institution and it wanted to remain influential, even survive, which mean that it had to compromise. It received funds from the state. The Prophet lived in a hostile environment. He was commissioned as a prophet at 40. He lived the next 13 years in Mecca, a hostile environment, a life of civil disobedience. He and his followers propagated their faith peacefully. Some Muslims lived in a hostile environment today— in Central Africa, for example. They were under attack from Christians. They must never resort to violence. Were they to accept martyrdom? He nodded, gravely. The second paradigm was the Abyssinian model. Muslims migrated there and were protected by a Christian king. They integrated and lived as equal citizens. They were part of the Abyssinian army. Al-Azhar had therefore ruled that it was permissible for a Muslim to join the U.S. Army. They were about fifteen in Abyssinia, and 40 who stayed behind in Mecca.[397] Muslims would fight other Muslims? If it happened, yes.

The third paradigm was that the Prophet migrated to Medina and formed the first Islamic State. In the constitution he outlined the rights and obligations of each citizen. There were minorities there, like in Egypt, where ten percent are Christians, or in Syria with its different faiths. The last paradigm was near the end of Mohammad's life when he lived in an almost total Muslim environment, like, say, in Indonesia today, where sharia was applicable. If it were applied in Egypt, it would raise serious issues for Christians. It was not enough to rule that it would be Islamic but was it workable. Al-Azhar was over 1,000 years old. The office of the grand mufti was 700 years old. They issued fatwas in nine languages, over 500,000 a year. Non-Muslims could apply for a ruling, in person, in a hotline free service, by email, fax or regular mail. A mufti, he or she—yes, it could be a woman—needed a degree in Islamic law from al-Azhar. He or she had to pass a training program. One must be scholarly and able to quote from the traditional sources. They taught communication, listening skills, introduction to political science, and medicine. They had to deal with medical issues: euthanasia, for example.

It was a matter of what Islam proposed and what modernity raised, not either/or. Islam was an expanding ideology, not a constricted understanding of clichés and individuals. They had a magnificent library of history and scholarship which other authorities did not have. Islam did not contradict democracy, but distinguished between it as an ideology, which they might not agree with, and as a tool. In the West they marketed democracy as anti-religious. It was a tool to bring the interests and welfare of people together. Historically, Islam was a tool.

How did they confront what led men to join al-Qaeda? You needed a stable state. They engaged these angry young men. They had rehabilitation programs. They were easy prey because of their economic and social

---

[397] Rodinson, "*Muhammed*," 113-116

conditions. His phone rang. It was the Grand Mufti. He had to go. That night I watched Azhar students demonstrating on television, fighting the tear gas.

A Son of the Ikhwan

Fahmy Howadi, in a sweater and jeans, sat on a sofa, draped with a rich colored textile, in his living room overlooking Cairo. The walls were filled with modern paintings from Egypt and Iraq.

There was a tribal Yemeni necklace on an end table, and a Yemeni knife on a hand-carved Egyptian coffee table. There were copper Persian lamps and Persian carpets on the hardwood floor.

He was the first Arabic-speaking journalist to go to Iran after the revolution. He wrote *Inside Iran.* He went to Afghanistan after the Communist revolution in 1978 and wrote *Happened in Afghanistan*, and *Soldiers of God in the Wrong Battle.* The Mujahideen and the Taliban were good, sincere Muslims, but they misunderstood Islamic rules and principles and were serving the wrong goal. Most of their leaders studied at Deoband. He couldn't imagine a tie between al-Qaeda and the Ikhwan. His father, Abdul Razzak, helped found the Ikhwan. Hassan al-Banna and other men felt there was a vacuum in the Muslim world. There was no center, no Vatican, as there was for Catholics. The British were putting pressure on Muslims in Ismailia and al-Banna saw the need to give them dignity. They needed an umbrella, someone to defend them, and Islam. The message was still there.

The principles he alluded to: that Islam was a total system with no separation between mosque and state; that it was based upon the Koran and the traditions of Mohammad, the Sunna; that it was applicable at all times and in all places, were that of the Deobandi. The Ikhwan were violent, he agreed. They fought the British and opposed Jewish immigration to Palestine. But al-Banna talked about bringing Shia and Sunni together. They started a magazine in Zamalek for this. The magazine ended, but the building was still there. The Ikhwan survived, still defending Islam.

There were secret branches, called the private sector.[398] They made mistakes, killing the Prime Minister, and a judge. Nasser had ties to the Ikhwan. There was a power struggle between them. There were Muslim

---

[398] Nazam al-Khas.

officers around him. The Ikhwan thought they could influence them. They tried to work with King Farouk, but many, committed to the equality in Islam, opposed the monarchy, and called for violence.[30] Some tried to start an insurrection. In 1948, the government banned the Ikhwan and put thousands in prison. In 1954, Nasser was speaking in Alexandria, and a man shot at him eight times, real or faked, no one knew. Nasser didn't flinch and his popularity soared. This gave him and the Free Officers, the latitude to destroy their competition. The Ikhwan survived, but the lines were drawn.

Howadi was arrested in 1954. He was 16, the youngest political prisoner in Egypt. They tortured his father, his brother and his sister's husband, but not him. Still, it was hard. He was released when he was 18 and felt like he was 60. It was a good experience in a way. He saw injustice and chose to work for the poor and against injustice. He had been a journalist for 60 years. He started writing for al-Ahram, but he couldn't live with himself if he kept working for the government, which was oppressing people. People thought he was Ikhwan, but he wasn't. Sadat didn't like his writing and sacked him. He went to Kuwait for six years and became a writer.

The minister of religion said elections were not welcome in Islam. He disagreed and Sadat banned him from writing. He returned to Kuwait and read Khomeini's books. When Sayyid Qutb was hanged in 1962, few people knew or cared. They were too enamored of Nasser's performance. In 1956, the U.S. prevented the World Bank from financing the Aswan Dam, and Nasser turned to the Soviet Union. Egypt changed. Qutb was influential in small circles. The media tried to demonize the Ikhwan, as they did today. He criticized some of Morsi's policies but because he did not insult him, he was seen as Ikhwan. Many secularists and liberals wanted Morsi to fail. They tried to find an independent, just one, even outsiders, to join the cabinet, but no one would. They had no choice but to put in their own people. The deep state—the military, the Department of the Interior, the bureaucracy—made Morsi fail.

The Ikhwan were active with the poor, some intellectuals, and controlled, through free elections, the unions. The government killed 3,000 in one week during the so-called Arab Spring. Sixteen thousand were wounded. Would their brothers and sons not want revenge? The leaders would resist, but not the young. There were 21,000 in prison. The media said they deserved to be there.

Al-Qaeda was a culture, not an organization. It, like the Haqqanis, was part of an ideology. They had fought the infidel invaders for 40 years now and were an inspiration. They fought for Islam. Three-quarters of the world's Arabs lived in Egypt. The Mujahideen and the Taliban were an inspiration here, so then would be the Haqqanis, for fighting for Islam.

What about the Sinai? He sighed. Under Morsi the Ikhwan, Hamas and the army worked together to control it. Now the army was fighting there. You would become a terrorist too to defend yourself. The people were all members of tribes. If you attack him, he was only a member of his family. There you had a tribe. You didn't need foreign fighters. The army ruled here.

Did Morsi call al-Zawahiri when he was in Pakistan? How could he do this? There were secret police all around him, and who were against him. One man there, Mahmoud Tataway, was ambassador to Iran, later assistant to the Foreign Minister. He was related to al-Zawahiri. When he was fighting Sadat and Mubarak Tataway was an ambassador. He would not have been in that position if he was helping him. No one listened to al-Zawahiri, or to his brother, Mohammad. There were no Shia here and so no Shia-Sunni battle. The groups waving the black flag of al-Qaeda were probably with the tribes.

What about al-Gamaá al-Islamiyya, and Islamic Jihad? Why, 30 years ago, did an Egyptian Army officer go to Afghanistan? Could there not be links here? Could not the ideology of protecting Islam against the West exist in the homeland of the Ikhwan and al-Zawahiri?

He couldn't say no. During the Morsi period, people on the blacklist returned from Afghanistan. Some were in prison. There were secret links here. He did not know about these things. One could find out but be careful. I really should be asking about the future of democracy. Since 1954 Egyptians had lived under military rule. The Ikhwan were banned in 1948 and spent the majority of their lives in jail. How could they be a political animal? You needed a healthy political system to create a modern state.

Two months later he went to the airport to go to a conference in Spain but was on a no-fly list.

1. Haqqani Mujahid (holy warrior) and pine boxes of U.S. ammuntion at Haqqani headquarters in Miram Shah, the Tribal Areas of Pakistan.

2. Preparing a wounded mujahid, shot by a Soviet helicopter gunship in eastern Afghanistan, for his journey by camel to a hospital in Pakistan.

3. A boy, in early Haqqani territory, proudly manning an anti-aircraft gun.

**4. The Haqqani compound at Shah-e-Khot (The king's place)
in Paktia Province.**

5. Inside the compound, a nervous Afghan army soldier who had defected two days before. Jalaluddin is in the white turban on the right.

6. The author, his interpreter, Mallem (teacher), in the room the author shared with British photojournalist Ken Guest, and Abdur Rahman, an Egyptian army major.

7. Preparing dinner of gritty rice, with bread, sometimes with a few greasy vegetables, sometimes with bits of gristle.

8. One of the Haqqani mujahideen.

9. Abdur Rahman, with some of Haqqani's men.

10. (Author second on the left) with Haqqani men in a tea house, en route, in the mountains.

11. Haqqani's men preparing mortars for an attack, later at dusk, on an Afghan army base.

**12. Jalaluddin and his men on a captured
Soviet T-54 tank at his arms cache higher up in the mountains.**

**13. Jalaluddin showing in the early days of the war,
his new AK 47 assault rifle with a scope.**

14. Jalaluddin and Abdur Rahman at a meeting in the mountains.

15. The author after racing Jalaluddin on the high plains.

16. The beginning of the growing Haqqani Mujahideen, and what today the U.S. calls The Haqqani Network.

17. One of their commanders.

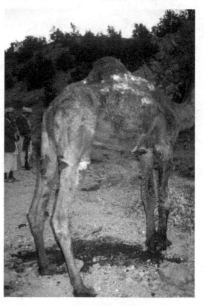

18. A camel minesweeper after stepping on a mine, blowing its foot off, saving the Haqqani Mujahideen, and the author, on his way back to Pakistan.

19. A village mullah/school teacher showing
the village cache of foreign-supplied ammunition and weapons.

20. Preparing an ambush. Jalaluddin is in the white turban on the left.

21. The author, two weeks later, before battle, in Kandahar.

22. The Haqqani Mujahidden becoming the large Haqqani Network.

Bin Laden's Filmmaker

Synods, which opened in 1880 was filled with men smoking, and reading the morning papers. A balding, heavyset man in his 70s in a blue suit, white shirt and tie, sat alone at a small round marble table, with a cup of tea. I will call him Amir. He spoke softly. He was not feeling well. I went to the counter, got a cup of tea and joined him.

He went to Afghanistan in 1986 and was there four years. He was close to bin Laden, to Haqqani, to all of them. I was trying to find a former army major, called Rahman, who was with Haqqani. He eyed me carefully. Haqqani went to the Emirates in 1980 a few weeks after the Soviet invasion. This man was probably Egyptian intelligence. It would not be his real name. He may have been one of many army officers in the Emirates, which would have sent him to help Haqqani, or to observe his tactics. He was always visiting the Emirates to attend conferences, and to raise money. Army officers were building the Emirates' army. It was the only professional link between Egypt and the Mujahideen.

What about his Arab wife? Many Arab women would be happy to meet and marry a proud, strong member of the Mujahideen, he replied. Haqqani was a famous commander fighting for Islam. The Emirates sent a general he knew, a jet pilot, to see Haqqani in 1990. He drank his tea.

It wasn't easy for him to talk. He had spent years in prison. In 2003, after he returned from America, Mubarak arrested him. He had a lot of videos of Osama and gave it to ABC television, but it refused to pay him. He stayed in a hotel in Crystal City. It was September 2002. He was sitting in his room the first day of Ramadan. He heard a helicopter and looked outside. There were police cars, a knock on the door, and men holding their badges up saying FBI. There were men with rifles. He stood there in his shorts, afraid. They interviewed him for five hours. They went through all his papers on a table, and relaxed. He had to stay and fight. A man gave him his card and said to call if he needed anything. They asked to borrow some of his tapes, which they would return by 10:00 the next morning. A man brought them at 9:55.

When he returned to Egypt, they put him in the Central State Security Prison. The head of security in Egypt came to his cell. He was sorry to see him like this. They had nothing on him. The Americans had them arrest him to force him to tell them where bin Laden was. He hadn't left Egypt in ten years. When he applied for a visa to go anywhere the word "wanted" came up. He was put on a blacklist in 1990. I asked him to start at the beginning. He was born in Cairo in 1946. At 16, after secondary school, he joined the army. He wanted to fight Egypt's enemies, including Israel. In 1962, there was the revolution in Yemen, and Egypt was going to fight there. They needed officers and compressed the three-year course at the military academy to two years. He became an officer at 18.

He didn't say that Egypt invaded Yemen. Afterwards he fought in the 1967 war against Israel. He was in a reconnaissance unit and crossed early behind enemy lines. He rubbed his forehead. It was hard. The war didn't end until 8 August 1970, when William Rogers arranged a cease fire.[399] They hated Nasser, nine of them, but it was his idea to overthrow him. He was in prison for five years. He looked down. Nasser died in 1970. He began to write in prison, entered one of his stories in a literary competition, and won first prize. After the 1973 October War, Sadat released them. His stories were in *al-Ahram.* The Minister of Culture congratulated him. Naguib Mahfouz, the Noble laurate, was supportive. He went to London and became a script writer for the BBC. He saw himself as an important writer one day helping the people. He became a documentary filmmaker and made 20 films in five years. The French came, could I imagine, the French, and asked him to make a film. He got married in 1984 and had a daughter.

In 1986, he took a crew to Afghanistan to film a documentary. He saw Russians burn whole villages. He lowered his voice. The military security court wanted to put him in prison for 25 years. He wanted to fight this regime because it caused their defeat, not Israel. Nasser kept sending soldiers, who were "ludicrously ill-prepared,"[400] draining the treasury. He was a captain. He wanted to address Nasser so he would know the truth. He refused to talk unless he was there. They arranged for him to talk by phone. They put it on the desk, but he refused. They called them "the Revolutionary Generation." The head of intelligence said if he talked to him, he was talking

---

[399] *Knesset.gov.il*, https://knesset.gov.il/lexicon/eng/rogers_eng.htm.
[400] Clark, *"Yemen: Dancing on the Heads of Snakes,"* 95

to Nasser. They worshipped him and were afraid they were going to lose the army.

Did he know al-Zawahiri?

They tortured him, and he came out an angry man. Three things changed al-Zawahiri. He knew Sayyid Qutb and found him to be a good, thoughtful Muslim. When Nasser killed him, Zawahiri was 16 or 17, a boy. Nasser told his head of intelligence his wife was angry, and he didn't sleep that night.[401] The 1967 war changed a generation of Arabs. The mindset in the press and in the streets was they would win in 24 hours. The army was destroyed.

Dr. al-Eryani, in Yemen, said it changed everyone. He nodded. It hurt every Muslim in the world. Afterwards, they were still poor, and there was no democracy, and Israel was making trouble for the Palestinians, like today. To Zawahiri, Nasser and Sadat were arrogant men who lost to Israel. He was at a university and met others like himself. It was because of the loss to Israel that he formed what became Islamic Jihad. He and bin Laden met at Jaji in Afghanistan where Osama formed his first unit. It was a camp at the summit. He dug a cave beneath it and built a clinic for the Mujahideen. Zawahiri assisted him. It was the fall 1986. He met both men there, but al-Zawahiri he knew only by his code name, Dr. Abd al-Muez. No one knew al-Zawahiri. Bin Laden was 26, al-Zawahiri 36.

The second time he saw al-Zawahiri was in March at the Battle of Jalalabad. He was working in a Kuwaiti hospital and brought Osama glucose because he had low blood pressure. It would get so bad he had to lie on the ground. He gave it to him intravenously. Jets were strafing them. General Hamid Gul had called for the Mujahideen, who only knew guerrilla war, to mount a conventional attack on Jalalabad. It turned into a four-month siege, and then defeat, the worst of Jihad. He shook his head angrily. Osama was a good and kind man and then Islamic Jihad moved its ideology to Afghanistan. Osama had money but no men. Zawahiri had armed, tough men, real fighters. He made a fist.

He became quiet. He had low blood pressure and needed something. He went to a glass case lined with pastries, and to the counter behind us and ordered a chocolate cake, and tea. He returned. Osama had 70 men, exactly.

---

[401] General Salah Nasr was head of the Egyptian Intelligence Directorate (Mukhabarat) from 1957-67. He retired, for health reasons, after the 1967 war.

He was there. About 50% of them were Egyptian. Osama said whenever he was looking for an engineer, a carpenter, an iron worker, they were all Egyptians. He would smile. The rest were Saudis and Yemenis.

Did he know Tariq al-Fadhli?

Osama sent him to Yemen to start al-Qaeda there. He was the only one who could verify this. He was there. They had to fight the communists. It was 1989, in Peshawar. They would begin with an international conference in Islamabad to announce jihad in South Yemen. Osama told him to contact the media. There was no contact with the CIA. Osama later called him here and said it was not a good time. He met Haqqani in 1985 when he went to Miram Shah to see some Arabs who were with him. He was an historical figure. The kings of all the Arabs were nothing against him. Bin Laden returned to Saudi Arabia. The government took his passport. Zawahiri became the leader of the Arabs. He went to Haqqani for support, probably on behalf of bin Laden. He himself returned home and went with his wife and daughter to Saudi Arabia for "*umrah*,"[402] to pray, and to visit the holy sites. Osama sent a car to the airport. They stayed in a flat next to him. They all slept on carpets. He shook his head. Osama liked to live simply.

He went to get another pastry and more tea and returned. Abdullah Azzam called to say he was coming. Osama was happy. Abdullah Azzam is coming, he exclaimed. They discussed the future of the Arab fighters. There was no plan. Osama said the Ikhwan refused to support them. It was dangerous. He was staying with the two most dangerous men in the world, who started the story that we were living. He had ties to the Ikhwan, but he used his own money to go to Afghanistan. Everyone respected that he came alone. Azzam was Ikhwan. The Saudis knew of their plans to go to Yemen. Azzam returned to Peshawar. Three weeks later he was dead. He said in 1988 they came to fight the communists, the first step to fight Israel. At that moment he knew Azzam was finished. He was Palestinian don't forget. He lost his home when the Israelis came.

In 1990, Amir boarded a plane to go on Haj. It taxied out to the runway, and then the pilot said they had to wait. A car came and he had to get off. He was wearing Haj clothes. They let him go. After that, they questioned him

---

[402] A lesser pilgrimage, generally three days, not as important as going on Haj, but considered meritorious.

all the time. The story of terrorism began with the death of Abdullah Azzam. He placed his hand on the table. Azzam had a charismatic personality, a PhD from al-Azhar, and was a professor at the Islamic University in Islamabad. He was on top. He brought Osama to Pakistan. He had to be killed. In 1987, Amir went to a conference in Islamabad organized by Jamiat-i-Islami, the Ikhwan party in Pakistan. Azzam and bin Laden were there. Bin Laden said he raised three million dollars in two weeks in America.

What about Haqqani? Jalaluddin was a good man, strong, clear, and brave. It was very rare to find a man like him. He was a fighter. He made a fist. Who was Mullah Omar against him? The Afghans needed someone they trusted. The only chance was for Haqqani to be president. He had ties to the Arabs, and everyone respected him. Omar was a private during Jihad with an RPG.[403] He paused. He didn't like the Taliban. They felt that only they knew the truth. In 1994, he went to Saudi Arabia to work. When he returned, they arrested him at the airport, took his passport and his archives. He leaned close. He knew someone I should meet. We had been talking for two hours and I had to leave.

I walked across a bridge over the Nile to a hotel, once an Ottoman palace to an outdoor cafe, like the Racing Club in the Bois de Boulogne, with wicker chairs and tables, and men and women in sunglasses, and linen. A European joined me. We ordered green tea. He was an investment banker in London and had worked in the Middle East and North Africa for years. He now advised clients on investments and business. There was a lot of money coming in, but the level of paranoia was high. Egypt was no longer sophisticated in the way in which it dealt with problems. It started in 1954 when the military came to power. The state became paranoid and the education level of the people got worse. It was too nationalistic.

He cohosted a program with a number of ambassadors after which he and an ambassador were walking down the street and a man came up close and told a policeman to move aside. He walked into traffic and stopped cars to cross the road. The army had pushed the Ministry of the Interior and the police into a corner. They listened to Abu Dhabi and Riyadh because they gave them money but were afraid of the Ikhwan. Everything had become sectarian, and hateful.

---

[403] Rocket Propelled Grenade Launcher, a ubiquitous Soviet weapon in Afghanistan.

Nearby, a woman with long dark hair, a gold necklace, white blouse, and another in a flowery dress and a wide brim hat drank their tea. There was wealthy Egypt, then the middle class which lived on $250 a month and demonstrated in Tahrir Square. The poor voted for the Ikhwan.

Western banks[404] and Saudi Arabia kept Egypt from another revolution. There was an undeclared war here. The state had the guns, but the Ikhwan had God. Behind us was a Coptic Church, with two high white crosses, like the minarets of Haqqani's mosque. The Copts rejected the belief that Jesus was both God and man, as agreed at the Council of Chalcedon in Turkey in 451, and in Greek Orthodox, Catholic, and Protestant churches. The Romans ruled here for 700 years. In 642 Amr ibn al-As led a Muslim army into Alexandria.

The Wahhabis made Egypt more conservative. Their influence was growing. Unless there was economic growth and open debate it would become like Eastern Europe. I must never leave my computer in my room. My phone would be monitored.

He was in a meeting where the host asked everyone to leave their phones in another room. Someone from the government called and said to move the phones back. Anti-Christian sentiment was growing. The waiter came over and said all Egyptians hated Obama because he supported the Ikhwan, and terrorism. We ended our meeting.

Two days later, I met Amir at Maison Thomas, which opened in 1922. A waiter in a white shirt, black vest, and white apron, came over. We ordered orange juice. He was trying to find the sister of a man who lived with the Taliban for ten years. He opened a copy of *Paris Match* to a photo spread of bin Laden, and him, and a photo of bin Laden after he had given himself a shot. He had so many pictures, so much footage, some of it never seen. He invited me to his home. No more phone calls or public meetings. He wrote the address and directions and left.

That evening, an interpreter, who I will call Sophia, who had worked for an American journalist, met me at an old restaurant with fans purring overhead. Why was I here? I began to talk. She put up her hand. They might have devises under the tables. They would kill me here. She talked about a

---

[404] Arwa Gaballa and Ali Abdelaty, "Egypt's Middle Class Faces Hardship as Austerity Bites," *Reuters* 21 Mar. 2018

correspondent they shot. We walked outside and she took the battery out of her phone. She was paranoid, but you learned that here. We walked across a bridge back over the Nile down into Zamalek, past a car with dark windows. "Police," she said. A man inside looked at us. "Secret police," she added. There was no license plate. They ruled here. There was not an ant that came in and they don't know it. I said I needed to go to the Sinai to find al-Qaeda. A journalist told me to have Hamas take me in. She said it was too dangerous. We took a table outside a restaurant. The man next to us smoked. She asked him to move and the table of young men did. Egyptians were nice, not all, but certainly most of them. She agreed, but they didn't tell the truth. They lived under a dictatorship, I said. They were afraid. "Exactly," she replied.

The following night I rode for half an hour through the city, as vast as Los Angeles, and the lights passed in a blur. I called and gave my phone to the taxi driver. A half hour later we stopped at an intersection. A man in his 40s with long curly hair, in a sport coat and jeans, was waiting. Amir asked him to show me a video. We entered an electronics store with a sagging wood floor, and old television monitors, and sat in a corner. A boy put a CD into a player. Bin Laden came on in a turban and a fatigue jacket, with a microphone. He appeared again with a long beard and a white kefeyyah, hanging loosely Salafi style. It was a famous speech, said the curly-haired man, the first time he said the real enemy was the West.

Abdullah Anas was next, with warm eyes and a bushy beard. "Jihad was now required," he preached. Other men came on, and then Abdullah Azzam, with a gaunt face, long beard, clutching a rifle, in his only interview, telling every Muslim he must go to Afghanistan to wage jihad. After this, bin Laden, al-Zawahiri and every suicide bomber held a rifle in a video. Hosafa, his son, a bright-faced young man, said they worked with the CIA to drive the Russians out, and then America decided they were terrorists. How did this happen? Azzam's wife, in an abaya, was next. Again Anas, who said the Afghans tried to separate the Arabs from the Afghans. The leader of the Ikhwan said they were building schools in Afghanistan, a university, and a military academy. We walked up the street. All those jihadists were crazy, said the curly haired man. His boss knew all of them from prison. The police were always putting him there. They stopped him at the airport every time he returned from Afghanistan. They were dogs.

"Ibn kelb," went the Arab curse, "You son of a dog."

They beat you and broke into your house. The Egyptians were cowards. Why did they worship all those gods in their history? They had no strength. The government bothered his family, and he had a little girl. His wife came from a good family. They forced a divorce. We entered Amir's apartment. He brought a tray with glasses of fresh orange juice and mango juice into his large living room. When he returned here sometimes, he saw that things had been moved around. Would the two women sitting on the bench say something? Would anyone in the store?

He was the one in danger. He wanted to write a book called the *Bin Laden Revolution*. It would be a history of the jihadi movement from the inside. Did he regret going to Afghanistan? He didn't answer.

The Reformed Islamist

Sophia stood on the sidewalk in front of Groppi's *Salon de the.*[405] In 1954 Nasser placed a bomb here to create insecurity.[406] No one was injured. We crossed the street and took an elevator to the office of Montasser al-Zayat, al-Zawahiri's lawyer. As we got off the lights went out. His assistant shrugged. This was Egypt. We had a meeting scheduled but he wasn't there. We took a taxi across the Nile. We walked up a busy street, with laundry hanging on balconies, entered a building, took a squeaky elevator to the sixth floor, and knocked on a door.

Professor Mustafa Fathy, a balding, stocky man in a white shirt, his sleeves rolled up, sat at his desk, a few plaques and framed photographs on the walls. He studied and taught the history of ideas in Islam. He was an Islamist, but the killings in Luxor, the work of al-Gamaá al-Islamiyya, (the Islamic groups) whose leader was not al-Zawahiri but Kamil Halib, made him recant. Al-Gammá and Islamic Jihad were founded by university students angry at Israel's victory in 1967, at the Ikhwan decision in 1970 to renounce violence, and at government corruption. The spiritual leader was Abdel-Rahman, the blind sheikh.

In 1959, students at the University of Michigan formed the Students for a Democratic Society, joined the civil rights movement, opposed the war in Vietnam, and from which emerged in 1969 the Weather Underground, like al-Gamaá, with their assassination and bombing campaign, but secular.

Fathy and his friends wanted to teach the poor that the political community paid a high price for violence. Mubarak cut their wings, using terrorism as justification. Like Nasser, he curbed the media, and his security apparatus penetrated all political parties, creating a dictatorship. He didn't say that Kermit Roosevelt, of the CIA, set up the apparatus. He lit a cigarette. The public, beat down for so long, did not understand. He wanted to show young men that they didn't have to stand on a street corner, preach hatred of America, and call for jihad, playing into the hands of the regime so that it could say to America, "Without us there would be chaos." Terrorism

---

[405] "Weekly.ahram.org.eg"
[406] *Groppi*, http://www.egy.com/landmarks/96-06-15.php.

was the gift that kept on giving, men said in Yemen.

There was the classic Muslim division: *Dar-el-Islam* vs. *Dar-el-Harb*.[407] It was too simplistic. In 1998, after bin Laden and Ayman formed their organization against Jews and Crusaders he saw that they were wrong. In Islamic jurisprudence it was wrong to kill people. Al-Zawahiri needed intellectual and psychological certainty. Islamic movements were social, not political. Theirs was a class war, for power and against arrogance, corruption, secularism, and U.S. policy. The Ikhwan were the *ruralization* of society. Nasser created rural communities around Cairo to kill the city, and to protect his coup. He sent an aide to Spain to learn how Franco did this. In 2007 Fathy visited a Kurd, a communist, in Iraq, who said Saddam tried to follow Franco, who brought in rural people in Spain to suffocate the cities because studies showed that revolutionary demands came from them.

Not everyone agreed with this. A friend, a former Wesleyan professor living in Madrid, wrote in response to my query. "After the Civil War (1936-39), the poor did migrate from the countryside to cities, but this was out of desperation. Large landholdings were carved up under the Second Republic and given to 'peasants,' but were returned to their original owners under Franco, and the landless migrated hoping to find work. They settled in shantytowns. They could not afford to live in the city. This migration began in earnest after 1959, when the economy was reformed, U.N. sanctions were removed, Spain signed an agreement for military bases with the U.S., and hard currency began pouring into the country. Families brought their values with them, but their children began to change."

It was, in reverse, like Mao Tse Tung's "Great Proletarian Cultural Revolution," sending the urban young and intellectuals in 1966 to the countryside to reeducate the masses to keep the revolution alive.

Rural men, said Fathy, especially of the mountains, felt superior to urban men. Both distrusted the other.[408] Freedom thrived in the mountains, said Schiller. Bin Laden liked the mountains. I thought of Jalauddin laughing, his voice deep in the night, as he grabbed my arm when I tripped on a rock in a stream. People migrated to the city because there was work

---

[407] The House of Islam and the House of War.
[408] Erik von Kuehnelt-Leddihn, *"The Menace of the Herd, or, Procrustes at Large"* (Auburn: Ludwig Von Mises Institute, 2007), 127

there bringing the mentality that you needed eight to ten children, Fathy explained. An Afghan told me you were not a man unless you had ten children, preferably boys, to form a militia.

Those who came to the cities forced out, or back, those who had fewer children. Cairo, like Sanaá, had overgrown its Ottoman borders. Peasants lived in apartment houses,[409] which became villages, and breeding grounds for radicalism.[410] Nageh Ibrahim, of al-Gamaá Islamiyya, who served over twenty years in prison for his role in Sadat's murder, said *Mein Kampf* affected his generation more than Said Qutb. He wanted to take over Egypt from the top, and impose Islam by force. Nasser aligned Egypt with China and the Soviet Union. But Sadat looked to Germany because Britain colonized Egypt. Leftist discourse controlled Egypt and made the West look like a monster. It was easy to influence people, who were so beaten down that they looked up to Hitler, who, like Leftists, and Islamists today stood up to the West.

Ibrahim would know who the army officer was who lived us in the mountains.

Fathy drew a parallel between President Pervez Musharraf in Pakistan, who, like Mubarak, and Saleh in Yemen, supported terrorism, and worked with the West at the same time. Leftists had ties to Nasser, but Sadat put them down. They came back in 1984, after his death. There was a tie between terrorism and the state in the Middle East. Sadat's murder was a riddle. Sophia agreed. The real assassin, Abu Gamel, was called as a witness in the trial, but then disappeared.

A famous Egyptian singer, a friend of Nasser's, wrote in his memoirs, to be published after his death, that he found it strange that the Egyptians loved Nasser, who lied to them, but hated Sadat, who was honest. It went back to Egypt's rural culture, which was based upon hatred. Villagers didn't read. They took their information from the media without looking into it.

Many Egyptians went to the Gulf, made money, and were grateful, but the media called them loud and showy. There was a huge amount of anti-

---

[409] Diane Singerman, *Cairo Contested: Governance, Urban Space, and Global Modernity* (Cairo: American University in Cairo Press, 2011, 146
[410] Alaa al-Aswayny's novel, *The Yacaubian Building*, (2004), made into a movie, captures this tragedy well.

American propaganda here. In the upper classes there was a great deal of French influence. They loved to look down on Americans, who were crude and unsophisticated, unlike Europeans, particularly the French. It was noble to praise the Soviets and to oppose the U.S. for supporting Israel, not acknowledging that France and the Soviet Union did also.

Arab states had receded back to tribal culture, which provided solidarity and kept their citizens down. It was getting to the point where, if the U.S. was to recite the *Shahada*,[411] that the Left and the upper classes would refute it. One had to follow the emir without questioning. He picked up a book by a Russian.[412] "In the south of Yemen, they received us with open arms, and in Laos. Why are our ideas accepted in backward countries, whereas in Eastern Europe we have to impose them with tanks?" Genocide and terrorism were directly linked to the collectivization regimes, which bred blind obedience. This was at the heart of the Egyptian regime, which believed that progress was possible without freedom.

Al-Zawahiri brought suicide bombing to Afghanistan and Pakistan.

It began, he replied, in 1985, when Sana Mahaydal, a teenage Lebanese Marxist, blew herself up in the middle of Israeli tanks. He used to write poetry about her. Suicide came from the Left. The Tamil in Sri Lanka were Marxists. He was a Trotskyite. How could one believe in God, and communism? There was a fine line between suicide and martyrdom. Sophia agreed. Morsi was an excellent example of rural culture, he responded. He talked simply and was not devious. The Islamist movement, to its detriment, was made up of men who studied the sciences. There were more engineers than sociologists.

The call came for *Maghrib*. He had to go to the mosque. Could al-Zawahiri and Haqqani work here? They could, but the Arab Spring was a set-back for al-Qaeda. The people saw they could overthrow a government without violence. Al-Zawahiri inherited what Zarqawi created in Iraq, but even he saw that he was too sectarian. For the first time Al-Qaeda withdrew legitimacy from one group and gave it to another. It was no longer a pyramid structure, but an umbrella. Al-Zawahiri lost control. Fathy watched Islamists

---

[411] The Shahadah, or Muslim profession of faith: "There is no God but God and Muhammad is his prophet."

[412] Alexi Vaselev, a former Middle East correspondent for Pravda, is at the Russian Academy of Sciences.

cheat on exams, and justify it, indicative of Egypt's low ethical standards. The theology of Egypt, stronger than religion, was that of continuation. Egypt was such an old civilization that it would keep going as it always had.

Why, in 1999, did the co-pilot of Egyptian Airlines flight 990 take over the plane, and, calling upon God, plunge it into the ocean?[413]

There were 33 army officers onboard. It was against military regulations to put more than ten on one flight. Mubarak went to Paris immediately afterwards. The suspicion was that U.S. intelligence had recruited three officers; or it was a trial run for 9/11. Mubarak was mad that the U.S. got in touch with the Ikhwan in 1995 and was afraid of U.S. infiltration.

Did he know Fahmy Howadi? Yes, his uncle, Amin Howadi, was once chief of intelligence. He told the story of George Blake, born in the Netherlands of a Dutch mother and an Egyptian Jewish father. His father died when he was a boy, and he lived with relatives here and attended a British school where his cousin founded the Egyptian Communist Party. He became a spy for MI6, and the KGB. I didn't know who I was dealing with.

What about a link between the army officer who lived with Haqqani, and Egypt?

Nasser's son in law, Ashraf Marowan, an arms dealer, was thrown from a window in London. A famous actress, Soad Hosani, was going to write in her memoirs how Egyptian intelligence used actors and actresses. She was thrown from a hotel window in 2007. I could dig, but it would be dangerous.

What were the ties between the Egyptian army and the Pakistani army?

Mohammad Hussein Tantawy, Defense Minister for 17 years, who ruled after Mubarak stepped down, was defense attaché in Islamabad. We walked up the street to a corner and caught a taxi. The military and intelligence people were orchestrating everything to send a message to the West that they were facing terrorism and needed money to combat this disease which threatened to overwhelm them. Al-Qaeda existed because the government kept the people down. At its core the Ikhwan wanted to reform society. They worked with King Farouk. Their troubles began when Nasser outlawed political parties and imprisoned and killed the Ikhwan. They were in charge

---

[413] William Langewiesche, "The Crash of EgyptAir 990," *The Atlantic*, 26 Mar. 2015

of sending men to Afghanistan. The husband of Sayed Qutb's sister was involved.

Again, I met Amir at Maison Thomas. He would take me to Alexandria to see Nageh Ibrahim but wanted too much money. Two days later he called. Ibrahim was coming to Cairo tomorrow. Sophia called. She had been trying to reach Ibrahim. I said Amir was with him the day before.

She warned me, I didn't know these people, or what they were up to. There was a man I wanted to see in Alexandria. A contact in the U.S. said he knew al-Zawahiri. My contact called a man named Hossam, a businessman and asked me to see him. We met at a café. An evening wind blew a palm tree nearby. He hated these people, but he would arrange a meeting. Fathy was afraid that they would harm me. The next morning, I called Amir. He had called Ibrahim three times but he didn't respond. He had to go to the hospital. I called Alexandria but the man's phone was still off. I would have to return.

London

He walked across the street, in a dark red velvet cap, a gray thobe, sunglasses, his beard orange with henna, and joined me at the cafe. I told him about my project. He looked at me carefully. I would write what he said. But would they listen? I said the same thing to Abdul Zindani, who agreed to see me, but got sick. He nodded. He knew Zindani.

Why was America the enemy of Muslims? Many men asked this question. Many Americans, since 9/11, were afraid of them. Most people in Cairo seemed to be happy that the army overthrew the Ikhwan. Where did I stay? I told him. People in Zamalek ate '*barasim*.' It was what donkeys ate. What about the Israeli lobby? It was the Bible, Judeo-Christian culture, the Holocaust, what I learned in the U.S. Senate. Jews voted. They had been persecuted for centuries and valued democracy. Pakistani leaders captured young Muslims and sold them to America, which put them in Guantanamo. Did we buy human beings because they were Muslim? Whether it was Mubarak, of Musharraf of Pakistan, or el-Sisi, it was the same; the U.S. was close to military dictators which kept the hopes of Muslims down.

We backed Muslims in Afghanistan and Bosnia, I said. If he were to fly to Cairo, the Americans would force the plane to land. The U.K. asked for the file of evidence against him, but the U.S. didn't have one. Egypt put pressure on the U.S. to put pressure on the U.K. to send him back. The judge said what he did they didn't know. The government put him in prison for eight months. The judge dropped the case. Here, they were independent. In the U.S., they followed the White House. He said on Arab television that Tony Blair was a dog of Bush.

He was not a part of any group, although he had ties to many people. Did I know Lynn Stewart? I knew of her, the lawyer who represented Omar Abdul Rahman, the spiritual leader of al-Gamma al-Islamiyya, the blind Sheikh, imprisoned for passing messages from him to them. He was charged in this case. Stewart sent him Sheikh Rahman's medical report, and he protested outside the U.S. Embassy. The U.S. said the report was wrong, but it came from a U.S. hospital. A paralegal to Rahman was American but the U.S. tapped his phone. It wanted to arrest him because he sent money to

Rahman's sons in Kabul. A judge said he sent large sums abroad to help terrorists. Scotland Yard did research. Did I think that al-Qaeda was looking for 100 pounds, the amount he sent to Rahman's son?

The U.S. killed him in a drone strike in 2011. I would learn that the man I was sitting with signed the letter of introduction that two al-Qaeda members used to kill Ahmed Shah Massoud, two days before 9/11.[414] He told Abdullah Anas that they asked him to sign it. He did, hoping to make money selling the interview to the media. He was trapped here, he said, like a bird in a cage. The only thing the U.S. had on him was a taped phone call. Everyone said America was fair. But America was against Muslims. He condemned the attacks on the British here. You could not kill a man because of his nationality. There was no justice in that.

What about Egypt? In general, the Ikhwan did not engage in violence, but you had to defend yourself. What about al-Qaeda in the Sinai? It was real but I was not to believe its statements.[415] The army spokesman controlled the media. Journalists were afraid. He gave me the name of a man to call to see Zindani. I told him about Rahman, the army major, but he didn't recognize his name. He told me to text him when I returned to Cairo and he would send a number that would enable me to get to Nageh Ibrahim.

He said Morsi wanted the Sinai to be quiet, but el-Sisi, a slave to America, and greedy for power, provoked the Ikhwan. He saw Sadat in a dream, and that he himself wore an Omega watch. He had visions of himself as a great, wealthy man, and the heir to Sadat.[416]

A man walked by and bowed his head. He nodded. What about the phone call between al-Zawahiri and Morsi? Were al-Qaeda and the Ikhwan linked? They played a fake recording on television. It was part of the state's black propaganda. After Morsi came to power, all the groups, including the Salafis, tried to rebuild the country, but the army was opposed. Al-Zawahiri was a cat corned in a room. Osama was a symbol. Al-Qaeda was dead. During Morsi's time 25 soldiers were killed in the Sinai. The army blamed terrorists. The intelligence service killed them. He gave me a man in Cairo to call. Yunus Khalis was fighting for his land. Haqqani, he didn't know.

---

[414] Abdullah Anas and Tam Hussein, "*To the Mountains: My Life in Jihad, from Algeria to Afghanistan*" (New York: Hurst, 2019), 246, 299.
[415] https://www.dni.gov/nctc/groups/ansar_bayt_al_maqdis.html.
[416] "Sisi: A New Nasser or a New Sadat?" *Coptic Solidarity* 5/25/2014

That night I went to an address on St. James Square. My agent and I had dinner in a room with large paintings of men in uniform, and battle scenes, the weight of great men and history, a feeling of darkness, and tradition. He was here on business. He urged me to quickly finish my work. I couldn't. I had become Ahab, driven to find Moby Dick. He was Jalaluddin. I walked across Pall Mall as men walked quickly, and taxis rushed by. I never felt this energy in the Middle East, where men were too beaten down.

Saudi Arabia

The airport in Riyadh was small and felt old and musty. There were half a dozen lines of Bangladeshis. Three hours they'd been waiting, said a man in his 30s. I moved to a white peoples' line. It moved quickly. Officials wore white thobes and red-checked headdresses like the member of al-Qaeda I saw with the Taliban in Kunar Province.

Outside, a man in a suit and tie held up a sign with my name. We drove on a modern highway with overhead lights through a rocky, sandy desert. He was Indian, had a degree in history, but teaching jobs paid poorly. It was midnight and there were SUVs parked on the hills, and families having a picnic. We reached Riyadh, with skyscrapers, one story buildings, construction sites, European car dealerships, and stores with designer names. The next morning, I entered the King Faisal Center for Research and Islamic Studies, a long white building, 1960s style, built by the Bin Laden Group Company. A South Asian took my card and called the man who invited me. I walked on linoleum floors under florescent lights, like in a municipal office in America, and took an elevator to the third floor. A man escorted me down a carpeted hallway to the office of Dr. Saud al-Sarhan, in his thirties, who had invited me. A servant brought a small cup of black coffee and a glass of water on a tray. He asked what my project was. I was taken by how much he knew about Haqqani and other Mujahideen. He wanted to talk about my kidnapping.

How much was I worth? I didn't like this. They wanted three men from Guantanamo and $1.5 million. He said I needed to talk with the British ambassador. There were reports that the Ikhwan had set up headquarters in the U.K. The Prime Minister asked the ambassador, considered an expert on Islamic groups, to do a study.

Saud took me across the hall to meet Prince Khalid Bin Saud al Faisal. He too wanted to talk about my captivity. He said I didn't seem so affected. I hated this. Saud left and Khalid called out and a man brought us tea. He went to St. Andrews in Delaware, then Princeton, invested in the record business and lived in Los Angeles for ten years. He had Jewish, Christian, Muslim friends, but he wasn't making any money. He came home, worked in the Ministry of Interior and then the Petroleum Ministry. Now he was head of external relations and partnerships with other think tanks. He believed in them, independent, but able to provide information, and influence policy. Driving wasn't important as was the need for freedom and opportunities. Most women didn't care about driving. I thought of a woman I met on the plane. Why drive when you could be chauffeured. Iran was their big problem, in Syria, Iraq, and now in Yemen. People thought they were too close to Ali Abdullah Saleh, but Yemen was on the edge of chaos. It had the same number of people as they did. Could I imagine? No infrastructure, terrorism, poverty, and now Iran was there. The Shia were Muslims, he was Muslim, and Sunni, and that was it. He prayed five times a day and read the Koran.

The Taliban wanted me to pray like a Wahhabi. What did I mean? I had to place my hands higher up on chest. They said I had to convert. He shook his head. These gestures meant nothing. Men did this to have power over ignorant people; they needed to show that they knew the truth. He waved his hand, Hanbali, Taymiyyah, there were many schools. I didn't say that Wahhabis taught my jailers. I said that there were similarities between what is called fundamentalist Christianity and fundamentalist Islam. They were almost identical, he responded. I suggested that he write about this. He stared at me coldly. I understood, yet al-Kurdi, and al-Fadhli, like the Taliban, and before them the Mujahideen, told me that Christians and Muslims were "of the book," meaning of all the Abrahamic faiths. I picked up a book on King Faisal sitting on a table. The call came for prayer. He didn't think that book was very good and took another from his bookshelf and gave it to me. It was in Arabic.[417] But I couldn't read Arabic, could I? I gave it back. I made a mistake. It was a gift, and I had rejected it. We shook hands and he disappeared into the back of his office.

A man took me to the next floor. As we got off the elevator there was a poster of pictures of Mohammad's footprint saved in gold, locks of his hair, the shirt that Fatima, his wife, wore from the Topkapi Palace in Istanbul. I was in the land of Mohammad.[418] The Saudis referred to their king as Custodian of the Two Holy Mosques, in Mecca and Medina. It was this that

---

[417] Vasiliev, "*The History of Saudi Arabia*"
[418] Bill Chappell, "World's Muslim Population Will Surpass Christians This Century, Pew Says," *NPR* 2 Apr. 2015

gave them their power. My escort introduced me to al-Sharif, a heavy-set man, in his 40s, with a thick beard, the liaison with foreign scholars. He studied in America. Did I believe that the Jews were involved in 9/11? I said Cantor-Fitzgerald, a part- Jewish firm, lost more people than any other. He said they were involved. He asked about my project. I was studying the ties between South Asia and the Middle East. We came to a smaller office. A woman in an abaya was finishing a phone call. Her name was Julia Claus, at the Free University of Berlin. She and Zina Sawaf, another scholar, were going for coffee. I was welcome to join them. We sat outside a coffee shop, while water vapors from an overhead pipe provided relief in the heat. Zina, from Beirut, was a PhD candidate in social anthropology. Julia pushed her abaya back showing her hair. Two men from the Institute walked by, looking over. Zina let her long hair fall down on her shoulders. Men thought they were naked when they did this. A man waved and kept walking. The women covered their hair. I looked at Khalid's card and told them what I had done. If I emailed him by tomorrow, I would be okay, said Zina. That evening I emailed him and thanked him for the book. I thanked Saud for inviting me. That night I went for a walk. Riyadh was a city of six million with futuristic skyscrapers, wide roads with sand on the edges, dusty cars, fast-food restaurants, and motorcycles screaming by. Nearly half the population owned their homes, and few were illiterate, but not everyone had access to drinking water. Many had no sewage facilities.[419] Cats foraged in piles of garbage.

I came back to my street, went to a small grocery store and bought fruit, yogurt and crackers, sat on a stone bench and ate. Across the way, a group of men, in white thobes and red-checked kefiyyahs, sat in a café drinking coffee and bottled water, their voices low in the night. High above us laborers shouted. A construction crane moved slowly.

The next morning Julia was setting at the café with Hamid, a former diplomat, having coffee. She was returning to Berlin. We bid her farewell. A white-haired man joined us. Hamid smoked Gitanes and his friend a cigarillo. He was a professor of Al-Andalus. A tall, striking woman in black high heels walked by her face uncovered. There was something sexy about an abaya, said the professor. Hamid agreed. Very sexy, but don't marry one, then you became a slave.

---

[419] *Arab News*, May 3, 2014.

Was I married? I traveled too much, a poor excuse. He put out his hand. I was a smart man. The really smart ones were the Mormons. Muslims could only have four, but they could have as many as they wanted. All those pretty Scandinavian women, blond hair, he shook his head. Two women came by their faces uncovered. The professor felt like he was in a different city sitting here. It was this closed street, with two cafes. He loved it. Where he lived, he never saw any women, ever. Who were these women? Hamid pointed to a building. They worked in the computer start-up companies around here. Women here were frustrated. They were no different from women anywhere. Everything went on here. You had to be in the right *milieu*, drawing the word out, saying that it was a chic, upper-class world of which he was not a part.

A newspaper reported that five men were sentenced to 32 years in prison and 4,500 lashes for having a Valentine's Day party, drinking, and dancing in a rented house with women unrelated to them. The Mutaween— the Commission for the Promotion of Virtue and Prevention of Vice, the police force created by Abdul Aziz, and adopted by the Mujahideen and the Taliban, to uphold Sharia—caught them. Be careful, Hamid advised, looking at a man with a broom by a garbage can. The professor asked why I was here. I was studying Islamic political movements. "Ah, an important subject." Did he know anyone I could talk to at the university? He shook his head. A Filipino who ran the coffee shop cleaned our table. He was a full- fledged dentist in the Philippines, said Hamid. Did he come here to make more money, asked the professor? He had a cousin who ran a hospital. Maybe he could help him. That was the way things worked here, said Hamid. You had to know someone. The professor was not going to help me.

What did they think of ISIS rising in Iraq? It would burn hard, but the fire wouldn't reach here. The professor agreed. Why not? They were quiet. Who were they? No answer. I sent a note to Nasrin, in Aden, asking if Tariq al-Fadhli or Ali al-Kurdi could help me. I asked Karim to contact Zarb. I was taking a chance. I didn't know who was on the Saudi payroll. That night when I returned to my hotel, there was no electricity. The manager, a Greek, and I sat outside, waiting for the owners. His wife refused to stay at home, or to cover herself. When she went out, men called her a whore and threw water bottles at her.

A woman had to wear canvas shoes in a mall so she didn't make noise.

Some uncovered, some with a diaphanous veil, glided by, like nuns in their habits, pushing strollers. Before Mohammed, the Bedouin buried baby girls in the sand. A boy could fight. There was little food or water to share in the desert. But Fatima rode a camel and saved Mohammad in battle. The *Saudi Gazette* said a court sentenced an expatriate marriage mediator to six months in prison, 50 lashes and deportation, for immoral unlawful activities and for acting as a pimp. Three other women were arrested, one with hashish. They had agreed to meet men for marriage without the presence of their male guardian. They brought people together to arrange a short-term marriage. A man could marry three women at a time.

There was no central electric grid in Riyadh, said the manager. Each building had its own cable hooked to a main transformer. My phone rang. A man said we had a mutual friend in Yemen. I preferred to talk in person. The next evening, he came to the hotel, his SUV covered with sand. In the desert the sand could be like flour. It would swallow me. A newspaper said 25% of Saudis had asthma from breathing polluted sandy air. We drove slowly in traffic. His family had five cars, one for every male. If women drove, there would be twice as many cars on the road. The city would come to a standstill. He drove up Olaya Street, at night like a racetrack. He went downside streets looking for a café he knew where he could smoke a shisha pipe. Was he from Riyadh? He was born here, but he was Palestinian. He had to be a Saudi, or related, to be a citizen. But the Saudis supported the Palestinians. That was for publicity. His grandfather came in 1948, but they would always be foreigners. When he met customers, he wore traditional clothes. If he took his headdress off, they could tell that he was not Saudi, but when he wore it, they couldn't see him clearly. He spoke with a Saudi accent and they couldn't tell.

I had never met a Muslim who liked the Saudis. They looked down on everyone. It was true. For centuries they lived in tents and all they saw every day was the desert, a few sheep and camels that they owned. Then one morning they woke up in a palace and they had half a million riyals in the bank. It was how it was supposed to be. There were no Muslims here. Alcohol was forbidden in Islam, but at least 90% of the people drank. A newspaper said 64,000 bottles of alcohol were confiscated in the first quarter of the year.

He went to university in Sana'a and met his wife who was close to

Zarb's wife. He parked by a compound with high walls and concertina wire on top. He took off his headdress and gave his ID card to a soldier in a booth behind a window. I gave him my passport. Inside there was a playground, apartment houses, and Filipino and Malaysian families with their children. In 2006, an al-Qaeda suicide bomber struck a compound for foreigners. Since then, it was illegal for a Saudi to enter one. His ID said he was Palestinian. This was the only place he felt free. We entered a café. Men and women were smoking water pipes. A man held up a sign. Everyone had to wear Western clothes. We drove to another café and I told him about my project. Underground groups existed here. He didn't know how to do this work. He would ask a cousin who worked in the media. I said to go carefully. A Yemeni ambassador told me that Saudi Arabia and Selah were involved in the fight between al-Qaeda and the Yemeni Army. I didn't believe that Al-Qaeda existed alone. He stared at me. The Saudis and the Gulf states were all involved in al-Qaeda. How did he know? He was positive. He would help me.

The next day I read in the *Arab News* about a former member of a jihadi group who made a film critical of those who recruited men to wage jihad in Syria. I emailed the reporter. Six months I had been pursuing the Haqqani Network in the Middle East, and I had little to show for it. A board member of the organization funding me questioned my thesis. I had to prove it.

Hamid took out a pack of Gauloise. First Gitanes, now Gauloise, they reminded me of my student days in Paris, of cafes at night, the Latin Americans in exile from military dictatorships, the Marxists holding forth. "What exactly was my project," he asked. Julia said I could trust him. I lived with Jalaluddin Haqqani during the Soviet war. I felt that he, with al-Zawahiri, had links to jihadi groups in the Middle East. This was important to the Americans and the Europeans, Hamid replied. The relationship between Pakistan and Saudi Arabia was the oldest, closest, and most enduring between the two countries. It was based upon mutual security. In 1967, Pakistan signed a pact with Saudi Arabia to defend the Kingdom; in the 1970s its pilots flew Saudi fighter jets. It stationed troops here.[420]

Hamid typed on his phone "beware of the goons." He meant the Mutaween. I must let my beard grow longer. I sent emails to the Palestinian,

---

[420] Fair, *"Fighting to the End,"* 83

but he didn't reply, or take my calls. I sent a note to Karim. Maybe they had observed him, he replied.

On April 30th, a newspaper ran a photograph under the headline "Battle-ready KSA warns enemies," of Crown Prince Salman standing in a covered cart reviewing troops at the conclusion of the nation's largest military exercise, Abdullah's Shield, with 130,000 soldiers. It was held near Iraq, in the Eastern Province, where the Shia lived, who could not join the army or the police. The Saudis were afraid that the Shia in Yemen would link up with the Shia there. Royalty from the Gulf, except Qatar, were in the reviewing stand, with the chief of staff of the Pakistani army. Saudi Arabia was one of the highest spenders on arms in the world.[421]

The next morning al-Sharif stood in front of my desk, holding up his phone showing a video, proof that no Jews were harmed in the 9/11 attacks. I told him to stop. "What exactly was my project?" Julia felt uneasy around him. Hamid thought he was a spy. I was studying Islamic political movements. He looked at me coldly. Be careful. What I was doing was dangerous.

It was late Thursday afternoon. I went down to the third floor to see Saud. It was dark. A Pakistani, in shalwar kameez, with short hair and a moustache, meaning military, possibly ISI, stared at me. What was I doing here? I worked here. Where? I told him. This floor was off-limits. I wanted to give Saud a book. I held it up. He was gone. I was the enemy here. I went back upstairs. I read an article. "Yemen says 37 al-Qaeda militants killed in fighting in Shabwa Province." I sent a note to Abdullah in the foreign ministry. Attacks on AQAP in Yemen proofs that there are many Qaedah in Yemen, he wrote, "AQAP is tailored by Saleh and Saudis." On May 5th Saudi Arabia said it had broken a terror cell of 62 people, 59 of whom were Saudis, one Yemeni, one Pakistani, and one Palestinian.

The assistant to Sheikh Salman al-Awdah, a scholar, with the Ikhwan, once in prison, now a television celebrity with millions of followers on Twitter, called to say that al-Awdah would see me. Zina, and Roxanne, a Syrian secretary, both wanted to be my interpreter. Al-Sharif found out and warned me not to go. I went to see Yaha bin Junaid, the director of research. The government was removing his books from the stores. It was a warning.

---

[421] "Global Military Spending Remains High at $1.7 Trillion," *SIPRI* 2 May 2018

Al-Awdah's assistant called to cancel.

The next morning Hamid was smoking, drinking coffee and eating a granola bar. I should be so happy to be an American. Never, in human history, had there been such a noble experiment as America. What was wrong? He was not sleeping well. A man in his late 40s, exuding a slick confidence, joined us. He was a plastic surgeon and had lived in Malibu. He asked for my card. Was I Jewish? Twice men had asked me. Hamid spoke to him. There was another journalist kidnapped, but he was killed. Yes, Daniel Pearl, he was Jewish. Why didn't they kill me? I wasn't sure why.

General George Marshall, Secretary of State under President Truman, who Truman felt was the greatest living American, opposed recognizing Israel. There were 30 million Arabs against 600,000 Jews, said James Forrestal, Secretary of Defense. Clark Clifford wrote in his memoirs that Truman often quoted the Bible, especially Deuteronomy 1:8: *"Behold, I have given up the land before you; go in and take possession of the land which the Lord hath sworn unto your fathers, to Abraham, to Isaac and to Jacob."* On May 14, 1948, Israel became a state. The U.S. and the Soviet Union recognized it.[422] Arab states attacked. Ruth Pearl, Daniel's mother was born in Baghdad, went to a French school, and spoke Arabic. Israel was founded, and her family left for Iran. Now they were the enemy, she said.

Abdullah, assistant to Prince Turki bin al-Faisal bin Abdulaziz al-Saud, director of the Institute, brought me into his office. How did I survive in Yemen? It was very dangerous there. I talked about Ali Hamid, his brother's friend, about the school I attended, the Houthis in the Old City, the signs, "Death to America." He shook his head. Yemen was such a dangerous, rough, unpredictable place. Al-Qaeda was there. Ali Abdullah Saleh invited them in and gave them room. They were tied to the tribes.

We heard a cough in the other room. Prince Turki, the youngest of King Feisal's eight sons, of medium height, with a short gray beard and wearing a white thobe, kefiyyah, and dark cloak with gold trim, came around his large hardwood desk, and we shook hands. There was a coffee table filled with books in front of his desk. He told me to sit there. There were dark wood-

---

[422] Amb. Richard Holbrooke served as Assistant Secretary of State for East Asian and Pacific Affairs (1977-81). "President Truman's Decision to Recognize Israel," *Jerusalem Center for Public Affairs* 6 May 2018, http://jcpa.org/article/president-truman%E2%80%99s-decision-to-recognize-israel/.

paneled walls, bookshelves, and a room behind us. Saud joined us. A servant came with a silver tray, a pot of coffee, and a pot of tea.

Who kidnapped me, the Afghan Taliban or the Pakistani Taliban? I briefly told him the story. Prince Turki was director general of Saudi Intelligence from 1977-2001. What was I doing now? I told him. What religion was I, if I had one, if he could ask? I grew up as a Plymouth Brethren, a small Protestant assembly. "Isolated in the central deserts, this little community of the godly, were the Plymouth Brethren of Islam," wrote an English author.[423]

I mentioned my ties to the Haqqanis which maybe helped keep me alive. I was here doing research on them. He leaned forward, smiling warmly. It was interesting. Jalaluddin, if he was alive, would be in his 80s. No, I said, he was in his 70s. No, 80s, of that he was certain. He had two sons, but he never met them. I told him about his first mosque and then his large one. I heard that he was married to an Arab, maybe a Yemeni, and was a wealthy man with many children. I glanced at the computer on his right, a laptop in front of him, a smart phone, and two stacks of books.

He knew Haqqani in the 1980s and thought then that he was a good leader among the second tier Pashtun Mujahideen. He didn't think he was ever that close to bin Laden, who the Haqqanis saw as a do-gooder, or that he was that close to the Taliban either, although they tried to recruit him to give them more legitimacy. It was during the late 1980s and early 1990s that he began to establish commercial links with the UAE. He thought they still existed. He didn't know if he was married to an Arab. He was interested in bringing people together, more conciliatory than others. He was a nationalist more than anything trying to protect his land and interests. He told the Americans when he was ambassador that it was wrong to take this man who was our ally and make him a terrorist. The military disagreed. By then they had invaded. Americans didn't generally listen to others.

Mikhail Gorbachev called the U. S. policy "the historical and political boomerang."[424] "The Americans were working in secret with those forces with whom they were now fighting. They should accept part of the blame.

---

[423] Lacey, "*The Kingdom: Arabia & the House of Sa'ud*," 56
[424] "Britain Should Pull out of Afghanistan, Says Gorbachev," *Independent* 27 Feb. 2011

Let them say so. I think God has some mechanism that he uses to punish those that make mistakes."

There was tribalism in Washington as there was in Afghanistan. He meant the Pentagon against the CIA; the CIA against the FBI; the State Department against the Pentagon, the Army, the Navy, the Air Force vying for funding. Haqqani came to see him in 1998 and asked for support for the Taliban. He told him to first give them bin Laden. Haqqani was their emissary? He had a ministerial position, trade or something, if he recalled correctly. Haqqani was more courageous than (Mullah) Omar who fled to Pakistan. He was not anywhere other than in his region. He didn't have access to any intelligence, but he didn't think that he was in the Middle East. The same went for al-Zawahiri, who seemed to be in Pakistan. He issued statements but ISIL and al-Nusra didn't pay attention. He didn't think that al-Qaeda in Yemen paid allegiance to him. Bin Laden was one of their own.

Why not? "Al-Zawahiri, an Egyptian?"[425] he raised his hands. It was Arabia against the Levant. Nasser wanted the Saudi oil fields.

He wouldn't be surprised if al-Qaeda, the Taliban, whichever they were, came from different countries, and with their wives, to Yemen. They had 450,000 illegal entries from Yemen last year, and that was of people they caught. If they came across the desert they could see them, but there was a 125-mile area in the mountains in which they couldn't. They came from East Africa, fleeing tribal warfare. The Americans and the French, using Djibouti as their base, were patrolling the sea, but with little success. He didn't think there was any movement across Africa, or that al-Qaeda had outside help.

Yemenis were fleeing to the Horn of Africa. This chaos helped al-Shabab in Somalia. The borders among Eritrea, Ethiopia, Kenya, Puntland, Somalia, Sudan, and Yemen, were open. He didn't know about movement out from the Tribal Areas, yes, there could be, of course. Pakistan had its hands full trying to have a government over which it had some influence in Kabul. I mentioned Pakistan's fear of invasion from the west. He agreed, and worried about a rising Hindu nationalism in India. He quoted Ahmad al-Bruni, who saw two types of Hindus, the uneducated who worshipped idols and believed in many gods and the educated who believed in one God. The

---

[425] "National Geographic's DNA Analysis Concludes That Egyptians Are Only 17% Arab," *Cairo Scene*

problem was the Durand Line. He would create a Marshall Plan for both sides of the border; build roads, schools, and medical clinics, to take away their poverty.

What about the Wahhabi schools? He didn't answer. With the border the Pashtuns were still divided. It was like the Rio Grande. He smiled. Texas was once part of Mexico. It could be like a federation, where people lived better, and had more security. There would be no need for the border. Afghanistan was the only country which voted against Pakistan joining the U.N., because of the border, he, too, like Babar, reminded me. They had problems with the Houthis, who were tied to Iran, and had attacked the Kingdom. They wanted to recreate their Imamate, but to do that they needed Iran, which backed them to further its power.

He accepted Foreign Minister al-Kirbi's numbers of three to four thousand al-Qaeda in Yemen. Many came by sea from the Tribal Areas, from East Africa and Somalia. They crossed into Iran. He told me to go to Abu Dhabi to learn more about Haqqani.

Abdul Majid al-Wahhab

The next day, Friday, men were wearing masks. According to the news, eight people died yesterday because of MERS, a coronavirus for which there was no cure. Ahmed smoked and read a paper. A black SUV pulled up and a man, six one, 180 pounds, early 40s, joined us. Hamid shook his fist at him. He was the cause of all their troubles. His name was Abdul Majid al-Shaikh, a direct descendent of Mohammad al-Wahhab.

We shook hands. He must be proud of being a direct descendent. I would like to talk to him, he was very proud of his family. He would explain the true Islam. Did I know anything about Wahhabism? I'd studied it. I'd been with the Taliban. He stared at me. The Taliban were idiots. I knew these men. They were proud to be Wahhabis, and he hated them. It was 10:30 time for prayers. "Goodbye priest," said Hamid. He was ruining the country. He walked away and came back. If someone said they understood his family, I was not to listen to any information about the Sheikh. Some would give me false information under his name. They hated Wahhabism. They were against Islam.

The next morning Hamid was at the cafe drinking black Americano. The priest was looking for me. He wasn't in either coffee shop. I needed to buy a mask. Hamid gave me directions to a pharmacy. I couldn't see more than 200 yards. It was like Ground Zero on 9/11. It came from here, Tariq told me in Sanaá. I bought three masks and returned. A lean man with a straggly beard and Hamid were talking intensely.

He was a journalist. Could he write freely? They robbed them of their fingers, their joy and pleasure, he replied. "He is the holy and I am the mundane," Hamid added. Al-Wahhab, wearing a mask, joined us. The road to Baghdad went through Khorasan, the journalist warned me, meaning Afghanistan. The Americans gave Iraq to Iran on a golden plate. Syria would become Afghanistan. Bashir al-Assad was related, through marriage, to the Saudi royal family. America was going to be in quicksand. Changes were coming. The fire would reach everyone—except Saudi Arabia. He waved goodbye.

I walked to the other café. The night before Abdul Majid sat with Hamid reading *Aristotle's Ethics.* In the 8th Century Arab Christians and Muslims were translating Aristotle and Plato into Arabic.[426] I said the West considered Wahhabism a violent sect of Islam. People had a misconception about al-Wahhab, he assured me. They changed his ideas and his principles for their own purposes. They took what they wanted, not the facts. Wahhabism wanted all people, all religions, whether Christian, Jewish, Buddhist, or Hindu, to live in harmony.

But the Wahhabis wanted to destroy the Prophet's home, because people worshipped there, and cemeteries, because people went to them, the first step to idol worship.

To kidnap was not Islam, he replied. That was terrorism. The message of Islam was to love the people. Islam was against terrorism. But his ancestor and Ibn-Saud formed an alliance to wage jihad. Yes, the two families came together to create a country. Together in battle they created Saudi Arabia. I was, in a way, Hamid said, talking to a descendent of Thomas Jefferson. Bin Laden was a terrorist, said Abdul Majid. The message of Islam was peace.

The Taliban who took me were Wahhabis. They taught them. The Taliban were not Wahhabis, he said firmly. How did Wahhabism deal with the changes in Saudi Arabia?

Islam was not against travel or entertainment. Thousands of people here went to America to study. He liked to travel and take what was good from one culture and adopt it in his own life. He was going soon with his family to the south of France. Yes, why not? He would not take what was against Islam. He would not lose control of his culture. He had to go now. We would talk again. I imagined him lying on a beach in Cannes.

Another man came, thin, late 50s, with dark gray, brown curly hair. When he was a boy, his father was the auctioneer in the vegetable market. There were three parts: the farmers, who grew the vegetables and watermelons; the driver, who brought the produce; and the landowner, who shared in the profits. In the 70s, there was a wheat shortage, and people became more religious. He went to America to study business at the University of Miami, and his cousin called. It was 1979. There was trouble in Mecca. He went to the airport to meet his cousin, who was flying in from

---

[426] Albert Hourani, *A History of the Arab Peoples,*76

Indiana. While waiting, he talked with an American. He, too, knew that something was happening in Mecca. He said the America that his grandparents wanted to build had changed. It was the same here.

It was the attempted coup, which helped lead to the Soviet invasion of Afghanistan, to the rise of the Salafis in Yemen, which led to war against the Zaydi Shia, and to the rise of the Houthis.

He was in the real estate business. When would I return to Cairo? He had an apartment there. We could all go together. It was a wonderful city, with all kinds of people, Muslims, Christians, everyone. Hamid wanted to go. He too wanted freedom.

A picture in the morning paper showed Pakistani and Saudi naval officers standing by the Pakistani submarine, Hamza[427] named after one of Mohammed's uncles, at al-Jubayl, on the east coast 100 miles from Iran, after their joint exercises. I asked Saud if I could see the Interior Minister, and the Foreign Minister. It would not be possible. A Yemeni gave me two relatives to call. One called back. If I couldn't explain over the phone what I wanted, he wouldn't meet me. Again, I told Saud that I wanted to talk. "God willing," he responded. Everything was in the hands of God, but God willing seemed to mean no. Patience, said the Incas, I learned in the Andes, was the supreme virtue.

Nasrin wrote that she had no news on al-Fadhli or al-Kurdi. A newspaper reported that al-Qaeda attacked an army post in Shabwa Province. Abdulrazzaq al-Jamal said al-Qaeda raised a black flag with the words, "There is no god but God and Muhammad is his Prophet," at the main police station in Azzan, the capital.

I reached General al-Turki, spokesman for the Ministry of Interior. He could see me next week. Yaha, my advisor, a kind, friendly man, was surprised that they would let me into the Ministry. I had a beard, but I didn't look like a terrorist. I wore one to be more acceptable, like carrying maswak. That night Hamid was smoking a Gauloise and eating a bar of mint chocolate. This country was obsessed with sex. Everything was forbidden and so it was bursting to come out. I didn't see this. It was my fault because I

---

[427] Hamza was Arabic for steadfast, and in Urdu, from the Turkish word for camp or army, the language that developed among the soldiers of different ethnicities of the Mughal armies, today the national language of Pakistan.

didn't talk to people. What was I supposed to do, go up to a woman in the mall? He laughed. No one would tell me the truth.

A hefty man in his 30s sat in my hotel lobby reading the paper. He was a filmmaker. What it was like to be one in Wahhabi Saudi Arabia? He told me to stop right there. He was a Wahhabi and didn't like violence. There were many forms of Islam. He was an artist, and a Wahhabi. Ever since he was a boy, he had been moved by film. In 1999, he and his friends started the first website on film. The Minister of Culture invited him to his office to discuss film. Through their website people found a community. He established a cinema page in *Al-Watan*, a prominent newspaper in the Arab world. In 2006, he became the first man to be invited on television to talk about cinema. He and his friends were supposed to be on for 45 minutes but were on for an hour and twenty minutes. Still, there were so many obstacles. A picture was haram for some people. They would not carry a banknote because it had a picture on it. They didn't want to anger God. To look at a picture was to glorify man, not God.

His goal was to promote this visual art and to show the beauty of his society to the world. The jihadis were against him, but he was less afraid of them now. The security services had done a great job. The Kingdom was safe. Had I seen Amadeus? Remember when Salieri said he wanted to please God with his music, yet Mozart, this vulgar, worldly man, God gave to him this great gift? He believed in God. He respected the religions of Christians, Jews, Hindus and Buddhists. Saudi Arabia was a religious country. Some said cinema would destroy religion. He studied mechanical engineering and worked for Aramco. Being a mechanical engineer, where he had to calculate how much weight a crane could bear, for example, helped him to plot scenes in his mind. He believed in his beautiful, strong, noble religion, which he wanted to show to the world. His faith had great values, which, if people followed them, would give them a better life.

My taxi arrived. The traffic flowed on freeways, like in Los Angles. I asked my driver where he was from. Pakistan. Where? Peshawar? There were 20,000 Pashtuns in Riyadh. "What about the Taliban?" Saudi Arabia was safe. Did he know of Jalaluddin Haqqani? He laughed. "Well?" He was quiet.

Summer was coming. There were heat waves on the highway. The Ministry of Interior loomed, like the Guggenheim in New York, with each floor a circle, twenty stories high, surrounded by a wall, with concrete barriers, soldiers behind machine guns, and pill boxes every thirty yards. We approached a white high rise next to the ministry, and a guard, in olive drab, waved us on.

"This terror cell, with links to extremist elements in Syria and Yemen, had been plotting to assassinate officials and attack government targets in the Kingdom and the region," said General al-Turki in a newspaper. "It was tied to the Islamic State of Iraq and the Levant (ISIL) in Syria,[428] and to Jabhat al-Nusra (al-Qaida), in Iraq. They had over $500,000 which they planned to use to smuggle arms from Yemen."

We drove around the complex and returned and the guard told us to stop. We called the assistant. He asked for my passport number. A guard came to the window, looked at my passport, and made a call. A guard escorted me into the high rise. It smelled of plaster and putty. A guard at a counter photocopied pages of my passport and gave it to a guard in olive drab. We rode to the sixth floor, where a general and a colonel, in Saudi dress, were waiting. We entered a large wood-paneled office. Major General Engineer Mansour Sultan al-Turki, in Saudi dress, came around his desk. There was a glass of water and glass of amber tea on a table in front. It was hot out. Each day it would get warmer up to 115 degrees at least, he said. Had air-conditioning made people softer? I had seen Frank Shakespeare's photograph of Abdul Aziz, and his men on camels with bandoleers, tough men in the desert.

Air conditioning imprisoned them and kept them inside. When they started to buy cars, the most important thing was the quality of the air-conditioning. The Japanese cars had the best and sold the most cars. Al-Turki smiled, drawing on his cigarette. They still confronted terrorism in the Kingdom. The threat was from al-Qaeda in Yemen, and Daesh in Iraq and Syria. They were increasing personnel and training. They had more border guards. Al-Qaeda could send people from Yemen.

They were trying to keep an eye on anything linked to any ideological activity that would lead to terrorism. They monitored the Internet and social media. They sent people to where al-Qaeda was approaching the population. They used people from the Ministry of Islamic Affairs and the Ministry of Education to educate the community. The trouble came from al-Qaeda, the

---

[428] Also called the Islamic State of Iraq and al-Sham, meaning Syria, ISIS

Muslim Brotherhood, Saudi Hezbollah, and the Houthis of Yemen. They caught the 59 Saudis because they were using Skype. They focused on Twitter accounts outside of the Kingdom used to recruit young people. They used videos from Syria which showed gruesome atrocities. "If you want to help these people, please send money." They provided a bank account. Most were in Kuwait or Turkey. They froze them or blocked transfers of money, but other accounts appeared. Saudis targeted others here. Terrorism only needed 200 people to cause trouble.

They had experience dealing with this because of Afghanistan. The difference was that there were 10-20 thousand Saudis who went there and now the number was smaller, and they had no training. This number was higher than any acknowledged by the U.S. People went to Syria and were lost. Today's generation inherited an interest from the past on the Internet and by listening to the Mujahideen. They had new laws on financing. There were no laws which allowed them to put the Mujahideen returning in prison, but now it was against the law to go to Syria. During the Afghan and Bosnian wars there were boxes in supermarkets where you could donate. There were pictures of children and you could adopt one for $100 and take care of this child by sending money. He paid 100 riyals a month. The money went to al-Qaeda.

Today, it was done secretly. Iran captured members of al-Qaeda when they fled after the U.S. bombing in 2001 from Afghanistan and was using these people. What was al-Qaeda doing in Iraq, targeting poor people in markets? Where did they learn to make the bombs? Al-Qaeda in Yemen had been approached by more experienced people. Here al-Qaeda was using young people to target the Saudis.

A former Yemeni ambassador to Riyadh, living in Cairo, told me that al-Qaeda leaders were all Saudis. If you were fleeing and took refuge with a tribe, they must sacrifice everything to protect you.[429] If not, it was a great shame. Al-Qaeda married into the tribes and convinced the sheikhs that they were protecting Islam from the West in Palestine, in Iraq and against U.S. drones, which were killing civilians.

What role did Wahhabism play in terrorism? When I talked about

---

[429] They provide "Alamonan," or safety.

Wahhabism, I must look instead at the Ikhwan.[430] It found in Afghanistan the al-Qaeda it could not find here. Terrorism was the marriage of the Ikhwan, and bin Laden's al-Qaeda. He couldn't say that Saudi Arabia gave Abdullah Azzam and other Ikhwan refuge when Nasser forced them to flee Egypt. The Ikhwan-Wahhabi alliance was born here.

"What changed the Mujahideen, and men like bin Laden, was the Ikhwan," the general added. They targeted them on three levels: the people, to raise money, and to spread their ideology. Those who brainwashed the young men had all been in Afghanistan. "The U.S. created al-Qaeda," Colonel Omar, in a white headdress, said "when the U.S. and Muslim countries worked with the Mujahideen."

"Wahhabism was a conviction and religious movement which rose when people were poor and isolated," said the general. Sheikh Mohammed traveled in Iraq and Egypt and went back to his people and said they were not practicing Islam properly, and he taught them. Wahhabism's history showed that it was a religious movement only. The tapes that they all listened to in the 1980s calling on men to wage jihad, came from Egypt. The ideology of the Ikhwan was propagated there in the 1980s and 90s, targeting the young who became terrorists. The Egyptians wanted to repeat this here. It is taken from Takfirism. They told the people that they were infidels because they didn't know the true Islam. His brother was with these people. You left here with no ideology, but you came back from Afghanistan with one. It was this ideology that they were fighting.

Where were people coming from? Surprisingly, they crossed Africa from Chad to here. Al-Qaeda had been hijacked by internecine warfare. If a group was loyal to al-Qaeda, it was a part of that family; if not, it was the enemy.

Who was behind it? The threat was coming from Syria and Yemen. Al-Zawahiri in Pakistan was focused on those countries. Al-Qaeda was a series of small groups, each with its own ideology, and leadership. It recruited young people with social problems.

I watched a video in Yemen of a man whispering as he filmed an SUV rushing a military base, men getting out, shooting others, speeding over a bumpy road, and as it approached a building, he got more excited, and then

---

[430] The Muslim Brotherhood.

an explosion, and a cloud of black smoke rose high. "Allah-o-Akbar," he kept repeating. They were a brotherhood. God was greater than the gods of money, of pleasure, of worldly success. They fought the invaders, the apostates, the corrupt, and the evil.

Al-Qaeda lived in congested areas where it was hard to find them. They explained to the people how and why they must be careful. They gave rewards. There was a number of people could call if they were suspicious. I'd heard in Aden that al-Qaeda smuggled women across the border. It was true. They were good with finances. If you got them emotionally involved, they were a big help. There was a woman in prison. Women could move within the female community, raising money, and recruiting. Al-Qaeda told young men they were not men; a woman was joining, and they were not. They wanted women to take care of their children. It was good propaganda.

He didn't know why in Syria and Iraq they always brought up Saudi Arabia as the main culprit. Iran felt it was the best way to destroy the Sunni image. We never heard about the Shia involvement in al-Qaeda's suicide bombings. Iran was using al-Qaeda. It was very complicated, and all behind the scenes.

Al-Qaeda is American Mumbo-Jumbo

I continued meeting people, hoping for a door to open. Alem, wearing a thobe, greeted me in his book-lined office, with degrees from prominent American universities on the wall. Did I want coffee or tea, with sugar or not? I had never in the Middle East been offered a choice. Sugar wasn't good for you I told Um Hussein, our cleaning lady, as she poured tea in the kitchen at CALES. "You can't change us," she said smiling.

Alem lectured me for walking to his office in the mid-day sun. I had to understand the traditional rhythm of the Arab farmer. He rose an hour before sunrise to begin his chores, prayed, had breakfast, worked in the fields until about 10:00, came home, took a nap, then went to midday prayers, and rested. When the sun was two-thirds in the sky, he prayed again, and then there were the sunset prayers. Today, they all had a Vitamin D deficiency. They needed more sun. Kids believed that cars could overcome anything. They drove out into the sand with a few bottles of water, got stuck, and died. They drove into wadis and drowned.[431] It happened all the time. They had lost their concept of nature and the natural skills to survive.

For a time, Abdul Aziz ibn Saud was a long-haired barefoot boy, like Mohammad, in the desert.

He knew how to track a camel, to live on dates and a bowl of camel's milk. Now young men raced fancy cars, sat in cafes, and princes lived in palaces. "The Bedu never doubted their superiority," wrote Thesiger. He asked some who had met Abdul Aziz how they addressed him.

'We called him Abdul Aziz how else would we call him except by his name? Why not "Your Majesty?" They were Bedu, they answered. They had no king but God.

Saudi society was the marriage of the Muslim Brotherhood and Wahhabism, Alem continued.

The creed was Asharism, an attempt to reconcile the non-rational with the rational, founded by Ali ibn Ismail al-Ashari (873-935) in Baghdad. He held that the attributes of God, the belief, for example, that God was

---

[431] Dry river beds that filled with water in a rainstorm.

everywhere, were different from his essence; the Koran was the eternal, uncreated word and essence of God; but the words that men used when reciting the Koran, and the ink and paper that they used to copy God's word, were created. There was no free will. There were no laws of nature; everything that happened was God's will. Man's destiny was written before the world was created; man did not think, but God thought through him.

"The Arab is by nature a fatalist," wrote Marine Corps Col. William Eddy, President Roosevelt's interpreter when he met Abdul Aziz on the USS Quincy in the Suez Canal. "He accepts what comes as a matter of course and as a gift from Allah"[432] Eddy, born of Presbyterian missionary parents in Beirut knew that a Christian was to follow the will of God.

There were the Mutazilah, the separatists,[433] who said God could do no evil. It was God's will that if you put a fire next to a cloth it would catch fire; God did this. They were an intellectual minority that believed that Sharia had to be based upon those hadith that were true eyewitness reports of the practices and saying of Mohammed.[4] They opposed the inequality, and the luxury of the Caliphate, that Muslims killed other Muslims. The true source of human happiness lay not in political power but in meditating on the Koran, in following God's will, in living a life of asceticism and reflection. Man was responsible for his acts, but because God was just, he gave man the power to live righteously. The caliphs must be held accountable for their deeds.

In the 1920s Hassan al-Banna went on pilgrimages to Mecca and Medina. In 1924, the Caliphate fell. In 1928 a few of the Ikhwan went to Arabia to teach. When Israel was founded, it meant the return of the Jews to the Holy Land and for Christians the advent of the Second Coming. To Muslims, it was, after the failure of the Crusades, the re-conquest. In 1952, the Ikhwan helped the Free Officers in their coup, but Nasser, afraid of their power, imprisoned, tortured and killed them. Other governments followed him. Those Ikhwan who could, fled to Saudi Arabia. Crown Prince Faisal could not allow Nasser, and his Pan-Arab socialism, to rule. He organized a bloc around "Islamic solidarity," making Islam the Kingdom's identity, the counter-ideology to Nasser's socialism. The royal family visited America and

---

[432] Rafiq A. Tschannen, "What Happened When Saudi King Abdul Aziz Met US President Roosevelt," *Muslim Times* 22 Feb. 2020
[433] *Dictionary of Islam*, 425

Europe, were seduced by their luxury and power, putting more pressure on the Wahhabis, who, with their desert, anti-Shia, anti-Sufi Puritanism, had to work with the streetwise, political Ikhwan to counter the West and Israel, a Western colonial outpost.

In 1958, a "Cold War"[434] began between the Egyptian-led Soviet-leaning socialists and Saudi Arabia's "Islamic bloc,"[435] allied with America. Faisal introduced radio and television, angering the Wahhabis, and used these weapons, with the Ikhwan, who had the credibility, from being imprisoned, and the ability, to lead a sophisticated propaganda war against him. After Nasser brought al-Azhar under his control, Saudi Arabia founded the Islamic University of Medina to compete against it. Taher, in Sanaá, said it was to teach foreigners Wahhabism which they would then preach in their home countries. It was like the People's Friendship University in Moscow, which became The Patrice Lumumba University, after the death of the Pan-African leader of the Congo, to teach foreigners communism, which they could teach in their countries.

The Ikhwan gained influence in Saudi universities. In 1962, the Saudis created the Muslim World League to propagate Wahhabism internationally, brought in al-Banna's son-in-law, Said Ramadan, and Maududi, founder of Jamaat-i-Islami, bringing Pakistan closer to Saudi Arabia. In 1965, Nasser accused the Ikhwan of conspiracy, and put thousands in concentration camps, among them Sayyid Qutb, born in 1906, who said he was really born in 1951 when he joined the Ikhwan.[436] He called Nasser a false god, who the Arab masses, beat down by colonialism, bowed to. They had to kill the Pharaoh. After Nasser hanged him in 1966, he became a martyr. In 1967, businessmen founded King Abdul Aziz University in Jeddah, where Abdullah Azzam and Mohammad Qutb, Syed's younger brother, became professors, where bin Laden studied. In October 1973, after the Yom Kippur-Ramadan War broke out, and Saudi Arabia reduced its oil production and raised prices, creating a vast new source of wealth, and long gas lines in America, the Saudis invested in U.S. banks, treasury bonds, and real estate.

---

[434] Malcolm Kerr, "*The Arab Cold War*" (Oxford: Oxford University Press, 1971)
[435] Stephane Lacroix, "*Awakening Islam*," (Cambridge: Harvard University Press, 2011), 41 Interview author, Paris 2014.
[436] Gilles Kepel, "*The Roots of Radical Islam*," (London: Saqi, 2005), 39

The Muslim World League fought communism,[437] sent out more Wahhabi missionaries, built madrasas in Yemen, and in the Tribal Areas.[438]

The Ikhwan built camps to teach boys the Koran, and sports. In Yemen, President al-Hamdi appointed Ali Abdullah Saleh to set up camps,[439] where Abdul Latif trained. A political social revivalist movement, called the Islamic Awakening,[440] rose against Wahhabism, and the lure of the West. Then Juhayman al-Utaybi's JSM, the Salafi Party that Commands Right and Forbids Wrong, rose.[441] The movement became more Sayyid Qutb than Hassan al-Banna. In 1975, the Mujahideen attacked Afghanistan. In 1977, General Zia ul-Haq seized power and afraid that if Pakistan did not become more Muslim it would become India again,[442] became "Fortress Islam."[443] After the 1978 Camp David Accords, Saudi Arabia paid Pakistan to put two battalions in the Gulf.[444] In 1979, Khomeini came to power, exciting the Shia in the eastern province, drawing Saudi Arabia closer to Pakistan. JSM attacked the Grand Mosque. The Soviet Union invaded Afghanistan. In 1982 Saudi Arabia paid for 50 F-15s that Pakistan acquired.[445] Its pilots flew Saudi aircraft.[446]

Alem, who was dismissive of American democracy, said the royal family was afraid that the Ikhwan would set up an alternative government. Salafism was tied to faithfulness to scripture.

Al-Qaeda, like the Kharijis, the Puritans of the 7th Century, came from the lowest classes. If al-Qaeda wanted to fight the West it would have a huge following here, but they couldn't do this by saying that the Saudi leaders were apostates.[447] "America's fear of al-Qaeda was mumbo-jumbo," he assured me. "It used it for political reasons. It was no more dangerous than a run-of-the-mill criminal enterprise." The former Yemeni ambassador to

---

[437] "Muslim World League," *Oxford Islamic Studies Online*
[438] Evgenii Novikov, "The World Muslim League: Agent of Wahhabi Propagation in Europe," *Jamestown* 20 Sept. 2016
[439] Lacroix, "*Awakening Islam*," 48-49
[440] Al-Sahwa al-Islamiyya.
[441] Al-Jamaa al-Salafiyya al-Muhrasiba (JSM).
[442] Kamal Dayar, *Tryst with Perfidy*,169
[443] Ibid, p. 168.
[444] Lacey, "*The Kingdom: Arabia & the House of Sa'ud*," 455
[445] *Christian Science Monitor* 12/6/82.
[446] Vasiliev, "*The History of Saudi Arabia*," 399
[447] Hourani, "*A History of the Arab Peoples*," 30-31

Riyadh said the same thing. Alem wasn't worried about Saudi Arabia, the only nation to create its own borders. It was an international sport to predict its demise. There was contempt in the Levant for the man of the desert, whom they saw as a country bumpkin, illiterate, and dangerous. Why did Egyptians blame America for its problems? He laughed. He would love to find one Arab intellectual, just one, who would say he was wrong. They blame the Ottomans, the Zionists, the colonialists, the Americans, the petrodollar. Egypt was living off its past grandeur, and current chaos. They would have to bankroll Egypt until it bankrupted them. Morsi was the most popular politician in Saudi Arabia.

That evening, at the café, I glanced at the truck, always there, 30 yards away, with a machine gun and four soldiers. A man joined me. He was a writer but worked in a ministry to support himself. I said General al-Turki, in the Interior Ministry, said they used the Ministry of Religious Affairs and the Department of Education to work with militants. He shook his head. It was a stupid idea to think that religious scholars had any influence on the new Mujahideen. They were outside the system. They got a diploma in order to get a job but were committed to their cause. None of the ministries had any influence. He was sad that almost everyone who joined seemed to be Saudi. It was the result of the extremist religious discourse, official and unofficial, which created of a new generation of fighters. Extremists, using social media, manipulated, and had a certain control, over society. They hit his family hard. Three of his cousins were killed in Syria. We were silent. This was why he agreed to meet. He was crying inside. He hated these men. They told the young that they needed to do this for Islam, and for Paradise. They kidnapped them. They didn't tell their parents but called them when they arrived in Syria. His aunts and uncles collapsed and were in shock for a month. They couldn't see anybody. Then they learned that their sons were killed. His eyes were sad. In a way, it was better. They didn't have to worry all the time. Every family whose son went to Syria suffered. He wrote to get his anger out, but he had to be careful. It was dangerous to go against the government.

The Desert

That Friday, Les Janka, a former Pentagon and White House official, working here, took me to old Riyadh, with baked mud walls, a souk, and the fort that Abdul Aziz, 21, and 29 of his friends attacked at dawn in 1902, his first battle to re-establish the Saud dynasty. Les took the highway toward Mecca. The land was rocky and covered with scrub grass. Rust red sand dunes appeared. He drove onto a gravel road down to a wadi. There were plastic bottles, rags, paper plates, a carpet, soft drink cans, and Styrofoam containers. We drove up into the hills and it was clean and silent and sand dunes rolled into the distance. I walked slowly in the heat. The desert, in Afghanistan, was bitter cold at night. Abdul Aziz and his men lived in the desert for a month before he was ready to attack. I walked over a hill and was alone and the wind burned my face. It was hard to walk. Mohammad meditated in a cave in the desert. This was where al-Wahhab told men that they had to return to the Koran. Jalaluddin and Ibrahim and their men prayed in the mud and the snow. Their sons, like those of Abdul Aziz, had to prove themselves, like all men, against their father. That evening I met again with al-Wahhab. I asked how his ancestor began.

Sheikh Mohammad ibn al-Wahhab's object was to declare Islam as the true faith, and to correct the people, who, because they were isolated, and backward, didn't know the real Islam. He wanted to show them the true way. Today everyone in the world blamed Wahhabism. It was always Wahhabism. They called Boko Haram Wahhabis. They were not. His ancestor learned about Islam from his father, Abdul Wahhab. As a boy he studied the Koran, struggled but over time found the true Islam. He never left Arabia. He found his calling, but his village rejected him. They didn't know the true Islam. They tried to kill him. He didn't say that he helped stone to death an adulteress, who had confessed, and they forced him to leave.

He became a preacher and developed a following. When he was about 40, he met al-Saud and they made an alliance. Al-Saud was the political leader, and his family was the religious leader. Together they created this state, Saudi Arabia. He leaned forward. Some in the family were trying to exploit Islam and distort it. In war, you were banned from cutting down a tree and from harming women or children. If you read Islam correctly you would see that it opposed violence. The Taliban banned education, and this was wrong. His raised his finger. The first word in the Koran was read *(ikra)*. Girls as well as boys? Yes, they were the same. Talk was nothing. He needed to see acts. But his ancestor, and Ibn Saud, fought the tribes. Yes, you had to fight to unify, and people fought you. You had to suffer, and to struggle to create a state.

Saudi Arabia was changing, but Wahhabism was still here. Everyone in the world blamed Wahhabism. Wahhabis were victims, like these boys who went to Syria. Bad men convinced them to go. The Ikhwan wanted power. This was political Islam. Men blamed Saudi Arabia, but everyone knew that America created al-Qaeda.

Hamid came in and went to a newspaper rack. Who were these men who were going to Syria? I asked. They were the children of the Wahhabis. Al-Wahhab closed his eyes. It wasn't true.

The café closed for *ashra*. I sat outside. The lights went on and Ahmed called. They were inside. I joined them. Another man arrived and sat next to me. He asked what I was doing. I told him. What was it exactly? The other men, except Hamid went outside. The question was, how did a person become a fundamentalist, and why? And why would militants, as I called them, come here when this place produced them? What exactly was I doing here? Hamid spoke to him. He stared at me. He didn't see how I could be here. They filmed me? He talked about beheadings. There was a network here, but it would be difficult to find people. It started in 1970. The people would be older. They were around Abdullah Azzam. They all shared the same background and ideology. Today people here supported the Taliban, as they supported the Mujahideen, and Arab Afghans, because of the ideology of jihad.

The Afghans say they were never colonized. The prime minister of India said Hindus had been emasculated by the Muslim invaders who ruled for 1,000 years. The Ikhwan and the Deobandi were born to give dignity to men living under British rule. Today, that feeling of impotence was still there. The enemy was a monarchy, a military dictatorship, a police state, and the neocolonialism of America. Saudis have little interest or understanding of the politics of Afghanistan or Pakistan, but they are interested in jihad, whether in Albania, Bosnia, or Somalia. Jihad is in their souls for two reasons: colonialism, and Israel. It was interesting that Vietnam could build ties to the West after decades of war, yet sizeable segments of Saudi Arabia were against this. He was surprised when he was in America to learn that Chinese, Vietnamese and other Asians considered the Arabs part of the West. We came from the same faith. Maybe that was why we kept fighting. The ideology of jihad has been constructed by people to serve their interests, national and tribal. They promoted the idea of jihad, using the poor and vulnerable, and sent these young men to their deaths to maintain their power.

Wasn't it dangerous to have these thoughts? It kept him on his toes. He was studying in America.

He went to the mosque for Friday prayers. Bush was bombing Afghanistan. The imam, a Pakistani migrant, new to America, was preaching. He said they had to support the president they were Americans. He finished his sermon and said in Arabic, "May God bless and keep the Mujahadeen."[448] Of course, he could have just said that because it was a standard way to end a sermon, so deep was jihad in them. Another time he went to a conservative mosque. Their faith did not prevent them from supporting their new Christian country. It taught Islam as it was practiced in the Middle East. It was too dangerous to say jihad. The owner turned off the lights. We sat at a table outside. Violence was rooted deep in them. When he went back to his village and talked to his young male relatives, they were soft-spoken and kind, but when he saw al-Qaeda in Syria, he said to himself they came from these people. Some of his relatives were in Syria. Others wanted to go. It was a way to success, even if a young man came from a wealthy family. He had three nieces with sons in their 20s. The first two were afraid because two of their sons said they wanted to go to Syria. The third was not afraid. The parents were all religious. He asked one father, "Why didn't his son want to go?" He raised his children in a way that they didn't believe in the way of jihad. They were all the same social status. If he said they needed to be strong, Muslims were weak, they were not what they were 1,000 years ago, and had to be like they once were, they would go. Did he want to promote a world view that called for jihad, or was he against it? One mother had sympathy for jihad. He clutched his fist against his chest. It was deep within her soul.

Today, a boy with a computer could develop ideas, and go without his family knowing. They were receptive to the ideology of Daesh. He talked to mothers who sought the acceptance of God, not the sweetness of life. The

---

[448] Allahumma Ensur Al- mujahadeen.

mass of believers in the country was shrinking, but there were many still, and they were aggressive. The jihad ideology was global. The Haqqanis once had an office here. There was fundraising here as there was in the 1980s when America and its allies were sending men to Afghanistan. Now it was a crime to do this without government permission. They were trapped by their ideology. There was no exit. This was an authoritarian state. You needed to be faithful more than skillful. This state was built upon this ideology. If you altered it you brought about its destruction. Jihad was in their hearts and souls. It was like Gorbachev. He changed the Soviet Union, and this brought about its destruction. There was a network here of Haqqani and al-Qaeda supporters. They believed in their ideology, not in the country.

The wind came up, and I could feel the sand. People were like these toys you could buy. You wound them up with a small key and they went around the table. They made them, not intentionally, but they did. I needed to find the gatekeeper. Who would let me in? My resume was my entry. The flags outside the hotel across the street stood straight out. The sand was in my eyes. A chair blew over. He told me to be careful, wished me well, and walked off into the wind.

Sartre's play *No Exit* was about three people trapped by one another, and the world, unable to think, to escape and be free, like those who felt jihad was a way to become a man. That night I sent a note to a Pashtun chief in the Tribal Areas. He sent me two names. I called one of them. I waited at a cafe with mists spraying over us. Two men, in their 40s, in western clothes arrived. They were Pashtuns. I was their guest. They had to be good hosts, like the Bedouin. We went to a restaurant, and I explained what I was doing. They were a community, they said. There were areas here that were like Pakistan, but the people were lambs. They knew about Haqqani and other Mujahideen leaders, of course. They had never heard of Haqqani recruiting here. People were educated, and wanted to talk, but they were afraid. You could not detach religion from the body. Every Pashtun was Muslim. He would not give up his faith. What existed in the Tribal Areas existed here. How could I find these men? I couldn't. Lower class people wore the same clothes that they wore in Pakistan. They didn't want to know anything new. They came from the same places as they did. The ideology was here.

But it was under siege. Yahya said fewer young people believed in God. It would be a problem for the Kingdom. He talked about the joys of having two wives. There was an Afghan at the Institute. He was just down the hall. Didn't anyone tell me?

No, men were polite, said hello, but kept their distance. I was an infidel.

The blinds were drawn and the walls were bare. Abdur Rahman, a tall, lean man with a light gray beard, sat at an empty desk. Habib, our Sudanese servant, brought in two glasses of tea. No one told him I was here. He was working on a paper on the re-institutionalization of science and technology in Islamic countries. He raised his finger. The Re was important. Maybe no one would read it, but he wanted to be at peace with himself. That was the key. He asked why I was here. I told him. He and Yunus Khalis were close. They were together one day and a man from the U.N. joined them. They asked for the maps showing where the Soviets placed their missiles during Jihad, but he wouldn't show them. The U.N. pretended to be neutral, but it was a Western organization. During the 1980s, he submitted reports to Crown Prince Salman,[449] in charge of aid to the Mujahideen. He agreed with Samuel Huntington that the West would be in an unending clash with Islamic Civilization, and with the rest of the world.[450] He looked at my card. And, the Council on Foreign Relations, that was the center. It was the enemy. I had to decide if I was on the side of the people or the establishment. There was a line between the two everywhere in the world.

How did he come here? He got a scholarship when he was 20, in 1962, and left Afghanistan for America. He went to a language school in Washington. He met a taxi driver who knew a prominent Afghan. He said the University of Maryland was a good school. He loved it there. He got a bachelor's, a master's, and a PhD. He had the highest admiration for Americans. They treated him exceptionally well. He had Saudi friends at the university. Through them he got a job at the Ministry of Planning. He said his father was a Member of Parliament, and Afghanistan's most prominent Pashtun poet. When he came here so much of this was desert; now look at all the Saudis had accomplished. During the Soviet war, the Palestinians took the Soviet line. Arafat said they had a right to invade.

Did he know Jalaluddin?

---

[449] Since 2015, King Salman bin Abdulaziz al Saud.
[450] Samuel P. Huntington and Brzeziński Zbigniew, "*The Clash of Civilizations and the Remaking of World Order*," *(*New York: Simon & Schuster, 2011)

He would come here to go on Haj or Umrah, or to raise money.[451] He said when they finished jihad in Afghanistan they had to go north to Central Asia. Why couldn't the Uzbeks or the Turkmens, who had been Muslims for 1,300 years, before the communists came be allowed to read the Koran, or go to their mosques? He and Haqqani were friends, but he didn't know where his main contact here was, or if he had married an Arab. I didn't like that he used suicide bombers. Did I remember the Kamikaze pilots? It was the asymmetry of power. In orthodox Muslim philosophy it was forbidden, but theologians today allowed it. Didn't drones kill children, too? There was no refined code of ethics. Arabs had a tenacious tie to their land, and no one could penetrate this. You had to live here for ten generations. King Faisal gave him citizenship, but he was still a guest. He and Prince Turki were the closest friends. The Iranians were arrogant. I was not to forget that the Pashtuns—the Yousafzai—wounded Alexander. I said I was with four Yousafzai around a campfire who said they wounded Alexander with an arrow in his leg. "He saw the blood running down his leg and said he realized for the first time that he was mortal," said Rahman. In the 1970s, the U.S. was tied to the Shah of Iran and to the dictators of Pakistan and didn't see the ferment brewing among the Afghans. They were poor and men preached about Communism. The Soviets invaded and the U.S. and Saudi Arabia relied on the Pakistanis, who armed themselves with nuclear arms while they had the U.S. in their back pocket. Yunus Khalis told him that when the Taliban formed, he wanted to move to Kandahar to be close to Mullah Omar so he could have some control over his policies, but Omar wouldn't have it. Prince Turki met him twice. He said he was ugly because he had lost one eye and had a high, whiny voice and an unpleasant personality. There was nothing there.

The next day, Rahman took me to lunch in a hotel restaurant. He had five daughters and one son.

His youngest daughter just died. He lowered his head. We were quiet. "We all love our children very much," he said softly. Haqqani was the most brilliant of the Mujahideen commanders, a humble, decent man. He should be even more so now. He had suffered so much. The Mujahideen didn't know the sacrifices they would have to make. If they did, they would have been humble, combined their forces, instead of competing, and prevented Pakistan

---

[451] *Dictionary of Islam, Umrah,*655

from controlling them. Hubris was the killer of humans and nations, and Afghanistan was the graveyard of them all. All the Taliban leaders came here except Omar. Jalaluddin did not need bin-Laden. He brought Rahman to a cave, and they walked for one kilometer. It was lined with munitions. He said if he died tomorrow, he would go to Hell because he had not fired one shot in Jihad. He fired some shells. Haqqani didn't want to kill Afghans, but to get soldiers to join them. I remembered an army defector in his thick gray uniform and the fear in his eyes. He used to see Jalaluddin all the time. He hadn't seen his financial man in 15 years. He'd forgotten his name. The ISI was a fly in the heat. It was everywhere, a daughter of the CIA. Haqqani sold his soul to Pakistan. His tribe was on both sides of the Durand Line. The border was nonsensical to him. The tribe was of the essence. The English were kaffirs. He almost spit the word out. In creating the Durand Line, they divided every tribe in two.

He looked at Afghan history 5,000 years old, at Zia ul Haq, the dictator, with the swagger stick under his arm. In the end, it was better to be with Pakistan, which, after all, was Muslim. Afghanistan and Pakistan were Sunni which was the determining factor. You could not compare Haqqani and other Mujahideen leaders to Ahmed Shah Durrani, who rose at a time when there was more freedom. Al-Zawahiri—he hated all of them. Go to the Arab world and fight. Why was he in that poor country, Pakistan? He could never forgive bin Laden. He could have done wonders if he tried to build Afghanistan. He had the charisma and the power. Afghanistan made America the sole superpower. As a good Judeo-Christian country, we had the duty to rebuild this nation. People looked at me an American, as a drug dealer for all the destruction that America had caused from Central America to Afghanistan.

That night Hamid and I met in the lobby of the Sheraton. A man, named Khaled, joined us. He gave a sack of books to Hamid, then turned to me. He learned English at a language school in San Francisco, the most beautiful city in America. Faisal bin Musaid, nephew to King Faisal, whom he shot in 1975, maybe because he was deranged, or because Faisal brought in radio and television, or to avenge the death of his brother, killed demonstrating against modernization, went to the same school. He was decapitated, a soul for a soul.[452] Khaled got a PhD in political sociology at UCLA. He was a professor,

---

[452] Al-Maídah, The Koran, 5:32.

but now a columnist for *al-Hayat*.[453] Hamid had to leave. Khaled wanted to go to the Italian restaurant in the hotel. He liked the pizza here. He began to talk about his book, *Wahhabism between Shirk and the Disintegration of the Tribe*, the best seller at the Riyadh Book Fair. The official version of the history of Saudi Arabia was that it was created to oppose *Shirk*, or idolatry, to associate anything with God, the great sin in Islam.[454] There could only be one God, Arab jihadis proclaim, holding one finger up for the cameras.

But was it true and where did Wahhabism come from? He went to the Wahhabi sources which no one had done. He found nothing in the collective mind in the 18th century that showed that shirk was widespread, no trace of it in popular expressions, in poetry, or in everyday life. The idea of the state created by the al-Saud family was false. It was al-Wahhab who came up with the idea. The traditional Salafi and fiqh (law) credo in central Arabia was to separate the religious and political realms. A religious figure was despised if he became political.

But Mohammad was a political and religious leader. Khomeini said Islam was a political religion. He agreed, but al-Wahhab went to al-Saud, the warrior, and political leader, not the other way around. His books were being withdrawn from the bookstores. Wahhabism was about the disintegration of the tribe. It took place over 300-400 years forced by climate changes. There were periods of no rain and people had to dig for water. They quit being nomads and became trapped in an urban world.

Al-Wahhab preached in his village, but he was too rigid and was forced to leave. In 1740, his father died. He took over as judge, but destroyed the tomb of one of Mohammad's companions, and again was forced to flee. He found refuge in al-Dariya, today a suburb of Riyadh, which his followers later likened to Mohammad reaching Medina. There, Mohammad ibn Saud protected him, and had his son marry his daughter in 1744, creating an alliance. Ibn Saud was king and al-Wahhab was the preacher, al-Sheikh al-Islam (the leader of Islam).

Each oasis was ruled by a clan, like Christian city states in Italy. Venice signed a trade treaty with Genghis Khan.

They would die to protect a guest and opposed inter-tribal marriage.

---

[453] Al Monitor: The Pulse of the Middle East, June 3, 2022
[454] Surah al-Ma-ida, The Koran, 5:72.

They fought or allied with other tribes. By marrying his son into another tribe, Ibn Saud broke this custom, and reignited a war, which Mohammad began a thousand years before, to create a new tribe, the Umma. Every man had to swear allegiance to al-Wahhab, and to pay a religious tax. He created the Mutaween to enforce his laws. In 1746, he called for jihad against all who opposed him. He and Saud raided weak villages and negotiated non-aggression pacts against larger tribes. He killed his enemies, but all who followed him were in "the army of God." In 1766, Ibn Saud was assassinated while praying, and his son, Abd al-Aziz ibn Saud replaced him. Their men rode two to a camel, with only water and barley flour, which they mixed for food. A new tribe was born.

Today Pakistan, using the Taliban, was following this plan, assassinating Pashtun tribal leaders, which was why the tribal chief in 2007 didn't want to take me to Miram Shah. To bring a guest would bring attention to himself. Pakistan wanted to destroy Pashtun tribal culture to create a new tribe loyal to Pakistan. By 2019, Pakistan had killed 1,500 Pashtun tribal elders, destroying 50% of the Pashtun tribes.[455] My jailer proudly told a story of a man killing his brother because he would not join the Taliban, his new tribe.

It was superficial, Khaled added, to say al-Wahhab cleansed the state of idolatry. Wahhabism was a religious movement, part of the state formation process. In the 18th Century, there was only religious education. At the end of Friday prayers, the imam praised the state. Tawhid, meaning the oneness of God, was the Shahada *"There is no god, but God and Mohammad is his Prophet."* But Tawhid also meant the unity and transcendence of God. For al-Wahhab this meant proclaiming the word of God, without an intermediary, and worshipping him, without one.[456] Martin Luther said this, creating the Protestant movement.

Wahhabi writers said there were different types of shirk: ascribing knowledge, or power, to anyone but God; worshipping anything or anyone but God; living or performing any ceremony, implying worship of anything but God. If you wanted to implement Sharia and Tawhid, you needed a unified political authority. Nomad tribes had two stages of development:

---

[455] Author interviews with Pashtun journalists and tribal leaders from the Tribal Belt of Pakistan and in eastern Afghanistan.
[456] Lacroix, *"Awakening Islam,"* 11

collective, when the whole tribe settled; and dispersive, when tribes broke up and settled with other tribes, which led to towns, to the rise of the Wahhabi movement, and to the Saudi state.

Wahhabism was born with the disintegration of the tribe. Al-Wahhab led the military and political campaign. Al-Saud was the political leader. They took Central Arabia and then the Hijaz—Mecca and Medina—drove the Ottomans out, and ruled Arabia. The Wahhabis never tried to take over the state. Bin Laden was not a Wahhabi. Wahhabism said you could not rebel against the state religion. He was a renegade, a jihadi Salafi disavowed by the Wahhabi establishment.

No wonder boys went to Syria and Afghanistan. I thought of the teenager in Saudi dress, with the Taliban. He was slight, but he carried a rifle and looked at me hard. He was a man.

In the 1960s Wahhabis and the Ikhwan interacted and a neo-Wahhabism developed. By outlawing the Ikhwan, the state was outlawing itself. Today they had a combination of state oppression, and U.S. policy. In the U.S. we had the pursuit of happiness, the enlightened America, he felt, yet we supported Israel which Saudis call a Judeo-Christian conspiracy against Islam. In 2002, the Arab Initiative[457] called for the recognition of Israel in exchange for the recognition of the Palestinians. The West ignored this, reinforcing their belief that the West hated the Arabs. If al-Zawahiri led al-Qaeda, then Haqqani was the intermediary. Afghanistan's Islamic roots were deep. The Abbasid Empire started in Khorasan.

What the West called radicalism, they called protecting their land. They were not radicals when they were fighting the Russians or the British in the 19th Century. The Americans came with the germ of nationalism, liberty, the nation state, and individualization. The U.S. was arrogant and greedy. It wanted people to be politically submissive and culturally Western. People admired those who went to Iraq and Syria. They were defending Islam and the Syrians, who were ignored by the West, and slighted by Iran, Hezbollah, and Russia. People saw the destroyed cities and dead babies on television. If al-Qaeda was the only one defending these people, so be it.

---

[457] "Arab Peace Initiative: Full Text," *Guardian* 28 March 2002

The Road to Sudan

Again, al-Sharif came and stood in front of my desk. Was bin Laden even a person, or was he someone America created, or the Israelis? How could four planes evade American security to reach those targets? Bin Laden admitted it. He shook his head. Rahman said the video in which bin Laden said this was photo-shopped. I went down the hall to see Majoob, a friendly curly-haired Sudanese scholar. Did he know about men coming from South Asia across the Arabian Sea. He sat on his desk. There was no difference among Eritrea, Sudan, Somalia, Puntland, or Ethiopia. They felt part of Arab world. They spoke Ge'ez, language of the Ethiopian Christian church, as they did in Yemen. Arabic was a mixture of Hindi and Persian. Yemeni merchants were in Suakin, the Sudanese port, and Khartoum. Many South Yemen leaders, and teachers, under the British, were either born in Sudan, or educated there. For centuries Muslim scholars traveled from Mecca to Baghdad, Cairo or Sana'a. Few knew the Koran and the Sunna—the only references they had---or could afford to pay for an education, which, irrespective of class, became, under colonialism, available to the masses. With modern education, Islam was no longer confined to the Ulema.[458] Anyone could consider himself a reference in Islam. He was not a master of physics, or of mathematics, but of the Koran and the Hadith. He was celebrated, and respected. Thousands now considered themselves a mufti, a guru, a teacher. For jihadis it was a way of life. It was a social movement, a free life, and you could go where there was trouble. You were not enlightened enough, or smart enough, to choose another way of living. The harm done by the West was nothing in comparison to the harm to your own people, most of whom were dead inside. Khartoum was a political and military center of terrorism in the Arab world. Haqqani and al-Qaeda were there.

The Sudanese embassy was crowded with veiled women and tall quiet men in prayer caps and thobes. I waited in line, filled out papers, and paid money. The next day, an officer asked why I wanted a visa. I wanted to go to Sudan. He gave me one.

---

[458] "One who knows." The learned, religious scholar s who by issuing fatwas and other decisions regulated the life, public and private, of a Muslim community.

These groups in the Middle East talked as if they had discovered Islam, Majoob continued. It had become the Arab world's only frame of reference. What achievements did they have in chemistry, physics, mathematics, economics, theater, or literature? Mahfouz wrote under a dictatorship. He had no depth, philosophy, or backbone. No one had one in this country. ISIL was stronger, more organized than what bin Laden and al-Zawahiri created, and closer to Europe. Abu al-Baghdadi was married to a Saudi, widowed when the state killed her husband in the Awakening.

This then, maybe, was why the fire would not come here. Al Baghdadi, a nom de guerre, was born Ibrahim al Badri, in Iraq. The al-Badri clan traces its lineage to the Quraysh, Mohammad's tribe, of Mecca. I wondered if his wife traced her lineage to Mecca also.

In Friday prayers here the imam will criticize Christians and Jews. His knowledge of the Koran and Hadith was limited. Recruitment was social, a question of their lack of rights. Young men needed to do something because they thought they were nothing. It was a form of self-realization. They were being manipulated.

A Typical Conservative Family

A black car with dark windows pulled over and I got in the back. Fatima, in an abaya, and I shook hands. Traffic was heavier now, and it was dustier entered a compound. Inside the house the walls were bare. There were three sofas, and a table, with nuts, dates, water, and tea. Her son, Faisal, in his 20s, came in. He majored in English literature in college. He loved Shakespeare. He had been working since he was 14 and because he needed a degree to get married, he had to keep working to earn enough money. If the girl you wanted to marry had a degree, and you didn't her parents would say no.

Al-Wahhab made sure that the lowest class was treated fairly. Women had to wear an abaya to prevent wealthy women from flaunting their clothes or jewelry in front of the poor.

He watched two women get out of a big car and throw plastic bottles and other garbage in the street. The garbage men, who got maybe 500 riyals[459] a day, would pick it up. Some of his friends admired how he took care of himself, but an equal number said that's why they had servants. They taught children to do something and then gave them a piece of candy, which led to a culture of bribery, Fatima said. They always wanted something for doing their job. In school, 90% of students didn't do their homework but when they did, they expected to be praised. Their teacher, a foreigner, said he wasn't going to praise them for just doing their job. Fatima asked how many religious classes he had. He counted to eleven.

Two girls walked in, Nasreen, in jeans and a sweater, her hair in a ponytail, shook hands firmly. Noor, in a sweater and pants, wore a scarf, was slighter and her handshake was soft. They had nothing in common, Nasreen said, but they loved one another. Her friends in her karate class couldn't believe that they were sisters. Hakim, in Saudi dress, came home and kissed his daughters on the check. The woman who arranged this said they were a normal conservative family. Nasreen said their parents never said they must cover or not. She chose to. In America everyone went their own way. Here you had a responsibility to your family. Noor served me tea and returned to

---

[459] About $40, one riyal in 2022 is about $.27.

her seat, her back straight, hands in her lap. She didn't feel any pressure in the U.S, or desire, to act American. His girls covered for God if they wanted, not for their parents, said their father. I wouldn't believe all that went on here, but they were not into that, said Nasreen. She liked horses. There was an underground basketball league for girls.

Hakim didn't drink and prayed five times a day, and he never had trouble doing business in America. It was the best country in the world. Faisal said people his age in America wanted to jettison their parents, whereas he and his sisters tried to please them. Here, there was no such thing as your own space. In the U.S. parents gave their kids room to develop, which was good. They pushed the individual. Here it was the family unit. It was Khaldun's "*asabiyya*." Hakim found the Americans open, they criticized themselves, a form of self-confidence. They might criticize the veil because it was different. Religion caused so much trouble. They were in the U.S. when 9/11 happened. He asked Fatima to take off her veil, but she refused. It was to protect her family. They were so afraid. There was so much misinformation in the West. In the Arab world, culture and tribalism ranked higher than religion. Social status was most important, said Faisal. Nasreen was talking with a Jordanian in school and a friend asked why was she talking to her? One tribe's blood was not as pure as another's, said Faisal.

There were three parameters Hakim added, cultural, religious and governmental. Before the 1970s, men and women mixed, and owned shops next to one another. Saudis drove taxis, picked up manure and everyone, for the most part, loved and respected one another. Everything changed with the influx of the oil money after the 1973 Arab Israeli war. A family could have an Egyptian driver. When he was a boy, he had an Egyptian teacher. He looked up to him. They all went to the funeral of his father's driver. Why did boys go to Syria to fight? It all came from the late 1970s. It had nothing to do with religion and everything to do with dictatorship. Their voices were not heard. They found satisfaction in Syria. One of his nephews was on his way. The police caught him and made them guarantee that he wouldn't go. He was not religious but felt that he was a slave. The royals ruled you. The battleground was a vent, a place to fight the dictatorship. They wanted freedom. A boy could drive at 12 because a mother needed a driver, but that was the only power he had. They had all been brainwashed in school to believe that America hated them. He told them that America supported the Mujahedeen in Afghanistan and the Muslims in Bosnia. They were surprised. They were easy prey for extremists.

Their leaders were not religious but intoxicated with their power. He was taught that in Islam you could not kill. The royal family used this religious vehicle to keep itself in power. When she was younger Nasreen said she had to walk on an Israeli flag to enter school. It was their doormat. They would a picture of a martyr with his face glowing, Faisal added. Hakim said it got worse after the first Gulf War. Bin Laden and his people began to raise their voices about the U.S. military presence here. He was trying to find someplace to rule, Sudan, Afghanistan, later South Yemen. They ruled by fear. Indonesia, the largest Muslim country in the world, became so through trade. All countries that did so had stayed Muslim, not through violence.

Most of Faisal's friends were agnostic, but they all had lost faith in the Mufti and in Islam. The others were zealots. They must destroy the infidels and the West. What created an extremist? Trust us, they said, they wanted to save our soul. He estimated that 30% of young men were potentially radical. A professor in Islamic studies could manipulate them. All were vulnerable. Noor had a friend who read a book on Hitler and said he was awesome he killed all those Jews.

She said he was a racist and would have come after them next. They studied the Prophet Muhammad and ended with the Ottoman Empire. They didn't study world history. The royal family ensured that the people hated the U.S. If they loved it, they would turn on them.

Then why did the government offer the King Abdullah Foreign Scholarship Program, which allowed thousands of students to go to American universities every year?

Twice Faisal said there was no social justice, the essence of Islam. Saudis hated it, said Hakim, when someone won because the royal family won all the time. They took all their freedoms away. No wonder boys went to Syria. If there were elections tomorrow the country would fall apart, Faisal added. Each tribe would take over its territory. People preferred to work for the government, so they didn't have to work. They were beaten down.

The royals could make things better by starting to be religious and stop drinking, his father added. The people were angry because of the hypocrisy yet were afraid of democracy. You want Libya, Syria, or Egypt? Jihad meant to fight for religious reasons. Mohammad, peace be unto him, had nothing to give the people and so he said if you fought to protect Islam you would go to Heaven. Now they had an army to fight for them, but the clerics talked of jihad. There were many types of jihads. The battle within yourself was mentioned far more in the Koran than any other. Why not say enough of jihad? Why did the government focus on what the U.S. did in Iraq? Why did it talk about Israel oppressing the Palestinians? Most of the public loved Morsi and hated el-Sisi. The royal family hated the Ikhwan out of fear.

Here, said Nasreen quietly, if you said the wrong thing, you would disappear. In the 1980s, Muslim countries let all these people go to Afghanistan to fight, then came al-Qaeda. Hakim said the brains were Egyptians, Algerians, and Tunisians. The government felt it could control other countries and influence the Muslim world by having Wahhabi missionaries get involved in politics, but not here.

We had talked for over three hours. It was 1:15 a.m. Outside a car was waiting, its engine running. Faisal drove through the empty streets. He was married to a woman who wasn't from their tribe, and he had to get divorced. Her blood wasn't pure. She was from a lesser tribe. Thesiger wrote that the Arabs cared more about the purity of blood than any race. The leaders told Faisal's father what would happen if he didn't get divorced. Did he still love her? He did very much. He wanted to work for the government. They needed to hold everyone together, if not the tribes would go their own way. He raced past sleek high rises and stores with designer names. It was a façade. The city was fighting the desert, and the Arabs fought one another. Mohammad tried to stop the fighting. A modern young man, driving an expensive European racing machine, could not marry the woman he loved.

The Rebel

Zina and I rode together in the back, and she laughed happy to be out. Our driver pulled into a compound. Dr. Madeha al-Ajroush rushed into her living room welcoming us warmly. The room was filled with photographs, paintings, and inlaid furniture from Egypt and Syria. She was a photographer, a psychotherapist, and the first woman to drive in Saudi Arabia. She brought a fresh fruit salad in a bowl and served us. She was married to her cousin, who was also her second cousin. A woman could not go outside her tribe. The "sahwa," the modern Islamists, those who grew out of the "Awakening," who were seen as liberal, said a woman's shoes should be made of rubber so that she was silent. One of her daughters was at the Cannes Film Festival. Her other daughter was retarded. She was sitting in the corner.

Many of Mohammad's first converts were women, drawn to Islam's call of equality. The Bedouin code required looking after weaker members of the tribe but was lost in the rush to make money in Mecca.[460] Women wore the *niktab* as protection. A woman could get divorced, but she needed a guardian with her before her papers could go through the court. Men signed them, but a woman used her thumb print. You could harm a Bangladeshi and an Indian woman, but you could not touch an American. How had life changed since the coup attempt in 1979? It was nightmare. Everything was the legacy of Juhayman and Khomeini.[461] It was part of an American and European plan to promote fundamentalism. Khomeini was living in France before going back to Iran. The CIA was considered all but omnipotent. In the 1960s there was a hippie abaya that came just below your waist and was all but transparent. The U.S. Embassy caused so much damage by sending a note to American women to wear a full-length abaya.

The radicalization of young men was in rural areas, among the unemployed, the dropouts, and the frustrated. They were vulnerable. The schools were useless. Once 80% of the population prayed five times a day; now atheism was growing, and people were expressing themselves on

---

[460] Karen Armstrong, *"Islam: A Short History"*(New Haven: Phoenix Press, 2009), 4
[461] Juhayman al-Utaybi: Leader of the 1979 attack on the Grand Mosque in Mecca.

Twitter. The government said you could not be atheist and that made it more popular. The feminist movement began in 1990. The religious establishment started a counter-campaign. The country was sensitive to the international media. When Obama came here, a car, with men in sunglasses, sat outside her home. You needed permission from the government to marry a foreign woman. A divorced woman got nothing. You could only work if your husband gave you permission. The Koran gave women the right to divorce, and to inherent centuries before Western women. Once, they fought alongside men, but later Arab patriarchy reasserted itself.[462]

She was going to a U.S. school in Kuala Lumpur. Her father was a diplomat. She was 10 and he said to her a woman was like a shoe. You used her until she wore out and then you threw her away. She was like a tissue. Her brother never said anything. She was in New York in the 1960s. She was 12 years old. The Hippie movement was going strong. She saw that a woman was allowed to talk, and that her voice could be heard. Her father said if she thought she could change society slowly, she was wrong. He wouldn't talk to her today. A marriage was designed to strengthen family ties, tribe, and wealth. She opened the door. They'd gone from being illiterates to college graduates in one generation. She was ostracized by her family.

A professor said for women in the village where he grew up jihad was deep within them. That was Bedouin culture, she explained. Women supported the *gauze* (raid), a tradition in that culture. The men brought back the booty. If women were caught, they became slaves. The word for woman was *wadu*, the classical word for honor. Her husband, in western clothes, a dean at the Arab Open University, joined us. In Islam it was jihad to provide for your family—protection, shelter, and food. You want to go to Afghanistan, and leave your home and women and children so you can go fight? So many men talked of jihad in Iraq, and Syria. Who were they to give the key to paradise to young men? Who gave them this power?

Madeha's photographs were on the wall, one of ancient hieroglyphics, of women dancing welcoming their men home from a raid.

---

[462] Armstrong, *"Islam: A Short History"*

Jamal Khashoggi

The NATO diplomat, sitting in a crowded lobby, confirmed that there was an air bridge between Aden and Istanbul. There was a similar bridge between Libya and Istanbul. Once in Turkey, the jihadis were shepherded through customs, and bussed down to the Syrian border. An Indian diplomat said this was exactly the way the Pakistanis would operate.

This meant that Turkey and Yemen were backing ISIS, and al-Nusrah, the al-Qaeda affiliate, in Syria. Saudi Arabia, which controlled Yemen, was involved. This was why Riyadh was not worried about ISIS reaching here. The Saudis and the Turks, like the U.S. and its allies in the 1980s, with Pakistan, were using young poor Afghans and Arabs to fight for them.

He said the Yemeni Republican Guard, trained by the U.S., once led by Saleh's son, was leading the fight against al-Qaeda, which meant that it would be left alone. Yemen was the Pashtunistan, meaning the Tribal Areas, of the Arab world, the Arab headquarters of al-Qaeda. Behind Yemen was Saudi Arabia. About 5,000 went to Syria. During the Soviet war there were many educated Afghan Arabs, but not now. The 60 or so men that the Ministry of the Interior found were ISIS. The Saudi population was pro ISIS. The Saudis hated me because I was an infidel. Theologically, I did not belong here. This was the holy land of Islam. Mohammad, one of their own, brought God's message to them. Before him, during *Jahiliyyah*, the time of darkness, Christians had their book, and the Jews had theirs, now the Arabs did also. Bin Laden was angry that the guardian of the two holy sites invited in the infidel U.S. Army, an unprecedented sign of weakness, a return to darkness, what Maududi called modernity.

That afternoon I flew to Bahrain, where 50 years ago men dove for pearls to earn a living. That night I sat on the hotel lawn, watching the World Cup on a giant screen while Arab and Western men sat at a bar drinking, smoking cigars and cigarettes, talking with the east Asian waitresses.

The next day, I went a sleek Italian restaurant overlooking the water for lunch. A slim Eastern European hostess, in a tight skirt, with short blond hair combed back, asked who I was meeting. I told her. She smiled and took me to a table by the window. Jamal Kashoggi, in a white thobe and headdress, with a black rope headband, the Bahraini uniform, and a three-day growth, arrived. A waiter came over. I ordered sparkling water and he ordered white wine. The waiter showed him the label, and he approved. This looked like a good place to do business. Yes, he liked it here. You could go upstairs and smoke cigars. He smoked cigars? Oh yes. But not in Riyadh? Oh yes, there were places, and it was not illegal. The Koran does not mention tobacco. It hadn't reached Arabia in the 8th Century. Al-Wahhab banned tobacco as Salafis did today. He told a story. The Muttawan, the ISIS of that day, the Wahhabi soldiers, told Abdul Aziz that tobacco should be banned from the kingdom. But then some merchants went to the King and said, but your Highness they had stocks of tobacco in their warehouses and if it was banned, they would lose a great deal of money. It would be bad for the economy. The King said to sell what they had in stock and that would be it. They had been selling what they had in stock since then. He asked for the menu.

The Arabs were the first to distill alcohol *(al-khul)*. Once, they and the Afghans made wine. In 1926, Abdul Aziz, bowing to the Wahhabis, and to increase his prestige among his followers banned it, like smoking.[463] Ramadan was coming. How different was it now?

Before electricity, when he was a child, he went to bed at midnight, got up at 4 a.m. to eat and then he went to school. Riyadh was a walled city until 1951. After the oil boom they changed. Toward the end of Ramadan, he went to bed at 4 a.m., woke up about 10, and went to work.

They had the longest vacation periods in the world. If there was a holiday or a special day on Wednesday, the King gave them the next day off, and therefore they had a very long weekend.

Our first course arrived and he leaned over, what was my project? Why was I here? I lived with Jalaluddin Haqqani in the 1980s. I talked about my project. We were old Afghan hands, part of the world of the Mujahideen. I could not do it. It was impossible. They would never let me get that close. The physical network was not important. It kept changing, and new men came up, older men died, and other men got killed, and new people replaced them. It was the history of the idea that was important. The mindset of the

---

[463] Vasiliev, *"The History of Saudi Arabia,"* 270-71

Afghans today was completely different from what it was during the 1980s. He was a journalist, but the word was then that he worked for Prince Turki, the head of Saudi intelligence. When he became ambassador to the U.S, he brought Jamal to Washington as an advisor.

Afghans were nobler in their fight in the 1980s. No one would kill Yunus Khalis. A suicide bomber killed Usted Rabbani. *"Usted,"* means professor, a sign of respect, showing how he felt about the Mujahideen. Now Afghans were killing one another indiscriminately. They did not kill one another especially women or children. They negotiated with men in the army. What changed the Afghan mindset, and the Muslim mindset that led to what ISIS was doing to people? This was what I had to do, find out what went wrong. He wished that he was courageous enough. He would write this to protect his country because it was the re-introduction of raw Wahhabism.

He was starting *al-Arab*, a television network, financed by Al-Waleed bin Talal, the Saudi royal businessman. He had over 200 employees. He liked cigars, fine wine, and this elegant restaurant, and was a graduate of Indiana State University, with friends in Europe and America, but he was an Arab who grew up without electricity. He admired the Afghans who waged jihad against the Soviets, who had little and didn't give in.

In 1931-32, there was a fight between the Ikhwan, as the Wahhabis called themselves, and Abdul Aziz, an actual fight. They became too strict and too violent and it took him two years to defeat them. I must read about this and then think of Boko Haram, and ISIS. They were against international laws, boundaries, and treaties, like ISIS. You couldn't invite ISIS to a peace conference in London or Berlin. The Matawan were against wires—the telegraph—the work of the devil. Abdul Aziz argued with them, and brought in the Ulema to talk with them, and it had no effect.[464] Al-Wahhab grew up in a black and white world where Muslims fought infidels. They were all Muslims with Abdul Aziz, but the Matawan saw others as infidels. You needed takfir. Did I understand this? I did, but I wanted him to talk. It came from kaffir and had its roots in Wahhabism. It meant to excommunicate and referred to those Muslims who other Muslims, like al-Wahhab, considered apostates because they didn't adhere to his guidelines for who was Muslim and who wasn't. Sayyid Qutb felt that Nasser, by

---

[464] A group of respected government Muslim scholars.

ordering the torture and murder of Muslims, was, by killing other Muslims, forbidden in the Koran, no longer Muslim, and could be killed. When the Afghans were fighting the Soviets, they fought other Afghans, even communists, but never called them kaffirs. The other great Saudi reformer to tackle them was King Faisal a mild, non-violent man who introduced television. There was so much opposition to this, and to labor laws. There was nothing in the Koran about labor laws. Everyone worked from morning until night. Faisal brought in a mild form of Wahhabism. The Wahhabis would argue with the Ulema, nice, pious Egyptian sheikhs, to try to open people's eyes, and provided scholarships to people.

Maybe King Faisal was mild, but in 1934 when he was Prince Faisal, he led Saudi troops against Yemen and wanted to attack Sana'a.[465]

Whether by coincidence or not they began to have troubles in their own countries, and they stayed. Faisal liked them and used them as advisors. Sheikh Mana al-Qattan, founder of the Saudi high judiciary, was Ikhwan.[466] Faisal was criticized today for bringing in the evil of the Ikhwan. They were celebrated then, but that was then. Abdullah Azzam was part of the Ikhwan who came later. Al-Zawahiri, maybe linked to them briefly when he was young, detested them and saw them as failures because they were not revolutionaries. He was Al-Gama'a al-Islamiyya[467] influenced by Qutb, whose religious roots were the Salafis, principal among them Ibn Tayimmah, who came of age during "The Time of Confrontation." He called for violence. What was Salafism? It was Wahhabism. If I scanned all radical movements that carried arms their Islamic background came from Saudi Arabia. He saw a link between the evolutionary Islamists of the 1970s, those who chose the Hanafi School, and the Wahhabis.

But the Haqqanis were, like most Afghans, Hanafi, the most liberal of the four schools of Islam. He agreed, but they were linked now to the Wahhabis. This was the evolution he was referring to, the change from Hanafi Afghanistan, when I had dinner one night with a family and the host asked me to marry one of his daughters, a laughing girl like her sisters, their faces uncovered. He talked about the influence of torture on al-Zawahiri. It showed that the Egyptian jailers, who were notorious for being cruel, were

---

[465] Vasiliev, "*The History of Saudi Arabia*," 286
[466] Muslim Brotherhood.
[467] The Islamic Group, or Groups.

kaffirs, with no respect for Muslims. Kaffir referred originally to Christians.[468] If he was an Islamist in Egypt, he would run away, or hide. It was just a matter of time before there was a revolution. The police were heavy-handed, and incompetent. Another group, made up of young men now meeting secretly, would rise.

There was a huge network supporting extremism in Saudi Arabia. He saw on You Tube where some boys had written ISIS on a wall. He shook his head, "the courage of that." Did he ever feel a desire to rise up? He smiled. He felt it in his childhood. It was the glory of Islam. It was the result of colonialism, British, and then American imperialism, the dictatorships, how the weak armies of the Middle East had insulted Islam. There were no role models for young men today, no leaders that you wanted to be like, or follow, fascist, or liberal, there was no one.

"No John Kennedy or Pierre Trudeau."

"Exactly," he replied emphatically. Maybe al-Baghdadi, the head of ISIS, what the West calls a terrorist organization, the enemy of Iran, Iraq, and Syria, but he was a leader standing up to the West. It did not understand the power of al-Baghdadi, or Haqqani, or the Taliban, who stood up for Islam, their weapon against the invader. Had the Arab Spring succeeded, extremism would have died. The youth were excited in Cairo. He went to a presentation by some of the leaders in a bookstore, and it was packed with young people. They had glory in their eyes. He shook his head sadly. Now there was silly dancing in the streets, and intellectuals insulting one another. Young people had lost hope, and radicals had taken charge.

It was a revolution of the youth, said Jasmine in Sanaá. Adults stole their revolution. America backed the adults. We glorified our revolution, and said the Mujahideen were like our founding fathers, but we were different now.

The Taliban told me that there were good Taliban and bad Taliban, that Pakistan used the good Taliban for its regional policy, and al-Qaeda internationally. The bad Taliban fought Pakistan. Did he know if the ISI was working with al-Zawahiri, the Haqqanis and other countries to send men out to fight? He thought for a minute. Intelligence people thought they were smart and could manipulate people. It was no secret that (Bashar al) Assad let people out of prison. He knew it would look bad to kill people walking in

---

[468] A coverer, one who hides the truth, *Dictionary of Islam* 258-259

the streets. There was no terrorism in Egypt, but they wanted it. It would give the army an enemy. Could Saudi Arabia arm ISIS? It had a popular base in the country. The government fought al-Qaeda in 2003, but not that harshly. If I went back to Riyadh and talked to religious people, I would have trouble. They, as Saudis, needed to free their minds. They hated the Shia and were intolerant of foreigners. If they sent the Mufti to Cambridge to give a talk, he would embarrass them. Saudi Arabia needed to open up, but it could not, not yet. It needed a transparent judiciary. The Arab Spring was all about people power, and the Saudis didn't want that.

Why was ISIS so popular?

There had been continuous failures for centuries. The Arab Spring was a class struggle. The Arab world had been ruled for 1,000 years by a ruling class. In Egypt the army had ruled since Mameluke times; in Algeria since 1991, and since before that in Syria. Armies had businesses and made money. Like the Egyptian and Pakistani armies, I said. He nodded. The Pakistani army was Saudi Arabia's most reliable protector. Then suddenly democracy emerged and gave the vote to generals' sons and daughters. When marginalized people rose up in Algiers, the ruling classes got angry. He was at a lunch in Algiers with high officials, and watched a man take a bread roll and put it on his plate and cut it with a knife and fork. A man, in a nice suit, looked at him with distain, and almost shuddered. The other man wore cheaper clothes. Who was this peasant? The ruling class in Egypt refused to give up power. His own government was on the wrong side of history. So was America. President Obama lost an important opportunity to help the people by not intervening in Syria, which could have led to a modern, successful Syria, even if it required a showdown with Saudi Arabia.

Al-Zawahiri and Haqqani today, he didn't know. After the U.S. withdrew from Afghanistan and it became Taliban or ISIS land and the Tajiks stood and fought, as the Shia would in Iraq, then al-Zawahiri would have someone to fight, but here ISIS was anti-al-Zawahiri. The al-Nusrah front, started by Mohammad al-Julani in Syria, was successful. ISIS saw an opportunity and al-Baghdadi ordered Julani to return. He refused and it led to a confrontation. Al-Zawahiri had to mediate. He said Julani should stay in Syria and that al-Baghdadi should go back to Iraq.

Baghdadi ignored him. Al-Zawahiri was forced to make a decision and lost power. He didn't have the charisma of bin Laden, who never told a branch of al-Qaeda what to do. Al-Zawahiri was put in a position that he could not win. He would let AQAP chose. The center for Salafi jihadists shifted from the Tribal Areas of Pakistan to the Levant.

Saudi Arabia was stuck between "our Islam," meaning Wahhabism, and that of others. Ask any Saudi what the root of ISIS was and he would say it was the Ikhwan. It was denial. It was obligatory. They should be proud of Wahhabism, but it was a different time. It was the Saudi superiority complex which led to Takfir. They felt that they were right, and that everyone else was wrong. The only network that existed was that of the Ikhwan. If a member wanted to go into business in Indonesia, there would be a man there to help him.

He used to see Jalaluddin all the time here. He was a traditional scholar. He married an Emirati and spoke fluent Arabic. Prince Turki told me to go to Abu Dhabi, the capital, but I felt it was wrong to try to find a man's wife first, instead of him. There was no suicide bombing during colonialization, he continued. Someone would place a bomb under a table in a restaurant where British, Dutch or French soldiers congregated. He was referring to *The Battle of Algiers.* In 2003, before the U.S. invaded Iraq, the Pentagon showed this film.[469] I saw it at the Army War College, and before that, as a student in Paris. Algerian women carried bombs in their purses and left them in cafes. Suicide bombing was the weapon of the Haqqanis, of ISIS, and the Taliban.

Khashoggi refused to let me pay. A year later, *al-Arab* was ready to broadcast. "We are going to be neutral; we are not taking sides," it said. "We are going to bring in all sides in any conflict because right now we have a conflict in almost every Arab country."[470] They were interviewing a Bahraini opposition leader, and *al-Arab* shut down. "The broadcast has been stopped for technical and administrative reasons and will be back on soon, God willing," *al-Arab* said in a statement. It never came back.

On August 14, I saw a Westerner, in a Guantanamo-type orange prison suit, his eyes strained, on his knees in the desert, on television. A man next to him, his face covered, with a knife, was ranting. The man on his knees

---

[469] Charles Paul Freund, "A New Look at the Battle of Algiers," *Slate* 27 Aug, 2003
[470] Ben Hubbard, "Channel in Bahrain Goes Silent after Giving Opposition Airtime," *New York Times*, 2 Feb. 2015

was courageous, holding his head up. He was trembling inside, praying maybe, thinking of his family. He wanted to be strong, for the pain to be short, and to die with dignity, for them. I learned that his name was Jim Foley, the first American journalist murdered by ISIS.

Sudan

The sun glistened on the Nile, winding through the plains. There were plots of green, canals, adobe houses, and two vehicles on a dirt road. At the airport a woman in a blue hijab checked my passport and asked softly if I had been here before. I went through two metal detectors and sat on the conveyor belt while 20 men prayed by a wall. The ATM didn't work. Sudan was under U.S. sanctions.[471] Outside, a man held up a piece of paper with what could be my name. It was hot inside his old car. He put a flashlight in his mouth and took out a wad of bills. In the bank five pounds for one dollar on the black market nine. He drove down dark streets and a dirt road to a house half-hidden in the trees. The clerk asked if I needed to change money. He left and my driver angrily said I was not to tell anyone what we did. Inas Ramily, my fixer, came, in jeans, high heels, and a hijab. It was safer here, she said, than a hotel.

The next day we stood by the river in Omdurman, south of Khartoum, by a dirt field and a high wire fence. People had been coming here for centuries to dance on the Prophet's birthday, and now on al-Mahdi's birthday, Inas said. Al-Mahdi, like Ali Hamid's ancestor in Sana'a, was chosen by God, at the end of time.[472] *"Even if there remains for the world one single day, God will extend it until He sends a man from the people of My House…whose name will be the same as mine, and the names of his father will be that of my father, He will fill the earth with equity and justice, just as it is now filled with tyranny and oppression."*[473] His tomb was ten yards away,[474] with a flag, black for jihad, green for Islam, red for the blood of martyrs, with a crescent and a spearhead, hanging over it. Inside, two men in white flowing jalabiyas prayed at his long-engraved wood coffin. A woman walked around praying. Wahhabis call praying at tombs idol worship.

---

[471] "Sanctions Programs and Country Information," *U.S. Department of the Treasury* 2 June 2022, Documents/sudan.tx.

[472] Hourani, *"A History of the Arab Peoples,"* 313

[473] Malise Ruthven, *"Islam in the World,"* (Oxford: Oxford University Press, 2006

[474] David Fromkin, *"A Peace to End All Peace,"* (New York: Avon, 1990), 97

About 150 miles north was an island called Abba where in 1881 Mohammad Ahmed ibn al-Sayyad Abd Allah, about 40, a Wahhabi ascetic, who called himself al-Mahdi,[475] influenced by earlier Mahdist revivalist movements in West Africa, a reaction to the economic and military dominance of European powers, set up camp. *"There was a strange splendor in his presence, an overwhelming passion in the torrent of his speech, a great orator, powerfully built, with fierce brown eyes and three tribal gashes on each cheek."*[476] Three times the Ottoman-Egyptian rulers of Sudan sent forces to capture him, and each time he defeated them. In 1882, the British invaded Egypt, calling those who resisted terrorists. "Oh Muslims, kill the Christians," men shouted, as they did in Delhi in 1857.[477] In 1884, London sent General Charles "Chinese" Gordon, who won fame in 1863 leading a guerrilla force in China in the Tai,Ping Rebellion, to evacuate people in Khartoum, and to bring order. For three months he evacuated women and children then al-Mahdi surrounded the city. Britain sent a relief force. Months passed and starvation grew.

In January 1885, three days before it arrived, al-Mahdi's forces, against his orders, killed Gordon. Prime Minister Salisbury called him a "Christian Martyr." In September 1898, an Anglo Egyptian army of 25,000, led by the Herbert Kitchener, fought al-Mahdi's army of 60,000 spearman and swordsmen with weapons taken from the Crusaders 600 years before, and riflemen in rows four miles wide, here in a "tremendous slaughter of Arabs."

His officers held a worship service at al-Mahdi's Caliphate, an adobe house twenty yards away, where a guard slept in the shade. Al-Mahdi [478] formed an Islamic state half the size of America.[479] In 1986, his descendant, al-Sadiq al-Mahdi, formed a coalition government with the National Democratic Front, founded by the Ikhwan, led by his brother-in-law, Hasan al-Turabi.

In 1989, General Omar Hassan al-Bashir, from a peasant family, and al-Turabi, overthrew the government and created a Muslim dictatorship, the second, after that founded by Khomeini, in the modern Muslim world. In

[475] Hourani, *"A History of the Arab Peoples,"* 313
[476] Ibid 313
[477] Ibid 205-208
[478] Vasiliev, *"The History of Saudi Arabia"* 156
[479] Hourani, *"A History of the Arab Peoples"* 313

1990, al-Turabi, after the Soviets left Afghanistan, hoping for a Pan-Islamic revivalism, created the Popular Arab Islamic Conference (PAIC), and invited bin Laden, al-Zawahiri,[480] Zindani, Jamaat-i-Islami, among 500 men, and groups.[481] Bin Laden moved here, built training camps, and with Sudanese intelligence, and al-Zawahiri, and Islamic Jihad, hit Sudanese and U.S. targets in Egypt and Somalia.[482] Al-Fahdli came, and Jalaluddin. In 1993 the U.S. listed Sudan as a state sponsor of terrorism. In 1995, Islamic Jihad and maybe al-Gamaá al-Islamiyya tried to kill Egyptian President Mubarak, after he landed in Ethiopia for a meeting of the Organization of African Unity.[483]

"The Mahhdiyya was a puritan who disapproved of dancing," Inas explained. Dr. Miriam Sadiqi al-Mahdi, his great, great granddaughter, an elegant, stately woman in flowing gray and tan clothes, joined us. The popular Islam here today was Malaki, from Morocco. But the center, to the Sudanese, was al-Hijaz. Politically, they spoke of Saudi Arabia, but religiously of Mecca, Medina, and al-Hijaz. The Wahhabis tried to conquer Sudan, but the Nubians, who were expert spearmen, said they would give them an option: In which eye would they like to be blinded? The Imam al-Mahdi fought colonization, to defend Sudan, a jihad to create a renewed Islam. She felt a responsibility and was a symbol of defiance. She, like her five sisters, had been in prison. She fought in the Ethiopian army. She had three daughters, and her husband said enough. If so, she wanted a divorce. They had another daughter, and twin boys.

In 1989, the Mujahedeen's victory in Afghanistan inspired the Muslim world. The government introduced Sharia. It used Islam to gain power and to reshape the Sudanese character. It made the Vatican office, symbol of the Crusaders, its headquarters. It said America was the enemy and invited militants here. All Sudanese were Salafi hurt by the Western fear of Islam. The Saudis put money into radio and television and in journals to compete with Iran. The imams were Saudis who treated women like criminals. The

---

[480] Hamid and Farrall, "*The Arabs at War in Afghanistan*," 204
[481] "Popular Arab and Islamic Congress," *Wikipedia* 13 Mar. 2022
[482] Steve Coll, "*Ghost Wars: The Secret History of the CIA, Afghanistan, and Bin Laden from the Soviet Invasion to September 10, 2001*," (New York: Penguin, 2004) 271
[483] Youssef, "Egyptian Group Says It Tried to Kill Mubarak," *New York Times* 5 July 1995

Sudanese are angry because they are not who they truly are. In 2010, there was a stand-off in front of the tomb between the police and young men. She put herself between the two sides, and a policeman attacked her. She had to have an operation. They could hit a girl for wearing pants. Any man could hit a woman. The people were poor and mostly unemployed. You had to belong to the right political party to get ahead. Young men were frustrated and joined armed groups.

Sudan was part of the Middle East, and Africa. The Saudis and the Gulf states used this to rule here. They backed Boko Haram and others to take the pressure off the Saudis elsewhere. When el-Sisi took power in Egypt, in 2013, the Ikhwan and Boko Haram came here. The government wanted to Islamize the world. It was the legacy of her ancestor. The Sudanese had two worlds in them, the West and Islam. If she went to a Sheikh, she was a woman, and humbled herself. If she pushed, she was seen as the devil. She was part of Pan-African Solidarity with women from Africa, and the world's women's movement. Her mother was a political force. She regulated what time she would be with Miriam's father in bed. She was so busy that she got women for him, yet she was never mentioned as a possible minister. Her name, Mariam, crossed religions. When she saw a priest or a monk she was humbled by their humility. *"Is not Hell the abode for all who are given to false pride?"*[484]

Jihad was a part of the Sudanese. In Medina, the Prophet said all the descendants of Adam were honored as the sons of God. How, then, were they to deal with the Chinese, who did not exist in their eyes? After the police hit her, her daughter, four years old, called President Bashir a traitor. She was a prominent rower now. She practiced on the Nile. Women fought with the Imam al-Mahdi. There were jihadists here, but they were hard to reach.

Inas and I approached al-Turabi's house half-hidden among the trees. A group of men sat in the shade. A man rose, shouted, and kissed my hand. Inside, al Turabi, a slim, striking man about 6' 2" in a white jalabiya, white turban, and scarf wrapped loosely around his neck, like men in Europe, came smiling, into his large air-conditioned sitting room. Al-Mahdi smiled, I read,

---

[484] The Koran (az-Zamar) 39:60

even as he was killing a man. He was 81,[485] looked about 60, wore wire rim glasses, had a trimmed beard, and bright eyes. He had a law degree from the University of Khartoum, a bachelor's and master's from Oxford, and a PhD from the Sorbonne. He was the founder of the National Islamic Front, leader of a worldwide Muslim movement, called the Lenin of Islam, and the Pope of Terrorism.

When I told him why he was here, he began to preach. Kaaba in Mecca meant cubic. Moses offered the first prayer there. In prayer they had to orient themselves toward God, who was beyond time, being, and space. He was everywhere and omnipotent. The debates at the University of Khartoum when he was a student were between communists and Muslims. During the Afghan-Soviet war he met with President Reagan. He didn't know the difference between Ethiopia and Sudan. In politics he oriented himself to God, and power. When he prayed, he focused on God, who saw on the inside. To begin, he washed his mouth because he may have said bad things, his ears because he may have heard bad things, his head because he may have read bad things, his feet because he may have gone to the wrong place, or the wrong way. Women had to be separate otherwise men would be distracted by them. But a woman, if she was more learned than the men, could be the Imam. In early Islam, they chose a woman to lead. He, like Hanbal and Taymiyyah, he said, was a fundamentalist, but not a Salafi, modern in his views on women. He taught himself German in prison so he could read Goethe.

Like Nasser, he tortured and killed prisoners. In 1989, he betrayed al-Sadiqi al-Mahdi and became President of the National Assembly. In 1991 he and Bashir introduced Sharia. What about his early life?

His great grandfather was an earthly man, simple and religious, his father was a judge. On his school vacations he began his other education traveling with him around the country. Britain founded Sudan in 1920. At the university[486] he overturned cars and called for independence from the Anglo- Egyptian colonization.[487] They became free in 1956, and joined the

---

[485] Millard Burr and Robert Collins. *"Revolutionary Sudan: Hasan Al-Turabi and the Islamist State, 1989-2000,"* (Leiden: Brill Academic Publishers), 2003
[486] Hourani, *"A History of the Arab Peoples,"* 302
[487] Rogan, *"The Arabs: A History,* 239- 241"

Arab League.[488] He joined the National Islamic Charter,[489] founded maybe by the Ikhwan.[490] It became the National Islamic Front, and may have been funded through a French initiative by Saudi Arabia, and the U.S. In America he met Afro-Americans who were Muslims, but they were embittered—he gritted his teeth—and embraced Islam to be against the whites. He had to write "Negro" on his immigration form. Islam meant submission to God. For whites it seemed to mean to the devil. But most Americans were welcoming. He went to a barber in Colorado, who heard his accent, and realized that he wasn't one of his slaves, and invited him in. Jihad was an effort, against an effort, in self- defense. You could be an aggressor. Dictatorships did not unite people, but they submitted to coercion. The Americans called the Afghans 'Freedom Fighters' now they called them terrorists. They told Prince Turki that everyone who went to fight was a potential terrorist. He told him that all their information was transferred to American computers. Bin Laden lived down the road. The Salafis, led by a Saudi, tried to kill him. He didn't know why. No one knew bin Laden. He was quiet, grew and sold vegetables. He built a road to the north.

Al-Turabi refused to acknowledge the al-Qaeda training camps, the passports he gave out, that bin Laden, whom he called the symbol of anti-Western forces in the world, and al-Zawahiri, planned terrorist attacks,[491] or that Sudan told Saudi Arabia[492] it could take him, or that it harbored and, maybe betrayed "Carlos the Jackal" to the French, worrying all those who had come to Khartoum that they might be next.[493] He wouldn't talk about the assassination attempt on Mubarak, nor answer any question about Haqqani.

The Ikhwan fought Israel, briefly. There were Jews and infidels in Mecca. ISIS didn't understand economics or foreign policy. As for Saudi Arabia, there was a very bad verse about monarchy in the Koran. He looked, as we sat there, but couldn't find the passage. The Saudis were Bedouin, their army rich, but weak. The fight today was a class struggle, like the Cold War.[494] He studied French in Britain and went to Paris. Yes, some of his zeal

---

[488] Lewis, "*The Middle East*" 258, 260
[489] https://Oxford Islamic studies.com/article/opr/t125/e1095.
[490] Lacey, "*Inside the Kingdom*," 66
[491] Coll, "*Ghost Wars*," 271
[492] Robert Lacey, *Inside the Kingdom* (New York: Penguin, 2009), p. 202.
[493] https://www.britannica.com/biography/Carlos-the-Jackal
[494] Interview, *Le Figaro*, 9/28/01.

came from living there, but *"Liberté, Eqalité, Fraternité,"*[495] it sounded glorious, but... he waved his hand. President Morsi never sent anyone to jail. The police academy was to be open to all, but it did not allow the lower classes in.

He was referring to an Egyptian novel,[496] movie and television series about a poor boy who wanted to be a policeman so that he could marry the girl he loved. They wouldn't let him in the academy, and he became a terrorist. The class struggle was a modern revivalism, from Europe across the Middle East, and revenge against colonialism, but it was too emotional. In Europe they were too few to be effective. The revivalists were like a bull with a red flag. There had to be a revivalism of the mind, a spiritual awakening. The Koran said to go out into the world. Muslims should become missionaries, not jihadis with a suicide vest. Initially he thought it was going to be through Islam. Soldiers only knew how to follow orders. The Salafis were against him because he was too modern. Wahhabis and Arab nationalists had the same base of support as Nasser. It was a fight for dignity, freedom, and equality against the West.

General Hamid Gul attended a PAIC conference. Al-Turabi may have brought bin Laden and Saddam Hussein together.[497] He said Mubarak was unequal to him intellectually.[498] Al-Lah meant the only God. Jesus was a priest revered by Muslims. Mohammad was the final prophet. He had a friend in Georgia named Carter, a Baptist.

Jimmy Carter first worked here in 1986. In 1999, he negotiated a peace agreement between Sudan and Uganda. He opposed the sanctions, imposed, in part, because American Christians felt that Christians in South Sudan were being enslaved by Muslims.[499] They hurt small businesses and the poor. In 2011, the South, more African than Arab, more Christian than Muslim, where most of Sudan's oil is located seceded from the north. Carter tried to end the war in Darfur, to help the poor, and to eradicate diseases.

---

[495] https://www.diplomatie.gouv.fr/en/coming-to-france/france-facts/symbols-of-the-republic/article/liberty-equality-fraternity
[496] The Yacobian Building, by Alaa al-Aswany, 2002
[497] Thomas Joscelyn, "The Pope of Terrorism, Part II," *Washington Examiner* 26 July 2005
[498] "Egyptian Group Says It Tried to Kill Mubarak," *New York Times* 5 July 1995
[499] "Report by Former U.S. President Jimmy Carter on Trip to Dubai and Sudan, Jan. 18-25, 2014

Each time Carter, a Christian, came here he met with the only Sunni revolutionary to take over a country.

Inas and I walked down the road to bin Laden's wood house, half-hidden in the trees. Al-Fadhli and Haqqani stayed here.

Gordon Memorial College, founded in 1902, with funds raised in part by Kitchener, to educate young men to work in the colonial government,[500] became in 1956, the University of Khartoum. There were tree-lined walkways, a rich green lawn, and red brick Moorish archways. Professor Atta El-Battahani, a lean man in western clothes, an expert in Islamic movement, sat in his airconditioned book-lined office. The Islamist movement began in the 1940s when Sudanese students in Cairo met the Ikhwan and returned home. Some were attracted to Fabianism, and a socialist revolution, others to a Marxist one, those linked to the Ikhwan wanted an Islamic one. Their base was small. This changed in the1960s when al-Turabi returned from Paris and said they must stop trying to educate the people to instead put pressure on the state. Many disagreed but al-Turabi, a skilled politician, built cells in the army, and Islamization crept in.

The students rebelled also was because after achieving independence from Britain in 1956, governments failed to provide economic and political stability, and Islam became the answer.

When the price of oil rose after 1973, Saudi Arabia and the Gulf monarchies poured money into Sudan. All a man had to do was grow a beard and say Allah-oh-Akbar and he could get a cheap loan. Thousands went to Saudi Arabia and to the Gulf to work. In the 1980s, during the war in Afghanistan, al-Turabi began to call for Sharia. Today Iran, in its cold war with Saudi Arabia, was encircling the Gulf. The Saudis were countering by investing in Pakistan, Iraq, Afghanistan, and Central Asia. General Bashir, to counter the Saudis, gave Iran access to Port Sudan, on the Red Sea, and to Yemen. Iran became Sudan's main arms supplier. When bin Laden, a Sunni, was here he met with an Iranian official who, at bin Laden's request, helped maybe to arrange an introduction to Hezbollah.[501] A former Egyptian army officer, Mohammad Zeidan, who went to Afghanistan and became Saif al-Adel, and joined al-Qaeda, came to Sudan with bin Laden, and from here

---

[500]Hourani, "*A History of the Arab Peoples,*" 302
[501] Soufan, "*Anatomy of Terror,*" 47-65

went to Lebanon and trained with Hezbollah. He and bin Laden looked, through Somalis they knew in Afghanistan, at Somalia. Al-Adel, it appears, went there with a team and fought in the 1993 Battle of Mogadishu.[502] In 1996, he flew with bin Laden to Jalalabad and lived near Yunus Khalis. Today, he is in Tehran.

Sudan, on the periphery of the Arab world, a poor nation, used Saudi Arabia. It was now, like Yemen and Egypt, using the threat of terror to frighten the U.S. to give money so that it could fight ISIS. When they brought bin Laden and others here, they provided houses, and watched them. After 9/11, Salah Gosh, the head of Sudanese intelligence went to the U.S.[503] In 2005, the CIA flew him to Washington because they were helping in the U.S. War on Terror.[504] In the 1990s Sudan supported Boko Haram, and al-Shabab in Somalia.

There were groups here, but it was too dangerous to dig. Was he afraid? He paused. It was like Communism in Russia, there was an unseen structure. He felt it around him. You don't know who the cleaner might be. When Bin Laden was here, a reporter asked him to describe the nature of the regime. He called it "a mixture of religion and organized crime." It used the threat of terrorism.

I tried to see Gosh. He asked Inas what my title was. I was a researcher. He said a researcher came here and saw him. He later found out he was CIA. He asked to see my resume. Inas gave it to him. He wouldn't see me. We went to see another professor, an expert on the Gulf, in black jeans and a bright, striped shirt. I will call him Tariq. Each monarchy was rich in oil or natural gas, he said, but dependent upon Pakistan and Sudan for soldiers, and British, French and U.S. bases for protection. The Bahrain army and the Qatar army were Pakistani armies. Omar al-Bashir was once military attaché to the Emirates (UAE). The population of Oman was 20 percent Baluch. The Omani army was almost all Baluch.

Alexander struggled coming home through Baluchistan, today a Pakistani province. The Chinese use Gwadar, the port near Iran.

The Pakistan army was linked to all the terrorist groups. In the 1960s

---

[502] "Battle of Mogadishu,1993" *Military Factory - Global Defense Reference,*
[503] *Sudan Tribune,* https://sudantribune.com/.
[504] Scott Shane, "C.I.A. Role in Visit of Sudan Intelligence Chief Causes Dispute within Administration," *New York Times* 18 June 2005.

and 70s, Pakistan, funded by Saudi Arabia and Qatar, promoted Wahhabi Islam across the Muslim world. The ISI was competing in the Gulf against India and looking out for Pakistani businesses. Those who had lived under dictatorships committed 90% of the major crimes. Indians were democratic and committed fewer crimes. Its caste system kept people in place. The Ikhwan were close to Turkey, Qatar and Yemen. China was using Sudan as a base from which to conquer Africa. Turkey, because of its Ottoman past, was important here. Radicals, financed by the Gulf, studied at Khartoum University in the 70s. Fully 90% went to Africa University, officially the International University of Africa, founded by Saudi Arabia and the Gulf states to train preachers and missionaries to educate Africans in Wahhabi Islam. I must go there. He would call his brother.

He paused. How did I get a visa? They didn't give out many. He asked Inas if she wanted to go abroad. He saw something in her. She needed to pursue a PhD. He gave her papers from his desk. She saw her name on a list. How did it get there? She wasn't in school. He said not to worry, standing over her. Maybe they could find her a scholarship. Two men came in. Tariq asked me to leave. I went downstairs and outside. Inas came and was quiet, with her head down, a single woman in a Salafi world.

The next day there was no electricity. At sundown, women in brightly colored clothes carrying food walked by the guesthouse. Dusk came. Judy, our cook, from Eritrea, stood in her rooftop kitchen. Below a group of men sat on a mat. The call came announcing the citing of the moon. The men ate quietly and then the call to prayer came. Judy brought a plate of rice and fresh fish. The wind came and the dust. Friday morning Judy invited me to go to church with her family. I had written an email, at her request, to a refugee organization in Canada. They had applied for asylum. An Ethiopian female guest and I took a rickshaw to a junction two miles away. Judy, her daughter, and her husband, their three-year old son, and John, a student, who worked the night shift at the front desk, arrived in a taxi. We took a dirt path dissected by a sewer into a large room with rows of people in plastic chairs. A man with a microphone walked back and forth onstage, praying. Men and women stood, their hands out, saying amen. He was casting out demons, said John. "Change was coming. We ask forgiveness, Lord," he prayed. A choir, in brown and gold robes, joined him. A man played keyboard, another monitored a console and they swayed and the music swept over us, a mixture of gospel, the Red Sea, and the Horn of Africa, passionate, melodic, hypnotic, and soothing. "No one is like you, Jesus," they sang, repeating this, and the music rose and fell, like an ocean.

Mohammad and his fifteen followers found refuge among Abyssinian Christians. A preacher, in a gray suit, tinted glasses, walked back and forth wiping his head with a towel. John translated. "They were one people. They had to stay together, and the Bible, the word of God, was their source." I had to go. John and I stood on a street corner trying to find a taxi. What kind of service that was? They were Pentecostals. Was it dangerous being a Christian? They had to be careful, but it was better than Eritrea, even if it was half eastern Orthodox. Judy's husband was in prison for four years. Pentecostalism began in Kansas in 1901. Pentecostals spoke in tongues, danced, believed in prophecy, divine healing, and that women could be leaders. They are one quarter of the world's two billion Christians.[505] Over 40% of Eritrea, across the Red Sea from Saudi Arabia, is Wahhabi. Every morning when I went up to the roof for breakfast Judy was there, reading the Bible. In America people were afraid of Islam, "wicked, violent, not of the same God."[506] Here, Pentecostalism was an evangelizing populist revivalist movement, like, in their way, the Tablighi.

That night Inas and I sat in a café planning the next day. Tariq liked her. She frowned. There were no such scholarships as he offered. He was going to investigate me. The following day, Houda, the guesthouse manager, and I drove past about forty men sitting under trees by the road, and then another group. They were Nigerians. They walked or paid money and rode in the back of trucks across half of Africa to beg. It was Ramadan, and people gave them money. They lived outside and didn't wash. We passed 50 women standing and sitting, rail thin, in colorful clothes, in the shade. Houda stopped by a grocery store. A little girl rushed over. A woman in a flowing gold and red garment, which you must be married to wear, who could make a small fortune as a model in the West, with a baby, came up. They looked like them, but when they talked, she knew they were from Nigeria, one of the largest oil exporters in the world.[507] She gave the girl a coin. Nigeria meant Boko Haram. Tariq said Boko Haram and al-Shabab studied here in

---

[505] "Church," *The Christian Church - Beliefs and Faith*, https://www.christianity
[506] Peter J. Boyer, "The Big Tent," *New Yorker* 22 Aug. 2005.
[507] *Central Intelligence Agency*, World Factbook

the 1990s. The government supported them and gave them passports. There wasn't a jihadi group it seemed anywhere that wasn't controlled by a government.

We went to see a newspaper editor and publisher. He was late and apologized. The traffic was bad, and it was hotter since they cut down the trees surround Khartoum. In 1989, after the Mujahideen victory in Afghanistan, the government wanted to bring for the first time in history all Muslims together, to create an Islamic renaissance, a new worldwide religious order, to regenerate Mohammad's true Islamic State.[508] They would fight the West, which included Egypt and Saudi Arabia. Al-Turabi got money from the Arab states. Kuwait, a nation of traders, was his biggest supporter. After 9/11, they got rid of everyone. The Arab Spring affected them. Did they need to think of a new way? Was it better to work with Christians? Should they change the concept that said they should look upon themselves as good and everyone else as bad? There was no jihadist mentality here. Everyone knew when a stranger was here, warning me, like Miriam. He had a responsibility as a journalist to tell the truth to help his country. He said on television that Sudan should recognize Israel. Once, he, too, I learned, followed al-Turabi, a messiah, who had returned to lead them. The next afternoon, I watched President Obama standing with Bowe Bergdahl's parents when he announced the exchange of five men from Guantanamo for their son. I remembered going to church with them in Idaho. Their faith gave them strength

Two days later, men ransacked the editor's office and beat him and his employees.

---

[508] Hassan Al-Turabi, "Interview with Sudanese Leaders Al-Turabi and Al-Attabani, 11/1994" http://www.africa.upenn.edu/Hornet/horn_sdn.html.

The Aristocrat

We drove slowly on a bumpy dirt road. A compound appeared, like a chateau in France, and all around in a field men and women bent over, like peasants in Millet's painting, hoeing in the heat.[509] A boy in a European soccer shirt opened an iron door and we passed a carport and a lawn, and entered a large home with bare walls and cushioned chairs. Ghazi Salah Uddin Atabani, a physician, with a PhD in biochemistry from Surrey University, former foreign minister, and a member of the Ikhwan, in a white jalabiya and turban, joined us.

We didn't say Christianist, so why Islamist? He preferred fundamentalist, as did al-Turabi. There were jihadis here. Arms smugglers were coming through. I would not find any jihadi links. He was a government minister when they hosted the PAIC, a follower of Turabi. The U.S. had taken over from Britain as the colonizer.[510] When al-Zawahiri came in 1986-87, he was under control. Bin Laden came in 1991 until '96. The U.S. wasn't interested. Al-Zawahiri went to Pakistan. The U.S. fought communism in Afghanistan because it was a more strategic location than Yemen. Sudanese went there. For some it was like a picnic, for others a battle for Islam. He never met anyone who was enthusiastic. The U.S. created the Mujahideen and encouraged people to go.

It seemed that when al-Zawahiri and bin Laden announced the World Islamic Front, in Haqqani territory in 1998 it came from the solidarity that they found here.

For Atabani, the PAIC was a fight for respect as a nation, and for Islam, against the West and its rich Arab allies, and their acolytes, like Egypt. After the Soviet Union fell, President George H.W. Bush spoke of a new world order, but al-Turabi called it a transition. The Arab world was in flux. The borders drawn by Britain and France would not hold. The Ikhwan had a wide, robust base, and could not be eradicated. If the jihadis went to the Sahel, to Darfur, to Niger, to Qatar, the ultra-religious among them could

---

[509] Jean-Francois Millet, *The Gleaners*, 1857. Musée d'Orsay, Paris.
[510] Hassan Al-Turabi. "Interview with Sudanese Leaders Al-Turabi and Al-Attabani, 11/1994, http://www.africa.upenn.edu/Hornet/horn_sdn.html.

bring havoc on Africa. Everything stemmed from the Mujahedeen. From Cairo to Yemen to Nigeria they formed alliances and smuggled men and weapons from Yemen across the Red Sea to Sudan. Al-Fadhli told me this also. They followed trade routes to Ethiopia, and Egypt, and from West Africa to Darfur to Egypt. Were the weapons from Iran going to Hamas,[511] or to Islamic Jihad?[512] Mokhtar Belmokhtar[513] the Arab Afghan leader of "al-Qaeda in the Islamic Maghreb,"[514] could be on their western border.[515] Al-Zawahiri had a strong presence here. The threat came from despair—the prevailing sentiment among the young.

They saw the West as established and economically stable; 95% of them lived in what the West called the Orient.[516] He too, had read *Orientalism*, Edward Said's book on the West's condescending view of the "Other," the romance of the Orient, of Flaubert's *Salome*. I must return to Cairo, a world center of intellectualism. He had no use for al-Zawahiri, al-Baghdadi, or Haqqani, who believed in the power of their will because it was God's will, an ailment of all religious people.

In 2020, the United Nations Food and Agriculture Organization would issue a reporting stating that that an estimated 32.3% of young people in the Arab world "did not have regular access to sufficient and nutritious food." On December 12, 2021, the FAO would state that since 2014, the percentage of undernourished Arabs increased 16%, and 91% over the last two decades. The World Bank, UNESCO and UNICEF stated that even before the Covid 19 Pandemic nearly two-thirds of Arab children, aged five to fourteen did not have access to a computer to learn remotely.[517] The World Inequalities Report of 2022 stated that the top 10% of the Arab Middle East and North

---

[511] "Israeli Attack' on Sudanese Arms Factory Offers Glimpse of Secret War," *Guardian* 25 Oct. 2012.

[512] Isabel Kershner, "Official Silence in Israel over Sudan's Accusations of Air Attack," *New York Times*, 25 Oct. 2012.

[513] Called Mr. Marlboro, for his alleged cigarette smuggling business, leader of "al-Mulathamun Battalion," or "Those Who sign in Blood," responsible for the 2013 attack on a natural gas facility in eastern Algeria.

[514] "Al-Qaeda in the Islamic Maghreb," *Council on Foreign Relations*

[515] "Notorious Algerian Terrorist, Mokhtar Belmokhtar, could Still Be Alive," *Council on Foreign Relations*.

[516] "Salammbô," *Encyclopædia Britannica*

[517] *UNICEF:* "An Entire Generation of Students Could Lose up to USD1 Trillion throughout the Course of Their Lives in Mena Due to covid19."

Africa controlled 58% of the region's income and that poor and vulnerable Arabs accounted for 2/3rds of the population. Nearly half of the youth in the Middle East and North Africa, could not find a job.

"The thing we need is a military organization of agents" [518]…Lenin

Inas stood silently in her old classroom and then we walked to the office of Professor Hassan Makki Mohamed Ahmed, at the International University of Africa. Ahmed, sitting in a black leather chair, put his book down.

The Islamic movement began here in the 1940s when Christian missionaries Christianized a woman. The key word was *Islamic*, which was not in the Koran, nor did it appear in any book until after the fall of the Caliphate in 1924. It began as a missionary movement. The Ikhwan came and found a group of like believers who had studied in Cairo. In 1949, they started the "Islamic Liberation Movement," an anti-colonial reaction to the communists who also wanted to get rid of the British. They were an extension of al-Mahdi's movement. British missionaries wanted to Christianize India,[519] and Sudan,[520] a form of colonialism. In the 1950s, the Ikhwan, the communists and the socialists saw that they had the same goals and organized a conference. The majority said they should call themselves "*Ikhwan al-Muslimin*," but as an Islamic nationalist movement.[521] Then Dr. Hassan al-Turabi came, his professor in law school.

Ahmed was imprisoned for his suspected involvement in a coup attempt. There he memorized the Koran, learned to translate Arabic to English and read Islamic history books. Their jailers provided whatever they needed. Friends sent books. He met politicians, union activists, soldiers, a German missionary, and learned from them. Al-Turabi was there for seven years and he never complained. Every day they waited for a visitor. It was so important to have someone come to see them. Al-Turabi had faith in God. He didn't want to show weakness. He never had a visitor. Initially, Ahmed saw the Ikhwan as an ideology, but in prison he learned about Islam. By watching al- Turabi, he found a way to live. He was imprisoned again in

---

[518] https://www.marxists.org/archive/cliff/works/1975/lenin1/chap04.htm.
[519] Dalrymple, "*The Last Mughal*" 9-10, 22, 58-70, 74-75
[520] Francis M. Deng, "Sudan - Civil War and Genocide: Disappearing Christians of the Middle East," *Middle East Forum*
[521] The Society of Muslim Brothers or The Muslim Brotherhood.

1973 for eight months. He was still a student. His father died and he had to get a job. He wanted to help his mother. He joined the Ikhwan. Al-Turabi sent him to preach and start cells around the country.

He worked in Darfur. Everyone had to donate five percent of his salary to the movement. He was pursuing an M.A. at Khartoum University at the same time. He wanted to research "Modern Islamic Revivalism." Al-Turabi liked his work in Darfur and wanted him to go elsewhere. He said no. He could not tell his family what he was doing or look for a job without an address. Al-Turabi was angry, but he had these things. He became a researcher here. The university funded him to go to Afghanistan to study the Mujahideen, and Iran to compare Sunni to Shia revivals.

He wrote to al-Turabi. "We cannot create an Islamic government through democracy; we can only do it through a coup d'état. There is no way to attain power unless by joining the military, but you must be cautious because it will be a military coup, not an Islamic coup." He became a revolutionary, in part drawing on what he learned from the Mujahideen. The political parties in Sudan were run by families, like a tribe. He was an outsider. He wrote a book about Islamic movements. The most important part was what he wrote to al-Turabi, who was upset because the military would read it. He said he created in General Bashir a Frankenstein. He was marginalized. It gave him the chance to leave. He joined the Islamic movement when he was 15. After 30 years he wanted to be free.

Bin Laden was not free but forced to come here as an investor to find jobs for the hundreds of Mujahideen who were being chased by Egyptian security forces. The Sudanese took at least $200 million from him. He built a highway 150 miles long. He and Bashir inaugurated it. Ahmed said if he wanted to save Islam to build a "Highway of Islam" to Ethiopia to open the land up to trade. He built the first 50 miles, and the U.S. said to expel him. He was the hen that gave birth every day with a golden egg, real money, cash. Al-Turabi was an Islamic leader, not bin Laden. Boko Haram's real name was "The Movement of the Followers of the traditions of the Prophet who are waging war against Innovations in the Religion."[522] It began in 1963 when a leader in the Islamic movement in Nigeria was killed, and then the prime minister. The Igbo tribe, which was Christian, mounted a coup

---

[522] Harakar al-Ansaw Sunni wa jihad Mura Bita.

because it felt that the new leader was threatening Christians. The south was Christian. The leader was trying to secure government jobs for the north, which was part of the Islamic world. Their leaders wanted to be closer to Sudan, Europe and Saudi Arabia, to help people go on Hajj, to study in the U.K. and the U.S., and to help women.

Everywhere, it always came back to the Mujahideen.

The Arabs were the first slavers, coming by camel across the desert. The Portuguese came to West Africa in the 15th century. In 1849, the British colonized what became Nigeria, dividing it between the Christian south and the Muslim north. In 1960 it became independent, but the army ruled. In 1967, Catholic Biafra[523] broke away. Civil war began. France, against Britain, and in its desire for oil, recognized Biafra. Medical students in Paris, upset that France, the U.N., and other nations were taking so long to intervene, and that there was not enough room in hospitals to practice, formed *"Médecins sans Frontières"* and went there.[524] The Salafis saw that France and the Catholic Church[525] recognized Biafra against the unity of Nigeria, a conspiracy against Islam. They could not create a peaceful Islamic Renaissance. They had to use Salafism. "People Committed to the Prophet's Teachings for Propagation and Jihad," rose in Borno.[526] In 2002, Muhammad Yusuf, who received a Koranic education in Chad and Niger, became the leader and changed the name to Boko Haram.[527] Boko came from *boto* (book), in Hausa, and *haram*.[528] Western books were un-Islamic. He was angry at government corruption, at the U.S. invasion of Afghanistan and Iraq; that it tortured prisoners and supported Israel against Muslim nations. He wanted to separate Muslims from Western civilization. The government killed him in 2009. His second, Abu-Bakr Sheekau took over. In 2012-13 Boko Haram trained with al-Qaeda in northern Mali. To the Salafis the war against Islam began in Biafra.[529] Al-Zawahiri was important, he

---

[523] "The Distorted Memory of Biafra," *Council on Foreign Relations*

[524] The founders explained this to the author in the 1980s

[525] "Exclusive: Real Reason France Supported Biafra during Nigerian Civil War," *Premium Times Nigeria*, 2 July 2017

[526] Jamaatu Ahlus-Sunnah Lidda 'Awati Wal jihad.

[527] Salaam, Abeeb Olufemi, "The Psychological Make-up of Mohammed Yusuf," 5 Nov. 2013.

[528] "Forbidden," or that which is unlawful.

[529] Michel Arseneault, "How France Armed Biafra's Bid to Break from Nigeria,"

emphasized, because the U.S. and Europe supported Israel, betraying the Arabs. He, too, saw the U.S. as a colonizer. Al-Baghdadi had not written anything. There was no growth, he might make a big explosion, and then vanish. Be careful.

There was one other man to see, Inas's uncle, Abdul Rahim Ali Mohamed Ibrahimi, a small, slight man, the founder of Africa University. He had a PhD from the University of Edinburgh in the literary structure of the verses in the Koran.[530] Men debated whether the Koran was poetry or just near to it. The unity was not in the number of chapters, of which there were 30,[531] but in the verses, which sometimes rhymed and sometimes didn't. When you studied a small unit of verse you could illuminate the whole Koran. He meant "*al-Batin*," that which is hidden, the inner level, one of the 99 names of God, only known by God. There was no authority anymore. Al-Azhar was the voice of the Egyptian government. Their way of life, centered on Islam, was being threatened by the web. Many fathers had discovered that their sons, who looked innocent, were in touch with groups online. They had discovered training camps, one, run by al-Shabab, when a bomb they were making went off. The youth were drawn to ISIS because it stood up to the West. The conflict in Palestine was central and unless it was resolved the people would revolt against every government. Abdullah Azzam was behind the creation of al-Qaeda. His fight was all about dignity. It was still all about dignity. Islamism was a class struggle. There were no reform movements, only wars and the dreams of young men. They wanted to be free and to prosper. Men who joined ISIS felt unfulfilled and disrespected, in part because of their age. They wanted adventure, and respect.

Be careful, he warned, ISIS did not rise by itself. There was a link between Boko Haram and an intelligence agency. Mariam al-Mahdi also warned me. The nucleus of Boko Harem was fundamentalist madrasa graduates. There were men underground but I should not try to find them. ISIS was also created by an intelligence agency. Professor Zindani said Saudi Arabia funded The University of Africa. Nigerian Muslims welcomed it. Before, education Africa had been associated with Christian missionaries. He wrote: "Al-Mahdi wanted to get rid of the secular Egyptian-Turkish elite

---

RFI, 25 May 2017
[530] "Ayah," is a sign or miracle in Arabic.
[531] A chapter is a "surah," literally a "row," or "series."

and their Christian representatives and replace them with a revolutionary Islamic state—a place for all true Muslims who were ready to cooperate in Jihad and the building of a Muslim state free from the evils of corruption and secularism. The Mahdiyya movement was a liberation theology, in part a reaction to the impotence of Muslim scholars.[532] Catholics, who established the Sudan Church in exile, collaborated with other European Churches and powers to distort the Mahdiyya image, mobilized international public opinion against it…which led to the destruction of the Mahdiyya Islamic state."[533] Most Sudanese call al-Mahdi the father of independence,[534] who united the tribes by an Islamic ideology, drove out the alien rulers, and created the foundations for a nation state. He saw himself as a re-newer of the true faith and as a successor of the Apostle of God, sent to recreate the community that Mohammad created in Medina with 130 followers.

In 1992, National Geographic asked me to travel the length and go to the source of the Amazon. Every day as I moved upstream in Brazil, I saw a small Pentecostal Church of God, next to a large cross, the sign of a Catholic mission, the populists competing against Catholicism as they competed against the Wahhabis in Eretria. Catholic priests, going against Rome, preached Liberation Theology, trying, like Mohammad, to help the poor.

---

[532] Hassan Makki Mohamed Ahmed, *Sudan: the Christian Design* (Markfield: The Islamic Foundation, 2007).
[533] Ibid.
[534] Abu-i- l'istiqlal.

Al-Gamma'a al-Islamiyya

I checked into a hotel near Tahrir Square and the next morning took a bus to Alexandria, and a taxi to the Corniche, with whitecaps on the water, the air invigorating, to a tourist hotel. I called a man and said I met a friend of his in London. He gave me directions to his office. The next day my taxi made its way down a dusty street filled with garbage, and broken cars. Two boys played in a dirt lot. We came to a small grocery store and two men in jeans and t-shirts, sitting outside asked who I was looking for. I told them. They were friendly and pointed up to a building. A burly man leaned over a balcony and told me come up. My instincts said he was friendly. Abu Samrah, rugged, bearded, with a warm smile, black, gray hair combed back, wore a short-striped sleeve shirt, jeans, and white sandals. His office had a white table and black chairs. The walls were bare. A teenage girl in an abaya, with her head down, his daughter, sat at the table. He introduced us. Her name was Jihad. She would be our translator.

He was a union leader for 15 years at the port. From 2002-2005 he called a strike every year demanding higher wages. The Ikhwan would not help them because he was al-Gamaá al-Islamiyya (AGI). They worked with them in the streets. In that they were one fist. He raised his fist, a longshoreman and a union leader. But they had differences. The Ikhwan talked with and trusted the Americans. He hated America. El-Sisi was America's man. He killed 6,000 people, more than Nasser. They wanted an Islamic revolution like Iran. The Ikhwan wanted a civil state and to be friends with America and Europe. They allowed television, whiskey, and for men and women to swim together. They were far away from Islam. El-Sisi was opposed to Hamas, and the Palestinians. He had killed them in the Sinai, admitting that AGI was there. They didn't want to help Hamas and the Ikhwan, but in other matters they were one hand. Again, he raised his fist, like he was giving a speech on the dock. Egypt had no power. Their power was that after the revolution they developed a strong heart. They were involved in the killing of Sadat. "Yes, we did that," he admitted. They gave 30 rifles to Mubarak. He looked at me.

He just said al-Gamaá-al-Islamiyya was involved in Sadat's assassination. Al-Zawahiri probably tried to kill Mubarak in Addis Ababa. He knew to hide under a chair, while Sadat, who chose him to be his vice president, sat with his head up, his chest out, dying with dignity. Mubarak, working with AGI, whose spiritual leader, the blind sheikh, not only betrayed the man who raised him up, but was involved in the 1993 bombing at the World Trade Center, and would now become president. And he was America's ally?

Did he know Abdur Rahman, the army major who came to see Haqqani? He didn't recognize his name. I had to bring a picture. Egypt made the Islamic revolutions in the world. The Ikhwan youth were disgusted with the leadership and were going to Iraq and Syria. Many left the Ikhwan, angry that el-Sisi killed so many in the streets, and wanting violence, had come to them. Wasn't it dangerous to talk? He wasn't worried. In 1995, they put down the gun, and el-Sisi left them alone. Their leader, Ayman al-Zawahiri, a good man, was the head of al-Qaeda now, but far away. Jihad was Egyptian. Egypt was its factory for two reasons: 1) Sayyidd Qutb and 2) the Koran. He picked it up from his desk, and read a passage, about the dictatorship of the Pharaohs, of Moses and Joseph. It was an example for any country. The Shah of Iran was a dictator, and so was Ali Bhutto, who Zia ul-Haq, a good Muslim, hanged. El-Sisi was a dictator killing his wife and sons in the streets. Egyptian men were ambassadors of jihad. He lifted his fist. They were like a bunch of grapes.

They were many groups, but all together. Jihad would be forever. If one group fell, another would rise. He was 54. He joined AGI when he was 35. The Ikhwan were too weak. Before, he liked music, and had a friend in New Jersey. They wrote to one another. He liked football. Then he read Sayyid Qutb and prayed more in the mosque. He joined AGI and the government put him in prison for five months. The Koran said the Jews were his enemy because they were God's enemy. They killed Christians and tried to kill Mohammad. Wherever there were Jews in the world, and they were everywhere, they created fire.

It was time for prayers. He had bad knees, from rheumatism. He prayed in a chair. They didn't hate Americans, but they hated the government because it helped el-Sisi and because through them, there was no justice. The Americans killed Muslims in Iraq, Syria, Afghanistan, Pakistan, and Yemen. Why? El-Sisi made sure there were no politics in Egypt, but they would fight politically. Al-Zawahiri left the order for them to choose the way. He wanted an Islamic government. The young wanted war because el-

Sisi killed so many people. The Ikhwan said their peace was better than the gun. El-Sisi loved blood, and he loved the throne. Abu Samrah didn't want a Syria here. There the army was against its people. He refused to fight the Egyptian army, which was strong only against its people. When el-Sisi was gone and a good man came in they would have hope. Why I was here? I told him. Alexandria was not Peshawar, but everyone who went to Iraq and Syria passed through here. He was forbidden to leave the country. They didn't want war, only justice without regards to religion whether Christian or Muslim. There was no difference. This was the Koran. He invited me to join them another time for dinner. He would have a friend come who he wanted me to meet.

Back in Cairo I met with a retired Yemeni ambassador in a tweed jacket. Salafism began in Egypt when the Mujahedeen returned from Afghanistan, he explained. They saw that the glory they went to find there wasn't here. You could see the Salafi changes in the mosques. The first line in all but one chapter in the Koran began with *"Bismillah il-Raham il-Rahim."*[535] This was how they began their prayers, but now the Salafis whispered the first line and began with the second phrase. It was not trivial. He asked imams about this, but they were quiet. It meant that the Salafis, tied to the Saudis, who supported el-Sisi, were gaining power.[536] Abu Samrah said their jihad began in 1974, when Wahhabi missionaries came here.

His son, in jeans and polo shirt, greeted me and led me into their living room. A soccer came was on television. Abu Samrah came with a man about 6'3," shaved head, in a white jalabiya, with an iron handshake, and hard eyes. He had been in prison for ten years and was just released. He had been fighting jihad. We sat at the dining room table and two women brought bowls of meat, potatoes and vegetables, and urged me to eat, to keep eating, and to eat more. His son wanted to fight, said Abu Samrah. He said no, but the young wouldn't listen. He would fight again, his friend said. Jihad never ended. I asked his son what he was going to do in life. He and his friends wanted to fight. It was time for jihad. It was dangerous. He shrugged. He, like Sirajuddin Haqqani, had to surpass his father. Dessert came, and coffee. They couldn't have been nicer, these men whose brethren massacred tourists at Luxor, and looked to al-Zawahiri. I was looking for networks. They were right here, but I hadn't found anything about the Haqqanis.

---

[535] "In the name of God, the most Gracious, the most Merciful."
[536] James Traub, "The Lighthouse Dims," *Foreign Policy*, 23 Dec. 2014

The Levant

It was September now and the weather was soft and warm. Amman, a city built on seven hills, like Rome, a village when in 1921, the British, after World War I, made it the capital of the Emirate of Transjordan.

During American colonial times, the Koran sold well in bookstores. Thomas Jefferson had one in his library. The colonies traded with the Ottoman Empire and people were curious about Islam, the faith of the pashas and the pirates of the Barbary States of North Africa, who raided U.S. merchant ships and took Americans captive. Jefferson, as Secretary of State, considered going to war.[537] In 1914, Britain and France, allied with Russia, went to war with Germany, allied with the Austro-Hungary Empire, and the Ottoman Empire. In April 1917 America entered the war on the side of Britain and France. In 1918, President Wilson called for an end "to the day of conquest and aggrandizement." The interests of the "colonized peoples were equal to those of the imperialist powers."[538] The Arabs at the Peace Conference looked to him,[539] the son and grandson of Presbyterian missionaries. He refused to declare war on the Ottoman Empire[540] to protect Christians and Christian schools. Western leaders were "profoundly ignorant about the Arabs; their information was derived entirely from the *Arabian Nights*,"[541] said Amir Faisal, commander of the Arab revolt against the Ottomans, a descendent of a great grandfather of Mohammad, whose clan, the Hashem, a subdivision of the Quraysh tribe, rules what is today the Hashemite Kingdom of Jordan.

Yusuf (Joseph) a Christian Palestinian businessman and I sat in a café. He and his brother had a grocery business in Iraq. In 1990, Iraq invaded Kuwait, and the U.N. Security Council imposed sanctions to force Saddam Hussein to disarm. The sanctions tightened in 1993, and Saddam rebelled. U.S. and British fighter jets responded. Saddam started a faith campaign and

---

[537] "Monticello," *First Barbary War*, https://www.monticello.org/site/research-and-collections/first-barbary-war.
[538] Rogan, "*The Arabs*," 193-94
[539] Hourani, "*A History of the Arab Peoples*," 316
[540] Ibid, 258-60
[541] Rogan, "*The Arabs*,"197

put Allah-oh-Akbar on the Iraqi flag. Women started to wear the veil and men grew beards. It was a particularly hot summer and Iraq, a secular country under Saddam, became, because of the hardship, and foreign pressure, religious. In 2003, President Bush, who felt that he had won in Afghanistan, withdrew forces and invaded Iraq. Insurgents fought back, particularly in Fallujah, north of Baghdad, where in 2004 the U.S. fought its hardest battles. The Iraqis who went to Afghanistan in the 1980s were from Fallujah.[542] The commander of the Black Banner Brigade, which led the fight, was Umar Hadid, born in 1971. He became a Salafi fighting Saddam Hussein and went to Afghanistan where he met Abu Musab al-Zarqawi, a nom de guerre of a man who grew up in a poor Salafi section of Zarqa, a blue-collar city next to Amman. His father died when he was 17 and he dropped out of school, became a street criminal and was imprisoned, and like al-Maududi, whose father died when he was young, found a home in fundamentalist and his case extremely violent Islam. In 1989, he flew to Afghanistan,[543] trained and maybe fought with al-Qaeda. He returned to Jordan, which, after given up its claims to land on the West Bank to Israel was pursing more peace initiatives, angering the Salafis, and the Palestinians.

Zarqawi joined those who wanted to overthrow King Hussein. Again, he was imprisoned.

In 1999, Hussein died, and his son Abdullah II became king, and al-Zarqawi was released. He returned to Afghanistan and met bin Laden. They didn't like one another, but Saif al-Adel convinced bin Laden to finance him. He trained men to fight Saddam, and Jordan. After 9/11, he fled to Iran, where Gulbuddin Hekmatyar, under the advice of General Babar, fled when the Taliban came to power, helped him to flee. In 2002, the first suicide bomber in Afghanistan blew himself up in a car in Gardez, the capital of Paktia Province, Haqqani territory. In 2003, Zarqawi attacked the Jordanian embassy in Baghdad, and then the Shia, blaming them for the Mongol conquest of Baghdad, and the Ottoman failure to conquer Europe.[544] He went to war against them. He sent the first suicide bomber to the U.N. compound, a symbol of the West. He founded ISIS.

---

[542] Soufan, "*Anatomy of Terror*," 114-115
[543] Ibid, 114-160
[544] Ibid. 130-132

Nicholas Berg

In 2003, Nicholas Berg, an entrepreneur and inventor, from Chester, Pennsylvania, went to Iraq to start a business. "He was a rebellious young man in that I was and am an atheist and Nicholas became devout," said his father, Michael Berg. "As a very young man, he embraced Tikkun Olam, which meant in Hebrew to repair or change the world, a community and a technology company, trying to help people in need. It was a call to social justice, a belief that you had an obligation to look out for the rest of humanity, wherever there was an injury." It began with Rabbi Akiva,[545] who taught men to "Love thy neighbor as thyself." Nick had a remarkably good outlook, Luke Lorenz, a boyhood friend, businessman and devout Catholic told me. He was so naïve, so trusting of human nature...he was all heart.

He went to Cornell, where he interviewed to join ROTC, not to join the military as a career, but as a way to serve. The woman who interviewed him kept a record of the interview. Years later, her son took Lorenz's class on becoming Catholic. Nick started to wear a Tsi-Tsit, a prayer vest, and a Yarmulke,[546] showing a growing spiritual life. His sophomore year, he went to East Africa in preparation for a project with the American Jewish World Service.[547] He worked with the Masai, teaching them how to make a well, lining the walls with bricks, and calculating how much it would cost. He returned to Cornell, where he conceived of the idea of building and repairing cell phone towers. He had good grades but left and eventually went to the University of Oklahoma, to learn how to build and repair them.

One night in 2001, he was taking a campus shuttle bus and another student asked if he could borrow his computer to send an email. It was Zacharias Moussaoui. Department of Justice reports show that in 2000 he received a letter to become a marketing consultant for In Focus Technology of Malaysia, in Europe and the U.K. He flew to Pakistan, and then to Oklahoma City. He was in Norman to attend flight school, using an email account he had set up in Malaysia. After 9/11 the FBI found Berg's email

---

[545] https://en.wikipedia.org/wiki/ Rabbi Akiva
[546] A cap that devout Jews wear to show their devotion to God.
[547] "American Jewish World Service," 1 June 2022

address on Moussaoui's computer and questioned him. He wondered to Lorenz if this would come back to haunt him. He set up, with family help, Prometheus Methods Tower Services. After the U.S. invaded Iraq, he went to a defense contractors' convention that the government hosted in a hotel near Washington and got all the necessary documents and licenses. "He was very open. He could understand and be with other people easily," Lorenz said. He went to Iraq and set up his business repairing towers. The U.S. Army asked who was this man, working alone, whose name on Moussaoui's computer? The Army put him in prison, but soon released him.

One of his best friends was getting married and he wanted to go to the wedding. The photographs emerged of U.S. soldiers torturing men in Abu Ghraib prison enraging the Arab world. He was out late one night coming home in a taxi in Mosul. It stopped at a checkpoint and an Iraqi policeman, surprised that he was alone, took him to a police station where the U.S. Army military police had an office. There was a JAG[548] officer there, his father said. The FBI talked to him. One agent happened to be from Chester, PA. In 2000, a series of pipe bombs exploded over a 20-month period near Philadelphia. The FBI asked Nick if he could make a pipe bomb. He said yes. Did he know any terrorists? Yes. They put him in prison. The Bergs contacted their congressman, Jim Gerlach, who said he should be there. His name was on Moussaoui's computer. He was released but missed the wedding. He wanted to go home to see his family and friends. He took a bus going to Amman. It stopped at a checkpoint, either official, or random.

Two men got on. "Nick carried the Hebrew Bible and the Koran with him," his father added, "and they took him off the bus." On May 2007, 2004, the video ran on television. Five men stood in a row, Zarqawi in the center, and Omar Hudid, and others of the Black Banner Brigade. Nick Berg sat on the floor; his hands tied. A man read a statement about U.S. soldiers at Abu Ghraib, and one of them grabbed Nick, age 26, and he screamed.

Judea Pearl, father of Daniel Pearl, urged Muslim leaders to denounce Berg's killing citing the Koran, "*We have prepared fire for the wrongdoers. The killers will be punished by Allah himself.*"[549] The war that began with the Arab invasion of Khorasan in the 8th Century and continued with the

---

[548] Judge Advocate General's Corp is the military's legal department.
[549] *Wall Street Journal* 5/18/04.

European colonization of India and the Middle East, and in 1970s in Pakistan and grew with the Soviet invasion and the U.S-Pakistani-Saudi program to recruit Arabs, which led to the Arabization of the war, continued. Michael Berg ran for Congress from Delaware. That people cared, that was what got him through the excruciating, gut-wrenching mental, and physical pain. What would Nick have accomplished in life? Lorenz asked. "Danny was an optimist," wrote Judea Pearl in 2009, "a true believer in the goodness of mankind." Michael Berg said the same about his son.

Al-Zarqawi, like Maudidi, like the Taliban, called democracy a western religion, where man deified man, not God. President George W. Bush, as Saddiqui in Deoband said called the war in Afghanistan a Crusade. The U.S. killed al-Zarqawi in 2006. Yusuf didn't know about underground movements. What concerned him more was the way the U.S. treated Arabs. He, like all Jordanians, aspired to have what was written in the U.S. Constitution: life, liberty, and the pursuit of happiness, but the U.S. did not want this. What ISIS was saying was what imams were saying in every mosque in Jordan. He introduced me to a Palestinian expert on Islamic movements, called Amir, who told us Muslims had been orphans for 100 years. Every child wanted a father and now they had one, and thanks to Abu al-Baghdadi, who had declared himself the Caliph. You couldn't be a true Muslim without a Khalifa. The king of Jordan, like the king in Morocco, relied upon his Hashemite lineage to stay in power. Abu Umar al-Qurayshi al Baghdadi[550] was a Quraysh. The Sunna said the Khalifa had to be a Quraysh. ISIS didn't need educated people. The toughest people came from the desert.

Yusuf said there was no way that you could tell his grandmother that her land in Jaffa was not hers. The Jordan River, "River of Dan," what the Arabs called "*esh-Sheria*," the "watering place," was 200 miles along, the border between Israel and Jordan, when I visited there a stream flowing through barren land, Judea in the Bible, in the south, and Samaria in the north, revered in Christianity, Islam, and Judaism. Yusuf was referring to what Palestinians call the *nakbah*, (catastrophe), when in 1948, thousands, like Abdullah Azzam's family, lost their homes, and became refugees. The Israelis and the Palestinians claimed this land. The Palestinian in Riyadh said the Saudis had a tenacious tie to their land. The Taliban chanted in their

---

[550] *Wikipedia* 2 Nov. 2021, https://es.wikipedia.org/wiki/Abu_Abdullah_al-Rashid_al-Baghdadi.

suicide recruitment tapes about their land. Prince Turki said Haqqani was focused on his land.

The next day, Amir came to Yusuf's office.[551] They had to fight Israel. It was elephant in the room, Yusuf said. Al-Qaeda would not exist, and ISIS would not exist, without Israel. In the 1980s, jihad was local, Amir explained. Because of the U.S. ties to Muslim dictatorships, they turned their focus to Afghanistan, where the U.S. was fighting the communists and wanted help. The Ikhwan, Saudi Arabia, Pakistan, UAE, and Egypt sent men. The strategy changed when al-Qaeda stopped focusing on the Arab states and went for the U.S., because it backed the dictatorships. The terrain of jihad became global. Abdullah Azzam, as the leader of the Arab Afghans, sought the support of Jalaluddin. Before 9/11 everyone worked together, now the jihadists worked separately. Amir lamented the divide between rich and the poor, who the dictators kept down. ISIS gave them hope. Al-Baghdadi had a PhD in Islamic history and the Koran in his heart. He knew Sharia. He worked with al-Zarqawi. What did I know about the Iranian diplomat kidnapped in Peshawar in 2008 and released two years later?[552]

I said Zawahiri negotiated his release, securing a transit route to the Middle East, where they could re-establish the Caliphate. That evening, the parents of Steven Sotloff, an American journalist, being held by ISIS, pleaded with his captors on television. Within days he, too, appeared in a video on his knees in the desert. A man stood next to him ranting with a knife. Steven Sotloff kept his back straight and his head up, a most courageous man.

Amir knew two ISIS men in Zarqa. I didn't want to see them, but I needed to know about a possible tie to the Haqqanis. I waited for a week, but Amir said he couldn't find the boys. I had to return to Afghanistan and find someone who was close to the Haqqanis and would know what they were doing, if anything, in the Middle East. The royal family was once the ruling clan of Mecca, said the taxi driver on the way to the airport. The British placed them in power. They were thieves. Every man I met in Amman said the same thing.

---

[551] *The Salafi discourse Transformation and its influence on International Relations—an al-Qaeda case study*, Arab Network for Research and Publishing, 2000.

[552] Alan Cowell, "Iranian Diplomat in Pakistan Is Freed," *New York Times* 3/30/ 2010.

Afghanistan
September 2014

Din Mohammad came to the Serena Hotel, and I told him the story of my kidnapping, and that Abdullah, who was behind it, killed his brother, Hajji Qadir, and that I knew this before I went and that I had come to apologize, to find out who was behind Abdullah, and to find people who would know about the Haqqanis and what they were doing. He listened and then explained that my information was wrong and told me what happened.[553] Our friendship remained intact. If I had come to him when he was governor of Nangarhar Province, he could have arranged for me to see Jalaluddin. The U.S. had captured his son, Anas. If people knew that I was trying to find out who kidnapped me, "they" would come after me. I had to leave immediately. I returned to New York. I read that the U.S. captured Anas Haqqani, and Hafiz Rashid, a Taliban commander responsible for suicide bombings, whose brother was released from Guantanamo as part of the Bowe Bergdahl exchange, in the Middle East. It was a signal that Arab governments were going to make it difficult for Afghan insurgents to raise funds.[554] They were in the hands of Afghan intelligence.

On November 11, Peter Kassig, a former U.S. Army Ranger, a convert to Islam, and an independent aid worker in Syria, was, like Jim Foley and Steven Sotloff, beheaded by ISIS. He, too, was strong to the end. Kayla Mueller, an aid worker from Arizona, was taken prisoner by ISIS. On December 3rd, I watched Luke Somers plead in a video on television for help. He was clean- shaven, wore western clothes, and looked healthy. It was sunny and there were green bushes behind him. He was probably in the South, being held by Al-Qaeda. They had never killed a hostage in Yemen, except in a rescue attempt.

Luke's mother and his younger brother, Jordan, pleaded for his life in a

---

[553] Jere Van Dyk, *"The Trade: My Journey into the Labyrinth of Political Kidnapping"* (New York: Public Affairs, 2017)
[554] Declan Walsh, "2 Haqqani Militant Leaders Are Captured, Afghan Officials Say," *New York Times* 16 Oct. 2014

video. On December 6, the U.S. launched its second rescue attempt. It became a firefight. A captor shot Luke, and Pierre Korkie, a South African school teacher. The U.S. didn't know that Korkie was there, nor that the charity he worked for had paid a ransom and he was to be released the next day.

In February 2015, I flew to Paris and Khadijah gave me the phone numbers for Yahya Abdallal Saleh, commander of Yemen's Central Security Forces, Ali Abdullah Saleh's nephew. I flew to Beirut and met him at a ski lodge, at his request, in the mountains. He drove me to his home. I asked him about Jalaluddin, and his Yemeni wife, and her tribe. He didn't know Haqqani. It didn't matter. They were not fighting one man, not bin Laden or al- Zawahiri, or one organization, but an ideology. He and his family invited me to stay for what was an enjoyable dinner. It was he who attacked "*Al-Ayyam*" in Aden. He said he worked with the U.S. military, and intelligence people. I returned to Kabul.

The street was bumpy and icy and empty. The taxi stopped in front of a large gray compound. I knocked on the door. Din Mohammad's aide welcomed me in and led me downstairs and opened a door. I walked in the dark across thick carpets toward the orange glow of a heater and sat on a sofa with a low table in front of me. I didn't feel anyone in the room. Gradually, I could see a few feet ahead. A generator started and the lights came on. There were two Afghan flags and small sofas lining the walls. A man brought a plate of nuts and dried raisons, and a thermos. Din Mohammad came in, wearing a prayer cap and a long thick multi-colored coat. We shook hands, leaning forward, and greeted one another in the Pashtun way. I liked his coat. He would get one for me. I told him no. By commenting on it I had made him say that. He was sorry to keep me waiting. They were talking until 11 o'clock last night. He was involved in the peace talks. I had come to talk to the man he knew who had information on Jalaluddin. He pressed a button on his table. His aide came, listened, left and returned with a phone. He made a call. I heard in Riyadh that Yunus Khalis was buried in Medina. It was true. The Saudis did this for two reasons: In 1991, when Saddam attacked Kuwait, they asked them to send a big group of Mujahideen to help them. Yunus Khalis was one of the few commanders to accept their request. Pakistan did not want the Mujahideen to go. Aslem Beg, the head of the ISI, delayed it as long as he could. Din Mohammad sent 300 men and two commanders to the Kuwaiti border at Khatji, where the

Iraqis attacked U.S. Forces, some of them women, and surrounded them. Saudi Arabia was very happy with Maulvi Khalis. A maulvi was a "learned man," a madrasa graduate. Yunus Khalis was his family's religious instructor, a minister, teacher, and tutor when he was a boy.

Secondly, Osama asked Yunus Khalis for a fatwa to attack the U.S. or the Saudi government, because U.S. soldiers were in their country. Khalis said no. The Saudis had the right to ask for help. They were being invaded, and they had a religious country following the precepts of Islam. Their laws were just. There was no need to attack them, or there would never be peace. The Saudis were grateful. Whenever any Afghan student wanted to go to Saudi Arabia to study, all they needed was a letter from Maulvi Khalis, and they would be granted admission. He was in China and Khalis called him to come back. It was 1996 or 97. He came all the way back to see him in Pakistan. Why did he call him? He didn't appear sick. His son was not a serious person. If he died outside of Afghanistan, he wanted him to bury him in Medina. If he died in Afghanistan, he wanted him to bury him in his village. His deepest wish was to be buried in Medina near the tomb of the Holy Prophet. He went to Saudi Arabia. He knew his time was coming. President Karzai said he would send a plane and bring him back here to die. His family said not to push them. Former president Rabbani said to bury him here. He died in Saudi Arabia, and they buried him near the Prophet.

Yunus Khalis had five sons by two wives. He was referring to Anwar ul-Haq Mujahid, his third son, in charge of the Tora Bora front when the U.S. was trying to find bin Laden. After his father died, he went to the Gulf and asked his father's friends to give him money. They said he should bring a letter from Mullah Omar and then they would help him. He said Omar had disappeared. They said to bring a letter from Jalaluddin Haqqani. They were in the same party and close and he could find him immediately. He went to him. He said to go fight with the Taliban. I heard that Yunus Khalis wanted to go to Kandahar to be closer to Mullah Omar. This was true. Three or four times they went there. Maulvi Khalis asked Omar why did he fight the Mujahideen? They were simple people, and he was making trouble for everyone. Omar said, when Khalis came, they would blame him. He fought them, I felt, because Pakistan was behind the Taliban, who were mostly Pashtun and wanted to guide them now to power.

Once, said Din Mohammad, they stayed at a Taliban guest house to talk about a cease-fire between the two groups. Mullah Omar refused to see him. The Taliban were afraid of Yunus Khalis. There was no one among them who had the courage to stand up to him. He led Jihad against the Russians, he was a strong person, and he was a powerful speaker. I remembered his deep voice, and commanding way. Din Mohammad smiled. He didn't have any ties with bin Laden until 1995 or 96. They weren't close. I asked about Rahman, the Egyptian army major. He would check his records. No one, strangely, seemed to know about this man.

Did the Sudanese director of an organization in Peshawar, who became the ambassador here, help bring bin Laden and Yunus Khalis together? He didn't know who gave permission for bin Laden to return. Gulbuddin Hekmatyar and Abdul Rasul Sayyaf, both of whom were powerful Mujahideen commanders, went to Sudan to see him. Then, Engineer Mahmud, a commander under Yunus Khalis, Maulvi Saznoor, who was under Sayyef, and Fazul Haq Mujahid, who was under Hekmatyar, went to Sudan and asked Osama to return.[555] These three commanders were close to the Arabs. Yunus Khalis was not close to them nor to Osama, not yet. Ahmad Shah Massoud and Sayyaf sent planeloads of arms and ammunition to President Bashir to fight Christians in the south. It was night and there were no lights when the Ariana planes, under the Afghan flag, came into Jalalabad.

Bin Laden stayed with Fazul Haq Mujahid, and then he went to see Yunus Khalis. The Arabs were afraid of Abdul Qadir, his brother, who didn't want them here. He knew that bin Laden would use his money to gain power. His brother was on one side, and the Arabs and their friends were on the other. All the Arabs, Abdullah Azzam, Abdul Majeed Zindani, had close relations with Jalaluddin. He was all the time up in the mountains fighting. From the very start of jihad, the Arabs were close to him. They would sit in front of him, almost worshipping him. Again, I asked about Rahman. He was quiet. Why did Jalaluddin marry a Yemeni?

He smiled again. He married an Arab because he would go to the UAE and go on television and talk about jihad. He had his big beard, and his strong presence was powerful. More than 100 girls were ready to marry a mujahid. They sent a list to Din Mohammad. It would bring them closer to

---

[555] Abdul Rasuf Sayyaf, Mujahideen commander, later a Member of Parliament.

God, they said. They would be fulfilling their obligation of jihad by marrying a strong mujahid of Afghanistan. Who killed Abdullah Azzam? Abdullah Anas in London said al-Zawahiri would have benefited. I knew Anas? He came here often. The meeting between the Taliban and him was in this room. It was hard to get information on Haqqani in the Middle East. I felt like I was betraying him and chasing a ghost. He told me to stop. Jalaluddin was focused on Afghanistan. He wanted to get rid of the Russians. All the Arabs were very respectful of him. He would go to the Gulf. His son, Anas, was in jail here now. The Americans grabbed him in the Gulf last year.

There were footsteps on the stairs. The door opened and a lean, older, swarthy man, about 6'1," in a black turban with silver trim, a thick olive drab shawl and black shalwar kameez, entered. He had a thick black beard and a scar on his left cheek. His eyes were deep in his face. The two men gently hugged one another, and shook hands, bringing their heads forward. Din Mohammad left. The man and I greeted one another. His name was Khalid Mangal. The Mangal were a sister clan of the Zadran, spread along both sides of the Afghan-Pakistani border.

The Haqqanis were a large family with enormous power, he began. Jalaluddin was America's friend once, now the Americans were trying to destroy him. They killed three of his sons. Either they or the Pakistanis killed Dr. Nasiruddin, who handled the family's fundraising in the Gulf. He was living under ISI protection. Was he a doctor? In their culture, in their villages, they called a man who knew about medicine and first aid and how to give injections, Doctor. Who killed him, and why? A Pakistani general asked him to move away from the border. Pakistan was under pressure from the U.S. Nasiruddin said until they reached the Attock River this was their land.

"*From the Attock to the Oxus, they were one nation,*" the Pashtuns sang[556] in their anthem, banned by Zia al-Haq, in Pakistan. They called the Indus the Attock. The Oxus River, today called the Amu Darya, was the northern border of Afghanistan, where the British drew the line against the Russians. They also called the Attock the "*Abaseen,*" father of the river, said

---

[556] Ali Wazir, "What Does the Pashtun Tahafuz (protection) Movement Want?" *Diplomat* 28 Apr. 2018

Mangal. Like, the Indians along the Columbia River, where I grew up, called it *Nch'i-Wana*, or the Big River. Amir Abdur Rahman[557] called Afghanistan "Yaghistan," the "Land of the Unruly... of the Free...of the Rebel... of the Insolent." "The insolence of the Afghan," wrote Louis Dupree, the Afghan scholar and archeologist, was not "the frustrated insolence of urbanized, dehumanized man in western society, but insolence without arrogance...of harsh freedoms set against a backdrop of rough mountains and deserts...of equality felt and practiced...of bravery past and bravery anticipated."[558]

Assad Durrani, Director General of the ISI from 1990-1992 said: "I am not sure why the Haqqanis were so high on western radars—for being more effective, or for their alleged ties to alQaeda. Many groups from elsewhere had come to the AfPak region, primarily to learn the art and to later employ it in their own area." Art, he called it, waging jihad.

Was Jalaluddin Deobandi or Wahhabi? He and his family were Deobandi. The ISI was using his beliefs. He felt that he was doing jihad. How did bin Laden return to Afghanistan? How close was he to Jalaluddin?

He and Ibrahim were close to bin Laden, but not as close as Abdullah Azzam. Azzam was his teacher in Saudi Arabia. So was Mohammad Qutb, Sayyid Qutb's younger brother. When bin Laden came here, he was an inexperienced young man. Azzam was like a father to him. He was a professor at the International Islamic University and the leader of all the Arabs here. He had money from Saudi Arabia that he gave out. They were closer to Gulbuddin, Rabbani and Sayyef, who were members of the Muslim Brotherhood. They were educated and more international than the other Mujahideen, and Azzam and bin Laden decided it was better to work with them. Yunus Khalis was sympathetic to the Ikhwan, but he was Hanafi Deobandi. Azzam worked with Ahmed Shah Massoud, who was also Ikhwan.

On April 28, 1992, the Mujahideen came to power and Afghanistan dissolved into civil war.

Kabul became a battlefield. In May or June, President Rabbani told his Interior Minister, Ahmed Shah Ahmadzai, to give bin Laden and 14 or 15 other Arabs Afghan citizenship. Ahmadzai said they were mujahideen and

---

[557] Rahman, Abdur. "*The Life of Abdur Rahman*," (Adamant Media Corporation,) 2001
[558] Dupree, "*Afghanistan*," xvii

helping us, but it was wrong to do this and it would be bad for Afghanistan. The Foreign Ministry was opposed also, but Rabbani gave him and the others Afghan passports. In May, after Jihad ended, Hekmatyar and Sayyaf went to see bin Laden in Sudan. Bin Laden agreed to work with their commanders, and Rabbani's commander. Their commanders went to see him, and he agreed to work with them. Bin Laden was afraid of Hajji Qadir, who he knew was powerful and who opposed him. Bin Laden was giving money to Hekmatyar, to Sayyaf, and Rabbani. They wanted to use bin Laden against Hajji Qadir. Bin Laden wanted to send a delegation to Afghanistan to make plans, but he was under too much pressure from the U.S., and he came with his family. He stayed with Engineer Mahmud, who was the powerful governor of Nangarhar, also under Yuns Khalis, who then became bin Laden's host. During Jihad, Yunus Khalis built houses a few hundred meters from his home. He called it the Yunus Khalis Colony. He advised bin Laden to stay there, but he wanted to live up in Tora Bora. It was Yunus Khalis' sons, who had studied in Saudi Arabia and were Salafi, who helped him escape.

After 9/11, after the Taliban were defeated, there was a vacuum here. Pakistan tried to find someone among all the commanders to lead Afghanistan. Mullah Omar went into hiding. Maybe Pakistan and America had an understanding. Jalaluddin led a delegation to Islamabad. There they decided to make Jalaluddin the Emir of Afghanistan. Pakistan was afraid of the Northern Alliance and wanted to use him against Ahmed Shah Massoud. They were afraid of Abdul Haq because he, like Karzai, had his own support. He was close to the West, particularly to the Americans. But he had also lost power. He had lived for four years in Dubai, doing business. Massoud had a great deal of power. He never left Afghanistan and the people respected him for this. Jalaluddin had spent the last four years with his wife and children in the UAE. He, also, did not have the support he once had. If you want to be powerful you need to live among the people.

Did the U.S. invite Jalaluddin to the embassy then in Islamabad? Mangal thought for a minute. It was possible. The ISI could have taken him there. He was once close to America. Maybe they both wanted him to be Emir. Before 9/11, when the Taliban took power, Jalaluddin wanted to fight them and went to Yunus Khalis. He advised him not to, and not to join them. He was opposed to inside fighting, but he didn't know how to stop them.

When the Taliban came, he left. He would take his Koran and turn the pages. There was nothing here about the Taliban. The Mujahideen were mentioned many times. Today he was in North Waziristan which had always been part of Afghanistan. He was home. Pakistan convinced him that the U.S. had replaced the Russians as the invaders. The Pakistanis and the Taliban used his name, but he had no real ties to them. The U.S. made him more important than he was. Maybe there were other reasons for this. If the Americans could solve this problem, they could solve all their problems here.

Why did the U.S. put Ibrahim in prison? Mangal nodded, it was true. Pacha Khan Zadran, a leader in their tribe, opposed the Haqqanis and convinced the Americans that the Haqqanis were their enemy. They were of the Mezi clan, born in the Wuze district in Paktia. Jalaladeen had a stroke recently and was partially paralyzed on his right side. He was in Miram Shah. He read the Koran and prayed. His sons made the decision on their operations.

Who killed Abdullah Azam? He didn't know. It could have been the CIA, or the Pakistanis, or the Mossad, there were many conspiracy theories. He was a threat to the security of many countries. He meant the power of the Afghan-Arabs.

Mangal rose. It was time for him to leave. Ten minutes later, Din Mohammad returned. His aide brought more tea. I asked how they began their jihad in the 1970s. He relaxed and smiled. He liked this question.

Yunus Khalis and he and Jalaluddin created the first jihadi center in Afghanistan in Khost, called Mustalbar. They, with Mutallah Khan, formed the first jihadi political party. Rabbani and Qazi Anas Rakat met with them in Peshawar. Abdul Haq was small then. One night they all went to Jalaluddin's house for dinner. His mother cooked for everyone. She said Abdul Haq was her child.

Jalaluddin's mother was the strong one in the family. They slept in Jalaluddin's house that night in Miram Shah. Abdul Qadir was there. They were one family. There were differences between Hekmatyar, and Rabbani. They asked everyone to reconcile and to have Yunus Khalis, the eldest among them, be their leader. He refused to have any part of Hekmatyar and started Hezb-i-Islami Khalis—the Khalis Islamic Party. They were four:

Jalaluddin, Khalis, Muktullah Khan and himself. There were almost no madrasas in Afghanistan. Then Nur Mohammad Taraki became the first communist president of Afghanistan.

Hekmatyar, an engineering student, founded Hezb-i-Islami. I had seen the minutes, in pencil, of its first meeting, confirming this. Din Mohammad, an intellectual, with a degree in Pashto literature, and a Master's, the thesis of which was the ties among Pashto, the Vedas, and Sanskrit, from Kabul University, cofounded Mustalbar. Unlike the other groups they did this outside the university. He walked around the room to get his blood circulating. He went to the Stanford medical clinic where they said his immune system was gone. He had taken too many anti-biotics when he was younger, and he had to stay there until they fixed it, which they did.

Two days later, Din Mohammad and two aides came to the Serena for lunch. He wanted me to sit next to him, not across from him. I was a Mujahid, one of them. He moved in his seat. He felt uncomfortable. He needed his bodyguards. Did he know Abdur Rahman, from Saudi Arabia? Yes, he came to Peshawar during the Taliban time and was angry that he didn't support them. He was living with his family in Peshawar. This was not his fight, he told Rahman, who appeared to be working for Saudi Arabia.

In June 2104, the Taliban attacked the airport in Karachi, the commercial capital of Pakistan, and the army, under pressure from the public, and the U.S., to clear the Tribal Areas, mounted a counter-terror campaign, but first moved the Haqqanis.[559] Maybe a million people in Waziristan became internal refugees. In revenge, the Taliban attacked the Army Public School in Peshawar, killing over 140 children and teachers. It was raw Wahhabism, it was Ibn Saud and al-Wahhab killing every man, woman and child in Karbala. Once, Pashtuns never attacked women and children, once Wahhabis were only in Arabia, once schoolgirls here laughed in the streets. The links between here and the Middle East were like trains rushing back and forth in the night and I was stuck standing at a station watching them pass.

---

[559] It was called "Zarb-e-Azb" or "Sharp and cutting," in Arabic and Urdu, referring to Mohammad's sword.

The Foreign Minister

Cars moved slowly and fumes rose. The snow fell on men in turbans and brown shawls crouched by the road. One man had a plastic leg. A woman stood by him digging into her purse. Traffic police wore face masks. There was a stoplight now, the modern world. We reached a large home. Men with bullet-proof vests, and AK 47s, stood in front of cement barriers, twenty feet high. A guard looked out from a high cement bunker. The living room had red carpets and modern paintings, a dining room table with chairs, a coffee table with German magazines a room more Western than Afghan, more intellectual than wealthy.

Dr. Rangin Spanta, former foreign minister, and national security advisor to President Hamid Karzai, who sat with us in Karzai's office when I interviewed him in 2008, wore a blue suit and a light blue shirt with cufflinks. There was green tea and bowls of nuts and dried fruit on a low glass table. He asked about my family name which led to a discussion of Aachen, near the Dutch border, where he lived and taught for years, the seat of Charlemagne, in German *"Karl des Grosse,"* descended from Charles Martel, who defeated Abdur Rahman in 732, and the exchange of gifts between Charlemagne, and Harund al-Rashid, the Abbasid Caliph, in 807, who sent an elephant, and people were happy, two great civilizations.

He grew up in Herat in a large landowning family, with strong Marxist beliefs, in human rights, equality, and opposition to feudalism. In Germany, he took part in student demonstrations, against the war in Vietnam, for social justice, the Soviet invasion of Czechoslovakia in 1968, and in the anti-colonialist movement. Today it was the opposite, a neo-liberalism, but where his fight then was for solidarity today it was for modernization and against theological fascism. He was happy that the Soviet Union was defeated in Afghanistan because there was no democracy here, but the alternative had become a religious fascism. He didn't know why the strategic policy makers had done to Afghanistan what they did, the wars, the destruction, the deaths by the hundreds of thousands, but he didn't want to talk about that. After 25 years of exile, he returned in March 2002 to find a country destroyed, not just the infrastructure and the institutions, but the traditional networks of tolerance, of rejecting violence, with nothing to replace it.

Once shopkeepers sat on their steps here drinking tea, once schoolgirls laughed in the streets, once there no blast barriers, or magnetic bombs.

There was destruction in Europe at the end of World War II, but it was replaced with the rule of law, solidarity, and humanism. Here to accept violence was normal, which was neither modern nor traditional. Before there were a small number of spies, for the Communists, the Iranians, Pakistan, and maybe a few with the C.I.A., but it was unacceptable to work for foreigners.

It was the end of your credibility. Now, there seemed to be a concentration of intelligence agencies and security companies. Afghans worked for them and didn't feel any shame or the need to hide this. It represented a change in their moral understanding of right and wrong. Intelligence gathering was one thing but to serve another nation was something else. People no longer believed in Afghanistan. Suddenly, there arrived wealthy Western news organizations, governments, and international agencies, offering a minimum of $100 a day for assistants, fixers, guards, translators, and other jobs. There was a gap between rural Afghanistan and the so-called elite. People worked for other countries justifying it in the name of religion. He meant the Mujahideen and Taliban commanders who received money from the Middle East, and from America, Russia, India, Iran, Pakistan, and the Europeans.

After 9/11, there was solidarity among other Western and Eastern nations with the U.S. There was a chance for Afghanistan. But there was no change. Until 2006, the U.S. came to fight al-Qaeda. There was no interest in nation building, or the emancipation of human rights. Finally, in 2012, there was an effort.[560] Afghans tried to build a democracy but with people who did not believe in it. The ethnic groups were divided. This explained the tensions today. The international community focused on fighting terrorism, but not the roots, or its causes. When he took over the foreign ministry in 2006, he gave a speech in which he said this strategy to fight terrorism was wrong. They had to eliminate the sanctuaries, the training centers, and the financial support. This could only be done with a strong liberal state, under the rule of law. Iran and Saudi Arabia were dictatorships, not strong liberal states like those of northern Europe. There was so much corruption now, as

---

[560] "Tokyo Conference on Afghanistan the Tokyo Declaration Partnership for Self-Reliance in Afghanistan from Transition to Transformation July 8, 2012

much as from the international community as from Afghans.

The U.S. considered Pakistan a strategic ally. After the U.S. killed bin Laden, he hoped that there would be a new approach, but the U.S. continued under President Obama to give billions of dollars to Pakistan to kill Afghans, and U.S. soldiers. Richard Holbrooke tried to remove Karzai by every trick and every means. It was unbearable for them. The destruction Holbrooke caused was irreparable. Madame Clinton tried to correct this and to rebuild trust, but the wound was too deep. Attacking Karzai, and his family, insulting him, saying that he took drugs was reprehensible. (Ambassador) Eikenberry called him an unreliable partner. He had 1000 criticisms of Karzai, but he was his friend. He didn't drink or smoke. Karzai made me wait until after evening prayers.

The hypocrisy of it all, that the U.S. claimed that it supported democracy. Today, people believed, as a result, in conspiracy theories, or that America was ignorant or incapable. Pakistan delivered some al-Qaeda people to America, but not high-level Taliban. The U.S. believed that nuclear weapons made you strong. He believed that you needed a strong state. Pakistan was weak, with separatist movements and sectarian warfare between Shia and Sunni, and corruption. Why the U.S. was pursuing its policy with Pakistan he didn't know. Some felt that it wanted to keep turmoil brewing in the region to keep pressure on China and Russia. He defended the U.S. for the deep cooperation that they had with it, but he was critical of its ignorance. The most corrupt ministers had the closest ties to the warlords, who had the best ties to the U.S. They needed a strategic partnership with America. There was no alternative if they were to fight terrorism. The Haqqani Network was not working for the ISI. It was the ISI. The U.S. had values to explain itself. It showed in World War I and World War II that it would defend those values against fascism and totalitarianism. Afghanistan also had values. It was 5,000 years old, a civilization with a Buddhist and Zoroastrian heritage.

Once there were large clay jugs, like those in Khartoum, filled with water, and a metal cup tied to a string by a tree in Herat and Kabul, like the horse-drawn carts, with bells tinkling, the smell of kababs grilling, and fresh flowers in small hotels and no guards outside.

Pakistan would tell you that they were Hindus until the Arabs came and turned them into Muslims. The Moguls ruled for 1,000 years and the

European colonists came. Afghanistan was the legacy of the Mogul Empire. Only two nations defined themselves as belonging to a single group, one Jewish the other Muslim, Israel and Pakistan. The Jews brought philosophy, enlightenment and humanity to Europe. There were many Jews in Herat once. He had two lovely grandchildren. His son married an Israeli from Jerusalem. She told Karzai that she couldn't come to Afghanistan. He asked why not. She had the wrong passport. There was no such thing, he replied. Everyone was welcome here. Pakistan was a fundamentalist military state. India was strong and Pakistan could not move east and therefore had to move west. It proudly called its nuclear arsenal the Islamic Atomic bomb. India and Pakistan were in competition, and it had to justify itself. It was a Hindu phobia. The Afghan ambassador to Canada was a Hindu and Pakistan demanded that they bring him home and eight months later they did. Pakistan wanted to restore the Mogul Empire and needed to export its values to Central Asia, to Afghanistan, and to other countries.

Islam was the main part of their history, which, from the sixth to the eighth century was militant Islam, then a people's Islam, until it became a state ideology. Egypt, through the Muslim Brotherhood, brought militant jihad here in the 1960s. Hekmatyar and Rabbani were Ikhwan. The suicide bombings came from the Arab jihadis, from the Tamal movement, and from Lebanon. The Marxist response to the Arab search for how to live in the world failed. The communist approach failed. The Islamist movement was rejecting the culture of modernity, secularism, emancipation of women, but defended the technical modernity of Kalashnikovs, and tanks. There were millions of educated, unemployed people standing in lines in Tehran and elsewhere. Their idols were bin Laden and al-Baghdadi. The integration of Muslims in Europe had failed, radicalizing the young.

I was listening to Tariq in Aden, to Majoob in Riyadh, to Khashoggi in Bahrain, to Atabani, and Ibrahami in Khartoum. That week there were reports that Kayla Mueller was killed.

The National Directorate of Security

The driver stopped at the front gate in front of giant concrete barriers. A man with a walkie-talkie took his place, smiled warmly and said Mullah Sab.[561] Soldiers stood in guard houses. He weaved past more barriers to the headquarters of the NDS.

Sami Sadat, in a coat and tie, and a colleague also in a suit, welcomed me. I didn't need to be afraid of Hekmatyar or Haqqani, said Sadat, smiling. In the past decade, the ANA (Afghan National Army), and the NDS, and other government institutions, and the media, were finding new ways to work with the world, fighting their enemies and seeking help from their allies. They were taking responsibility for their security. Secondly, for the first time, Afghanistan had transferred power from one elected leader to another. The people made a choice. But the Taliban, its backers, and the Haqqanis, didn't want democracy. Thirdly, by signing the Bilateral Security Agreement (BSA), they had established a strategic relationship with the United States,[562] which would advise, equip, sustain, and train Afghan forces but no longer engage in combat, unless both sides agreed. The U.S. would stay until at least 2024. All three of these programs brought threats because their allies had now left them alone on the front lines.

The Taliban, an umbrella organization, the Peshawar Shura (Council), Hezb-i-Islami, which Hekmatyar founded in 1973, that part which held allegiance to al-Qaeda and to IMU (Islamic Movement of Uzbekistan), Lashkar-i-Taiba, and the many other jihadi organizations, were their main threat.[563] The goal of the ISI was to retake the southeast provinces. Pakistan then would be able to say that all Taliban camps had moved from Pakistan to Afghanistan. The Haqqani Network sent 21 suicide bombers and then a truck with 21 tons of explosives, with layers of concrete on top to cause more damage, which hit the NDS compound in Ghazni, near the Islamic Museum. The destruction was one kilometer wide. Last year they mounted attacks in Kabul, Jalalabad and in Kandahar, to get media attention.

---

[561] Mullah Sab means respected elderly priest.
[562] A BSA provided the terms by which the U.S. agreed to keep its armed forces in a country, granting it immunity from prosecution.
[563] Hezb-i-Islami: "The Islamic Party." Lashkar-i-Taiba: "The Militia of the Pure."

They struck in Kandahar, far from where U.S. policymakers said they were operating and they hit the U.S. Consulate in Herat near the Iranian border.

Anas Haqqani, captured in the Middle East, was in prison in Kabul.[564] He admitted that the ANA had sustained unprecedented causalities. All they had was their chest, it was their shield.

In the 1980s, a man was not a man unless he stood and fought. In 2007, a Talip placed a Soviet machine gun on a rock to fire on the overwhelming force of U.S. solders 100 yards away. If he died, like so many in his unit, he lamented, he would go to Paradise.

The Quetta Shura was in disarray, with competing factions vying for power. Mullah Omar was probably dead. He was emotionally, spiritually and operationally dead for five years. Taliban commanders wanted to meet their Emir but not one had seen him in five years.[565] Some were joining ISIS showing that the Taliban were not a nationalistic, religious force, like the Mujahideen, but a sophisticated proxy army equipped by Pakistan. The men who attacked the Serena,[566] wore size 12 and 13 shoes, with munitions and pistols in the heels. They wanted to sabotage the 2014 election by killing the monitors staying there. There was a deadlier attack after the election, at the Hotel Intercontinental. The Haqqanis were behind it.[567] They had killed four of Haqqani's sons, and one had been arrested. There was one to go.

He meant Sirajuddin Haqqani, the Taliban military commander.

The Haqqanis received money from businessmen and princes in the Gulf. The Arabs were in Pakistan, but their battlefield was here. They were closer to Haqqani than to the Taliban or to the ISI. Haqqani sent fund collecting teams to the Gulf. The Mujahideen fought a holy war. For the Taliban the rules of engagement were defined by money, and indoctrination. Pakistan paid for each Afghan soldier, and for each U.S. soldier, that they killed. The Taliban told me the same thing. Haqqani was sending men to Iraq and Syria. The NDS was tracing them. Sadat, like Tariq al-Fadhli, said

---

[564] Declan Walsh, "2 Haqqani Militant Leaders Are Captured, Afghan Officials Say," *New York Times* 16 Oct. 2014

[565] "Profile: Mullah Mohammed Omar," *BBC News* 29 July 2015

[566] "Taliban Gunmen Kill Nine Civilians in Attack at Kabul's Serena Hotel," *Guardian* 21 Mar, 2014

[567] Mujib Mashal and Fatima Faizi, "Siege at Kabul Hotel Caps a Violent 24 Hours in Afghanistan," *New York Times* 21 Jan. 2018

there were many routes from here and Pakistan to the Middle East. Al-Qaeda was stronger than ISIS in Yemen and Europe. He thought Haqqani's wife was Yemeni.

My driver approached Massoud Circle and as we drove around it, he said softly that his father was killed here by a suicide bomber. He lived in Herat, but there were no jobs there and he, as the oldest son, had to support his family. The Haqqanis killed his father.

Ibrahim Haqqani

Pakistan

A week passed. It was early afternoon, and I was sitting in a room with my guide in a guest house in Islamabad. Her phone rang. They were here. I walked outside as the gate opened and a white SUV with tinted windows entered the compound. The driver, in a brown Chitrali hat, stared ahead.[568] A burly man, a solid six feet, in a white salwar kameez, with a black beard, a black and white striped headdress hanging loosely, Salafi style, stepped down and walked toward me smiling warmly as I walked towards him. It was Ibrahim Haqqani. We hugged one another gently. A man about 21, in a leather jacket, and black salwar kameez came around the other side, smiling, and we shook hands. He said he called himself John. We had talked on the phone arranging this meeting. We walked inside.

A half a dozen men sat watching us, one saying, with his smile, not to worry. We walked down a hallway, entered a small room and Ibrahim sat in a chair and I sat next to him. Fatima sat opposite us. John sat by his father. Ibrahim and I smiled at one another, remembering the past. He looked at the cover of my book on my time with the Mujahideen. It was a photograph of Jalaluddin and some of his men sitting on a Russian tank. I brought it for him and Jalaluddin. I gave him another photograph of Jalaluddin, and then one of Din Mohammad and me. He pushed it away. He couldn't look at him. He was with the U.S. and the Afghan government now. We were quite for a minute and then we began to talk about our time in the mountains. I said I was writing a book about them. I told John on the phone. Ibrahim talked about when they took me higher up into the mountains to an arms cache and where they kept their artillery, and the tank.

He had never driven it, but he taught himself, with God's help, to start it, and drive it. He smiled, happily. I remembered the tree branches covering the tank, the loud rumbling engine, the gray smoke billowing out and Ibrahim shouting and raising his arms high. We talked about that afternoon.

---

[568] The pancake like felt hat worn by Afghans and Pakistanis is said to have originated in Chitral, northeast Pakistan.

Jalaluddin and I raced horses across the plains, laughing in the wind. I thought of a little girl I saw one morning near our compound at Shah-e-Khot. She had stringy hair and was standing by a fire, with a kettle on it, in front of a cave.

He talked about a battle they fought before I arrived. I thought of the men with their six-shot bolt action Lee Enfield rifles, the same rifle that U.S. soldiers used in the Civil War. Only Jalaluddin and few others had AK-47s. The U.S. had just begun to supply them with weapons and ammunition. I asked why they chose to live there. They were born in Saran, a village in the Kando Kali district, of the Wuzi clan, of the Zadran. It was a four hour walk from Saran to Shah-e-Khot, on the other side of the mountain. It was their first camp. The Soviets bombed and strafed the valley, and everyone fled to Pakistan. I remembered a man and woman, a teenage girl smiling, and a younger boy, and a donkey carrying a small load on the path walking east. My guide and I kept walking west. The valley was empty, and I could hear my footsteps echoing in the silence. We entered the high-walled compound, and there were small campfires, and men sitting around them, and a horse and a donkey. We talked more that time. What did their father do? He was a common village man. He was a wood cutter and sold goats. He jumped two decades ahead. When the U.S. invaded, they had three houses in a compound in Saran, but the U.S. bombed and destroyed everything. They were three brothers now. Ismail was martyred at Zermat near Khost. He was angry. Once we were allies and now the U.S. was trying to destroy them. I asked about their youth. I wanted to start at the beginning. I didn't ask this before.

Jalaluddin would accompany their father to the mosque for morning prayers. When he was old enough Ibrahim joined them. They had breakfast afterwards, bread and sometimes an egg. He remembered losing his baby teeth. When he was older, he would go with their father, helping him carry wood, or to watch the goats. When he was about nine, he went with Jalaluddin to another village to study. There were no madrasas in their area, and very few in Afghanistan. They lived in a hujra and then in a mosque where they studied, and mullahs gave them food.

A hujra is a male guest room. Almost every village has one where a traveler can stay for a night, eat, and go on his way. It is part of *"melmastia,"* or hospitality, like that of the Bedouin. A man is judged, as Tariq al-Fadhli's uncle wanted to be judged, by his generosity. Jalaluddin had been interested in religious studies since he was a boy and became his teacher more than the mullahs. They stayed there for two years. He didn't like to study. They went home to their village periodically. When he was about twelve, they went to Khost. It was more like a madrasa, but they didn't use that word. It was called an *anjuman* (association), a place where some mullahs created a school. There were 40 rooms and he and Jalaluddin shared a room. The food was free. They were there for a year, but went home twice, for a month, each time. They were taught the Hanafi School, which was what had been taught in Afghanistan for centuries. They were Hanafi today. They were not opposed to statues.

He was telling me that they would have kept the great Buddhist statues at Bamiyan that the Taliban destroyed with artillery, in March 2001. They were not the Taliban. But he wore a Salafi headdress, like an Arab, when he arrived. Maybe it was a disguise on the road. He now wore a prayer cap, which had long been common here.

From Khost, Jalaluddin went to Dar-ul Uloom Jamia Haqqania in Peshawar for his final year. It was at the Haqqania seminary that he took the name Haqqani. Haq meant truth. Haqqaniyet was a truth teller. After graduation Jalaluddin returned to Saran, where he built his first mosque. It was in the last year of Zahir Shah's reign. Samuel ul-Haq, the founder of Haqqania, asked him to stay another year and teach, and he did this.

Daoud Khan overthrew Zahir Shah in 1973. The Communists began to come to their area. They were divided into the Parcham (flag) and the Khaliq (people), both urban and members of the (Communist) People's Democratic Party of Afghanistan, founded in 1965 in the home of Nur Mohammad Taraki (1917-1979).[569] Parcham advocated a gradual turn; the Khaliq were more radical. Jalaluddin, in building a mosque, in his village, or maybe by the paved road near Khost, was taking a stand. A man came in with a tray of green tea in small glasses, a plate of cookies and a small bowl of sugar. Ibrahim took tea only. Once we lived on gritty rice, bread, and tea. A doctor said he was putting on weight. He fingered his prayer beads.

They showed a film in Kabul about religious students versus communist students who said there was no God. Word of this film made its way to their

---

[569] Rosanne Klass, "*Afghanistan: The Great Game Revisited*" (Washington: Freedom House), 1987, 412-24

village. Communists were giving out pamphlets. They studied them in order to counter them. They researched the Koran and talked to the people. The communists were gaining popularity. They went to religious scholars and said they had to counter this. Communists held protests in Khost, attacked mosques and destroyed Korans. It was two years before the coup against Daoud. They organized a counterdemonstration with 6,000 people and marched to Khost to see the governor. I calculated that when they were boys, they walked twenty miles through the mountains and down on the paved road, if it was paved then, to Khost, ten miles from the border, the same distance they would have walked with their 6,000 followers. The communists, with help from the KGB, overthrew Daoud and killed him and his family in the Arg Palace, in April 1978. In 2008, Karzai's chief of staff showed me the hallway by the stairs, next to his office, where they were killed.

After the coup Jalaluddin and Ibrahim led the demonstration on the same route and down the dirt lane, lined with poplars, opposite Khost, to the governor's house. They gave him a list of all the communists in their area and asked him to hand them over and they would be fair with them. They would deal with them according to Islam. Ibrahim paused. He was happy. Finally, their true history would come out.

The governor said to give him two months. They would deal with this, according to the constitution, in Gardez. It was the capital of Paktia Province of which Khost was then a part. In 1985, the communist government created Khost Province. He said the entire movement against communism started there. If this was true it meant that the Haqqanis, in 1973, not the Mujahideen, created by Pakistan and funded, it appeared, by the U.S., when they launched their first attack in 1975, started the rural Afghan resistance. There were communist factions in the Daoud government, Ibrahim said. They helped him come to power. Brezhnev told them to stop fighting and to work together. There were communists in Khost today They had Russian passports, and apartments in Moscow, which funded them. There were Communists in the government. I would soon hear this from tribal leaders.

He and Jalaluddin met with religious leaders and tribal elders to start a national underground movement to counter them. They recruited 70 people to begin a military campaign, but Daoud had an effective secret police, and threw them into Damazang, the oldest and worst prison in Kabul. He and Jalaluddin and some of their men studied the jail and saw that the only way to get their friends out was to dig a tunnel. They rented a house one kilometer away and began to dig, working in two-hour shifts, three men at a time, over two months. Finally, they were ready and told their men where to go where they would break through the floor. They had a car waiting at the house. A truck came, delivering food for the prison and drove over the tunnel and it gave way and the truck fell into the hole. They brought in two tanks and went over the ground where the tunnel was. There were twelve of them, and they had to run. He sat quietly. Daoud built Pol-i-Charki expressly so that he could move the 70 men into it. After four months, it was ready and Daoud moved them. Two and half months later he moved them to a military base north of Kabul and hanged them. Ibrahim paused. This was important. The truth would finally come out.

Pol-i-Charki, run by KhAD, the State Information Services, precursor to the NDS, was synonymous with torture.[570] Mohammad Najibullah, a member of the PDPA, was head of KhAD, and then president of the Communist government from 1989-1992, when the Mujahideen killed him and his brother and hanged them in a traffic circle.

Gulbuddin Hekmatyar and other future Mujahideen leaders were out in the rural areas opposing the Communists, and came and met with them, Ibrahim continued. Their stronghold was Loya Paktia. When anyone was in trouble, they brought them there for protection. It was still their stronghold. He meant Paktia, Khost and Paktika provinces. Herodotus called this area "the country of Paktuike," the most warlike of the Indians. "The Paktues wore cloaks of skin and carried the bow of their country, and the dagger."[571]

They decided to mount another coup. They contacted General Naseerallah Babar, the governor of Peshawar. They wanted financial support and a safe refuge in Pakistan. They felt their movement would motivate Afghanistan's ally, India to move against Pakistan. They convinced Pakistan to back them. The Russians wanted to reach the warm waters of the Arabian Sea. The Pakistanis gave them 70,000 rupees. Most importantly, they had a place to go where they would be safe. When they felt secure with Pakistan, they began to collect alms from their village to plan their coup. They went to

---

[570] Hassan M. Kakar, *"Afghanistan: The Soviet Invasion and the Afghan Response, 1979-1982"* (Berkeley, University of California Press, 1995)
[571] Caroe, *"The Pathans,"* 28-29, 441-4. In 1975, the exchange rate was $1 for 9.9 Pakistani rupees.

Darra with the funds that Pakistan gave them and bought weapons.

Darra had an aura then of the Old West, with dirt streets, and gun-shops, where men manufactured all kinds of weapons, and the gunfire was loud as they tested them.

They told the government whenever they went there the make and year of their vehicle and the license plate number so they could travel freely. They prepared their next coup. It would begin at midnight. Just before, their man, General Saifur Rahman, was arrested with some of his men. Others fled to the countryside. Daoud had spies everywhere. They gave up trying to overthrow him and in 1977 started their guerrilla war. They were separate from other Mujahideen. They fought for four years without training. Since the last war against the British there was no law against carrying arms along the border.

In the 19th Century, Europeans, based in Oman smuggled arms to Arabia and Persia. By the 20th Century the borderlands of British India were their most lucrative markets.[572]

When they started damaging the government, the Pakistanis finally got interested in their movement. General Babar invited them to Pakistan, gave them space for refugees, and more money and arms. In 1976, Prime Minister Ali Bhutto went to Kabul to rebuild trust with Afghanistan, and Daoud went to Lahore. He wanted to resolve the border dispute. While all this was going on Pakistan was supporting them. Babar, now the governor of the Northwest Frontier Province[573] introduced them to the ISI. Pakistan provided passports, ID cards and visas. They introduced them to Saudi Arabia where they began to raise money. By 1978, they were networking in the Arab world, mainly in Saudi Arabia and the UAE. The Arabs at first didn't understand that they were under threat. They knew some Arabic through their Koranic studies, and some Urdu.[574] Afghans working in Saudi Arabia also helped them. Their informants in the Daoud government told them to try to get an RPG,[575] which was a very effective weapon. They asked Pakistan for one, but it was afraid to give it to them. They said to show them one and they would take it to Darra, and have it made there, but Pakistan still said no. He talked, for

---

[572] *Friday Times*, Lahore, Pakistan, May 17-23, 2019.
[573] Today called Khyber Pakhtunkhwa.
[574] Urdu is the variant of Hindustani, used by Muslims, official language of Pakistan.
[575] Russia manufactured Rocket Propelled Grenade Launcher.

half an hour, like it was yesterday, about a battle against an elite force that Daoud sent to fight them. By God's grace they won and took the RPGs from the Afghan forces. They were so happy. The Mujahideen proudly carried the old, never new, Russian made rocket-propelled grenade launchers on their shoulders, as the Taliban do today.

Ibrahim got up to pray. John, who said he taught himself English on the Internet, but got fed up with social media, and stopped, stood up with him. The Americans picked him up and put him in Bagram for two months. He wasn't doing anything wrong, and they released him. His father finished praying. He got his shoes for him and gave him his scarf back. Then John prayed. Ibrahim looked at my book again, and then one about my kidnapping.[576] I was trying to get to them, but I was betrayed. I used Jalaluddin's name hoping that it would keep me alive. Ibrahim listened carefully. He didn't know about this. They were not involved. Kidnappings could have a good outcome, or they could end in disaster.

They took their RPGs to Pakistan and asked for more of them. The Pakistanis came back and said to give them the RPGs. They said not unless they guaranteed to give them back. Pakistan gave them some Chinese RPGs, AK-47s, and artillery. After the Soviets came, the ISI introduced them to the Chinese, and to the Americans. They, and Saudi Arabia, supported them. They could go anywhere in Pakistan. He went to Germany, and America, for medical treatment. I asked about the Egyptian, Rahman. Many men came to get their picture taken with Jalaluddin so that they could go back and say they fought the good fight. He shook his head. They were innocent people. No one, I realized, was going to tell me who Rahman was.

After the Soviet war, Jalaluddin lived with his wife, who was Yemeni, in Abu Dhabi. He had three sons and a daughter with her. Other Mujahideen leaders went to other countries. Hekmatyar was the only one who stayed. He and Mullah Omar hated one another. Jalaluddin didn't want to be the leader of Afghanistan. Hamid Karzai became the leader of all the Mujahideen groups. But a year after unification, there was more infighting. The ISI told them to get rid of certain men, and to put others in power. Yunus Khalis left to study in a madrasa in Darra. Jalaluddin wrote and asked him to come to Peshawar, and they would support him. They took his picture to show the

---

[576] Jere Van Dyk, "Captive My Time as a Prisoner of the Taliban," 2010

people that he was their leader. Gulbuddin and other leaders had their pictures taken. He laughed. Every man, except Jalaluddin, wanted to be king. Jalaluddin called all six Mujahideen leaders: Hekmatyar, Mujadidi, Rabbani, Gailani, Mohammad Nabi, and Yunus Khalis, to Peshawar.[577] He brought in Rasul Sayyaf, linked to the ISI, and to Saudi Arabia, and made him the leader of Afghanistan for eight months. Rahman in Riyadh said this was his and Haqqani's biggest mistake.

Sayyaf was the Muslim Brotherhood, spoke fluent Arabic and was a commanding speaker, but he kept millions of dollars that the Saudis and Gulf States sent for the Mujahideen. This was what led to their breakup.[578] The ISI was involved, and Jalaluddin secretly kept them informed, so was Saudi Arabia. The U.N. tried to make Jalaluddin the leader of Afghanistan. Peter Tomsen led a delegation to see him.[579] The ISI pressured him to become president. When he refused, the ISI was upset. As a true Muslim if you become president then you would become a different person, and it would destroy you. You would have to go against your faith. People would come to Jalaluddin asking questions and he would say read the Koran. Everything was there, and in the Hadith. He, as a guerrilla fighter, and as a man who shunned becoming the leader, became respected throughout the Muslim world. He was known as a tactician, and a political thinker, and he was clean, politically. He never sought power. He always turned it down. He only wanted what was best for the country. There were very few Arabs around at the beginning. The Arabs saw their long hair and thought that they were barbarians. Don't forget, they had to convince them of their jihad. When the Arabs fought and prayed with them, they didn't think that they were proper Muslims, but then they saw the sacrifices that they were making, and the more time they spent with them, they saw that they were truer to their faith than they were. They stayed true to their Hanafi beliefs. The more Jalaluddin interacted with others, the stronger he became in his

---

[577] Gulabadeen Hekmatyar, The Islamic Party of Afghanistan; Professor Sibjatullah Mujadidi, The National Front for the Rescue of Afghanistan; Professor Burnhuddin Rabbani, The Islamic Society of Afghanistan; Pir Sayed Ahmad Galaini, The National Islamic Front of Afghanistan; Maulawi Mohammad Nabi Mohammadi, The Islamic Movement of Afghanistan; Mohammad Yunus Khalis, The Khalis Islamic Party.

[578] Klass, "*Afghanistan*," 401. Sayyaf, The Islamic Union to Free Afghanistan.

[579] Tomsen, "*The Wars of Afghanistan*," 2011

beliefs. He was always committed to his own house, and to have Sharia here.

What about his Yemeni wife? Didn't she make him think about the Arab world? He laughed. The main point was that of all the Mujahideen leaders, he was the most important. If they had listened to him, and chosen one leader, there would not have been a civil war. It was not his outreach to the world, but his fame, because of his example, that extended out to the world, and touched all who came to see him. Only Yunus Khalis and Jalaluddin said that they were the leaders of Jihad, not of the country. Jalaluddin wanted to create a Shura and for the leaders to follow Sharia and to send good, clean, pious men throughout the country to talk of Sharia. In Islam as soon as you sought something you disqualified yourself.

The Arabs came to fight. They didn't involve them in politics. They gave them money to buy weapons, and they, the Arabs, did charity work. But Jalaluddin had to be involved with the Arabs. Ibrahim was exasperated. I knew how these things worked, he admonished me. Who gave them passports, and who brought them here? Jalaluddin was just one person. He was not sending them out into the world. The U.S. was trying to create war within the Muslim world. It used Osama bin Laden and Jalaluddin to make them the bad men in the world. How did bin Laden come here, but via Pakistan and the United States? How was it possible that the world's superpower could let one man send five planes to attack America? During Jihad, the world came to salute Jalaluddin. Westerners sent him gifts and congratulated him. They used him to break the Russians. He was the best commander some said in the world. He was the best person in the world to a great many people. But this best person in the world had not changed nor had he changed his way of thinking, his way of life, and who he was. But they were now calling him a terrorist, and said he had no morals. They tried to turn him into a bad person to create war in the world. The Americans replaced the Russians. Foreigners and non-Muslims came during the Russian time, and today it was the same. They didn't accept the Russians, and they didn't accept the Americans. Over 1.5 million people lost their lives during Jihad. The U.S. was here under the exact premise. The West wanted to control Afghanistan. The people felt that it was a way to surround China, to keep Russia out, and to extract their mineral wealth.

He was quiet again, tired and upset from getting worked up. I said the U.S. came under a U.N. mandate. He ignored me. They wanted to establish

Sharia and an Islamic state. They had been deprived of their freedom and of their right to do this. If he fought the Russians, he was a good person. If he fought America, he was a terrorist. In the same place and for the same reasons they found themselves fighting the Americans. They fought the Russians because of what they found in the Koran and for the same reason they fought the Americans. They brought in Karzai, as the Russians brought in Karmal.[580] Babrak Karmal, who Rahman in Riyadh said he saw years before preaching in a mosque, meaning that he was an amoral, ambitious hypocrite, was the communist leader of Afghanistan during Jihad, to Ibrahim, and to the West, a Russian puppet. The new Afghan Constitution was a Western imposed document. They wanted Shari'ah. The U.S. brought in Abdul Haq after 9/11 to be president of Afghanistan, Ibrahim continued. After the Taliban killed him, the U.S. went to Karzai. If Abdul Haq had come on his own Jalaluddin would have supported him. Even if there was one American here it was one too many. They were not looking for revenge for the 1.5 million who were killed, they wanted their homeland back. Why were all those Americans in his home? Again, he was quiet for a minute.

Did they have Bowe Bergdahl?

Twice, he met with Obama's man and said no to a deal. The ISI was at both meetings. He skyped into the Oval Office. I pondered this. This once poor teenage guerrilla fighter had skyped, he just said, into the Oval Office. The U.N. was involved in the soldier's release. When they released the five men from Guantanamo, the agreement was that the families would be allowed to meet with them. Anas and Khalid went to see them, and the CIA, reneging on the U.S. commitment, kidnapped them. The Americans were traitors. He trusted me and not them. He had waited four days to see me. He asked if I could guarantee their safety in Dubai to talk about this. I said I didn't work for the government. They made the decisions on the soldier in Khost. He never met him. He was captured by Mullah Sangeen, one of the men linked to them. They were on a demining patrol, that was his understanding, and he was trailing behind the others. Two men came up to him and threw a blanket over him and got him away.

The U.S. reports said Bergdahl went AWOL. Sangeen's men, it appeared, told a different story.

---

[580] "Babrak Karmal," *Encyclopædia Britannica*

When the Taliban came, they were not interested in going back to the Mujahideen or to the Taliban. They didn't want to work with anyone. Jalaluddin got many offers to join the Taliban.

The ISI pressed them. They never heard of Mullah Omar but learned that he was a bodyguard to Mohammad Nabi. Three times they sent a team to do research on him. He was a small man during Jihad, but they found nothing bad about him. Jalaluddin agreed to join them, but they had to impose Sharia. They agreed. They then brought the leaders from around the country to Kandahar. They decided that Omar would be their leader until peace was established. Omar agreed with this. When they came to power, they made Jalaluddin Minister of Border and Tribal Affairs. He should have been given a much more powerful position, people said, but because of jealousy they gave him this. He wasn't interested but couldn't refuse the job. It was so they could say that he was with them. He spent his time in Abu Dhabi or in Saudi Arabia. Ibrahim said he did most of the work. Khalil, another brother, I was told later, shared it with him.

Did they know about 9/11 beforehand?

When it occurred, he and Jalaluddin were listening to the radio. Jalaluddin said this was going to be very bad for Afghanistan They had no idea this attack was coming. Three times I asked this question over the next four years. Each time he said no. Why did the Americans bomb them after 9/11? Three times they came, killing women and children, but they never touched Mullah Omar. To the U.S. he was not a terrorist, but they were. They believed, therefore, that Omar was America's man. The first attack was at their house in Kabul in Wazir Akbar Khan. This surprised me. It was an upscale diplomatic enclave. The U.S. hit the kitchen with a rocket. Jalaluddin moved to another house, and they hit that house. They hit a car and killed two of Ibrahim's bodyguards. The U.S. killed their younger brother, Ismail, in Gardez, and 17 other people, including five children and seven women, and his cousin. When the rockets came Ismail jumped out the window and escaped in one of four cars, but the U.S. planes hit all of them. That same year, at Ramadan, 130 people gathered at their mosque one night to read the Koran, which was their practice, before evening prayers. For two hours the U.S. bombed them, so that they could not even take out the wounded. Why, he asked plaintively, did the U.S. do this to them? I didn't know what to say.

Was Pacha Khan Zadran involved?

When the Americans arrived, Pasha Khan Zadran told them that he had a force of 50,000, and not to use Haqqani. The U.S. gave him money, satellite phones and walkie-talkies. He was 100% certain that Zadran got the U.S. to bomb them. He gave them specific details. He was jealous of them. He had the power to call in airstrikes. After 9/11, Omar sent a delegation to Peshawar, to Islamabad, and to Jalaladeen, who met with the head of the ISI and asked him to tell the Americans not to bomb Afghanistan. The Americans gave Zadran a letter saying he was governor of Paktia Province. He said if anyone didn't like this, he would have them bombed. When President Karzai appointed another man to be governor, Zadran fired artillery on Gardez when the official governor refused his demands to leave.

I had heard this story many times. I met Zadran in March 2002 after the battle of Shah-e-Khot, after he declared himself the governor of Loya Paktia, when I went to Khost to Haqqani's mosque. He was sitting at the end of the beautiful poplar-lined dirt road in the governor's mansion, with a big smile, and men around him and outside a dozen men laughing in their thick U.S. parkas with fur lining, made for troops probably in Alaska, tooling around, fishtailing in courtyard in Toyota pickups, like teenagers on a Saturday night in America.

In 2006, I met a man in Kabul who told me that he accompanied Jalaluddin to the U.S. Embassy in Islamabad. If he did go, Ibrahim replied, he didn't tell him. How could he not know? Other men told me he went there. I said I wanted to see Jalaluddin. He smiled obliquely.

Jalaluddin and other members of the Zadran decided to hold a council of tribal elders to end criminal activity after the Taliban fell. They put together a convoy and drove from Kabul to the village where it would be held. Jalaluddin would attend a funeral and then join them. He came the next day in a convoy of 20 cars, arrived late, and went to a secret place to stay. He said they would hold a council meeting the next night. That night someone called in an airstrike on their mosque in Miram Shah and killed the 130 people. It was Ramadan and the next morning they were preparing for *suhur* (predawn meal) and the U.S. bombed them in their village in Afghanistan, killing nine people and eight guards outside and two inside. The roof fell in and Jalaluddin was injured but they took him away to safety. I thought of the former mujahid in 2007 who came up to me after our elaborate lunch with the tribal leaders, angry at me. He helped pull Jalaluddin from the rubble. They came back to establish peace and to start a new government and the Americans tried to kill them, Ibrahim said bitterly. The room was silent.

There were no suicide bombings during Jihad. It was forbidden in Pashtunwali to kill women and children in war.[581] Why did they use suicide bombers, especially children, to kill innocent people?

The U.S. used drone strikes all the time. Did the Americans ever ask if there were going to be women and children inside? In 1965, during the Kashmir War between India and Pakistan, India said it would have breakfast tomorrow in Lahore. They were going to send tanks across the border. Ayub Khan, the Pakistani chief of staff, asked, how were they going to stop them? They had to find soldiers who had neither wives nor mothers. They found 18 men and strapped bombs around them and gave them guns and sent them to the road the tanks were going to take. They shot their pistols at the tanks, and the Indians saw that there was no resistance, and kept coming. There were 180 million Pakistanis alive today because of those 18 boys. The Fedayeen of Afghanistan came into being in order to defend the people, and to save the future generation from going down without Islam. The five pillars of jihad were not safe without Islam. The roof was jihad, and the room then was secure. Jihad was the roof over the teachings of Islam. In this room, there were four walls and a roof, but without the roof, without jihad, nothing was safe. Jihad kept Islam safe. There were no five pillars without jihad. This came directly from God.

But if they killed innocent children...Ibrahim cut me off. "If you desecrated the Koran in any way, it was the worst thing, for it was the word of God."

He called them the "Fedayeen," Arabic, and Persian, for "he who sacrifices himself." I thought of Alia, in Sana'a, talking about her older brother, and the "Fedayeen." The Arab war was here.

America had forced them into this. If a non-believer did something to the Koran, even picked it up in the wrong way, this was bad; if you picked it up to defend yourself then you could do it, but never let an unbeliever do this. Everything was to protect the future generations. Who had brought them to this point? I repeat, he said, raising his voice, who had brought them

---

[581] Pashtunwali: the unwritten tribal code of the Pashtuns.

to this point? If a non-believer was in a mosque, you could destroy it. You could destroy the Koran. You could do anything to a mosque and the Koran to protect the future generations. If a kaffir went to the Prophet, you could kill him because he was here to destroy Islam, and your future. He touched my arm gently, his voice soft now. Who had brought them to this point that they had to strap bombs to their children to protect themselves? He was passionate, again, like a preacher. Then he spoke softly. He was not a crazy man. The Koran and Islamic teaching allowed this. They did this to keep their faith alive. It was defensive. The Americans had drones without humans in them and they could do anything they wanted to them, and they couldn't do anything about it. They didn't need suicide bombers during the Soviet time, but this was all they had now to protect themselves, and their way of life.

I thought of Ali al-Kurdi in Aden. Once, men fought equally. America fought from the sky. It was cowardly to kill a man with a drone. Come down and fight like a man. The Americans killed indiscriminately, everyone, women and children, just to kill one person, his brother, Jalaluddin.

They didn't pressure anyone. Until the last minute they could walk away. They realized that this was the most effective thing they had. The Americans came up with the name Haqqani Network. Their real name was the "Haqqani Mujahideen." They were just those who came together as a group for jihad. They only wanted freedom for Afghanistan. They had never gone to anyone else's country, and, God willing, they would never have to. Afghanistan was their home. They would do anything to protect it. This was mandatory. In their family Jalaluddin Sab was the eldest and because of his age—he was 72 now—and because he had a stroke and could not talk well and was weak, Sirajuddin was his representative. Yes, they called him the Khalifa.

They were four brothers: Jalaladeen, Hajji Ibrahim, Shaheed (martyr) Ismail, and Hajji Khalil Rahman. Jalaluddin had four sons by his first wife: Nasiruddin, Shaheed; Badruddin, Shaheed; Mohammad, Shaheed; Sirajuddin, the Khalifa. From his Yemeni wife there was Muhammad Omar; Abdul Aziz; Hamza, Anas, Abdullah, Abdullah Rahman and Huzaifa. A man brought in food. He drank his Sprite. It was strange to see him eating a chicken sandwich and holding an American soft drink. I wanted him to be up in the mountains with a rifle.

Yes, ISIS was here. They were trying to figure them out. They were

Wahhabis. They didn't know what they wanted. Like they did with Mullah Omar, they were doing research. In their religion there was no such thing as mass murders or the desecration of artifacts or statues. ISIS was not of the same religion as they were, and they had no interest in them. It was now up to Mullah Omar to decide what to do about them. Was he alive? As far as they knew, he was. Did ISIS or the Arabs or the Chechens come to them to get inspiration and training?

He sat back. It was untrue, completely. If anyone came to them, they sent them to whatever government group they were assigned to. If they were against the Islamic Emirate, they threw them out. They did not deviate from the Koran, and they stuck to their beliefs. They didn't rob or murder even Sikhs or Hindus but defended their rights. They didn't want to force people to accept Sharia, but to reason with them. Americans could come back, to work, or as guests. The U.S. had laws and they had to abide by its rules, and so it was the same for visitors here.

People said they had a business empire. He relaxed and smiled. He was the only one who did business. He bought and sold properties in Pakistan. It was the truth. Only God knew the truth. They had two houses and two families.

We had been talking for over eight hours. It was past midnight. I ended the meeting. Again, I said I wanted to see Jalaluddin. Ibrahim and I embraced gently. John told me to stay in the room. My guide and I waited and then went outside. The moon was bright, and everyone was gone.

The Islamic State

It was April and the rain pounded on the roof and the wind blew. Already the monsoon had arrived. Asfand, in a dark salwar kameez, with a cigarette, sat cross-legged, his stomach out, his hair long. He opened his laptop. In late 2014, a three-man delegation from al-Baghdadi crossed Iran to Baluchistan.[582] They arrived in South Waziristan, on November 12th. It was the first official visit by Daesh.[583] They went to North Waziristan, then to Khyber Agency, up to Mohmand Agency, across to Nangahar Province in Afghanistan, and up to Kunar and Nuristan, to spread Islam according to ISIS.[584]

He turned his laptop. There was a wide riverbed, and sunlight shining through the trees. A male chorus chanted and a hundred horsemen in single file, some carrying the black flag of ISIS came, and then a line of men holding their rifles high. The chanting rose and they came in slow motion, and the chorus was loud. The horsemen and the riflemen walked two abreast. The men, many with long hair, showing their commitment, and black turbans, like Mohammad wore, sat on the ground. A former Taliban commander, in his 40s, his beard trimmed, in an army jacket, announced the emir for each Tribal Area, and for each province in Afghanistan.[585] They placed their hands together, like athletes before a game, and pledged to live and die for Abdul Moktar al-Baghdadi.

They left the Taliban and needed money and Daesh was a rich organization, Asfand explained. They shouted Allah-ah-Akbar, and a man fired his rifle. Another held up a sword and addressed the camera. A dozen horsemen raced toward us, and the chanting was loud. Asfund said Pakistan did not want ISIS in its territory and would assign Haqqani and al-Qaeda to get rid of it. Pakistan created many Taliban groups, to divide and rule them better, but it could not control them, and now ISIS was here. The groups had splintered, and each belonged to a different tribe.

---

[582] Al-Zubar al-Kuwati, Farden al-Ansari, and Seikh Yusuf of Saudi Arabia.
[583] Al-Dawla al-Islamiya fee al-Iraq wa al-Sham.
[584] Gospel comes from godspel in Old English.
[585] Hafiz Saeed Khar.

On 15 June, the Army launched *"Zarb al-Zab"* in North Waziristan, but not before moving the Haqqanis away. After the attack on the Army Public School, on December 16, last year, when the Taliban killed 132 children, and for which the TTP took credit, the army said there was no longer a difference between good Taliban and bad Taliban.[586] A month later, the Uighurs of the East Turkistan Islamic Movement (ETIM), from Sinkiang, who fled to Pakistan, moved their 600-700 families to where the Haqqanis were. The Pakistani Air Force, probably under Chinese pressure, bombed them, killing some Haqqani people. He talked about Arabs of al-Qaeda linked to the Haqqanis, the IMU (Islamic Movement of Uzbekistan) and its offshoot, IJU (Islamic Jihad Union). Recep Erdogen, the president of Turkey, praised the Uighurs.[587] They were fighting in Syria. The Haqqanis, along with Jaish Mohammad, Ansar-ul-Mujahideen, linked to Boko Haram, the IMU and IMJ, all under the ISI, helped thousands of the Mujahideen, Taliban, Arabs and Uighurs--move there. Prince Bandar, head of Saudi intelligence, was trying to assassinate Bashir al-Assad. Ayman al-Zawahiri's younger brother, Mohammad, in prison, was guiding those who were with al-Qaeda (al-Nusrah) in Syria. A fighter from Syria told Asfand that Ayman's brother was their leader.

How could I prove this? I couldn't.

He told Mohammad Khorasan, spokesman for the Pakistani Taliban, that they had lost so many to ISIS that they were now weak. ISIS was paying hundreds of thousands of dollars to the groups. The Haqqanis were linked to every group in the Tribal Areas, and in Afghanistan. There were many Europeans who came from 2009-2011 across Iran, where they met with Saif al Adel and Hamza bin Laden. Asfand confirmed that in 2008 al-Qaeda kidnapped the commercial attaché at the Iranian consulate in Peshawar,[588] and that Al-Zawahiri negotiated his release[589] in exchange for access to a route across Iran. During the 2014 exodus, hundreds of men went by boat from Baluchistan to Iran and on to Syria. Sirajuddin was the Khalifa for the

---

[586] Tahreek-e-Taliban, Pakistan
[587] Uran Botobekov, "China's Nightmare: Xinjiang Jihadists Go Global," *Diplomat* 17 Aug. 2016,
[588] Rferl, "Iranian Diplomat Kidnapped in Pakistan City of Peshawar," *RadioFree Europe/RadioLiberty* 13 Nov. 2008.
[589] Alan Cowell, "Iranian Diplomat in Pakistan Is Freed," *New York Times* 30 Mar. 2010

entire Tribal Areas and eastern Afghanistan. The Haqqanis were the most powerful Pashtun family now. A former parliamentarian, who worked with them, sold honey. ISIS didn't like to kill only a few people. They wanted to create real terror to show real power. The emir of the TTP in Peshawar was the master planner of the Army Public School attack.[590] It was his way to show that he was worthy of ISIS. Asfand closed his laptop. The rain came down and the world seemed dark all around us.

Khashoggi was right. ISIS was raw Wahhabism.

How did he work with these people and stay alive? He addressed each leader as 'Emir Sab' and showed respect, and they in turn gave him respect. They wanted publicity. In North Waziristan, forty percent of the population was of the Darwar tribe and 60% were Wazir, totaling between 1.4-1.6 million. In South Waziristan, 60% were Mehsud and 40% Wazir. He agreed that every chief knew the number of people in his tribe, who went to a madrasa, and to the inch where his land began and ended. He knew everything that happened on his land.

Over 1,000 Pashtun tribal leaders had been assassinated by militants and unknown people, since 9/11. In every village there were five to ten maliks (leaders), who, like the militants, were on the Pakistani payroll. Before the latest military operation many Uzbeks, Chechens, Tajiks, Arabs and Uighurs, linked to al-Qaeda, and one another, were killed. After the army school bombing an ISI source told him the Prime Minister went to Saudi Arabia and asked the government to stop sending money here. Pakistan sent its G-3 assault rifle,[591] manufactured in Taxila, to Saudi Arabia. Pakistan sent the same rifle to Iran and Syria, part of its Islamist agenda.

The Haqqanis were the main facilitators in Afghanistan and Pakistan for the international jihadi groups. If the U.S. left Afghanistan, Sirajuddin would become the Khalifa of the whole country. In Loya Paktia, the Taliban were fighting ISIS. Mullah Omar was dead, but Jalaluddin was alive, and his son was alive. America had delisted the Taliban, probably to negotiate, or use them. The TTP had links with Somalia pirates and started websites and radio stations there. Al-Qaeda sent arms. Hamid Gul, the former head of the ISI, was involved. His son, Abdullah, named after Abdullah Gul, the Turkish

---

[590] Omar Mansur of the Tareek-e-Taliban
[591]"Standard Rifle of Pakistan Army: The G3 Assault Rifle,"

foreign minister, was taking over. Asfand explained how the Afghan Taliban crossed into Pakistan and Pakistani Taliban crossed into Afghanistan. He showed where the Haqqani commanders were in the Tribal Areas, and in Afghanistan. Naisruddin established the Taliban office in Qatar. The Yemeni side of the family facilitated the move. They raised money in the Gulf. It went through him, but he was dead now.

In the early 1970s Pakistan decided that it needed people to work for them in Afghanistan. The British told Pakistan to focus on the mullahs. If you gave them five rupees, they were yours. You could not manipulate a tribe, but you could a mullah, one reason why they were assassinating all the sheikhs. There were no madrasas then in Afghanistan. Mullahs went to Pakistan to study, and the ISI trained them and gave them salaries.

I felt that the ISI probably recruited Jalaluddin at Dar ul-Uloom.

During Daoud Khan's time Pakistan was paying mullahs. It gave Haqqani money and weapons. Pakistan was afraid of Daoud, who wanted to return the Tribal Areas to Afghanistan. Haqqani's goal was the Pakistani Project Implementation to rule Afghanistan and Central Asia. Those who joined al-Qaeda, or ISIS, were fighting for one goal: to go to Paradise. The mastermind of the suicide bombers was Qari Hussein Mehsud, a cousin of Hekmatullah Mehsud, the Taliban leader.[592] He said he could prepare a man for suicide in under 30 minutes. Asfand watched him preach to 60-70 boys and young men in a room for about 25 minutes about Paradise, the drones, and U.S. Forces committing atrocities against Muslims, and why the U.S. and Pakistan tortured and killed people. He asked who would be next for a suicide attack. They all raised their hands. He chose two and they were happy, but others looked worried. Why not them? What had they done wrong? Three days later the two boys, between 14 and 16, attacked in Peshawar. He asked Hussein, why was he killing children? He was not killing them. He was sending them to Paradise. Many people agreed with him.

Pakistan was attacking them for U.S. dollars. In Islamic thinking there were seven levels of Paradise. If you killed a U.S. soldier or citizen you went to the top level, a Pakistani a lower level. One man was using children 10-12 years old to kill security forces. Most suicide attacks were for revenge. One man had two or three children and one left to go to school. The Taliban said

---

[592] Hekmatullah Mehsud was killed in a U.S. drone strike in 2013.

they were praying that his son would achieve Paradise. He asked why. He had become a suicide bomber. The man and his wife cried. They didn't know that he had been taken from them. If America wasn't here, or stopped sending money, there wouldn't be war.

The people liked suicide bombers because they are taking revenge against America. The Jordanian's attack on the CIA agents in Khost was the first attack on U.S. forces by "the cream of the crop," the Tehrek-i-Taliban.[593] All the money the U.S. sent to Islamabad for the refugees displaced by "*Zarb al-Zab*" went to the government.[594] It was using the tribal people to get money from the U.S, which was killing them by the government. The war since 9/11 had been a Tsunami against the people. When the people died the U.S. gave money to aid their families. If the Taliban died the U.S. gave money to bolster the security forces for doing a good job. If the security forces had trouble, the U.S. sent money to help them even more.

Al-Zawahiri's brother wanted to create Lashkar-Ghazwa-Khorasan in the Middle East and move it here. It would become Lashkar-Ghazwa-e-Hind, the umbrella organization for South Asia to fight ISIS to rule Khorasan. "It was inevitable," said Haif M. Saeed,[595] leader of Lashkar-e-Taiba, which attacked Mumbai in 2008.

The Ghazwa Hind was the great battle that would come, said a Hadith, between Hindus and Muslims, in India, for control of Kashmir and India. Pakistan would lead the revived Muslim Mogul Empire. In Islamic thinking, the final battle was the Battle of Khorasan, mentioned in the Koran. The Khorasan Lashkar (militia) would lead this battle. ISIS would carry the black flag. After this all the people would be under Muslim rule.

The editor in Riyadh warned me that the road to the Middle East ran through Khorasan.

---

[593] Laura Rozen, "Jordanian Double Agent Killed CIA Officers in Khost," *Politico*
[594] Farhan Zahid, "The Successes and Failures of Pakistan's Operation Zarb-e-Azb," *Jamestown*, 20 Sept. 2016
[595] Praveen Swami, "The Lashkar Project." *The Indian Express*, 10 Dec. 2014

Pacha Khan Zadran

Two soldiers stood in the snow a foot deep behind a barrier blocking the road. They let us pass. Two other guards stood outside a compound. We followed a narrow brick path to a house in back, took off our shoes, entered and sat on a carpet. A heater glowed in the center of the room. Pacha Khan Zadran, with a thick black moustache, entered with a small boy. His eyes were not as proud as before, but his voice was strong. He looked to be in his late 70s. His son was three. His house was guarded well. In 2005, a bomb hit here, he replied.

Who was behind it? He waved his hand. He'd had three suicide attacks on him. It was a sign of his power that his enemies would send men to attack him. It was Haqqani. He was the enemy of all the people. He was running a proxy war against the West. He was ISI. His own people had been defending Afghanistan from the Taliban since the beginning. His problem with Jalaluddin Haqqani began when he rose with the Taliban. He couldn't say that Haqqani, a poor boy, had risen above him, a tribal aristocrat, and become famous and powerful during Jihad.

He supported King Zahir Shah, in exile in Rome, during Jihad, and was not part of any group. The U.S. found him to be very effective. He was in the camp of Afghanistan. Jalaluddin was in the ISI camp. He sold himself to another country.

Why would Haqqani work for the ISI?

He liked power, cars and money. It had nothing to do with Islam. Anyone who was Muslim would not do as he did. He didn't know anything about his businesses. His son, Sirajuddin, was considered the Khalifa of his region. Most of the suicide attacks along the whole of eastern Afghanistan were his.

Where did the suicide attacks, which did not exist during Jihad, came from?

During Jihad, the Mujahideen did not want to kill civilians. What they were doing now killing little children was not Islam. The center of suicide bombing was Pakistan.

But he, using a satellite phone, provided by the U.S., told the Americans, after 9/11, to attack Haqqani. Was this not true?

"How many people had Haqqani killed?" he replied. He didn't push him to the ISI. From the beginning, Rabbani, Hekmatyar and Haqqani were not independent. When you were all part of the ISI network it was difficult to release yourself from that. When Haqqani went with the Taliban after their fall he went against him.

But he, Zadran, more than once called in air strikes on Haqqani, killing members of his family, which turned him against the U.S. Was I wrong?

He was quiet. After the fall of the Taliban, he was in charge of Khost, Paktia and Paktika provinces. Haqqani and the Taliban were in these three provinces. He called a jirga,[596] and invited Haqqani, his brothers and sons and gave them time to give up their arms and surrender. If they wanted to fight, he said, this place was not for them. They went to Pakistan.

He was trying, in post 9/11 Afghanistan, to reassert his authority over the Haqqanis.

No, it wasn't true. He gave 600 men to the Americans to fight the Taliban, and Hekmatyar. The U.S. asked if he wanted to start a bombing campaign against the Taliban. He said no. They would kill women and children. He did not tell the Americans to bomb Haqqani, he said emphatically.

After I first met with Zadran in 2002 at the governor's house in Khost, I saw him in 2003 at his checkpoint on the road. His men were accused of extorting money from truck drivers coming from Pakistan. They moved back as a U.S. Army convey came toward us.

The Defense Minister of Pakistan said without the Haqqani Network there could be no peace talks. Haqqani did what they told him to do. Al-Qaeda and Pakistan were together. Militants from Tajikistan, Uzbekistan and other countries were there, part of the Haqqani Network. Why did the U.S. not attack them either here or in Pakistan? Pakistan was supporting them. Pakistan was supporting the U.S. and tricking it. We should look at the interests of Haqqani as the same as those of Pakistan. Al-Qaeda and Haqqani had a common ideology, under the control of the ISI, which asked him,

---

[596] A tribal council of elders.

Zadran, to work with them during Jihad and he said no. Haqqani joined the ISI during this time. He had a Pakistani ID card. Pakistan gave him a house on a military base in Miram Shah. They were living in Rawalpindi today, the headquarters of the army. Who was paying for these houses? During Jihad, Saudi Arabia supported the Haqqanis, and still did.

An Afghan journalist told me that he was on an army base in Rawalpindi. This, if true, was why Ibrahim wouldn't let me see him. A tribal chief told me he was colonel in the army.

He didn't know anything about their trucking business or rental properties, but he condemned them. The biggest problem was that the U.S. did not know what to do. If it wanted to stabilize Afghanistan it should put one person in charge of a zone. If the U.S. gave him money and put him in charge, he would make it impossible for one Talib to come into his zone. In the beginning he asked the U.S. to attack Haqqani and the Taliban. You had arms, and the artillery, so just destroy them, but you didn't do it. You brought this war to Washington.

Again, he admitted, to his credit, that he told the U.S. to attack the Haqqanis, which turned them against the U.S. It had become a war of revenge, a power struggle, a class war, a form of solidarity with men from the Horn of Africa to Europe. Zadran said 15 men from his tribe were waiting to see him.

Turquoise Mountain

Late afternoon, in Murad Khan, in old Kabul, the sun fading over the hills, a wide courtyard, a green lawn in the summer, white with snow now, surrounded by a 19th Century adobe and wood compound, with lattice windows, the Afghanistan Strategic Studies Center. The founder, Davood Moridian sat at his desk, a bokara with a small fire crackling in the silence. It was old Afghanistan. It was the safest place in Kabul, he assured me, The Pakistani embassy was down from him 50 yards away.

The key question here was what was the U.S. intention toward the Haqqanis and the other militant groups? Policy makers in Central Asia, China, and in the Middle East did not trust the U.S. The ISI felt that the U.S. maintained the Afghan Taliban to put pressure on Pakistan to hand over its nuclear weapons. China felt that the U.S. was using the Uighurs, Turkic speaking people, once Buddhist, from Sinkiang (Western Territories), in the 1930s under Soviet control, called East Turkistan until 1949, who had become militant under Chinese pressure to give up Islam. Many fled to Badakhshan Province, Afghanistan, to destabilize Sinkiang. India, Russia, and Central Asian states felt the U.S. was not sincere in fighting terrorism.

U.S. officials he talked to laughed and said this was all paranoia and conspiracy theories.

Many Arabs said the West was behind al-Qaeda and ISIS, I said. It was ridiculous. The U.S. could not ignore this, he countered, but must alienate this suspicion, not reject it as paranoia. It had made many blunders, but the Afghans had accepted this, but they would not accept that you had refused for so long to declare the Haqqani Network a terrorist group.[597] They could accept that you killed so many innocent people, it wasn't easy, but they could not accept your arrogance and insincerity. The U.S., over a period of 40 years, has been here to protect itself. It was now a transactional relationship. America gave them money in exchange for military bases. In the case of the U.S.-Pakistani relationship an incompetent America had been outmaneuvered and outsmarted by a duplicitous Pakistan. The U.S. gave

---

[597] "State Department Dubs Haqqani Network Terrorists, 'Sopranos of the Afghan War'." *PBS* 7 Sept. 2012

Pakistan money, and it gave sanctuary to your enemies. The U.S. was desperate after 9/11 and Pakistan gave you access to bases and land routes into Afghanistan. We fought the Taliban, giving them legitimacy.

It was what Afghans called a lipstick war. We were putting a pretty face on an ugly reality. Why were the TTP[598] and now the Haqqani Network, terrorists, but not the Afghan Taliban? He, a Tajik, was afraid of what was coming. Empirically, the Taliban were the most dangerous terrorist group in the world. The elite Pashtuns in Kabul were afraid of them. He, too, talked about Pakistan's assassination program against Pashtun leaders. The U.S. had become the neocolonial power here, as it was in the Middle East, supporting President Ashraf Ghani, a former employee of the World Bank, a symbol of Western power, married to a Christian, imposing its rule. President Karzai, a Pashtun, told his vice president, Marshall Fahim, a Tajik, not to put pressure on him. The Taliban were part of his army. Fahim, a former Mujahid had the Mujahideen on his side. There was a balance of power, and terror. There was solidarity among the Mujahideen. They were respected throughout the country.

They defeated, with U.S. help, the Soviet Red Army. There was the Tajik-led Northern Alliance and the Pashtun Southern Alliance. The role of Saudi Arabia was to protect the kingdom and to delegitimize anything that would threaten it, the Ikhwan, or democracy, and, secondly, to find a place for its clergy to operate outside the kingdom. Prince Turki, when he was head of Saudi intelligence, brought jihadist leaders to his office and asked if they wanted to live in the Kingdom or go to Paradise. If they wanted to live at home they would give them a house, and all they had to do was not fight. If they wanted to go to Paradise, they would give them a passport and send them to Afghanistan. It was a de-radicalization program. For potential troublemakers, whether devout princes or mullahs, you needed a theatre where they could spend their money and energy outside the kingdom. It was an outsourcing policy. He smiled.

The Saudis had trained enough Afghan fighters by now. Thousands had studied in Saudi Arabia. The Saudis were building mosques here when they needed schools and hospitals. Moridian, like Rangin Spanta, said Pakistan saw itself as the successor to the Mogul Empire. It wanted to conquer

---

[598] Tahreek-e-Taliban

Muslim Central Asia. In Washington, it played the victim, but with Afghans it played the imperialist. If I went to the Pakistani army headquarters in Rawalpindi, I would see a portrait outside of all the Muslim armies that had fought in India. The army named all its missiles after the names of Muslim rulers who went from Afghanistan to India and of whom Pakistan claimed ownership. Islamabad provided an Islamic army to Saudi Arabia and it in turn provided an ideology and financing. Saudi money going to Pakistan went mostly to religious political parties. Forty years of war had degraded the Americans, Afghans and Pakistanis. It was the Arabization and the Islamization of Afghanistan.

This was the "why" that Khashoggi talked about.

Hekmatyar and Haqqani were wealthy. Their own interests were most important to them. The viciousness of IS was the evolution of this industry, like the evolution of the iPhone. At first there was the Nokia, then the iPhone and now there were more advanced phones. In the same way we were seeing jihadist groups evolve. It was the stagnation of Islamic Civilization. IS was justified in its burning of a hostage because they burned people during Mohammad's time.[599] This was an internal debate that they, as Muslims, needed to have. The IS and Taliban violence was linked to the past.

Yes, it was Ibn Taymiyya, it was al-Wahhab, and Ibn Saud at Karbala.

There were many interpretations and sects in Islam. How many different churches were there in America? In Atlanta, near CNN, he saw seven on one street. ISIS was using Khorasan, the ancient Islamic name for Afghanistan. Abu Muslim Khorasan was a leader in the Abbasid period. ISIS appointed a Tajik as a district governor in Syria to replicate the one in Khorasan.

He recalled the old yellow Shah-Shamshera, (King of Two Swords) mosque, that sat by the Kabul River. He was an Arab who people said used two swords to slaughter Afghans. Al-Qaeda and the Taliban were popular here. Which was more appealing to Afghan customers? It depended upon who was more vulnerable. The manpower was here. Afghans owned the "brand." They defeated the Russians and were on the way to defeating the Americans. There was huge respect for them throughout the Arab world. He

---

[599] Muath Kasasbeh, Jordanian fighter pilot burned to death in a cage in January 2015.

was invited to Israel and while in Jerusalem he met a Palestinian who found out he was Afghan and gave him a big hug. The uniform of ISIS was Afghan clothes, the salwar kameez. ISIS forced children to wear these clothes. Thousands of Arabs were killed here when they brought Islam. When the Taliban came the people said it was the second victory over the Arabs. The Islamic State brought the third Arab invasion. The average Afghan felt that the U.S. had lost the war here. Vietnam was an American war. The U.S. lost over 4,000 people, and spent a trillion dollars, but its diplomats, politicians, the military, even Obama, called it Bush's war. Now Trump called it Obama's war. There was no owner.

The compound where we sat was called Turquoise Mountain, after a Buddhist city before the Arabs came. Once, Kabul was called Paris of the East, now it was lined with blast barriers.

We talked about Iran. I said Rafsanjani's son was making regular trips to Saudi Arabia, flying, like Saudi princes, to private airfields. Rafsanjani had always been close to the royal family, he replied. The Iranians played good cop, bad cop.[600] Why had the U.S. and Pakistan elevated Haqqani to such a high position? He was only powerful in a small, eastern part of Afghanistan. I reminded him that the Haqqanis attacked the U.S. Consulate, in Herat, on the Iranian border. Haqqani owned a shopping center in Islamabad, he replied. I must see it.

---

[600] Ali Akbar Rafsanjani, a disciple of Khomeini, was president of Iran from 1989-1997. He died in 2017 at 82.

The Taliban Military Council

The lights spread out, Dubai at night, like Los Angeles. Sami pointed to a boat leaving for Iran. There were many Pashtuns here, but I would never see one working as a domestic, a servant, a janitor, or involved in prostitution. They didn't like barbers, although they got their hair cut. They hated singers but liked to listen to people sing. If you were a barber, then you must marry your daughter to one. If your grandfather was a barber people would know that.

His phone rang. His friend was waiting for us on a corner. He was rail thin, had a soft voice and a gentle manner, but so did Hekmatyar. He was afraid to be seen with me. I walked behind them to an Iranian restaurant and after dinner to the hotel and sat in the lobby. They took the elevator upstairs and I sat in a chair. I saw a man with a phone cord in his ear standing at the elevators. He wasn't there before. I went to the elevator, and he said good evening. I asked Sami's friend what it was like to live here. There was a bar downstairs and a dozen women in short skirts in the lobby. There were many temptations, he said. You had to suppress your evil desires.

Sami's friend was on the Taliban Military Council. He owned a small bakery. They were feeding the people. There was no connection with women. They bought bread and left. He had two wives. He would have four if he could afford it. He was a maulvi and an expert in Sharia. A talib was a divinity student.[601] He studied at the Noor Madrasa (School of Light) in Ghazni. Then he went to the Haqqania madrasa in Peshawar where his teacher was the 25th generation recipient of the Hadith, and he was the 26th since Mohammad taught. There were 300 in his class in 1992. He was fighting the communists in Afghanistan, and it took him ten years to graduate. He was wounded badly. He ran his hand across his chest and right arm. He was the first in his unit of 16 men to enter Ghazni. It was 1996. From there they marched on Kabul. There were 2,000 in a class at Haqqania now. Not everyone could be a talib but anyone could be a mujahid. He meant that you had to have studied at a madrasa. A mujahid did not have to.

---

[601] *Dictionary of Islam*, 626

The Afghan Taliban had a structure during the Mujahideen time. The leadership was made up of religious scholars. They ran a government. The Pakistani Taliban was created by others. He meant Pakistan. The Taliban were working here secretly. Eventually, they would rule Afghanistan. They didn't have any intention to go beyond there. They had enmity with the Russians. They would not have a lifetime of enmity with the Americans, who were believers. The Koran said they could marry other people of the book. He meant Christians and Jews, they of the Abrahamic faiths. They had a hard time with Hindus, who believed in so many strange gods, and with the Chinese. They could help America against them, and the Russians. They had no choice but to work with Pakistan. It was not straight, but it could not avoid America's power. It benefited from working with the Americans. The Taliban understood that it was not an honest friendship. Yes, Arabs still trained with them and fought in the Middle East. Why not? If Afghans could go live in America, why couldn't people come and live and train with them? Abu Zarqawi, God bless him, was in Afghanistan. Abu Bakr al Baghdadi was there for six years. So was Abu Zubayda,[602] of al-Qaeda, a small dark-skinned man, like a Punjabi, but he was Yemeni, and smart.

Yemenis also said he was Yemeni. He was Palestinian it appears, brought up in Saudi Arabia.

Jalaluddin merged with them. They were closer to him than to Yunus Khalis, who was Ikhwan.

He gave Mullah Omar an AK-47, nothing more. "Khalis, Hekmatyar, Rabbani and Sayyaf were all Ikhwan," Sami interjected. When Jalaluddin was Minster of Border and Tribal Affairs, Khalil and Ibrahim shared the role as minister. Jalaluddin would come to big meetings, and everyone would be interested to hear what he had to say. The Taliban could not have taken Kabul without him. Twice they attacked from the south and failed. Jalaluddin came and drew a map to show how to surround Kabul and attack from Bagram, in the north, which they did, and took Kabul. He was the Massoud-level commander for the Pashtuns. During the civil war, after the Soviets left, the Arabs joined the Taliban, gave them some money, but not much, and followed their rules. There were no problems between bin Laden and Mullah Omar. Osama pledged loyalty to him, so did al-Zawahiri. Had I

---

[602] "The Guantánamo Docket," *New York Times* 18 May 2021

ever heard him say anything against the Taliban?

What about the statements of al-Baghdadi against Mullah Omar? They considered al-Zawahiri much higher as a Muslim scholar and spiritual leader than al-Baghdadi. He, like Haqqani, controlled a lot of territory, but neither was a spiritual leader. Haqqani said to Omar, even if his coat was just hanging there, he was his leader. After the U.S. starting bombing Afghanistan, Omar said he would give everything to Jalaluddin, but he said no. Al-Baghdadi had power in the Arab world only because of the Shi'a-Sunni split. There were more Arabs around Jalaluddin because he was a good man, and humble. He did not fight in the civil war. The Arabs respected them because they gave up everything to protect bin Laden and to fight for their country, and they never gave in. The Taliban inspired Daesh. The Haqqanis and Daesh were dedicated to an Islamic state. It was all one from Afghanistan to the Middle East.

Finally, I thought, this was what I was looking for.

The Haqqanis were the most powerful Pashtun family in the world. Arabs, some wealthier than a state, loved, admired, and supported Jalaluddin, who, unlike them, did something important as a Muslim, fighting the greatest powers of our time, the Soviet Union, and America. There was strong support from Arabia to Egypt for Afghans because they sheltered bin Laden, who gave up an easy life to fight for Islam and were waging jihad against the Americans. The Taliban respected those from Mecca and Medina. But of all the non-Arabs who came to the holy cities the only ones the Arabs there respected were Afghans. That was why there were a lot of ex-Mujahideen and Taliban living here. If there was no U.S. pressure, I would see people in the streets raising money for them. Wasn't I afraid being here?

The Taliban used suicide bombers, going against Pashtun culture. How could they do this?

They had no choice. The U.S. was so strong that there was little that they could do to resist. No one was obligated to become a member of the Fedayeen. In Ramadan, if you were traveling, you didn't have to fast; in the same way, you did not have to become a martyr. People chose to do this. It was honorable and respected. They were Shaheed.

They were martyrs, martyrs, or witness, in Greek, a witness for God. A shaheed, like a martyr, went directly to Heaven and did not have to wait for Judgment Day. St. Augustine said the power of martyrdom depended upon the cause for which you died. Ibrahim said it was to protect the faith. In Rome, early Christians had to decide whether to die or deny their faith. The Talmud said man should prefer martyrdom to idolatry, sexual immorality, and murder.[603] Clement of Rome called martyrs God's athletes vying for the eternal prize. T.S. Elliot called martyrdom "the design of God, for his love of man, to warn them and to lead them back to his ways." In Taliban suicide recruitment tapes men chant slowly, saying goodbye to their mothers. They chant about their land. Pope Francis said martyrdom "is the air of the life of a Christian."[604] For al-Qaeda, the Haqqanis, ISIS, and the Taliban, it is a weapon.

Since the U.S. burned their homes and bombed them, they had to kill them. Their emir could order them to kill in any way he chose. Was I not afraid to meet with him? Twice now, he asked. The Bible said those who stood firm, and according to Tacitus, Nero killed thousands,[605] reigned in Heaven a thousand years.[606] During World War II, Franz Jagerstatter, a Catholic Austrian farmer,[607] was guillotined for refusing to pledge allegiance to Hitler; so was Sophie Scholl,[608] a student in Munich. Pope Benedict canonized Jagerstatter and said martyrdom was an act of supreme love, based upon the death of Jesus. In 2009, the Taliban kidnapped Piotr Stnaczak, a Polish geologist, and asked him to convert to Islam, but he, a Catholic, said no. They admired him but beheaded him. Siddiqui in Deoband said all that Muslims wanted to do was to die. Freud, a secular man, said human beings wished for death as they did for sex, and to procreate.[609]

Sanaá Mehaydali, the teenage Lebanese bomber, was dispatched by the Syrian Socialist National Party. Dhandu, who in 1991 knelt before Prime Minister Rajiv Gandhi, and detonated her bomb, was fighting for the secular Liberation Tigers of Tamil Eelam.

Judgment Day (*Ashrat-a-sur*) was coming, said the talib. A super non-

[603] Sanhedrin 74a.
[604] "Pope's General Audience: English Summary," *Vatican News*, 11 Dec. 2019
[605] *Encyclopedia Britannica*, vol. 14 (1967 ed.), p. 984.
[606] Revelation 20:4
[607] "*A Hidden Life*," 2019 Film, written and directed by Terrence Malik
[608] "Sophie Scholl," *Wikipedia*, 25 May 2022,
[609] Armstrong, "*The Battle for God*," 2000, 136

Muslim nation would come to Khorasan. This was America. People went to Afghanistan to fight the Americans and now that force would rise from Khorasan and move to greater Shams (the Levant) where there would be the final battle. Then they would go to Medina. The kaffirs would attack there, and the Shia would join them. Their flags and their turbans would be black. The battle would be between the Shia, who were not true Muslims, and the infidels. The last battle would be atheists vs. non-atheists. The Army of Khorasan was forming now in Afghanistan. The Taliban saw the Afghan turbans and clothes that ISIS wore. They were all Mujahideen.

Had he changed living in Dubai? He accepted that by nature human beings were social and didn't like to live in isolation. Before he came here, he would not shake hands with a non-Muslim, but now he would even hug him. They lived in a land of dust and dirt and needed money to survive. Before, groups got together, but now they raised money individually, secretly. They never asked people to fight for them. Pakistan was helping them, but they were not looking for money from Pakistan. They didn't like to have foreigners on the front lines. They themselves should be in the front. Did not Haqqani, by marrying an Arab, have doors open to him? Of course, once a man married into another family, or a woman, it created a bond. If he went to a village where his daughter lived, he would be welcomed and treated with respect. Jalaluddin and his wife, and Khalil and Ibrahim came here often. They were Zadran, a large, influential tribe and the Haqqanis despite the American efforts to kill them were still a large family. It started when Pakistan introduced Jalaluddin to important people in the Arab world. The Americans bombed his mosque near Khost and killed Afghans, Arabs, Pakistanis, all were inside. It was during Ramadan. Sami said he pointed out the cemetery to me. There was a special smell, like perfume, but I couldn't smell it because I was an infidel.

"Why had I come here, taking this risk?" he asked again. I wanted people to understand one another. The best message was that a man was treated well by the Taliban and told the world. That was success. Sami must have said they captured me. The government came for him after the U.S. invasion. He had been married four days. He only had a pistol and was ready to be martyred and would kill as many as he could before he died. His family said he had to surrender. He was in a prison, built by Government Security Services, from 2002-2006. He had been the director there and the guards saluted him when he arrived, and then they tortured him. There was no dignity in torture. They tied his hands and feet and left him like that for over a year. Once, it was so cold there was ice on his handcuffs. They beat him and his blood and his clothes and parts of his skin stuck to him. He prayed and recited verses from the Koran and he never felt pain. Neither was he afraid. They believed, as Taliban, if someone was going to be martyred, there would be no pain. He never saw the sun and he never felt pain. God was with him. He married a second time and didn't have a chance to be with his wife. This bothered him more than the torture. The head of the NDS was from his village. When he came here the government questioned him. A Pashtun could not hide.

Yes, Jalaluddin went to Khartoum. They were all brothers there. The Taliban did not want to be part of ISIS. They did not want to destroy everything to build a state.

Why did General Gul say on television that Jalaluddin was more Pakistani than a Pakistani?

Hamid Gul was an old friend. Haqqani was very important and he and his family had more freedom and facilities than anyone else. Pakistan didn't need help from the Haqqanis here. They did not have businesses here.

The NDS said the Haqqanis were training and sending people to Iraq and Syria and that they were tracking them. Al-Qaeda was their biggest problem. NDS said this so that America would stay. The Taliban had no international intentions. They had enough problems at home.

I noticed that when I said "al-Qaeda," he said "We..."

All the groups were linked. Officially, they had not received nor responded to anything from al-Baghdadi. They were not sending people to the Middle East. They had a responsibility in Afghanistan. They could not attack America if they wanted to. They could help the U.S. against China and Russia. Even with mineral extraction. The U.S. was fighting Pakistan's war, dividing the Pashtun nation. Pakistan destroyed the Buddhist statues. Pakistani scholars made it known that they shouldn't be there and this made it into the minds of Afghan scholars. The Pakistani goal was to isolate the Taliban from the international community. It was using them like a dog. America threw them in front of the dog that was Pakistan. After the Soviet war the U.S. left and Afghanistan fell into chaos. Pakistan helped them win the civil war, and to come to power. They used Pakistan. He had a house there worth 5,000 rupees. If he pounded a nail into the side and it split it would crumble. He needed a home to survive. The Arab monarchies depended upon Pakistani engineers and soldiers.

It was after two in the morning. I had to go. What should I call him? He put his index finger to his lips. "Abu Ahmed al-Medini," he would be the son of Ahmed from Medina.

The next day, March 26, the monarchies of Bahrain, Kuwait, Qatar and the United Arab Emirates, and Saudi Arabia, began bombing the Houthis in Yemen. Yemenis were fleeing to the Horn of Africa. Zindani fled to Saudi Arabia. Al-Fadhli was in hiding. The Houthis were hunting for Ali Mohsen. Saleh warned Saudi Arabia which lost to the Houthis in a border dispute in 2009, not to invade. How could the Houthis, 20% of the population, take Sanaá, or move south through areas controlled by Sunni tribes? Saleh was helping them. They, allied with the Iranians, called their onslaught, this "blessed uprising," this "Islamic Awakening," mocking the "Sahwa," of Saudi Arabia, which used the same words. The Saudi jihadi movement rose from the Sahwa. U.S. ships patrolled the sea lanes. U.S. forces were in Djibouti. U.S. planes refueled Saudi and UAE planes in the air against Yemen.

I returned to New York. There was a packet from the National Counterterrorism Center, inviting former hostages and the families of those who were killed, to Washington to discuss the new U.S. Hostage policy, the result, in part, of phone calls we received and the conversations we had.

In June we met at the National Counterterrorism Center. Lisa Monaco, chief counterterrorism advisor to President Obama, stood as the families whose children were murdered, emotionally, painfully, politely, poured their hearts out, angry that the government wouldn't help them. She said there were Americans being held hostage mostly in Latin America. The Haqqanis were holding five people. I didn't know this. The next day we met at the White House with President Obama and Vice President Biden. I told officials that I had met with the Haqqanis.

The Scion

Pakistan

It was spring, 2017. Osman, in a tight blue suit, was holding a long cigarette. Two days ago, he asked if I would call Walt Monroe, who, according to the news, worked for MI6. I called him. He said the ISI had taken Ibrahim into custody. The Haqqanis wanted Anas back and would kidnap anyone, especially an American, to help them. Had I been in contact with his son? I said yes. I wondered why Ibrahim was under arrest, why Walt wanted to know about John, and how Osman knew Walt.

The ambassador came down the hallway, in a bright-colored sari, attractive, with two men behind her. Osman stood and pushed his cigarette into an ashtray. He said I had been kidnapped by the Taliban. She was horrified. She told one of her aides, in a tweed jacket, to buy my book. We talked for a few minutes, and she left. I would get a visa. I asked Osman for an application. He said to go online. I told officials in Washington that I was going to return to see the Haqqanis. They were classified as a terrorist organization. If they kidnapped me, it would put pressure on the government to negotiate and this would get in the way of other initiatives. Pakistan or the Haqqanis could be luring me into a trap.

In 2012 the Haqqanis kidnapped Caitlan Coleman, and Joshua Boyle, her Canadian husband. They had three children, born in captivity. In 2016, they kidnapped Kevin King, an American, and Timothy Weeks, an Australian, instructors at the American University of Kabul.

I flew to Islamabad, and went to the Serena Hotel, a modern Mogul palace. South Asian music played in the background. My phone rang, and I went out by the pool, a cerulean blue in the evening light. John's voice was deeper than two years ago. Where was I? I told him. Was Fatima with me? I hadn't seen her yet. She was going to call him, then me and we would all meet tomorrow. Whatever time and place we agreed upon, he would be there. I called her. She had called John. It wasn't him. His voice had changed if it was even him. Maybe she was right to be worried. She would call John in the morning. I went swimming to break my jetlag. Fatima called

again and said she would not go. It was someone else on the phone. She
knew his voice. They'd talked on the phone enough in the last two years. I
brought her in to translate. She told him, whoever it was, that he sounded
completely different. Her head was going *bing bing bing*. She would not
meet him for coffee. There were ambushes here all the time. He said he
would meet the next day, but then cancelled before they could pick a place.
Why? So many people before they were to leave the country, committed
suicide. Visitors were murdered and the papers called it suicide. John was
very comfortable with her. They had met three or four times. Now that I was
here why hadn't he contacted her? Getting me to the airport would be dicey.
She couldn't think of leaving. She had to take care of her father.

She called the next morning. She was going to arrange a place to meet,
just in case. She called at noon. She found a place and talked to John. She
called an hour later. She and Hafiz were waiting outside. She was only going
part way. Hafiz stopped at a shopping center. She got out of the car, and I
felt alone, nervous, and freer. We drove slowly down a leafy empty street
with high compounds on both sides. There was no one visible. We stopped
at an iron gate. On one side a man was raking leaves and putting them in a
barrel. Another man opened the gate, and we entered a courtyard. Two
teenagers studying a phone looked up. A man in jeans, and a starched white
shirt, and long black hair, took my hand in his. A lean man, with short hair, a
moustache, in shalwar kameez, and a sport coat, the ISI uniform, sat in a
chair with a glass of tea, looking down. He was my guard. A thin man in his
30s took me down a hall and to a room. I sat in a sagging sofa and put my
papers on a coffee table. He returned with a bottle of mineral water and
glasses. Hafiz came in and said he would be outside. He gave me his phone
number. The thin man returned and said my friends were here.

John was getting out of a small sedan and came around smiling. Ibrahim
and I hugged one another gently. We followed the thin man inside. Father
and son sat across from me. Ibrahim saw that I was nervous. "Don't worry
about anything," he said warmly. "You helped us during the Soviet war. If
the whole world is your enemy, you are not my enemy. If you have no
friends in the world, you can always come and stay with us. You are our
friend." I felt a wave of relief flow through me. I had come back to talk
about my book, to see if they found out who kidnapped me, and why, and to
talk about the hostages.

Did Jalaluddin study in Kabul? Were they always on their own?

Their friend Maulvi Habib Rahman, and Qazi Hussein Ahmed, introduced them to General Babar in Pakistan. Rahman was his teacher in Kabul. Ibrahim and Jalaluddin met Rabbani and the others there.[610] They were never there with Hekmatyar. I talked about my meetings in Washington. I learned that they wanted to exchange their hostages for Anas and Khalid. The Americans and the Taliban both cared about their hostages, Ibrahim replied. Both sides talked with one another. The Haqqanis, by holding Bowe Bergdahl, had negotiated, through Qatar, with the United States. It was the first time that the U.S. recognized the Taliban. They agreed to exchange the soldier for five men from Guantanamo. Again, I asked how they captured him. Mullah Sangeen captured him and gave him to Sirajuddin, who informed the Emirates of Islamic Afghanistan. They wanted to exchange him for the prisoners. He was detained for four years. The leaders told Sangeen to treat him better than his own family. He kept him in his own house. There were only women and children there. He escaped once, at lunch, and hid in a tree for three days. The Emirates of Islamic Afghanistan informed the U.S. that he was in custody. The people who had him took money three times for three videos.

Publicly, the U.S. did not pay ransoms,[611] although the George W. Bush administration did for two American missionaries taken in the Philippines.[612] Lt. Col. Jason Amerine, a decorated Green Beret, tasked by the Pentagon to "think outside of the box," told a few of us sitting at a table in a hotel in Washington in 2015, of his efforts to try to find a way to free Bergdahl.[613] He was very impressed with Haqqani's counter-intelligence network.

Again, how did they capture Bergdahl? The soldiers were walking 20 meters apart in single file. They were in Paktika Province. The Taliban were waiting. He was walking in the front, and they grabbed him and put a blanket over him and took him up into the mountains. Before he said

---

[610] Burhanuddin Rabbani, Tajik, former President of Afghanistan 1992-2001

[611] "Does the U.S. No-Concessions Policy Deter Kidnappings of Americans?" *Rand*

[612] Gracia Burnham, "*In the Presence of My Enemies*," (Carol Stream: Tyndale Momentum, 2010).

[613] Jennifer Griffin and Lucas Tomlinson, "Green Beret: I Was Punished for Revealing Hostage Recovery Problems," *Military.com* 31 Oct. 2017

Bergdahl was behind everyone. Jalaluddin, he said again, never wanted to become a leader, nor did he want to be one today. The sons made the decisions, Monroe said, but they would inform their father. If so Jalaluddin knew about the suicide bombings.

If, in their religion, someone wanted to become a leader, this desire was the curse of God. At the end of the Najibullah Communist regime, NATO and the whole world asked Jalaluddin to become leader of Afghanistan, and he said no. Without a leader, your jihad was nothing. You could not go up into the mountain alone. There were clashes starting. Jalaluddin went again to Yunus Khalis and said he was going to do jihad and Khalis had to be emir. Until he died Maulvi Khalis would be his leader. Jalaluddin was the most famous and most active of the Mujahideen leaders, but he was never on his own. They had no choice but to fight.

What about the Arabs? When the others came to help them with the passion they brought to fight for Allah, they—the Mujahideen—could not help but respect them and to welcome them. The foreigners wanted to be in the front lines, to be martyred, the same as Jalaluddin who never wanted to sit in Peshawar. He was never interested in politics. Every party leader wanted to be in touch with him because he was always up in the mountains fighting. Russia and then America created this fear of him. The Americans hid their own thoughts. They, the Haqqanis, only want sharia for Afghanistan. The Americans had, for their own, unknown, reasons, created this image of the power of the Haqqanis.

Abdul Rahim, the Mujahideen spokesmen, ambassador to the U.S., and President Ghani's first choice for vice president, said we would never find Mullah Omar. Maybe we raised Haqqani so high to create another leader. Fatima said John's mother didn't like it that he went out into the city. She was afraid and wanted him to stay at home. He was her youngest son.

The relationship at the time between the Arabs and them was good, as it was today, Ibrahim continued. After the American invasion the foreigners came again, for jihad, to help them. After the U.S. fought in Iraq, Syria and then Bosnia, jihad became necessary there. NATO fought on behalf of Muslims in Bosnia and Herzegovina, I added.[614] "Most foreigners started

---

[614] Bosnia and Herzegovina were part of Yugoslavia, with a majority Muslim and large Orthodox Christian (Serbian) and small Catholic (Croatian) population. It

fighting in Tajikistan, Uzbekistan, all along the northern Afghan border," Ibrahim replied. Then, after Bosnia, Pakistan decided to help. Al-Medini said it sent men to fight there.

Did they feel a desire to take jihad abroad? They never wanted to go to another country. They never sent anyone anywhere else. When the American war started it was necessary to fight jihad here. They started then to build madrasas. Even when Hekmatyar and Massoud were fighting over Kabul they, the Haqqanis, only wanted peace. The two former students, in their lust for power, what Ibrahim called "the curse of God," destroyed part of Kabul. Pakistan supplied the rockets that Hekmatyar, called "the Butcher of Kabul," rained on the city.

"Prime Minister Zulfikar Ali Bhutto told me that the Durand Line Agreement was expiring in 1993, so Afghanistan had to be destabilized because Afghanistan will demand its territories from the Durand Line to the Indus River," General Babar told a Pakistani journalist.[615] Babar told me it was why he created the Afghan cell, and the Mujahideen. He told the journalist that he invited Hekmatyar, Massoud, Rabbani and other "religious youngsters" to Pakistan. He met them at Bala Hisar, the fort, built by Babur, in 1516. Her gave them money and 3.03 rifles. "Together they started to burn Afghanistan and destabilize Afghanistan so much that the Soviet Union burned it more. Now, Afghanistan would never have the power to demand the removal of the Durand Line. This was the service that he performed for Pakistan."

General Babar died in 2011. In February 2017, Hekmatyar walked, after over 20 years in Pakistan, with President Ghani and other leaders to a welcoming ceremony in Kabul.[616] He signed a peace agreement, and spoke to the large audience, this Trojan horse.

They brought maulvis together, under great strain, to talk peace, but to no avail, said Ibrahim.

Massoud tried to kill Jalaluddin three or four times. He worked with the French and the Russians.

---

broke up June 25, 1991. The Soviet Union fell on December 26, and they declared independence.
[615] Mashal Khan Takka, "The Five Evils Who Destroyed Afghanistan," *Voice Times* 7 Oct. 2016
[616] "Afghan Warlord Hekmatyar Returns to Kabul After Peace Deal," *BBC News* 4 May 2017

Jalaluddin was the biggest wall for Massoud. He wanted to move south and was using Haji Qadir, and Hazrat Ali, another commander, to do this, against Pakistan, and Jalaluddin was stopping them. Din Mohammad said his brother, Qadir, joined Massoud. He couldn't tell his brother what to do.

After four and a half hours, Ibrahim apologized and said he had to go. I said a man had come to me about an American agent who disappeared in Iran in 2007. His family believed that he was in Pakistan. His name was Robert Levinson. Did they know of him? Ibrahim looked at me blankly.

I walked him and John to their car. I didn't see anyone. We gently hugged one another. As they drove away, he turned and waved goodbye.

For two weeks I waited in the Serena, trapped in a golden cage. Once it was easy to walk in the streets, but now I never saw a foreigner walking here. A man in a suit stood at a podium by each elevator bank. They were like the women standing at a podium on each floor at the Hotel Metropole in Leningrad, today St. Petersburg, watching us, there to compete in the U.S. vs. Russia Track and Field meet in the Cold War.

I called the Haqqanis every day. They called back, but they couldn't see me. My visa would soon expire. On May 31, a truck blew up near the German embassy in Kabul killing over 150 people and wounding 413, the worst suicide bombing in Afghanistan, the worst since October 23, 1983, when Hezbollah detonated its bombs at the U.S. Marine Corps barracks in Beirut killing 241 Marines and sailors, the worst Marine Corps toll since Iwo Jima in 1945. Another truck detonated at the French army barracks killing 58 paratroopers.[617]

The next day, John called. They had been away and were back. His father was busy and couldn't make it. I didn't want to see them, but I had work to do. The evening was balmy. Fatima called. John called and had come to town to see me before I left. They picked a spot where they had met before. She drove through the city, crowded with traffic. I wondered if we were being followed. The café, with waiters in black shirts and jeans, played western music. John called, where were we? He was in a different café. We drove to a shopping enclave, walked up stairs, past a guard in black boots, and with a rifle. John was standing, in a white shirt, khakis, a small beard now. We sat at his table by a window.

---

[617] "1983 Beirut Barracks Bombings," *Encyclopædia Britannica*

He apologized that his father was unable to meet. We ordered green tea. I asked if he had any information on who was behind my kidnapping. He took all the information I gave them and passed it on. It was so long ago, and people were not using their real names and it was hard to find them, but they were looking. No group, I believed now, after my time in the Middle East, operated alone. John was at home, with people his age and older talking over the music, eating, drinking tea, and soft drinks. A man, in his 30s, in shalwar kameez interrupted us, and talked to John. He excused himself and they went to another table. The man introduced him to a woman, in a dress, who looked western. They shook hands and the three of them talked. John returned.

He was afraid of that. He was sorry. He didn't want to be recognized.

They were eight feet away. Fatima asked if he was married. Maybe this summer he would get married, he smiled sheepishly. He didn't want to, before. He'd lived many lives—prison, war, that life—he pointed in the distance, meaning his family—this life, meaning the café. His family was pressuring him. Why was he spending time with those people? He was torn, I felt, between the demands of his family, and the lure, like that of most young men, of freedom. Why did the U.S. not want to do anything about an exchange? They were ready. Why did I come all this way? I came for my book, and to try to resolve the hostage problem. I didn't work for the government. It was loud and we leaned close as we talked.

Daniel Pearl, the first American journalist kidnapped in Pakistan after 9/11 was killed in 2002 in Karachi by al-Qaeda. I was next, but the Taliban released me. Since then, the U.S. took its time, knowing, I felt, that they would not kill a U.S. hostage. He nodded. The Americans were very lackadaisical. They sent demands, but they were not in any rush. The Obama administration wanted to do something to resolve this, but this new administration was not trying. Things needed to happen quickly. Things were getting hotter and hotter every day. I was impressed that he knew the word lackadaisical. By meeting with us alone, he was showing that he was rising in his family. I kept thinking about the suicide attack. John said the American and Canadian family and the American and Australian professors were being treated well. They wanted them to go back to their homes, the children especially. They felt for them. The U.S. was not being sincere with the families. They were willing to do an exchange. It wasn't about money.

Fatima brought up what his father said that I was their friend always, the only foreigner who could get to them anytime I wanted to. John nodded. It was true. She asked about Paul Overby, an American writer. I remembered him, I thought, a smiling, soft-spoken fellow. He returned to Kabul in 2014 and took a bus to Khost to cross the border to interview Sirajuddin. He disappeared. John said they never had him. I knew his wife and wanted to solve this mystery.

John returned to Anas. There would be no deal without his release. The Afghan government was a department of the U.S. and would do what the U.S. said. The U.S. was trying to pressure them. They did not do it, the attack in Kabul, but they were being blamed.

Sometimes Anas called. Jalaluddin wanted his son back, and Sirajuddin wanted his brother home. John didn't like Americans because they played with his head and changed him in prison. He was there for two months and ten days. It was hard. A male and female soldier came every day to interrogate him, although they were good to him. He could decide about the hostages. So many people were trying to get to them, everyone saying they knew someone who knew someone, but it was all ten to fifteen degrees of people away. Only I could get to them directly. People were getting money from governments claiming that they could get to them. If we could come to an agreement, they would release the children. This was a political exchange. The families were innocent civilians.

He talked, as his father had, about the letter that the U.S. gave them saying if any relative wanted to go to Doha to see the men released from Guantanamo, they would be allowed to do this. The U.S. lied and kidnapped their relatives. The U.S. was not straight in its dealings.

Why did they call Sirajuddin the Khalifa? He didn't respond. Right now, their focus was on Afghanistan. They wanted it to be free. The Afghans knew only war. One day maybe, if this war didn't end, it would go to the West. The West liked war. It was the first time that I saw him angry. Every day, technology advanced, just as the way in which they worked changed. If people thought that they were just men who wore turbans, they had moved on. Unless the U.S. ceased its involvement in Afghanistan, it would get worse. What did the U.S. want in Afghanistan?

It wanted peace, democracy and no al-Qaeda. He scoffed. Did we still believe that al-Qaeda was there? He assured me they weren't. I said I had seen al-Qaeda with the Taliban in 2008 in the mountains. Why did the U.S. want democracy? The Afghans didn't want this; they wanted Sharia. They wanted freedom. They wanted their own land for themselves. The U.S. knew that there was no al-Qaeda in Afghanistan. They were not associated with it. They were fighting ISIS. They told me they would, and they were. He returned to the hostages. It was a good way to test one another. The first step was to see if both sides could do this. Why wouldn't the U.S. talk with them? In 2012 it declared them a terrorist organization. He nodded. They wanted the freedom to travel to Dubai to build trust. They would let the grandparents come to see the children, but I had to bring a letter from the U.S. government.

He told his mother that he wanted to go out. The others got upset when he wore Western clothes or spoke English. They asked why he was being like the enemy. Nasiruddin used to leave his laptop and his phone for him. He taught himself how to use them. He liked that laptop. The Media said his uncle oversaw finances, business ventures, and fund-raising in the Middle East.[618] When he was 13 or 14 and was on Yahoo, he created a chat room. He made the rules and said there would be no bad language and they would be respectful to others. Some guy created problems and he forced him off. A girl called and she wanted to be his friend. He was scared. He didn't know how to talk to girls. She said it was fine they could just talk. He fell in love with her, and never saw her. He smiled, embarrassed. She had a boyfriend, and he was a hacker. He found out that she was calling him and said he would come after him and destroy him. He found out that John was a Pathan and said he was a brother. He would spare him. It was the first time that anyone had power over him, and it made him angry, and he was determined to beat him and stop him, and that was why he became a hacker. The other man came and talked to him. He taught himself English. He went to a class twice, but he spoke better English than the teacher, and quit. His father spoke Dari, Pashto, Urdu and Arabic. The Americans were surprised that he spoke English. He would speak to them with a Russian accent and they would get confused. He liked Charlie, a soldier. I reminded him of him. Otherwise, he didn't like Americans. It was Ramadan and he would stay up until Serer, at 3:15 and then to sleep. It was 1:30 a.m. He had to go. I paid,

---

[618] M. Ilyas Khan, "Nasiruddin Haqqani: Who Shot the Militant at the Bakery?" *BBC News* 12 Nov. 2013

over his objections. Outside, there was a line of teenagers and people in their 20s and 30s. They were not those who went to bed early and fought the infidel. We walked down to a landing. He would wait here. He took out a cigarette. We shook hands goodbye.

ISIS

Turkey

I flew to Istanbul. Twenty yards from my hotel, a dozen fit, vigorous men with short hair were clearing the cobblestone enclave and putting up long tables and chairs. My fixer, Engin, said the government was bringing in people from poor sections of the city to serve them Iftar. Recep Erdogan, the populist Islamist President, who wanted to create a neo-Ottoman Empire, was using religious poor, like Nasser, and Mao in his way, to take over this part of Istanbul, of cafes, small restaurants, tattooed men, western music, and women with cigarettes.

On July 10, 2021, Erdogan would lead the prayers in the reconverted Holy Hagia Sophia (Divine Wisdom) Grand Mosque, built by Justinian in 537 A.D. as the Church of Hagia Sophia, the great Cathedral of Constantinople, which became, with the Ottoman conquest in 1453 a mosque, as mosques in Spain built by the Arabs were converted into churches. Erdogan was photographed in 1985 with Hekmatyar, whom he invited to Istanbul. In 2021 he invited the Taliban publicly to a peace conference, without telling them in private, and they refused to come.

Engin drove on busy roadways with aggressive drivers to *Milleyet*, the largest newspaper in Turkey, to meet Bunyamin Aygun, in a black t-shirt, and a shirt with the sleeves rolled up, and black jeans. In November 2013, he crossed into Syria, covering the revolution against Bashir al-Assad, and was kidnapped by ISIS. They killed his fixer, who was with the Free Syrian Army (FSA), deserters from the Syrian army led by former officers, backed by Turkey. He never prayed or went to a mosque. After he was rescued, 40 days later, he still didn't know how to pray,[619] but he knew enough about Islam to know that his captors weren't following Islamic principles. He read the Koran to see if they were following the true Islam, as they called it. In one verse it said to kill your enemies. They took this verse and said they were making jihad. They could kill them, take their women and their possessions.

---

[619] "Held by Is for 40 Days, a Turkish Photographer Tells His Story." *Al*, https://www.al-monitor.com

He saw that in truth you could only kill if someone was making war against you. The Koran said to kill one person was to kill all of humanity. They killed people as if they were mosquitoes. The Koran said they must be just to those they captured, but they burned POWs by putting their heads in ovens. They tied people with electric cables, hanged them from the ceiling, peeled off their skin, hit their arms and legs, and broke their bones, to intimidate them and make them talk.

This was raw Wahhabism, it was the "the Terror,"[620] when "citizens" massacred thousands, beheaded the aristocracy, carried their heads and hearts on a pike, and women cut up their bodies and held up the pieces, like al-Qaeda holding up a boy's hand in Yemen, the Nazis burning humans in ovens, Japanese cannibalism in World War II, Lt. William Calley and his men in Vietnam,[621] Sgt. Robert Bales in Kandahar,[622] al-Qaeda slaughtering Daniel Pearl, ISIS burning to death a Syrian pilot in a cage.

These were shopkeepers, auto mechanics and tire repairmen. They tortured him, but he wouldn't say what they did. They played good cop, bad cop. Every night his guards bound his wrists tightly with plastic handcuffs, which cut him and Uncle, as he called him, a Turk, from Germany, came and loosened them and moved his arms from behind his back to the front and took off his blindfold. It was winter and he brought him hot tea but interrogated him in his own way. Uncle wrote to the prosecuting priest to appeal his execution, who announced that he was an apostate, and had to die. Only, they, of ISIS, were true Muslims. Uncle belonged to the family of jihadists. He made a fortune and decided to devote his life and money to jihad. He went to Afghanistan and joined al-Qaeda, fought for ten years and was captured, imprisoned for six months by the Americans, and released. He was, if this was true, a professional jihadi, for some a Paladin, for Mahjoob, a man of no principles.

Every time they tortured him, after 30 minutes, when he didn't think he could take it much longer, Uncle appeared. He called it "a project," a way for them to soften him up before he gently interrogated him. His appeal had

---

[620] Clery et al. *A Journal of the Terror: Being an Account of the Occurrences in the Temple during the Confinement of Louis XVI.* (Cambridge: Folio Society, Cambridge University Press, 1955), p.22.
[621] "Lt. William Calley Charged for My Lai Massacre," *History.com* 16 Nov. 2009
[622] Sarah Sicard et al, "Army Times, Independent News for Soldiers"

been rejected and Uncle would execute him, honorably, by cutting his throat. He did not want him to die, ignobly, by a firing squad. The next day Uncle was killed in battle. They brought his body to him. He saw the bullet hole in his head. He was a real martyr, they said. You could smell his blood, which smelled like perfume. Aygun had to smell him. Uncle, a deracinated Turk, found a brotherhood and a home. Their jihad moved to Iraq. They cooperated with al-Qaeda, and al-Nusrah. They had differences and the professional jihadis moved to ISIS. They insisted that he join them. They would make him a suicide bomber. There were men from all around the world. They were in the Philippines. He meant the Abu Sayyaf, in honor of Rasul Abdul Sayyaf, in Afghanistan. ISIS was a global jihadi organization backed by some countries: Muslim, Christian, and Jewish, but he wouldn't say who. ISIS became strong because of Assad, directed by a force under his direction. When his forces pulled back, they left their guns and ammunition.

Why didn't they attack Israel, he asked? His antisemitism made me distrust him. When ISIS took Mosul, it became the umbrella organization for people who wanted revenge against the U.S. for invading their lands, for the relatives of soldiers killed, and for Sunni tribesmen who were shunted aside. Each leader had a profession. Uncle was artillery. They made explosives. He was going to be the emir of his territory. He told men on the phone in Turkey that they were creating a good country, come join them. If they lost, they would go underground. They are all over southern Turkey, but al-Qaeda was stronger. It did not kill randomly. ISIS was a cell system, but if al-Baghdadi didn't like something, it wouldn't happen. When ISIS took Mosul, he saw the footage of piles of money from the central bank. They sold oil for three years from Raqqa. Assad bought most of it for his planes, tanks, and buses. The ISIS men idolized bin Laden, one of the richest men in the world, they said, who spent his money on jihad and for poor Muslims. They would accept al-Zawahiri. They asked about his photos in his laptop of the coup in Egypt. He said the Ikhwan came to power through elections, but they did not look to Egypt. Most were from Chechnya. They were quiet, kept separate, covered their hair and faces and stayed out of photographs. They were good fighters, got things done, and were famous as suicide bombers. Most of the Turks were from Germany. There were many Moroccans, many from France, then Belgium and Austria. They read books on how to be a good jihadi. They woke up, prayed, fought, ate, prayed, and slept. Their only connection was with their phones and texting—no singing, no newspapers, no television, no fun.

There were large demonstrations calling for his release, putting pressure on the government. Turkish intelligence, with the FSA, fought for 4 ½ days for him. ISIS didn't know it was a rescue operation. They said they knew they had hostages and said to give them only one, an Israeli agent, and let them execute him, and they could go. They released him.

An ISIS Commander

Ahmad, 25, a soft-spoken Syrian, with a ponytail, in jeans and a white shirt, and I flew to Gaziantep, near the Syrian border and went to a hotel. He called his contact and I rented a conference room, walked around the lobby, looked for separate entrances, and checked the scanner at the front door. It was still Ramadan and the streets were empty. That night we sat at a large blond wood table with black chairs. Ahmad stared at me. He had lived under ISIS, in Aleppo, 60 miles away, before his father sneaked his family away at night to their village. They were Kurds who were fighting ISIS. They came at night shouting *allah-oh-Akbar*, and said there was nothing to be afraid of, and they should stay in their homes. They did whatever ISIS said, praying five times a day. They were all very afraid.

The ISIS man wouldn't do anything here, unless he came with others, I hoped. I hoped he couldn't get a knife or a pistol through the scanner. He could have sympathizers in the hotel. He would come after *Iftar*, and after prayers again in the mosque, and *Tarrawi*, when they read every night for a month one of the 30 chapters of the Koran. This was when the U.S. bombed the Haqqanis, and Jalaluddin, for the first time, felt that he was going to die. It was that night that he told son, Sirajuddin, that he was the Khalifa, his successor.

At 10:00 p.m. Ahmad's phone rang. He answered. He would be here in ten minutes. He went upstairs. At 10:30 he returned, and behind him was a man, in his 30s, about 6"1," slim, in a tight black suit, gray shirt, a trim beard, the lines precise, his hair short on the sides with a combed top, like men in New York. We shook hands and he sat on the side. I sat at the head table, and Ahmad sat between us. I thanked him for agreeing to see us. There would be no cameras, or names. I wanted to learn about his life and to learn from his point of view. His name was Mohammad Sayif, he said quickly. I asked him to start at the beginning. I wanted to know what he wanted to be in life when he was a boy. I wanted to know, but didn't ask, when and how his dreams were destroyed that he would join ISIS. He stared at me, filled with intensity. He wanted to be a lawyer. He loved studying, but he did it to become a policeman. He wanted to do legally what he had been in the army. I didn't know what he meant but didn't dwell on this and later wished I had.

He studied in the university and then went to al-Azhar where he got a graduate degree in Shari'ah. What writers influenced him? He couldn't name one. I mentioned Sayyid Qutb. He knew of him, but it was the Koran more than anything that was his authority. After al-Azhar he returned to Damascus for his final year of studies. He was a *stagière*, a graduate assistant. Syria was a French colony after World War I and he, like Ahmad, studied Arabic and French in school. It was 2011, and he was teaching a class on the beginning of the Ottoman Caliphate. He was trying to describe this time, the beginning of the Islamic world. The professor disagreed and said no, it was a war, and the beginning of the Ottomans. The doctor said to read only what was in the text. They knew better than he did. Mohammad had studied and read the history books, and knew he was wrong. He said, 'no doctor.' The professor called security and six policemen came and took him to prison, what they called the "Palestinian Club." They tortured him for three months. His career was over. He stared at me hard. His father had to pay the equivalent of $260,000 to bribe the guards to get him out. They changed his life in prison.

"A man disagreed with a chemistry teacher, who was a member of the Assad family, and he disappeared," Ahmad added. "They would take you to your aunt's house is what people said."

Syria was a dictatorship. They didn't have the rights to talk, to discuss, to be free, Mohammad said almost softly, in despair as much as in anger. He started working for his father selling cars. Demonstrations were beginning against the regime of Bashir al-Assad. He proposed to his father's sister's daughter, and they got engaged. His fiancé was walking in a demonstration and a sniper shot her in the head. She died immediately. I stopped writing. He stared at me coldly.

What young man wouldn't go to war?

The revolution had started, and his father decided to go to their village, called Ashra. The government had a file on him, and officials asked him to come see them, but he ignored them. It was war now between his family and the state. His clan, the Ashiri, numbered about 6,700 and from them his father formed a militia of 600 men, and became the leader. Every family in Syria was expected to have a gun. In August, they attacked and surrounded an old tobacco factory which the army was using. They told the soldiers that they would let them go but they had to leave their weapons, which were

1980s vintage, behind. If they didn't, they would die. The soldiers signed everything over to them and left. He was in the militia he said proudly, his eyes wide, staring. He was getting revenge. Before, he was a quiet, peaceful person. They were a kind family, but the government had pushed their backs to the wall. They saw how they could set up check points and through them control a road. Soon, they secured it for 50 kilometers from their village to Aleppo. He spoke in sharp, staccato sentences. His phone rang five or six times. He glanced at it, like Abdul Latif, and continued. The government took all his rights, and so he fought them. If they, as Syrians, were not allowed to talk, they would assert their rights.

This was six years ago. He was 22. In 2012 the revolution grew. Other militias formed and became active. Pressure on Assad increased. Officers and soldiers were deserting. Assad turned to Iran for help and it, and its proxy, Hezbollah, entered the war and it went from becoming one of the people against the government to a war between Sunni and Shia. Iran, too, was getting its revenge, against America. He again pointed out that he and his family didn't start this war. They wanted their rights and to be equal men among others.

I heard this in every Arab country, young men deprived of opportunities, kept down by men in power, losing hope, and in anger they fought back, using Islam to give them strength, as it gave the Mujahideen, the Taliban, and the Haqqanis. They didn't want these outsiders, Iran and Hezbollah, here, and so they fought them. But their family militia wasn't enough. They were upset at the Shia drinking alcohol in mosques and denigrating the companions of the Prophet. Did he mean the Salafis? He nodded, the pious ones, their founding fathers. He and his family, in need of greater strength, created *Ketab-al-le-Jalaini-al-Islami*. "To fight against what is wrong." The complexion of the revolution was changing and becoming a religious war. Soldiers from Menagh, an air force base near Aleppo, were firing artillery and mortars on their positions. They had to neutralize them. The base was in a wide plain, but they surrounded it. It was dangerous.

They were exposed and couldn't attack without heavy weapons. In 2013, his father met with the leaders of *al-Nusrah*,[623] and *al-Hawarj*, those of the Black Flag, to ask for their help.

A waiter came and asked if we wanted anything. We ordered coffee and

---

[623] Al-Qaeda

Mohammad drank his quickly. I glanced at his shining black patent leather shoes, his bare ankles, his suit, and perfectly combed hair. He looked too hip, too urban, to be a fighter. Only his large marron ring gave him away, the sign of a jihadi. He was now a full-time guerrilla fighter. There were men in his family who were high-ranking officers in Assad's army, and they taught him how to fight. They laid siege to the air base for four months. Men of the Black Flag joined them. Their goal was to get the soldiers to flee, and to take their weapons. They interrogated 350 soldiers and told them to go home to their families. They interrogated their senior officers, nothing personal, only to find out where they were hiding their weapons. They had a depot underneath the runway. On June 8, 2013, his family and the foreign fighters, hardened, well- trained men, attacked the base, and got the weapons. They were now one with the fundamentalists.

Their next goal was to take Kuweirez Air Force Base, near Aleppo, to protect themselves, and the civilians now under their control. They got ammunition from Turkey and with their new weapons took the base. Turkey, maybe because they were getting too powerful, stopped supplying them, and they returned to protecting their villages. He, and his group of 200 men, all from his family, left their militia and contacted other jihadi groups, mainly because they had more modern weapons. His father had ties to the Turkish government, which was happy that they were attacking Syrian forces. They joined al-Hawar. They were more religious and taught them about Sharia and fiqh and other religious subjects and he felt that he was now living a fuller life. He felt stronger. Everyone was Syrian. Their trainers were Algerians, Chechens, and Iraqis, especially Chechens. They taught them how to be fit, how to fire their weapons, even tanks. He felt like he was living with perfect brothers, fighting and living the right life. By the end of 2013 other jihadi groups heard about them. The Free Syrian Army started to join them. More soldiers joined. They began to call themselves the Islamic State in Iraq and Shams (ISIS).

Was their leader al-Baghdadi? They didn't know him, but they were ordered to choose him as their leader. Of their original group of 200 men, 13 had been killed, 17 wounded, and 170 were strong. They wanted to fight al-Assad. They were all educated men. They knew what they wanted. Did they feel a tie to other groups beyond Syria, like the Taliban, and al-Qaeda? They did this for Islam. It was their conviction that they were fighting for Islam, like the Mujahideen who fought the Russians in Afghanistan, like the Taliban who were fighting the Americans. They were the same, like al-Qaeda, all fighting under the same flag. After their successes over the next two months, they began to create a sharia legal system, a police department to remove other jihadi groups, and to become bigger. They were getting rid of the *al-murtaddin*.[624] They said they could join them or stay in their houses, but they would take their weapons. His family learned about this and was happy. They were still fighting and protecting themselves, and they were not harming civilians.

He became a policeman but asked for a new mission. On May 5, 2015, they got their orders, to attack Syrian forces in Asfiri. They were 170 men with 200 behind them. They had MR15s and M16s from Iraq. Only 25 of them survived. He was shot in the leg. His father, with his connections in the Turkish military, sent him to Ankara for treatment. He showed me a photograph of an MR15 and said during this battle that their weapons didn't work, but later they did when they were home. They discovered that there was a chip inside controlled by a computer. They were now afraid of the men who sent them on this mission. They felt even more like a brotherhood, under siege sometimes, paranoid, separate from everyone around them, and more determined than ever. When they liberated Syria, they would go to Iraq and fight for Islam there. He would go anywhere for Islam. He was like the Taliban I met in the mountains who said they would go anywhere, even Azerbaijan.

He knew not to look to or even care about the leaders of Islam today, especially those who became famous Al-Zawahiri, Zarqawi or al-Baghdadi, men who sought to lead and be in the limelight. The true leader was in the shadows and should be in the shadows. He who sought to be the leader, by definition, could not be the leader. Did he know of Jalaluddin Haqqani? "Yes," he replied, like him. He knew him as a great jihadi leader, a person who didn't seek to be the leader. It was the ideology which counted, not the people.

This, I finally saw, as Ibrahim said, was Jalaluddin's power. It was his example. This was the Haqqani Network in the greater Middle East.

They were all fighting for Islam, not for personal glory. They of the Islamic State were following the Koran, not al-Baghdadi. Mohammad was a normal person. They did not follow him, but only what they needed, which

---

[624] apostates

was Islam. The *Kalimah* (The Word)—"There is no god but God, and Mohammad is the Apostle of God"— was their proclamation of faith. Mohammad was not their leader, but God's messenger. It was hard now. He was wounded and couldn't fight. He strode in vigorously and he sat straight, and seemed healthy and strong, but they had been defeated and had to create a new force. They were underground now and were planning the future. There were ISIS men all over southern Turkey. The government didn't know how many. It was a crime to talk to an ISIS fighter.

All human beings were brothers and Islam was a religion of love, said Mohammad. There was no difference among Sunni, Shia, Christian, and Jew.

We were all brothers we were all one. God sent humans to his earth, not to America or Iraq, not to a single country. He was trying to make everyone understand this. They were not terrorists. They didn't think about Islam all in one place, but an Islam that ruled over all other religions while respecting all of them. They felt that they and Jalaluddin Haqqani, for example, were the same. This was Islam.

It was nearly 1:30 in the morning. We had been talking for almost three hours. His eyes looked tired. He admitted that he was. He asked if he could go. He had to keep his head down in Turkey. He had fasted, eaten Iftar, and then gone to the mosque before coming here. We shook hands firmly. He smiled for the first time. We would talk again. He left as quickly as he came. The next morning Ahmad and I sat in Tahmis Kahvesi, a café from 1635, drinking tea. Fans purred overhead. The Haqqani Network stretched, through the example set by Jalaluddin, from Pakistan to Yemen to Syria to Turkey. His son, Sirajuddin, and his nephew John wanted Sharia.

Jamal Khashoggi said young men in the Middle East had no one to look up to. Mohammad, the ISIS commander, looked up to Jalaluddin, so did Tariq al-Fadhli. Ali al-Kurdi wanted to protect him. The U.S. tried to kill him, and his family, but it couldn't kill his message. He fought for his faith, and he never gave in.

We stood in line at the airport. The ticket agent said Ahmad, because he was carrying a Syrian passport, could not board the plane. I said we flew here from Istanbul. He and his family lived there. The agent wouldn't budge. Ahmad would straighten this out. He asked for my passport.

Ten minutes later he came over. Could I come with him? I wore a khaki suit, no tie, had gray hair and an unkempt beard. I joined Ahmad with two men in civilian clothes, one holding our passports. A soldier, with a rifle, and a pistol, came and stood next to me. They didn't like all the stamps in my passport and all the places I'd been. Why did I use that passport? It was against the law to talk with a fundamentalist, Ahmed reminded me. Even though Turkey, I thought, brought in men on flights from Libya and Yemen so they could fight in Syria. "Why didn't I have another passport?" he asked plaintively. They would not let him get on the plane. He would have to take a bus, a 16-hour ride, back. One of the men spoke to him. They wanted to know if I had ever been to Europe. "A hundred times," I said glibly. A man gave me my passport. "You, no problem," he said. My picture showed me with short dark hair in a suit and tie. I met last night with an ISIS commander. Ahmad was no longer a young man in a cafe telling me stories. He was older now, and afraid. I told him to take the first bus, and I would see him in the morning. Did he need money? He said no. I smiled politely at the agent. He gave me a hard look. I got a small refund on Ahmad's ticket, went back to the check-in line and the woman was friendly, checked me in and pointed toward the gate. I stood in line. A woman took my passport and slowly turned the pages talking in Turkish. I responded in English. She looked at me hard. Finally, she returned my passport, and I passed through the scanner. I had to leave this country as soon as possible.

Back in the U.S., I met with people on the National Security Council. I called Jim Coleman, Caitlan's father and said the Haqqanis would allow them to see their grandchildren. He called back a few days later to say that he and his wife wanted to go see them. I sent a message to the Haqqanis. They were ready, but the government felt that I was interfering. That October, the U.S. said, according to newspapers, a drone picked up unclear images of a woman with small children in a militant camp in the Tribal Areas of Pakistan. Soon thereafter a car was seen taking them away. The U.S. said it thought that the images were of Caitlan Coleman and her children. The U.S. ambassador told the Pakistani government if it did not resolve this kidnapping then the U.S. would. There was a SEAL team standing by. Newspapers said the Pakistani army confronted the kidnappers, there was a shootout, and the Boyle-Coleman family was released.[625]

---

[625] Adam Goldman and Eric Schmitt, "Navy Seals Were Ready If Pakistan Failed to Free Family Held as Hostages," *New York Times* 17 Oct. 2017

No guard would allow a hostage to go outside with a drone overhead, nor would the Pakistani army fight the Haqqanis. I told the acting hostage czar that I didn't believe a word of the story. She was silent. I had breakfast with an FBI agent in Washington. There was no way they were going to allow the family to go to Pakistan. That fall, John went to Oslo to meet with the U.S. to talk about other hostages. He called and said there was an older American there. The Americans called him Mr. Ambassador. He, and others, asked him to release the hostages. They would not give anything in return. It was of waste of time. I passed this message to the government. An official said to tell the Haqqanis that they had not responded to the U.S. request. I told John.

The U.S. arranged another meeting in Oslo. John called again. The last time they went for walks in the woods and the ambassador asked why couldn't they release the hostages as a goodwill gesture? He threw the travel documents away. I relayed this message. The official said there was a lot going on.

In September 2018, the Taliban announced that Jalaluddin died. John sent a note saying he died in Paktika Province. I knew that he couldn't tell me truth. They weren't officially in Pakistan. I was sad that I never saw Jalaluddin again. I would remember him as he was when I was young. Ibrahim had assured me that they were Hanafi, as their friends did, yet they, to me, were part Wahhabi now also, killing, with suicide bombers, innocent Afghan men, women, and children, like the Wahhabis did in Arabia and the Levant. The U.S. no longer supplied them with weapons with which to fight the Soviets. Jalaluddin, one of my guides told me, called American soldiers "Crusaders," what the Arabs called the Europeans who fought them over Jerusalem. In 1829, the Plymouth Brethren sent missionaries from London to Baghdad. After 9/11, the U.S. bombed there. Din Mohammad told me that in the first Gulf War, Saudi Arabia asked Yunus Khalis to send the Mujahideen to help them. He sent 300 men, who, he said, helped save American soldiers, including women, who were surrounded by Saddam Hussein's army. I didn't know this.

In 2003, American Christians, completely political now, overwhelmingly supported the U.S invasion of Iraq. Sirajuddin was determined, like his grandfather who defeated the British, like his father who defeated the Russians, to defeat the Americans. This had become, indeed, a religious war. Sirajuddin, with a bounty on his head, was military commander of the Taliban, and the Khalifa of the Haqqani Network.

The Power of the Tribe

On October 2, Jamal Khashoggi was murdered at the Saudi Arabian consulate in Istanbul.

In November, I met in Washington with an ambassador and part of the team involved in the peace talks, at the State Department. The ambassador was frustrated that the CIA didn't know anything about the Haqqanis and wanted to know what I could tell them. It was the tribal warfare in Washington that Prince Turki talked about. I hesitated. I didn't work for the government. I didn't ask to meet just to give information but felt that I could help in a small way. I had access to the Haqqanis and no other foreigner did. I couldn't betray them. I was trapped in the middle.

They didn't like private citizens running around trying to free hostages, said the ambassador. I knew Paul Overby, I replied. The room was silent. It had been nearly five years since he disappeared. I gave the team some information. The ambassador sent a note to Zalmay Khalilzad, the head of the U.S. delegation at the peace talks. I had contacted him before. In April 2019, I told the ambassador's assistant that I was going to return to Afghanistan. It was arranged for me to meet with others at State. I flew to London and met with Yassar Siri. He agreed that the Islamic Group killed Sadat. He didn't trust the Islamic State. Al-Baghadid was too interested in money and power. Only Jalaluddin did not seek these things. He followed the Koran. Siri wanted an Islamic revolution in Eygpt, like that in Iran.

Hassan Noman, the head of the Socialist Party in Yemen was now the ambassador to London. He said no Saudi could have gone to Afghanistan to fight without the permission of Prince Turki. King Abdullah and President Hadi of Yemen, living in Riyadh, let al-Houthi attack and humiliate Ali Abdullah Salah and Islah. Iran was not involved. The UAE was using al-Qaeda to fight the Houthis.

The main question was what kind of state did the Yemeni people want? How do they stabilize the country? There were so many religious factions. He was the speaker of the House in Parliament and they couldn't even agree on one item of Sharia. Each man worships God in his own way. When you talk about a civil state they look upon you as a kaffir. China, Russia and Iran are all there, creating turmoil. Saudi Arabia is trying to counter Iran.

Abdullah Anas and I met in our same hotel restaurant next to the motorcycle repair shop. I mentioned that I had seen Yassar Siri. He got upset. They found a letter in the bag of the two Tunisians who killed Massoud in 2001 which said they were journalists there on behalf of the Arab News. Siri signed the letter. Anas called him and asked why. Siri said the Tunisians had come to him and he signed it hoping to sell the interview to television stations and he could make money. He realized that Siri had been duped, but he didn't seem convinced. His great friend, Ahmed Shah Massoud, was dead, "Siri is fighting for power," he said shaking his head. Anas, once head of foreign relations for the Islamic Salvation Front, in Algeria, once knew power.

Islamabad
May 2019

My car approached the compound. John, standing outside, wore a red and white checked kefiyyeh tied in the back, like an Arab jihadi. I never saw him dress like this and he made me nervous. We shook hands. Ibrahim got out of the back seat of a car, and we gently hugged one another. He held me closely. He felt it in his heart, he said. A few men watched us. One, with a narrow beard, led us inside a house to a room. John put our phones under two pillows on a bed. This, too, was new.

We sat facing one another. I said I met with officials at the State Department, then flew to Kabul and met Rob D'Imaco, head of the FBI at the embassy, and a man named Ted, holding some papers for me to sign freeing the government of any responsibility should I get kidnapped. I signed them and Ted sighed in relief. Rob and I talked and he told me about his work infiltrating the Mafia in Miami. He told me that they had just transferred Anas to another prison and asked me to tell the Haqqanis that they were treating him well. He gave me a code name and told me to stay in close contact. Ted walked me to the front gate and we talked for a while. He told me to stay in close contact with Rob, and to report back to him.

I went to see Mangal, the tribal chief. I felt that the Haqqanis sometimes lied to me, and that they had to, to protect themselves. I needed someone, close to them, who could answer questions I had. He gave me the name of Sirajuddin's best friend and told him that he could tell me everything. I will call him Abdullah.

I summarized some of this for Ibrahim. As Fatima and John translated, he smiled, and raised his finger. Yes, he knew this. He was in contact with Anas; the U.S. transferred him to another prison. He was indirectly in contact with Ted. When he was in prison at Bagram Air base, Ted came to see him to talk about peace. When he got out in 2004 Ted came again, along with his friends, to talk about peace. I listened. After I signed the papers, Ted walked me to the embassy gate and told me to stay in contact with Rob. I wondered if this was the same Ted.

In 2006, Ibrahim continued, Ted again contacted him, and he invited him here. But Ted and his friends wanted to meet in Dubai. They met there. He brought Shams, whose father had been with Jalaluddin as his translator. Ted asked what they wanted. Ibrahim was clear with him. They never wanted the Russians in Afghanistan and they never wanted the Americans there, and they wanted Sharia. He and Ted held detailed talks in Dubai. The problem was the foreigners on their land. After the Americans left, maybe they would invite some back as quests, but all foreigners had to leave. They told Ted and his friends to take this to the highest level in the U.S. government. If they had a different offer from what they wanted, they needn't bother to get in touch. Ibrahim and his party took this information to General Pasha, head of the ISI, and asked if Pakistan could help them.[626]

Pasha talked to his leadership, and they agreed with this view. Ibrahim asked if Pakistan could be the go-between. Did it have enough strength? Pasha came back and said yes. This was in 2006 and 20007. Obama came to power in 2008 and they met in Dubai with three of his people: a political person, a man from the Defense Department, and someone from the CIA. Ibrahim, a Taliban translator, General Pasha, and an ISI man, were there. Ibrahim talked with Obama on a video call into the Oval Office. They had many exchanges with the Obama administration. "They were involving me," he said, "but then," he smiled, Trump came in and everything went cold.

Then Trump's people reached out to Ted and brought him in. Ted got in touch with Shams, who got in touch with them. Ibrahim said they wanted to deal with the hostages, and they wanted the same thing that they told the Obama people. The Trump people didn't understand, and he had to clarify that Afghanistan was an independent country and its own people would decide its fate, and no one else. Trump's people said they wanted to meet again. Ibrahim said they would meet them in any third country. Ibrahim and Shams contacted the Norwegian ambassador to Kabul. Then Ibrahim went to Pakistani officials and they arranged a meeting in Oslo to discuss hostages, and peace. This was in 2017. They talked with other Afghans. It was the same time that I had come to them again. After this, John kept me informed. He brought a copy of the letter which the U.S. gave them which said any member of the families of those released from Guantanamo, in exchange for the U.S. soldier (Bowe Bergdahl), could pass back and forth freely through Dubai.

---

[626] The Inter-Service Intelligence Directorate

Then the CIA kidnapped Anas, his nephew. "How could you do this?" he asked me again. "The CIA reneged on its commitment." Again, I pondered that Ibrahim, once a young man in the mountains, said he negotiated directly into the Oval Office.

The policy of the Trump Administration would sink. Obama's policies were working and Trump's policies were ruining everything. They had two or three meetings in Oslo, but the head of the ISI got upset because they were at a high level and Pakistan said it wanted its people to be there. The U.S. said no, and they had to pull out. The U.S. kept inviting them to Oslo and Pakistan said it wanted to be involved and came to their compound and took six of their people, and their passports. He sat there, thinking about this.

John kept me informed of their meetings in Oslo, of walks in a forest, where the old man, as he described him, the Ambassador, kept asking, why, as a humanitarian gesture, they didn't release the hostages. The U.S. invited him to come again. He tore up the travel documents. It was a waste of time. The U.S. was playing with them. When he was in prison in Bagram in 2002, Ibrahim said, the U.S. asked who he knew in the U.S. He said three people: Charlie Wilson, Charles Schnabel,[627] and me. Ted couldn't come to Pakistan, and Ibrahim couldn't go visit him. Only I had slipped between the cracks. I felt that the ISI knew. The CIA wanted him to be able to travel. Pakistan said no. It refused to allow them to meet separately with a U.S. delegation. Pakistan had raided their house twice now, once with women there. It was humiliating. Again, he was silent. After the U.S. invasion in October 2001, when all they wanted was peace, the U.S. began to kill them, and finally they moved their daughters to the Middle East, away from the American bombs, to try to preserve their future as a family. Twice he told me this. Plus, Pakistan was showing them that the Haqqanis worked for Pakistan. They were trapped, but they were on their land, as the Saudis were in the Hijaz, as al-Mahdi was in Sudan, as Abu Samrah was in Egypt, as the tribes of Yemen were. Pakistan wanted to keep them hidden behind a curtain, Ibrahim said. He couldn't pick up and move his family to another country. They were a separate front from the Taliban. He had never had anyone translate properly so that his thoughts came across clearly. They couldn't talk on the phone. In 40 years, he had never been able to speak freely. His only concern was his country and his family. For the first time I

---

[627] Chief aide to Congressman Charlie Wilson

saw sadness in him. "It was the cost of the cause," Abdullah said softly. To America they were now terrorists. They were, attacking hotels, killing innocent people with truck bombs, hundreds and hundreds of them. To themselves they were fighting for Sharia. We called them freedom fighters once, like our founding fathers. I once saw them as like the Indians I daydreamed about when I sat on our front lawn and looked at our horses in the field down below, and across the Columbia River and rode with them, my hair long, and my chest bare, holding my rifle high. I remembered racing Jalaluddin and laughing in the wind.

Kabul

I returned to Kabul and reported on the hostages to the FBI. I worked with them and talked to the Haqqanis about Paul Overby, and Robert Levinson. On a recommendation I went to see Hashmat Ghani Amadzai, chief of the Amadzai, the largest Pashtun tribe, brother of Ashraf Ghani, the President. There were four guards out front and Hekmatyar's compound was next door. We talked in his large sitting room.

He said Ibrahim contacted him in 2003. He was always the softer face of the Haqqanis. He wanted to make a deal to bring Jalaluddin to Afghanistan. All he wanted was security. Ghani talked to President Karzai but he wouldn't do it. He was too cocky. Tom Ford had called him the most elegant man in the world, and he wouldn't see him. The Haqqanis were finished, Karzai said. They all knew what Jalaluddin was capable of, said Hashmat. Haqqani sent a delegation to Khost and one to Kandahar. He worked with another man, who was now in Guantanamo.

Jalaluddin didn't get upset until the U.S. bombed his house and killed so many of their women and children, especially their daughters. The U.S. didn't understand that Pacha Khan Zadran, in truth his brother, gave the U.S. Army the information and they attacked the Haqqanis' home. American generals did not, after 19 years, know how to fight in a tribal culture. They hadn't been trained to do it. They asked the U.S. and the U.K. to train their army officers before but they refused, feeling it was beneath them. They were both afraid of upsetting Pakistan. They said get in line behind Pakistan. Instead, they sent their officers to the Soviet Union. Jalaluddin's wife was the powerhouse in the family. Like, I thought, his mother, Ladonna. Jalaluddin, the famous guerrilla warrior, was at a gathering in 1988 in the Emirates and a young Yemeni woman came up to him and said she would marry him. His wife had just died and he married her. She was an excellent fundraiser. She worked in Oman, which was not easy place to fundraise. It was she who introduced the Haqqanis to the Iranians.

He explained how Pakistani President Musharraf in 2005 began to use Haqqani again. The Pakistanis killed Nasiruddin. He was getting too cocky, one of the few who really understood fundraising and the Middle East. In the

1980s and 90s the Haqqanis owned a transportation company and then a construction company, but neither one did very well.

Ghani said yes, smiling proudly, the Amadzai were Kuchis. I remembered being with the Mujahideen in the desert at night and a caravan came by us, and a little girl in wood crib looked down from the camel and a barefoot man next to her walked deep in the sand, and then they were gone. There were three types: the settled Kuchis, who had a summer home in one place and a winter home in another; the half Kuchis who still moved and had some animals; and the herders, who continued as always. The last caravan in his family was in 1916. The Kuchis were the richest of all the Pashtuns. They had the camels, the goods, and they owned the caravansaries. They were, I saw, like the Saba of Yemen two thousand years ago. After their last caravan, he started an international trucking business and then he bought Reefers, the refrigerator trucks in the Middle East. In the 15th Century, Babur gave them a palace in Sarg, in Logar Province, which was still there. The property had been taken over by fourteen governments, but always returned to them. The peace talks were important for the Pashtuns, and Pakistan didn't like it. A tribal structure could be changed with the help of accepted, educated families, but it required patience. The U.S. never had any patience. The tribe was still the most important entity in Afghanistan. As it was, I learned, in Arabia. The Constitution was important, but a judge would tell you to go to the tribal Jirga to solve your problem. It was much faster, much more efficient and didn't cost anything. The Taliban were doing the same and had been for a long time.

Pakistan was trying to destroy the Pashtun tribes, and replace them with a new tribe, the Umma, like al-Wahhab in Arabia. When I was a boy, my father told me when I met an Indian to always ask the name of his tribe. They were proud of their tribe. So were they here and in Arabia.

For Jalaluddin to kill Karzai would be fair game, said Hashmat. Karzai took a helicopter down to Loya Paktia for a campaign trip, and Jalaluddin fired one rocket at him, and he left immediately. He smiled. His convey was getting ready to return to Kabul, but Jalaluddin said his men would go ahead. His convey had to move slowly. He asked why? He learned that Jalaluddin's men were clearing the road of mines. Jalaluddin was at home along what Pakistan and America call the border region, what Afghans call Afghanistan. He, like the Haqqanis, had no use for the Durand Line. This, said Hashmat, is what frightened Pakistan. One reason why the Haqqanis were so powerful was because when they gave their word, they kept it. They were close to the ruling family in Qatar, which was competing against its big brother, Saudi Arabia. The ISI didn't really like Haqqani because he was not completely obedient. He did not want to sit in Peshawar. He was always up in the mountains fighting, independent of Pakistan, and of Yunus Khalis. He was the real Pashtun warrior. The Haqqanis kept all the tribal ties, and they would keep them.

It was a son of a tribal chief, through another chief, who brought me back to them. The U.S. insulted them, blowing their houses up, killing their women and children, focusing on this, said Ghani. The information the U.S. received was always on the women and children.

The U.S., ignorant of what they were doing, blindly followed the Haqqani's tribal enemies. They had shifted, as a result of the Americans bombardments, all their daughters to the Middle East. They were educated and spoke English. They were never in the honey business. Ibrahim said the same thing. Why, then, did my contact, the expert in the White House, tell me they did?

After two hours Hashmat escorted me to the door. Outside there were rows of classic European and American cars sitting under a series of carports, and beyond them carports of new SUVs, and Land Rovers. He was a wealthy man, a Kuchi, a nomad, as the Haqqanis were Zadran.

I kept working with the embassy, on the missing Americans, and the hostages. The FBI began to pay my expenses, but I had to return to New York. A few weeks later, the FBI sent three people up to take me to lunch. They wanted to know who my contacts were. My friends were afraid and wanted to remain anonymous. That November, John called. They were going to exchange the hostages, but there was a problem. Could I come over quickly and help them. I didn't work for the government, I said again. He called again. Four times he called. I sent a text message to Rob. He said the U.S. had no contact with the Haqqanis. I became the intermediary between the government and the Haqqanis. The release took place and Kevin King and Timothy Weeks, after three years in captivity, were exchanged for Anas Haqqanis and Khalid Rashid.

Three months later, David Rohde, also a former hostage, held by the

Haqqanis, sent me an email. He was talking to Kevin King who said hello. In the 1980s he came from Los Angeles to see me, with a lawyer, to option my book *In Afghanistan*, and I turned him down. It all came back to me. When my book came out, a famous actor said he wanted to make a movie about it. I told my literary agent, who said he didn't deal with Hollywood. The actor invited me to his home for dinner and introduced me to a famous actress, a lovely woman. I got another agent, who took me to dinner at a hip New York restaurant. I felt uncomfortable. Kevin called and said he wanted to option my book. He took the night flight from Los Angeles and we met in my apartment. He wanted to give me $500 to option it. I liked him and admired him for crossing the country to see me, taking a chance. I wanted to work with him, but the actor was still there. It was the lure of Hollywood, the opposite of my upbringing. I told Kevin no, reluctantly. The agent went to Los Angeles and returned and said, "Better my book was called *In North Dakota*." For years, I was upset that I turned Kevin down. Now 35 years later, I paid him back.

In January 2020 New York City became the epicenter of the Covid epidemic in America. John called from Pakistan to see how I was doing. They were worried about me.

On August 15th, the Haqqani militia came up from Logar Province, in the southeast, and took Kabul, Abdul Rahim, the former Mujahideen spokesman and ambassador to the U.S., told me. President Ashraf Ghani fled the country. His family, Din Mohammad said months before, was packed and waiting. Qatar, where the Taliban had their headquarters, was against him. The Taliban, Rahim explained, came up from Kandahar after the Haqqanis. They can't believe, Abdullah marveled, that they took 34 provinces in 11 days. That Friday, Khalil Haqqani entered the old, venerable Kul-e-Kheshti (brick bridge) Mosque on the north bank of the Kabul River, with four suicide bombers, his bodyguards, he said. He spoke, holding a rifle. The worshippers, sitting on the floor, their rifles beside them, listened in awe.

On February 23rd, 2002, Sirajuddin, 41, the former military commander of the Taliban, now Minister of the Interior, and the Khalifa of the Haqqanis, went with his young brother Anas, 30, Ghilzai Pashtuns, from eastern Afghanistan to Kandahar, home of the Taliban, and of Ahmed Shah Durrani, founder of the Durrani Empire, and modern Afghanistan, and of the powerful Durrani aristocracy, and of Mullah Omar, founding leader of the

Taliban. There for the first time since 2008, when the U.S. declared him a specially designated global terrorist, Sirajuddin showed his face publicly and gave a speech before the largest crowd in memory where he announced that they alone, a separate front Ibrahim told me, in their common struggle against the infidel invaders, sent 1570 suicide bombers to Paradise. He was saying, Abdullah explained, that they too had sacrificed and were in solidarity with the Islamic Emirate. He established himself that day, Abdullah said.

On June 22, 2022, an earthquake struck eastern Afghanistan in Haqqani territory, and over 1,000 Afghans died. Anas, showing his authority, tweeted that "the government was working within its capabilities and they hoped that the international community and aid agencies would help their people in their dire situation." "The Saudis invited him to go on Hajj," Abdullah said. "They wanted to meet him and to introduce him to others." His mother was Yemeni. He was already part of the Arab world. "Mullah Omar was respected," Abdullah added, "throughout the Arab world for sacrificing his government to protect Osama bin Laden. Sirajuddin was respected also. Anas was the future." Both men were becoming, like their father, famous throughout the Middle East.

Postscript

On July 31, the CIA killed Ayman al-Zawahiri, the head of al-Qaida, in a drone attack in Kabul. The New York Times reported that "Officials have said that he had moved back to Afghanistan earlier this year after American forces left." A tribal leader called and said that he was moved from Pakistan to a house on his land after bin laden was killed. He saw him in the 2014 but had to keep quiet. He was moved after that. Abdullah said al-Qaida leaders had been close to the Haqqanis, but reminded me that their senior people were in Iran, and that al-Zawahiri was possibly there. He said that Mullah Yaqoob, the Defense Minister, had been meeting with the Americans in Qatar. On August 7, Abdul Wali, a promionent Pakistani Taliban commander, who was behind my kidnapping in 2008 in the Tribal Areas, and who Abdullah called a bad man, and because he, like other Taliban leaders, rode in an armored car, was killed not by a car bomb, but by a drone, in Afghanistan near the Pakistani border.

Index

CPSIA information can be obtained
at www.ICGtesting.com
Printed in the USA
LVHW081403040223
738683LV00023B/961/J